Normative Aesthetics

Normative Aesthetics

Sundry writings and occasional lectures

CALVIN G. SEERVELD

Edited by
John H. Kok

DORDT COLLEGE PRESS

Cover design by Willem Hart
Layout by Carla Goslinga

Copyright © 2014 Calvin G. Seerveld

Fragmentary portions of this book may be freely used by those who are interested in sharing the author's insights and observations, so long as the material is not pirated for monetary gain and so long as proper credit is visibly given to the publisher and the author. Others, and those who wish to use larger sections of text, must seek written permission from the publisher.

Dordt College Press   www.dordt.edu/dordt_press
498 Fourth Avenue NE
Sioux Center, Iowa, 51250
United States of America

ISBN: 978-1-940567-00-6

Printed in the United States of America

The Library of Congress Cataloguing-in-Publication Data is on file with the Library of Congress, Washington D.C.

Library of Congress Control Number: 2014934726

Cover: The emblem of being offered a piece of freshly cut, multi-grained brown bread instead of a stone hints at the calling of doing philosophical aesthetics: systematic reflection on the nature and task of human imaginative life will be normative when the thought is wholesome, edible, worth chewing, and builds the body of a community with joyful shalom.

Table of Contents

Author's Dedication i

Editor's Foreword
    by John H. Kok iii

Introduction to this book
    (Un)Timely Voyage: Calvin Seerveld's Normative Aesthetics
      by Lambert Zuidervaart xiii

1. The Halo of Human Imaginativity 1

2. Imaginativity 27

3. Dooyeweerd's Legacy for Aesthetics: Modal law theory 45

4. Joy, Style, and Aesthetic Imperatives, with the Biblical 81
    Meaning of Clothes and Games in the Christian Life

5. Ordinary Aesthetic Life: Humor, tastes, and "taking a break" 111

6. Both More and Less Than a Matter of Taste 135

7. Christian Aesthetic Bread for the World 145

8. The Place for Imaginative Grit and Everlasting 169
    Art in God's World

9. The Relation of the Arts to the Presentation of Truth 219

10. A Turnabout in Aesthetics to Understanding 233

11. Philosophical Aesthetics at Home with the Lord: 259
     An untimely valedictory

12. A Review: *Kants Kunsttheorie* 285

13. A Review: *Truth and Method* 289

List of illustrations 297

Index 303

Abbreviations used throughout this volume:

RA Calvin G. Seerveld, *Redemptive Art in Society: Sundry writings and occasional lectures*, edited by John H. Kok. Sioux Center, IA: Dordt College Press, 2014.

CP Calvin G. Seerveld, *Cultural Problems in Western Society: Sundry writings and occasional lectures*, edited by John H. Kok. Sioux Center, IA: Dordt College Press, 2014.

AH Calvin G. Seerveld, *Art History Revisited: Sundry writings and occasional lectures*, edited by John H. Kok. Sioux Center, IA: Dordt College Press, 2014.

CE Calvin G. Seerveld, *Cultural Education and History Writing: Sundry writings and occasional lectures*, edited by John H. Kok. Sioux Center, IA: Dordt College Press, 2014.

BSt Calvin G. Seerveld, *Biblical Studies and Wisdom for Living: Sundry writings and occasional lectures*, edited by John H. Kok. Sioux Center, IA: Dordt College Press, 2014.

Author's Dedication

Laus Deo! This work is done. The six books edited by John Kok collect with illustrations all sorts of miscellaneous writings and lectures for special occasions I have presented throughout my lifetime. By publishing them at Dordt College Press editor Kok has made my limited contribution to the tradition of Reformational christian reflection available for a younger generation to chew on and test for insight. I am deeply grateful.

Almost all the texts collected here were written to be heard. So the compact, paratactic style (common to Jean Calvin and Theodore Adorno) is often dense, like poetry, rhetorically insistent, and takes getting used to when a mere reader faces the transcript rather than that he or she be a listener to its oral presentation. The occasionality of the pieces has been important to me too. When you connect with a specific audience somewhere at a certain time, the "occasional" speech, Gadamer contends (*Wahrheit und Methode*, I,2,ii,b), carries over in its performative character beyond the occasion, with a surplus of reality and meaning; the text was not a speculative, argued abstraction.

Helpful to prospective readers might be my mentioning that many of these lectures were given at festive occasions, people conferences, where there was a sense of human leisure time to listen eagerly, digest slowly, and discuss. The presentations were not constricted to the 20 minutes of a tight academic format.

I am aware that the upfront, frequent references to Bible passages may put off some readers. But I am not using the references to show off "proof texts," but am just being normally open about what is running through my consciousness. The translations offered of the various biblical passages are my own responsibility.

Professor Dr. John Kok has been an incredible editor: personal, professional, meticulous, considerate, undaunted by numerous obstacles. His indefatigable sleuthing for images in the public domain, his internet detective acumen in tracking down sources, and utter perseverance in nailing down details, has given a luster to these books beyond anything I could have imagined. Like an angel he has often protected me from myself and, with his staff of Carla Goslinga and Sarah Moss, has augmented and enhanced the materials I provided with a sure aesthetic touch, high editorial competence, and production follow-through. My gratitude will remain outstanding, so long as I live, for his service, which has indeed tried to make my efforts accessible and fruitful.

I thank the colleagues who wrote introductions to the various segments of the books, which show there is a community of scholarship that has been afoot in our lifetimes. Lambert Zuidervaart, Adrienne Dengerink-Chaplin, Barbara Carvill, Dirk van den Berg, Henry Luttikhuizen, Doug Blomberg, Gideon Strauss, Craig Bartholomew, and Peter S. Smith are friends whose critique has buoyed me through the years (Psalm 141:4–5). There are also many other encouragers, especially Willem Hart, and all the venues that invited me to present these writings and lectures, for which I am grateful.

Special thanks go to John and Jenny Hultink of Paideia Press for a subvention that has made possible the plethora of images while keeping the price of the books reasonable. His generous gift aims to give a public voice to material that promotes living a daily life dedicated to the compassionate Rule of Jesus Christ in the world. Would that more donors had this vision.

Finally these books, such as they are, are dedicated to my wife Inès, who with Griselda-like patience and steadfast strength has stood with me as her husband for more than 56 years, through good times and through hard times. She provided for our three children—Anya, Gioia, and Luke—during the years when I was closeted in the study or away on speaking tours more than was right. She has given me an uncommon peace of a sure biblical quietness, a redeeming forgiveness, and lasting love that our Lord has blessed. Without her my life would have been thin. My hope is that these animated books will long remain a tribute to your steady care and selfless love for me, Inès, our family, and the many students who miraculously entered our lives.

Toronto
January 2014 AD

Calvin and Inès Naudin ten Cate-Seerveld at home in Toronto, 2006
(photo by Jeanne Brackman-Daniels)

Calvin Seerveld and John Kok
Dordt College 4 November 2013

Editor's Foreword

John H. Kok

While editing these six books (almost 2,000 pages, with more than 450 images) and readying them for simultaneous publication has taken longer than I had expected, doing so has been, all told, a wonderfully rich experience—quite simply an honor and a privilege. When Calvin Seerveld sought the advice of a few friends back in February 2010 as to the viability of such a collection, I could only agree with their response: "a marvelous idea and a splendid project!"

My desire as editor was to get published, in addition to his many other books, what Calvin Seerveld has done in a variety of areas that is worthwhile for a younger generation. Many of these 100+ chapters are already available in print for those who know where to look, but, in addition to having them all "under one roof," a particularly attractive component of these six books is the 30+ unpublished lectures from over the years that are available here for the first, for those who would like to also have access to what he has been thinking and delivering in public over the years.

I am deeply thankful to those who did such a wonderful job of introducing these books.

- Seerveld is convinced that philosophical aesthetics—systematic reflection on the nature and task of human imaginative life—will be normative when the thought is wholesome, edible, worth chewing, and builds the body of a community with joyful *shalom*. **Normative Aesthetics** (*NA*), introduced by Lambert Zuidervaart, aims to spell out some of what this aesthetic imperative means for human imaginative acts, for the arts, and for other acts and institutions where aesthetic functions play a role.

- Art, for Seerveld, belongs to the very infrastructure of a good society, in the same way that a country's economy, transportation system, or media network do: "With a vital artistic infrastructure priming its inhabitants' imaginativity, a society can dress its wounds and be able to clothe and mitigate what otherwise might become naked technocratic deeds." **Redemptive Art in Society** (*RA*), introduced by Adrienne

Dengerink Chaplin, addresses the need for Christian public artistry and ways in which Christians can be stewards of art.

- ***Cultural Problems in Western Society*** (*CP*), introduced by Barbara Carvill, explores the unfavorable conditions in which European society and its Christian artists find themselves today. Seerveld masterfully locates current quandaries in the large timeframe stretching from Ancient Greece to the present, all the while introducing normative alternatives that are biblically oriented. The artwork of mostly twentieth century and contemporary artists that Seerveld includes exemplify the kind of redemptive, modern, Christian art he is advocating.

- The essays in ***Art History Revisited*** (*AH*), introduced by Dirk van den Berg and Henry Luttikhuizen, follow a general course from the historiography of philosophy to the historiography of art and aesthetics to analyses of individual artists like Antoine Watteau and Gerald Folkerts and the theory and practice of artist/aestheticians like William Hogarth and Anton Raphael Mengs. As this selection of essays attests, Seerveld is both well-versed in the history of art and has made significant contributions to this field as well.

- Seerveld sees a central role in education for "understanding and developing history," but then "history" not as rote rehearsal of what has transpired but as past and present events in their complex interrelation. Education is inevitably an induction into our cultural heritage; conceived ecumenically, in the spirit of loving our neighbors and their "mistaken visions," wherever and whenever they may be. But as ***Cultural Education and History Writing*** (*CE*) makes plain, we are initiators—culture-makers, shapers of history, and also history-keepers—as much as we are inductees. These seventeen essays are introduced by Doug Blomberg and Gideon Strauss. And finally:

- In the talks, lyrics, and articles in ***Biblical Studies and Wisdom for Living*** (*BSt*), introduced by Craig Bartholomew and Peter S. Smith, Seerveld opens Scripture in a variety of life contexts in which God's people find themselves today. In both his professional studies and popular lectures, Seerveld seeks to explicate, both devoutly and playfully, a biblical wisdom for daily living, convinced as he is that the Holy Spirit-given biblical writings bespeak God's everlasting care and wisdom for us corporeal mortals.

Throughout, the first page of each chapter indicates where the text was first published or delivered. Each book also includes an index and a list of the illustrations included in the text.

— Editor's Foreword —

I also want to thank Willem Hart for his excellent work—collaborating with Seerveld—on the books' covers. As Seerveld notes in *BSt*: "Designer Willem Hart . . . is an unsung saint, I think, who was incredibly important in the development of almost all the Canadian Reformational institutions in existence. . . ."

Here at Dordt College many others have also lent a helping hand. Early on Julie Andree helped digitalize a number of texts, and most recently Mia Kornelis is helping with website materials, including easy links (see www.dordt.edu/DCPimagesSeerveld) to color renderings of many of the illustrations used throughout these books. Sarah Moss was most helpful over the course of more than two years in preparing and reviewing texts and tracking down images in the public domain. Benjamin Kornelis contributed his skills of notation and lyrics layout for songs in *CE* and *BSt*, and Dordt's Computer Services folks served me well with the necessary Dutch, German, French, and Italian MSWord® dictionaries that I needed to check and correct citations and footnotes throughout. Carla Goslinga desires special mention—she patiently rendered and revised her InDesign® layout of the text (which also includes Greek, Hebrew, and Inuit) and was primarily responsible for preparing and placing the images and diagrams throughout the text. Thanks also go to my wife Sanneke—too often "working on Seerveld" was the reason that other good things just did not happen. Hopefully my "retirement" will change that in ways that we both have yet to discover.

I also want to thank the many artists that have graciously granted Dordt College Press permission to reproduce work(s) of theirs in black and white (and in many cases in color on the web—see the url. above). Further from home, but aids that I have come to also deeply appreciate are: the Google.com "search engine" and particularly its advanced_ image_search capabilities—very helpful and simply amazing.

But most of all my thanks go out to Dr. Calvin Seerveld. While appreciating his biblical wisdom and reformational passion from the get-go when I was a student of his at Trinity Christian College in the late 1960's, our contacts and relationship have grown with the years. Our reconnecting began when I was a student at the Free University in Amsterdam (1971–1983). His youngest, Luke, was a student of mine during my first years (starting in 1983) at Dordt College. Seerveld spoke at his son's graduation ceremony in 1985, and since that time our contact gradually increased. He wrote sporadically (I admittedly less so), often to share texts/lectures that he had prepared, or simply just a postcard update (see below)—always using a splash of colorful stamps. We, in turn, were able to invite him to come to Dordt many times, often—one time, in 1999, for a whole week—to participate in my Philosophical Aesthetics course and to deliver public lectures on related topics to boot.

Cal, although you definitely allowed me to "do my thing" as editor, I also deeply appreciated your willingness to review what I delivered back to you and your encouragement along the way, often along the lines of "Haast U langzaam" (You can better do something well but slowly than bungle what needs doing because of haste). I also thank you for sharing some of your emotive responses with me regarding what was in the process of becoming (again). E.g., you e-mailed me once: "Maybe I'm getting senile. Because the spoken manuscripts bring back such vivid memories of when the pieces were delivered, it almost makes me cry. So what you are doing is a most generous, in a strange way, comforting deed to me. I hope God keeps me going until the whole effort is completed." I am delighted that God has allowed you and Inès to live to see the day of this project's completion: a lifetime of hard work once again blessed with sunshine. God bless!

I recommend to those readers who are not familiar with the work of Calvin Seerveld these two introductions: "Transforming Aesthetics: Reflections on the work of Calvin G. Seerveld," by Lambert Zuidervaart, in *Pledges of Jubilee: Essays on the arts and culture, in honor of Calvin G. Seerveld*, Lambert Zuidervaart and Henry Luttikhuizen, eds. (Grand Rapids: Eerdmans, 1995), 1–22, and "*Bread* and not Stones: An introduction to the thought of Calvin Seerveld," by Craig Bartholomew and Gideon

— EDITOR'S FOREWORD —

Strauss, in *In the Fields of the Lord: A Calvin Seerveld reader*, Craig Bartholomew, ed. (Carlisle/Toronto: Piquant/Tuppence Press, 2000), 3–22.

For those who are not familiar with Cal Seerveld's background, I close with a brief biography that also gently contextualizes the topics Seerveld engages in these six books.

Calvin George Seerveld is Senior Member in philosophical aesthetics, emeritus, at the graduate Institute for Christians Studies in Toronto. Born to Christian parents in 1930 in West Sayville, Long Island, New York, he later studied philosophy, literature, and classical languages at Calvin College (B.A.) and the University of Michigan (M.A.). After several years of study in the Netherlands under D.H.Th. Vollenhoven, S.U. Zuidema, and G. Kuiper, in Switzerland under Karl Jaspers, Oscar Cullmann, and Karl Barth, and in Rome, Italy, under Carlo Antoni, he received the Ph.D. in philosophy and comparative literature from the Free University of Amsterdam in 1958. He is married (1956) to Dutch born Inès Cécile Naudin ten Cate; they have three children.

Dr. Seerveld taught undergraduate philosophy and literature at Belhaven College, Mississippi (1958–1959) and at Trinity Christian College in the Chicago area (1959–1972) before specializing in aesthetics at the Institute for Christian Studies (1972–1995). Throughout the years he has given lectures in many places on the difference the biblical Christian faith can make in performing, interpreting, and understanding human artistry and artwork in society. An abiding concern of Seerveld has been to show that good artwork—painterly artwork, theatre, poetry, and music—is called by God to be a gift to one's neighbors, to enrich their insight into the often unnoticed marvels of God's world (see, e.g., *RA* and his *Bearing Fresh Olive Leaves: Alternative steps in Understanding Art* –2000).

Seerveld was instrumental in shaping the contours of Christian philosophy in the curriculum of Trinity Christian College when that college began in 1959. He has lectured in many colleges and teachers' conferences on the nature and task of Christian education as conceived in the thought tradition of the Calvinian Reformation, as distinct from but appreciative of the Roman Catholic scholastic tradition of reflection, and aware of Evangelical theological attempts to have a robust apologetics on hand in advanced education. Seerveld's emphasis has been on presenting a biblically driven Christian *philosophical* orientation that, from a certain thetical standpoint, invites reshaping the conceptions of others, instead of leading with negative critique of what others think. A permanent focus of Seerveld's professional writing has been to forge a conception of history and history writing that critically melds the insights and categories of Reformational Christian thinkers Herman Dooyeweerd and Dirk Vollenhoven into a working methodology that makes a difference for understanding the encyclopedic setting and significant contribution of particular thinkers to the development of philosophical reflection. He recommends a "glocal" vision (a bifocal, global and local awareness) in our human attempts to be faithful history-keepers (see, e.g., *CE*).

At the Institute for Christian Studies Seerveld's research and teaching concentrated on the study of fundamental categories in the systematics of philosophical aesthetics, such as imaginativity, artistic taste, and the playful aesthetic life (see, e.g., this volume –*NA*– and his *Rainbows for the Fallen World: Aesthetic life and artistic task* –1980/2005). His concern has always been to examine and discern the meaning of ordinary creatural matters like subtleties, quirks, and surprises that trouble and enrich our lives and can lead to artistry in the light of the biblical testimony to the compassionate lordship and truth of Jesus Christ.

Besides philosophical aesthetics, Dr. Seerveld also explored problems in the historiography and critical theory of art. His cartographic methodology works out of Vollenhoven's "problem-historical" conception of the history of philosophy, modified to deal with artworks. For several years Seerveld focused his research and professional writing on artistry buoyed by the European Enlightenment. His partiality for picaresque William Hogarth, as serious aesthetician as well as artist, and for Anton Raphael Mengs, signals Seerveld's eye for the idiosyncratic figures in art history. His study of the neglected art historian Kurt Badt with Lorenz Dittmann at the Universität des Saarlandes in Saarbrücken, Germany, and giving serious narrative exposition to young Christian voices like British Peter S. Smith and Canadian Gerald Folkerts are attempts to give examples of what deserves attention to round out what constitutes the art historical world (see *AH*).

Seerveld has a European penchant for multiple languages and the history of Western culture. His research sabbaticals have been spent at Heidelberg Universität studying with Gerhard von Rad, Claus Westermann, and Hans-Georg Gadamer (1966–1967), in the musea of München (1981), in the archives of the Bibliothèque Nationale in Paris, working on Watteau (1986), and until recently he has been a frequent summer reader every couple years at the Warburg Institute, University of London, since 1973. Recurring invitations (the first in 1997) to speak at the Christian Artists International conferences held in the Netherlands were likewise an occasion for Seerveld to wrestle with the ferment of different European nations' and national cultures' struggles to discover what economic, and possibly political, integration might entail for artist unions in the different countries. These, he found, are practically a mandala for the troubles and opportunities facing working, professional artists in Western society (see *CP*).

Although literature and philosophy were his major areas of study, Seerveld has kept biblical theology as a supplemental hobby. He learned classical Greek at Calvin College and later studied the biblical Newer Testament under Oscar Cullmann at Basel Universität (1953–1954), where he learned Hebrew under Walter Baumgartner. Later he continued Older Testament studies under Gerhard von Rad in Heidelberg (1966–1967) and Hans-Joachim Kraus in München (1981).

Of special interest to Seerveld are the "wisdom literature" texts of the Older Testament, and the book of the Psalms. His original translation and oratorio arrangement (with cantor Ina Lohr) of *The Song of Songs* has been performed around the world. Currently he is busy with a performative translation of Ecclesiastes as a chorus of multiple voices. He served as a "poet" member of the committee that spent ten years developing a *Psalter Hymnal* for the Christian Reformed Church of North America (1977–1986), and has versified various psalms for Genevan tunes and sturdy Welsh melodies. Seerveld is particularly interested in biblical laments and has composed several Blues melodies for God's people, to balance their "praise songs."

Both Seerveld's professional studies and popular lectures have sought to explicate, both devoutly and playfully, a biblical wisdom for daily living (see, e.g., *BSt*).[1] And what he suggests regarding others, holds for himself as well, I'd say:

> ... a *way*-of-life in-the-world [is] a subconscious habit of activities beaten out in the press of daily life that marks their kind of whole integrity and that shows itself notably in crises. A people's way-of-life holds elements of style, a language, training, mores, temperament, mentality, and other kinds of matters kaleidoscopically together, and receives its over-all imprimatur from the faith-commitment underlying and leading the whole. But a way-of-life is not sacrosanct just because it is fundamentally shaped by a faith-commitment. Touch a person's way-of-life, alter a family's way-of-life, for good or ill, and you change quite drastically the exercise of their humanity. (*NA* 86)

---

[1] Earlier books with this cachet are *Take Hold of God and Pull* (1967, rev. ed. 1999), *How to Read the Bible to Hear God Speak* (1979, revised expanded ed. 2003), *In the Fields of the Lord: a Seerveld Reader* (2000), *Voicing God's Psalms* (with CD, 2005), and a lecture-recital CD, *The Gift of Genevan Psalmody for Today: Sprung from its historical context*, with Stephanie Martin directing Pax Christi Chorale (2011).

INTRODUCTION

(UN)TIMELY VOYAGE:
CALVIN SEERVELD'S NORMATIVE AESTHETICS

by Lambert Zuidervaart

To develop a systematic normative aesthetics is not fashionable. It resists the mainstreams of contemporary Western thought, where a postmetaphysical turn in both analytic and continental philosophy makes scholars suspicious toward comprehensive claims about societal principles, including what is aesthetically or artistically good. It also runs counter to a consumerist and instrumentalist mentality that permeates Western culture, where people often base their decisions and actions on what they like and what works for them. It even troubles the waters of many religious communities, which tend either to consider aesthetic concerns peripheral to true faith or to regard normative pronouncements as unduly dogmatic.

Calvin Seerveld has not worried about being fashionable. He has not sought to swim with the philosophical currents, to give people what they want, or to conform to contemporary religious patterns. Instead he has tried to enrich a reformational tradition of thought that raises critical questions about Western culture and works out a Kupyerian vision of the Christian faith. The result, as this volume demonstrates, is a robustly normative conception of the arts and culture and an unapologetically systematic approach to philosophical aesthetics.

The scope and ambition of Seerveld's work in this field show up in the public lecture he gave to begin his years as a faculty member at the Institute for Christian Studies (ICS), the graduate school for interdisciplinary philosophy where he taught for more than two decades (1972–1995). His inaugural address calls for "a turnabout in aesthetics to understanding."[2] Like many of his public lectures, the address opens and closes with freshly translated readings from the Hebrew and Christian scriptures, illustrating

---

2 See "A Turnabout in Aesthetics to Understanding" in the current volume, pp. 233–58. Hereafter citations from essays in this volume will be in-text. Seerveld delivered his inaugural address on October 14, 1972. ICS published it in 1974 as Institute for Christian Studies Publication No. 1.

in practice what it means to do philosophy that is "scripturally directed." The "understanding" to which aesthetics should turn is the divine Wisdom that, accordingly to Seerveld's translation of Proverbs 8, has played throughout God's creation from the very beginning. It is to this Wisdom, manifesting itself in creation, scripture, and Jesus Christ, that Seerveld wants his aesthetics to respond. For the normative task of aesthetics is to give "a winsome account of the aesthetic hold the Lord God has for creaturely existence" so that people can "order their everyday lives more obediently" (p. 242). Such an aesthetics can be a blessing, he says, not only to Christian believers but also to artists, scholars, social institutions, and society as such.

The stakes for Seerveld's normative aesthetics are high. Historically, he notes, the study of aesthetics has not had a proper home in the Western academy, and the arts and aesthetic life have not found a legitimate place in Western society. Nor have Christians done much to change this historical predicament. Yet they must, he insists, because the arts and aesthetic life are good gifts from God that should contribute to human flourishing.

Seerveld's response is to claim that normative aesthetics has a "rightful task," in three respects (pp. 243–252):

1. To map out the structure of aesthetic life, its relationships with other aspects of life and society, and the normative principles that hold for aesthetic life (Seerveld calls this mapping exercise "modal aesthetics").
2. To develop a general theory and historiography of the arts, both in their differences and in their common features, and to indicate their proper tasks and roles in human life.
3. To study the principles that should guide arts criticism and literary criticism and thereby to indicate the proper tasks of professional critics, journalists, and educators in these areas (a study Seerveld calls "hermeneutics").

To those who think that the arts defy theoretical analysis or that such study is an elitist enterprise, Seerveld has a twofold reply: first, "art is no more recalcitrant to analysis than a salmon's nervous system" (p. 246), and, second, the right kind of "committed aesthetics," in pursuing Wisdom, will be humble enough to serve artists, critics, and their publics. The many articles in this volume that started out as public lectures for nonacademic audiences show his own commitment to providing a serviceable aesthetics.

Seerveld has not shied away from the hard work of systematic philosophical reflection, however, nor has he shirked the responsibility to address fellow scholars. Two essays stand out in this regard.[3] "Dooyeweerd's Legacy for Aesthetics," first published in 1985, builds a systematic framework for Seerveld's aesthetics from the reformational ontology developed at the VU University Amsterdam by Dirk Vollenhoven and, especially, Herman Dooyeweerd. Seerveld derives several key insights from Vollenhoven and Dooyeweerd: that "the aesthetic" is one of the (fifteen) interrelated dimensions ("modal law-spheres") of creation; that the discipline of aesthetics should study this dimension in all its manifestations; and that the arts constitute a distinct multidimensional realm of cultural products, practices, and relations that are "qualified" (i.e., definitively characterized) by aesthetic concerns. Seerveld differs from the founders of reformational philosophy in two respects, for reasons he explains. First, he characterizes the aesthetic dimension in terms of "allusivity" or "imaginativity" rather than harmony or beauty. Second, he considers the aesthetic dimension more fundamental to human experience (i.e., earlier in the order of modal law-spheres) than Vollenhoven and Dooyeweerd do. Yet Seerveld retains, indeed strengthens, the conviction that Christian scholars should contribute to an "inner reformation" of academic disciplines, including philosophy.[4]

Two years later Seerveld published an article on "Imaginativity" in *Faith and Philosophy*, the leading journal for Christian philosophers in North America. There he lays out the central claims of his systematic normative aesthetics and indicates how they provide a redemptive response to the "pivotal errors" in Western thought about art and the aesthetic dimension. Briefly, the pivotal errors are to disparage (Plato), to misconceive (Aristotle, Aquinas, Kant), or to exaggerate (Coleridge, Schelling, anti-rationalist theologians) the nature and role of imagination. Seerveld counters this entire tradition by identifying "imagining" as an irreducible mode of ordinary human functions—the aesthetic mode. It is distinct from, albeit related to, "sense perceiving or image constructing or conceptual functioning" (p. 31). Aesthetic functioning is characterized by the activity of

---

[3] In addition to the two essays discussed, which were addressed primarily to other Christian scholars, one should turn to "Both More and Less Than a Matter of Taste" and the two book reviews at the end of this volume to see how Seerveld raises his normative aesthetic concerns in the pluralistic contexts of philosophy as a profession.

[4] "Dooyeweerd's Legacy for Aesthetics" may be read as a companion piece to "Modal Aesthetic Theory: Preliminary Questions with an Opening Hypothesis," in Seerveld's *Rainbows for the Fallen World: Aesthetic life and artistic task* (Toronto: Tuppence Press, 1980), pp. 104-137, an essay originally written for *Hearing and Doing: Philosophical essays dedicated to H. Evan Runner*, edited by John Kraay and Anthony Tol (Toronto: Wedge Publishing Foundation, 1979), pp. 263-94. "Modal Aesthetic Theory" gives a more substantial argument for replacing "beauty" with "allusiveness" as the "qualifying function of art."

"making-believe." All creatures are open to our acts of imagining or making-believe: all creatures have aesthetic object-functions, and all humans (and perhaps some other creatures) have aesthetic subject-functions. Even God's unchanging ordinances for all creatures and their relationships can be imagined. Moreover, all that is "imaginativable" (whether objects, subjects, or laws) and all acts of imagining are themselves governed by God's aesthetic law or creational ordinance, whose meaning human beings need to disclose as an "aesthetic imperative." Seerveld articulates this aesthetic imperative as follows: "note or present or perform the nuances there be playfully; present what a given state of affairs is like; transform dissimilars into a similative surprise; and do this as praise of God, with care for things, in winsome service to all and sundry" (p. 39). That is how to love God and one's neighbor in aesthetic life, he says, and it can be a blessing. All of us do well to accept and nurture God's gift of imaginativity "as an avenue for joy" (p. 44), for "humans are created to be imaginative before God's face" (p. 1).

The challenge for Seerveld's normative aesthetics is to spell out what this aesthetic imperative means for human imaginative acts, for the arts, and for the other acts and institutions where aesthetic functions play a role. Beginning with the first article, titled "The Halo of Human Imagination," several essays in this volume give passionate and thickly textured articulations of the aesthetic imperative in ordinary life—in style of life, including clothes and games, for example (see "Joy, Style, and Aesthetic Imperatives"), or in leisure, humor, and aesthetic taste (see "Ordinary Aesthetic Life").[5]

Other essays explore what the aesthetic imperative implies for artists, who are to give leadership in aesthetic life as "professional imaginators . . . making nuanced human knowledge serviceable to the neighbors in God's world" (p. 10). After explaining why "allusivity" is better than "beauty" as a norm for good art, the essay "Christian Aesthetic Bread for the World" catalogues several ways in which art can and does violate this norm, namely, through subaesthetic, para-aesthetic, anaesthetic, and anti-aesthetic approaches. Similarly, "The Place for Imaginative Grit and Everlasting Art" pinpoints the traditional worldviews and contemporary spirits that confront those who wish to follow the aesthetic norm, including the spirits of pragmatism, agnosticism, utopianism, and anarchistic nihilism.[6]

---

5 For a schematic presentation of Seerveld's multi-layered conception of the aesthetic imperative, see Diagram 4 (p. 152) in the essay "Christian Aesthetic Bread for the World." It is interesting to compare this diagram with an earlier schema of "functions of aesthetic-life subjectivity" on the right-hand side of the diagram "A Christian Tin-Can Model of the Human Creature," in the essay "The Fundamental Importance of Imaginativity within Schooling," *Rainbows for the Fallen World*, p. 143.

6 Seerveld's term for utopianism is "fundamentalistic neo-idealism" (p. 179).

"The Relation of the Arts to the Presentation of Truth," chronologically the earliest essay in this volume (1971), offers a reformational conception of truth and shows how the imaginative knowledge provided by art can present and embody the Truth. Throughout these essays Seerveld gives many examples of artists and artworks that, in his judgment, do indeed offer aesthetic bread, not stones.

Seerveld, too, wishes to offer bread, not stones—philosophical bread for a needy world. That is how he formulates his vision of scholarship in "Philosophical Aesthetics at Home with the Lord," the valedictory address he gave in 1995 to conclude his years as a faculty member at ICS. The aim of "obedient Christian scholarship," he writes, is "to give the next generation food for thought as *they* covenant with the LORD in our *dürftige Zeit* [impoverished time]" (p. 260).[7] Blending cultural sensitivity with passionate commitment, Seerveld calls for scholarship that meets three requirements. First, it must be "scripturally directed," guided by a vision of God, creation, and human life provided by "the Holy Spirited Bible" (p. 261). Second, it should be historically informed, well-versed in foreign languages, comprehensive in scope, culturally critical, and relevant. Third, it needs to be an interdisciplinary and communal endeavor. Scholars who meet these requirements will "give away wise untimely counsel to those caught in our cultural times of disarray" (p. 271)—wise counsel, because such scholars will pursue Wisdom; untimely, because, as Seerveld says about his own valedictory remarks, such teaching and research "are not fashionable, do not fit in with the times, and might be considered out-of-step with the current drummers drumming" (p. 260).

Then, in appreciative response to *Pledges of Jubilee*, the volume published to honor him upon his retirement, Seerveld formulates five issues that need attention from the next generation of reformational scholars in aesthetics and the arts (pp. 272–277):[8]

1. To explain the unique character of aesthetic knowledge and truth.
2. To provide a general ontology of the arts.

---

7 The phrase "*dürftige Zeit*," which comes from Martin Heidegger, is translated as "time of need" in William Barrett, *Time of Need: Forms of imagination in the Twentieth Century* (New York: Harper & Row, 1972). Perhaps more than any other book, Barrett's *Irrational Man: A study in existential philosophy* (Garden City, NY: Doubleday, 1958) introduced Heidegger and existential philosophy to an entire generation of North American students in the 1960s and 1970s.

8 For attempts to take up several of these issues, see the two companion volumes by Lambert Zuidervaart, *Artistic Truth: Aesthetics, discourse, and imaginative disclosure* (Cambridge: Cambridge University Press, 2004) and *Art in Public: Politics, economics, and a democratic culture* (Cambridge: Cambridge University Press, 2011).

3. To sort out proper relationships between the arts and public culture.
4. To fashion historiographies that point out the "horizons of spirited vision" that enfold artistic developments.
5. To give a genuinely philosophical account of culture that does not rest content with a mere "theology of the arts."

In retrospect, we can see that Seerveld's instructions for the next generation encapsulate the unfashionable concerns of his normative aesthetics. Moving against contemporary philosophical currents, he points his scholarship toward a God-given aesthetic ordinance that shines from the very structure of creation, culture, and human life. Unbowed by the onrushing winds of consumerism and instrumentalism, he calls attention to the imperative to be imaginative in the arts and daily life. Appealing to the scriptures that should guide his own community of faith, he urges Christians to abandon both their theologically insular yachts and their aesthetically impoverished rowboats. This collection of essays, like all of Seerveld's scholarship, charts an unfashionable direction for exploration, construction, and critique, a direction not only for scholarship but also for the arts and aesthetic life. If Seerveld's hopes are fulfilled, his readers will find blessings by joining him on this untimely yet oh-so-timely voyage.

Lambert Zuidervaart
Professor of Philosophy
Institute for Christian Studies and University of Toronto

THE HALO OF HUMAN IMAGINATIVITY

In the beginning one day soon after God had created man and woman the LORD took them for a walk, a little earlier than usual, while the sun was still bright.

After an hour or so, when they stopped to set tea near a brook, they made a little fire first from fallen olive branches and twigs. While aroma of jasmine wafted pleasantly into their nostrils, the LORD did a curious thing. God stooped to rub two wetted fingers of the left hand in the wood ashes and smeared the ash over the poised thumb and circled forefinger of the right hand.

As Eve and Adam watched, the LORD God blew gently across the film of soapy water on the fingers, and a lovely, round, shimmering, colorful creature floated into the sunlit air.

The LORD performed the miracle a second time, while the man and the woman sipped their herbal tea in wonderment.

"Give it a name," said God.

So Adam and Eve called this creature "bubbles," and taught it to their grandchildren.

The story I just told is true to Scripture in disclosing the creatural feature of human nature we may call imaginativity.

Biblical orientation:
humans are created to be imaginative before God's face
The Bible reveals that the majestic, sovereign, merciful, and gracious LORD of Exodus 34:6–7 and Isaiah 40 delighted in tumultuous rainstorms, which brought forth tufts of grass in desert lands (Job 38:25–27); the LORD followed with fascination how young lions hid themselves to stalk prey for food (Job 38:39–41); the LORD enjoyed God's creation of fantastic animals like the horned female mountain goat gently crouching to deliver her young (Job 39:1–4), and watched snorting, fearless Arabian horses pawing the ground (Job 39:19–25), even before humans existed,

---

This lecture, adjusted over time, was first delivered at the Oxford Conference sponsored by the C. S. Lewis Foundation in July 1991 at Keble College, later in Sydney, Australia in 1999 and in Jackson, Tennessee in 2009. It is also translated/published in Greek and Korean.

says Job 38:4–39:30.

The LORD made trees, which normally outlive humans, to give birth in the spring while naked to leaves, green leaves which gradually turn into a breathing coat of many colors before they die to sail through the air to the earth. Only God could be so imaginative as to make a tree. And it's not just exotic animals that boggle one's imagination, like Australian platypuses or the huge, incongruous, lumbering, amphibious turtles that fascinated Darwin in the Galapagos Islands, or Atlantic Ocean seaboard lobsters, which swim gracefully backwards, tail first, or the churlish peacocks God created for Flannery O'Conner to cherish, to the consternation of her mother: God created ordinary chickens to eat kernels of yellow corn to form brown eggs beside red wheelbarrows near glazed rain water on which so much depends. The LORD God of the universe, who rules the nations of the world, stooped to fashion cows who turn green grass into white milk, which when drunk builds human bones—amazing! No wonder the punch line to the book of Jonah lists as a reason the LORD wanted to save the wicked, pagan city of Nineveh was the presence of its cows (Jonah 4:11).

Because Adam and Eve and their progeny were enabled to say "No" to God, as well as "Thank You," God's enduring, outstanding invitation to women and men to tend and joy in the garden of creation, as you know, has produced feats at odds with one another. Miriam choreographed a jubilant dance of thanksgiving to the LORD on the banks of the Red Sea, which pleased God (Exodus 15:19–21), but God's people took their Egyptian gold to fashion a molten Calf on a pedestal to be their ostensible leader, with fatal consequences (Exodus 32). And the Bible details results of good and bad imagination for millennia of history.

The point of our listening to Scripture on creation for direction at the outset is to become conscience-clear and certain that sinful imagination is not definitive for the gift of God that human imaginativity is, any more than proud autonomous reasoning illustrates the norm for obedient thinking that engenders wisdom. I do not want to argue from the Bible that because God prescribed for the high priest's ephod blue threaded pomegranates (Exodus 28:33)—which do not exist on trees—therefore non-representational painting is kosher; nor would I pit the final, X-rated chapters 17–21 of the book of Judges against Philippians 4:8 in a debate about what artists may treat.[1] Dogmatic tenets of Scripture have their

---

1   I know that such *argumenta ad hominem evangelicum* (cf. Hans Rookmaaker, *Modern Art and the Death of a Culture* in *The Complete Works of Hans Rookmaaker* [Cailise: Piquant, 2003], 5: 148–154; Francis A. Schaeffer, *Art and the Bible* [Downers Grove:

place in our confessional life, but the way to have holy Scripture lead us to and in our human tasks on earth in history is not to stare at it cross-eyed, but have the Scriptures in full voice speak to our hearts, ring in our ears, fill our consciousness until the Holy Spirit convicts us as a body that how God made us creatures in the beginning is good, very good. **And God made us to be imaginative.**

The Bible itself spills over imaginatively. Whether it be the exciting, true, apocalyptic story of Numbers 22–24, a fable by embattled statesman Jotham (Judges 9:1–21), the terse, stichomythic drama of Wisdom versus Foolishness in the paragraphs of Proverbs (1,9), the history of Naamen the Syrian teaching the prophet Elisha a word from God (2 Kings 5), the poignant parables of rabbi Jesus (for example, Matthew 13), the visions of Ezekiel and Zechariah and John on Patmos: such imaginatively brimful writing may be hard on Rationalists who want their knowledge in propositional form, and can be mistaken by Romantics as licensed *gnosis*, but the Bible as God-speaking literature is bread for the world, and for God's folk who receive its imaginative revelation as bona fide knowledge of God's great deeds and guidance to save us from our sinful selves.

To teach the Bible as literature has always struck me like teaching economics for its mathematics, because you miss what's crucial—the compelling call of the Lord to repentance and adoption into the family of God. But **the Bible is God speaking literarily, imaginatively**. As I read it, the Bible does not support a *via negativa* approach toward God, although it is so that the Lord's way of doing things transcends our creaturely ways (Isaiah 55:8–9): when the Bible likens the Lord God to a mother (Psalm 131, Isaiah 49:14–18), to a judge (Genesis 18:16–33, Psalm 75:6–8), to a rock (Psalm 95:1–2, 1 Corinthians 10:1–5), to a husband (Hosea 2), to a landlord-banker (Matthew 25:1–13), to a moth! eating away our most coveted possession (Psalm 39:7–11), to a man roused from drunken sleep when God's people are in desperate straits (Psalm 78:56–66). Such imaginative comparisons are not just fanciful glosses, but tell me truthfully what my God, the Holy One, is like. Scripture tells me concretely of the God of Abraham, Isaac, and Jacob, as Pascal said, the covenanting Lord of the riffraff like Samson and Jephthah, not to forget Rahab, who by faith made it into Hebrews 11. The Scriptures give

---

InterVarsity, 1973], 12–14) have freed people to take the artistic talents of their children seriously, and for that I am thankful to God. It is not the best way, however, I believe, to have Scripture train us in discerning God's will to be discovered in creational revelation.

me deeply insightful, poignant knowledge when I am told as a lost sheep that the God of the universe is the good shepherd looking for me (John 10:1–18, Psalm 23).

I'm just saying: the fact that the very way God's authoritative Word for human life is booked, with the LORD's evident approval (2 Timothy 3:16–17!), reinforces this initial basic truth that we human creatures all live, move, and have our meaning under the Almighty LORD's injunction to be imaginative, to bewonder dappled things, finches' wings, whatever is fickle, freckled, sweet, sour, adazzle, dim, and to heighten our awareness of that chorus of praise in creation by our unselfconsciously echoing, "golden echoing," the thesaurus of inventive initiative with which the LORD has entrusted us humans.

Imaginativity is making-believe and doing as-if, a blessing that provides nuanced knowledge

The crux of imagining as an irreducible kind of human activity is found in making-believe, as we say, in doing as-if. I am not yet talking about artistic activity. **Imagining is more elementary than making art**, is a more primary functioning, as when children make mud pies, play house, or walk on stilts as if they be fragile praying mantis giants. Having fun and fooling around are normally constitutive factors of imagining. A person busy imaginatively is liable to notice or concoct strange resemblances that remain allusive but fascinate, poised with metaphoric insight: if you were as melancholic lonely as Shakespeare's Jacques in *As You Like It* in a foreign country and happened upon an amorous couple, you might see that a kiss is simply a pleasant sucking way to transmit germs.

Fantasy is rudimentary imagining, whether it be the whiling pastime of discovering profiles in cloud formations as you lie on your back on a river bank in the summer sun, or make up the conversation between an elderly dragon and a friendly witch whose broomstick is broken. The **wit to tell jokes** is an enriched form of human imaginativity in action, whether it be dirty jokes or the kind, laughter-inducing tales the medieval jester told who, because he had only empty pockets, decided to give his jokes to God as a sweet-smelling offering. When you **entertain** your neighbor or plan an **adventure**, one's imaginativity comes to the fore; and hints of surprise will dartle like grace notes around the meal and conversation, or remain hidden in the plan until unexpectedly, like something whimsical, there it is! startling you gently into a pleased or puzzled smile. **Games** are congealed springs of imagining, occasions for persons to make-believe somebody is "IT," or to act as if you have a powerful queen to protect your one-step-at-a-time, hobbled king in chess. . . .

I could go on in describing this zone of full-bodied human activity topped up as imagining, but I have said enough perhaps to make the point convincing that there is a specific ontic structuring to human nature that sets us up, among all the other ways we are, to make-believe and act as-if, thanks to God's creative Word, "Let there be imaginativity to my human creatures!" How we men and women respond to this embedded gift of God, whether we gladly give it away in Christ's name, wrap it up and bury it like a bone in a hole in the ground, or thumb our imaginative nose in God's face, needs discussion too. But right now, on the import of the biblical truth of creation, we need to realize that every human creature—Asian, European, South American, atheist, pietist Christian, intellectual deconstructivist, New-Age spiritualist: no man or woman can jump out of his or her imaginative nature.

Although I cannot develop a full-blown, biblically framed anthropology here, it is important for my argument still coming that I call your attention to the fact that **this quality of imaginativity characteristic of humans resides in all the other ways the Lord created us to be too.** Imagining is of a different order than feeling or thinking, digesting food or showing loyalty; to be busy imagining is different than speaking or being friendly. But all the varied ways we bodily exist in God's world are inter-related. So, if you are imaginativity-anemic or hyper as a person, it influences the way you think, make promises, show emotional empathy and physio-organic spontaneity or not. I do not propose surgeons make imaginative guesses at which organ to excise when they pick up the scalpel, nor that theologians rest with fanciful hunches on exegesis of texts. And I do not hold that there is a lockstep consequence between the proportion of imagination one has and its effect on one's speech or friendships, comparable to the amount of blood or yellow bile in one's system, to use the old-fashioned humor psychology. But one's speaking and love-making and ability to implement plans are deeply colored by the caliber and exercise or atrophied lack of muscle tone to a person's imagining. Would to God that a supple, sanctified imagining had more priority in mothers and fathers' parenting of children, in judges' sentencing of criminal offenders, in the diplomacy of heads of state bound to bring justice to citizens.

I am just mentioning this interweaving of imaginativity in our other acts not typically defined by imagining to keep our focused reflection in context.[2] The implication of my remarks is that **artists do not have a cor-**

---

2 Cf. Wallace Stevens, "Imagination as Value," in *The Necessary Angel: Essays on reality*

ner or monopoly on imagination just because imaginativity is of special concern and prominence in artistry. Every walk of human life has a styleful moment and betrays richness or poverty of nuances—evidence that imaginativity is subterraneanly at work, or at a loss, within one's habit of greeting other persons, carrying on business transactions, or wrestling with the Lord in prayer.

And the good news about imagining is that it is not a stupendous, extraordinary jewel in the crown of humanity, but is a much more modest gift, infrastructural, you might say, to human nature, integral, not exclusive or optional. Imaginativity is in the neighborhood of whistling, winks, and blowing bubbles. What would life be without whistling when you are happy or afraid? If a speaker has no winks in his or her words but only stares and blinks statements at you, is that a way to love your audience? Blowing bubbles takes time, the kind of ample, unhurried, fascinating, leisural time a well-organized workaholic probably would find frivolous; yet when strangers held the hands of Jewish children, as Elie Wiesel reports, and told them stories as they made the last walk to the gas chambers of Auschwitz, blowing bubbles with them, as it were, lifting them out of their predicament, you can catch a sense of the blessing packed into God's little gift to us humans of imagining.

I know imagination can be devious and cruel, like clothes, or overwhelmingly powerful and breath-taking on occasion, but in the beginning we do well to fashion a humbled conception of imaginativity, to give imagination its creatural place in creation, with its own limited splendor, responsibility, and authority. **Imagination is a good God-given way humans explore and gain knowledge of nuances in the world**, embody and share such satisfying knowledge. I don't mean decorative "filler" for perceived facts and argued analysis. Imaginative knowledge gets into the crevices of things, ferrets out hidden riches, discovers the wrinkles in a face, the pot-holes in an intrigue, conjures up fabulous monsters or unicorns, dwells on the lambent sheen or the penumbra of shadows to the tangled skein of somebody's life. That's why there is this sparkle around making-believe, doing as-if, being merry with metaphor: realities often unnoticed, but important realities like the shadow-side of respectability or the courage in bashfulness, silent tears and quiet acts of love, which inhere being alive in God's world, are picked up, framed, as it were, surprising us and making all those who have eyes to see and ears to hear such bona fide, incisive knowledge of concrete reality wiser.

God's exuberant joy in playing around with humankind in the be-

---

and the imagination (London: Faber & Faber, 1951), 146–47.

ginning of creation (cf. Proverbs 8:30–31) is the biblical grounding for my saying that it is wrong for anyone to neglect so choice a gift, or to dull, damage, or pervert your neighbor's imagination. I have seen an adult in anger at a young person's harmless, mischievous prank full of originality dress down the child, as the colloquial idiom goes, and clip the little one's imaginative wings even before it could fly. Such stunting of imaginativity is a serious evil since, because the misdeed is often not recognized as evil, it is therefore seldom repented of.

It is so that one person is more imaginative than another. Some of us may be born color-blind, turn tone-deaf, remain gawky, be humorless—imaginatively handicapped. But such creatural blemishes only give me the opening to introduce the ministry, as I understand it, of professional imaginators—artists, including poets and song-writers.

A Platonist philosophical tradition distrusts imagination
I can pinpoint how the Platonist curse against images has embedded itself in the English language on imagination by referring to Romans 1:21 in the King James translation of the Bible. The crux of Paul's argument there is that those who are suppressing the truth of God's revelation in creation underneath their injustice, are inexcusable in terms of submitting to God because, in their firsthand creational experience of God's grace, they did not honor God as God, and were not thankful to God, "but became vain in their imaginations, and their foolish heart was darkened" (Romans 1:18–21). The Scripture rendered "imaginations" in King James' English is διαλογισμοῖς, vain in their "deliberate reasonings"! (cf. also 2 Corinthians 10:5). And the influential King James translation (1611) is consistent in other relevant passages, calling any "formations (*Gestalten*) of a person's inward, intentional designs" that are evil (cf. Genesis 6:5, Lamentations 3:60) "imaginations." The primary meaning in English of "imagination" is (quoting the *Oxford English Dictionary*), "what does not correspond to the reality of things, hence vain, false," with a secondary meaning documented already in Coverdale's 1535 Bible translation, "scheming, plot, fanciful project."

The Platonic position condemned images as perceptual errors, illusions, and artists who wasted time making mirages, imaginary things, unless such phantasms taught morality, were poor citizens of the polis. **Plato's error, in my judgment, was to identify a solid feature of God's good creation, namely, the sensible and handicrafted, as the locus of evil one should shun.** Thinkers of the Church have often been tempted to adopt this otherworldly stance, modified to be sure, to mitigate the localization of evil.³ Somehow, in the Platonizing process, the commandment not to worship homemade gods, **idols** (Exodus 20:1–7; cf. Isaiah 44:1–22), slipped a notch into becoming a prohibition against making **images**, thereby certifying depreciation of imagining. A tough strand in Talmudic studies,⁴ and much Islamic teaching about godly activity reinforced the suspect character of images and imagination.

I'll not rehearse the history, but a problem remaindered from the Platonic tradition christianized, which still bedevils us, is that in common parlance "imaginary" and "fiction" refer to what is not true, or at least a matter that is not present and needing to be accounted for. From everything I've said so far you know I believe we need to find a way to turnaround this old preconception, because **imaginative knowledge can deepen our grasp of God's world and bring a dimension of praise and love to bear in society otherwise missing.**

> ... Love is not love
> Which alters when it alteration finds,
> Or bends with the remover to remove:
> O, no! it is an ever-fixed mark. ...
> Love's not Time's fool, though rosy lips and cheeks
> Within his bending sickle's compass come. ...

It's the lilt in the language, the hesitating yet pulsing, steady rhythm set up by the alliteration, sibilants, and negatives, that testify to the durance of betrothed love through sickness and health, prosperity and want, aging, sin, and forgiveness: it takes the allusivity of poetry and what goes on imaginatively in-between the lines and diction, as it were, to get at the reality, the truth of vowed commitment between two fragile human beings. I do not want to introduce a tiresome polemic between poetry and prose, since straight talk and legal precision have their own particular glory. It's just—let me put it this way—if there be no more imaginative, subjunctive play in our speech, we people will forfeit the knowledge of such polite, deferential courtesy in human communication. (How often do we use the subjunctive mood in our fast e-mail communications?)

---

3 Thomas Aquinas taught that *sensualitatis inclinatio* is a troubling *fomes*—kindling, tinderbox for sin (*Summa Theologica* I–II q.91 a.2 *resp.*); but sin comes only from a deliberate act of free will not subject to reason; *natura humana per peccatum non est totaliter corrupta* (*Summa Theologica* I–II q.109 a.2 *resp.*). Young John Calvin keen *ad aedificandam pietatem* in the faithful, rather than dwelling on anthropological subtleties, stresses the complete derangement of the whole human nature by sin: *neque enim appetitus inferior eum* [Adam] *illexit, sed arcem ipsam mentis occupavit nefanda impietas, & ad cor intimum penetravit superba* (*Institutio Christianae Religionis* (II,1,9).

4 Richard Kearney, *The Wake of Imagination* (Oxford: Hutchinson, 1988), 43–49.

The mystical Romantic movement adores imagination as revelation
A second major, wayward philosophical tack that thwarts, I think, our taking God's creation of imaginativity in humans seriously in **its limited order of glory** for our christian living and learning is the tradition that credits imagination with supra-rational γνῶσις, as a kind of inspired, ecstatic entry into mysteries that transcend ordinary mortality. Plato uses the prophetess Diotima of Mantinea's speech in his *Symposium* to delineate the erotic ascent of the initiate soul up from pederasty to a final contemplative transfixion before "the great Ocean of Beauty," "Beauty itself" (209e5–212a7); and Aristotle eulogizes the contemplative energy of divine reason in us, exhorting humans in the *Nichomachaean Ethics* to strain "to make ourselves immortal" (1177b1–1178a2). The imageless, deiformic, superhuman illumination exalted by Plato and Aristotle was not called "imagination" but contemplative activity. Church thinkers christened its NeoPlatonic Plotinian version into the *visio Dei*,[5] and mystics, christian and otherwise, have believed in being transported—"beside themselves"—into the presence of The Hidden One to receive special revelations, like oracles. The movement of Western European Romantic Idealism adopted, secularized, and converted this age-old, visionary quest to meet God into a messianic humanism: they championed the god-like intuitive knowledge and creativity of genius, especially artistic genius, and called this power *produktive Einbildungskraft* (Fichte), *intellektuelle Anschauung* (Schelling), secondary esemplastic imagination (Coleridge).

I need to tred carefully here because my Reformation-Calvinian faith tradition, augmented Lutheran, partial to the Dutch-Rembrandt focus, thrives best in an earthy, gutsy christianity, and feels ill at ease with soul ascent, extra-biblical communications, "victorious living" and rapture. I'm willing to learn. But for me the Holy Spirit leads and works intimately out of Scripture, which is imaginatively intelligible. I don't want to step out of the Platonic frying pan of imagination into a Promethean fire. Personally, my "visions" of God stay close to Isaiah 6. Actually God is closest to me in the LORD's voice. I hear God speak in different tones of Hannah or Deborah's songs (1 Samuel 2:1–10, Judges 5), Psalm 39, 110, 2, 91, the prophet Isaiah, Amos, the Newer Testament texts of Romans, Hebrews: not daemonic voices, but by my dwelling intently and at length in the Word written I hear my Lord speak comfortingly, remonstratively, pleading—God's got good voice!

---

5   Cf. Augustine, *Confessions* IX, 10:23–26.

A current fusion of these two positions judges imagination to be powerful and sinister

Confronting us in our generation is a curious fusion of these two major philosophical aberrations I have mentioned—denigrating and over-rating imagination. Jean Baudrillard's (1984) lecture on "The Evil Demon of Images,"[6] epitomizes a current, Manichaean evaluation of imagination as powerful and sinister: images have almost occult power to bewitch people into believing the images are more real than ordinary reality—cinematic passion is made more real than my own mundane love-life—so imagination enslaves people to a satisfying unreality, hyperreality, while the real world goes to hell. The gospel of Fichte—human egos create the world—has perversely come true with a Sartrean twist: we thought we were Pygmalions sculpting beautiful Galateas, but our pathological creative human imagination has brought us Frankenstein's monsters! Our imagination has completely vaporized creational reality into culture, the work of our hands, and all of us, artist, technician, as well as viewer, have become facsimiles of Narcissus staring at ourselves in a hall of mirrors. For example, if we think that the highly selected TV images called "news" be reality, we are fools—

I leave our contemporary fix with imagination hang here for now, and shall try to show in closing how artistic imagination can hold a blessing, so that we neither disparage God's good gift nor idolize its power, and also not damn it because of its demonic captivity, but joy in redeeming its originary glory and ministry.

Artistic imagination is a professional imagining called to provide nuanced knowledge for one's neighbors out of love for God

Artists, including poets and website designers, I believe, are called by God to give leadership in practicing the integral human ability of being imaginative; **artists become professional imaginators in making nuanced knowledge serviceable to the neighbors in God's world.**

I have no truck with *le mystique d'artiste* because artistry is ordinary work like collecting and disposing the garbage of a city, or surgically removing somebody's gall bladder, or raising a new barn on the prairies, or drafting a treaty between belligerents after a war. Artists are persons who take their native gift to be imaginative, which is common to all women and men—which a budding artist may be endowed with in a special measure—and then by disciplined training deepen their imaginative

---

6   *The Evil Demon of Images*, translated by Paul Patton & Paul Foss (University of Sydney, Australia: Power Institute of Fine Arts), 13–34.

ability until they are able to fashion objects and events that take on their own objective and eventful identity defined by **the aesthetic quality of allusive, as-if simulation**[7] that I described earlier.[8] **Art objects and artistic performances have the quality of being composed/constructed/performed entities whose skillful, symbolific disclosure of innovative conjunctures of meaning elicit the neighbors' imaginativity.**

That's a touch of jargon to be philosophically precise, and it means this: while the LORD calls everyone to be imaginative, and to be thoughtful, and emotional, and just, and generous, according to God's creational will, the LORD blesses only some to become professional artists or theorists, professional counselors, statesmen and women, or business entrepreneurs. To become "professional"—I want to avoid the ancient class-loaded distinction of trades in competition with "liberal arts"—to become a **"professional" means for me that you have the leisure to be intensely busy continually in caring for and mastering the complexities of a specific service in God's world for which you willingly give your life time.** All professionals begin as apprentices; some practitioners remain amateurs, and other apprentices persist until they become master craftsmen and women as sales persons, jurists, psychiatrists, philosophers, or design artists—each with their own zone of creatural glory and authority.

Artists, poets, novelists, as professional imaginators are normal workers, in the creational sense of collecting manna daily by the sweat of their brows. Artists as professional imaginators, say I as a theorist, are laborers specialized in collecting nuances in God's world and in presenting out of love for God those fascinating quirks and quarks or deep-seated meanings as tasty manna to one's own kin and neighbors (cf. Romans 13:8–10). Artists as professional imaginators are leaders in imagining, and that entails, from a biblical perspective, artists take the lead in the diaconal work—leadership is ministering!—of opening up anyone, especially the imaginatively handicapped who only want to know what is exact, clear, indubitable (straight-laced brothers and sisters or technocratized neighbors who want things simple, left or right, up or down): open them up to the wonderful, alluring, subtle riches within and around us as God's creatures.

Let me illustrate briefly what I mean by knowledge of nuances: not

---

7 "Similation" is a coinage by Karl Aschenbrenner, defined as "The power of making apt comparisons. . . ." *The Concepts of Criticism* (Dordrecht: Reidel, 1974), 313–19.
8 Cf. C. Seerveld, "Imaginativity," *Faith and Philosophy* 4:1 (1987): 49–53 {infra pp. 35–39}.

logical, not sensed facts, but imaginative knowledge.

Puer natus est nobis [#1]—The *do-sol* melodic interval opening the festive Christmas morning mass, without saying it, exuberantly says it all: "It's a boy!"—God has stooped to our weakness so we may be raised

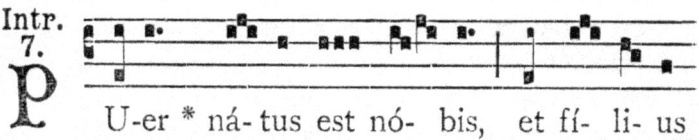

[#1] *Puer natus est*, Gregorian chant introit for the Christmas mass

up to newness of life! Or *la-mi*: the Phrygian mode of Gregorian chant, close to the format of pained seriousness the Jews used to declaim the book of Job casts whatever words fill its exquisite sorrowful melodic line with oxymoronic hopeful groaning (cf. Genevan Psalm 51)—**mi sol sol la mi sol sol re fa mi**—nuanced knowledge, preverbal, preconceptual, chiaroscuro **knowledge.**

The earlier fifth-century AD faithful in Ravenna were not only at-

[#2] *The Good Shepherd*, Ravenna mosaics in Mausoleum of Galla Placidia, c.450-500 AD

tended in the mausoleum of Galla Placidia by the shepherd of Psalm 23 caressing inquisitive sheep [#2], but also by a deep-blue vaulted sky filled with hundreds and hundreds of stars blinking like heavenly snowflakes, creating a warm, comforting architectural feel in the place. The animals

[#3] *Deer and shrubs*, detail, Ravenna mosaics in Mausoleum of Galla Placidia, c.450-500 AD

here and there on the walls [#3] are not composed for taxonomic identification but to capture a sense of uncursed Eden where a deer does not thirst for water but has its belly caressed by tendrils of lovely, curlicue flowers, as if all creation renewed embraces those who die in the Lord.

These artists used their artisanry unobtrusively to lead in joy, cradle hurts, and brush away tears, to raise the spirits of the community they served, that is, lead them into the bona fide imaginative knowledge, which often comes upon you unawares and fills in the chinks of your life.

Geoffrey Chaucer's *Canterbury Tales* entertained his courtly readers with the rough-and-tumble horseplay of peevery between adults comically fixed in their ways, which Chaucer honestly exposes, gentled in humor, framed in a homely piety that invokes God's blessing as easily as one spits to show disgust. The prioress is a gentle nun with the dainty name of Eglentyne, chaste mouthpiece for ruthful stories of unsullied creatures who are harmed and hurt; but Chaucer lovingly dimples in her own weaknesses—having her wimple fluted, and speaking French.

The hearty wife of Bath who has gone on pilgrimages like package tours and has worn out and out-lived five husbands, a coarse, sensual woman of enormous vitality, shameless aggressiveness, and incorrigible garrulity, ends her Arthurian tale of romance with a prayer:

> Jhesu Crist us sende
> Housbondes meeke, yonge, and fresh abedde,
> And grace t'overbyde hem that we wedde;
> And eek I praye Jhesu shorte hir lyves
> That wol nat be governed by hir wyves. . . . (III,1258–62)

To be bawdy with gentility and reverent with humor is rare, but the unsecularized mentality of the poet Chaucer deftly reveals *la gloire et la misère de l'homme*, the mixed bag of aspirations we earthlings are.

John Bunyan's more solitary pilgrim, or Bunyan's 1684 poetic conversation between "The Sinner and the [filthy] Spider," stand out from the chapbooks of the day and pamphlets of sects lambasting sects with a sunny humor, sharp eye for concrete lived life, and a colloquial idiom that makes Apollyon almost seem like a nickname.

> Then he [Christian] was frightened, and he felt inclined to run back; but suddenly he remembered that no armor had been given him for his back, and that, should he run, it would probably be worse for him than for him to stand his ground. So he kept as boldly on as possible. . . .

Puritan Calvinist Bunyan's candid narrative unmasks the humbug in ev-

[#4] Willem Claesz Heda, *Still Life*, oil painting, 1633

eryman, and without heroicizing vivifies resolve against the temptation of fear so precisely you can almost feel it in the small of your back.

A *Still life* with overturned dish and partially eaten pastry (1633) by Willem Claesz Heda gives burnished pewter and translucent glass on a tabletop highlighted halos of quiet splendor [#4]. The tipped plate, rumpled white cloth, and lemon peel drying out, footnotes of *memento mori*, still glory in the texture of fruit, glass, metal, baked goods, and teach the eye to come to rest and to joy in how grace can illumine mean, inanimate objects with unspeakable repose.

Most everyone knows by sight Rembrandt's [#5] syndics of the cloth guild with servant interrupted, as it were, at business, where the black cut of the clothes, rich conservative table covering, and dignified bal-

[#5] Rembrandt, *De Staalmeesters,* oil painting, 1662

anced demeanor catches the committed economic thrift shining through their eyes, or, as Léon Wencelius of Swarthmore College commented two generations ago, "the Calvinist view of vocation" of these illustrious burghers.[9] And artist Rembrandt could touch a butchered ox [#6] (1655)

---

9   Léon Wencelius, *Calvin et Rembrandt* (Paris: Société d'Édition "Les belles lettres," 1937), 49–53, 130–50, 227–36. E.g., "Nous avons vu combine les portraits, par la profondeur de l'alarment spiritual tout imprégna de lumière, par le dynamisme qui les anime, semblent être l'expression d'une vocation qui a son sens détermina.... Les médecins de la *Leçon d'anatomie*, les arquebusiers, les drapiers reflètent tous une vocation spécifique que doit s'accomplir dans une forme donnée ... qui tous, le savons, doivent pour Calvin faire briller la gloire de Créateur" (230).

[#6] Rembrandt, *The Flayed Ox*, oil painting on wood, 1655

hanging in the back room with a fleshy grandeur worthy of the psalms that dwarfs the woman peeking through the doorway. Much less well known is Rembrandt's imaginative engraving of human intercourse [#7]: the couple, in the private recesses of their canopied bed, are busy at their love-making; it's all very normal, *gezellig*, untidy, connected. If you look closely, the woman has an extra arm. With two hands she clasps her man

— The Halo of Human Imaginativity —

[#7] Rembrandt, *The Bedstead*, etching, 1646

to her body, but the third, extra arm—like a seraph?—rests quietly on the bed covers. A redemptive touch, I'd like to say, whereby Rembrandt genially, off-handedly, intimates how ungainly and awkward we humans had better be in the physical intercourse of our love.

Georges Rouault did not look the other way when he saw the ugly ravages of sin on human creatures: this is how you paint in watercolor the nuances of misery, flecks of blue and rose on the body suggesting the cold, the bruises of being roughly manhandled, with the bitter falseness of putting a gay red flower in your hair, *fille au miroir*, sitting on moth-eaten furniture [#8]. Rouault's artistic imagination has rendered compassionately the sad knowledge of the cruelty of self-gratifying male abuse at

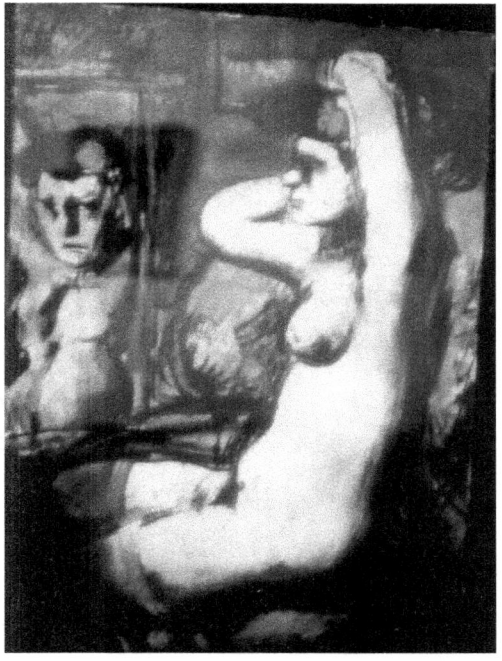

[#8] Georges Rouault, *Fille au miroir*, watercolor, 1906

large in the world of God's creation.

New York City Christine Anderson (Fulbright scholar in Berlin)

[#9] Christine Anderson, *Historical Dislocations: the Expulsion (after Masaccio)*,
oil painting, 1987, New York City

[#9] quotes Masaccio's fresco [*BSt* #21] with powerful effect: the monotonous grid of a housing development is a place of banishment! Middle-class sameness which is nowhere because it is everywhere is a result of the curse? [#10] When Michelangelo's *David*—David in the Bible fought

[#10] Christine Anderson, *The Standoff: surveying the Philistines*,
oil painting, 1988, New York City

the Philistines—when *David* towers over the standardized, colorless family ranch home, you realize even its cherished detachment is a mark of the Philistines; so we paint bright tropical colors on the van used for the annual vacation trek to get away from it all, a somewhat wistful, forlorn *memento Paradisus*.

Canadian Ed Hagedorn [#11] constructs a huge, eight foot by eight foot piece that shows the tanks of petrochemical installations standing like unreal ghosts silhouetted against a pale, befouled green-blue sky, looking like deadly missiles set to shoot off into outer space; underneath is the reality of sewage pipes and muck, refuse, clogged deposits, on top of which filth grasses and flowers still miraculously grow—amazing grace!

[#11] Ed Hagedoorn, *New Growth*, acrylic painting, pipe, mixed media, 1970, Colbourne, Ontario [now destroyed]

Australian Warren Breninger [#12] portrays a woman drained of energy after pushing forth a baby—muscles contracting—exhausted from straining in labor. The somewhat swollen features highlighted by an unreal shine of white like sweat and grounded by the rough black frame underneath as if one is reduced to the basics of humanity in such an ordeal cast the tired woman into stark relief. The black-blue [#13] across the cheeks and mouth hint at soreness, while the wisps of leaves in the dark seem

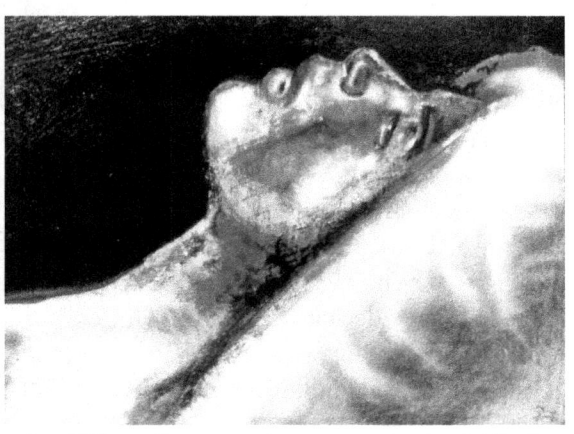

[#12] Warren Breninger, *Art as a metaphor for childbirth, no. 2*, photography/painting, 1986, North Frankston, Victoria, Australia

[#13] Warren Breninger, *Art as a metaphor for childbirth, no. 1*, photography/painting, 1986, North Frankston, Victoria, Australia

to dance and skip wistfully, as if easier times might wait in the wings. There is a sense of distance and uncompromising estrangement in the piece, which yet shows a fascination with the ordeal of bringing forth life. There is softness and love, as I see it, within the hardness. Its wry title, *Art as a metaphor for childbirth*, wants to say, I think, "That's me too as artist, as (christian) artist, my friend."

Murmurs of the Heart [#14] by Joyce Recker in Toronto uses precious purple heart wood with chicken wire to form a delicate, lovely rib cage, doubling as a cathedral, for a levitated heart of a rock caressed smooth by wind and water, as if pulsing above kindling that keeps it suspended, alive. There is something private and protected, warm and gentle, but sharply pointed and precarious about the whole ensemble. I'd play Anton Webern's music nearby, to complement the murmuring heart's exacting, chaste, crucial finesse.

[#14] Joyce Recker, *Murmurs of the Heart*, purple heart wood, found rock, chicken wire, 1990, Toronto

[#15] Britt Wikström, *Seagull I*, bronze, 1984, Rotterdam

Seagull I [#15] in bronze by the Dutch sculptor Britt Wikström shows the gracious alighting movement of this tough, wizened bird, taut body and tail, under the strong wings folding like canvas sails as the webbed feet grip the slippery rock. *Seagull II* [#16] shows the scavenger ready for flight, poised for lift-off, where the raised wings give a cathedral soaring to the creature, a phoenix about to rise again.

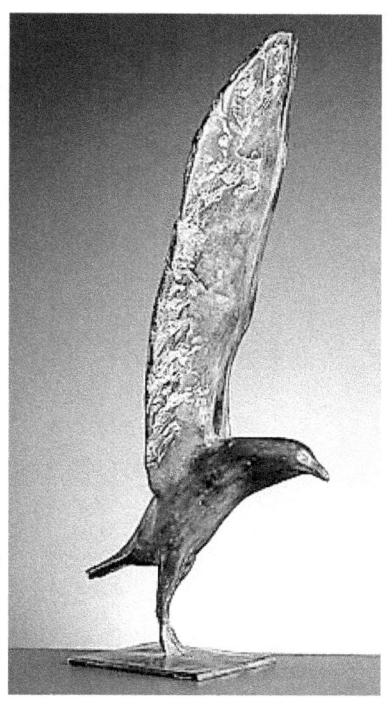

[#16] Britt Wikström, *Seagull II*, bronze, 1985

> My heart in hiding
> Stirred for a bird,—the achieve of,
> the mastery of the thing!

Woman [#17] has the slenderness of a dancer, long legs and body, neck, arms extended to their limit, as if reaching for something beyond—raised mouth, nose, eyes beseeching? while the capped hands form an arc arresting what fain would be, closing off this supple, vulnerable (almost African) figure with a waiting composure. Brit Wikström collects her livelihood by teaching, making mosaic [#18] murals in schools, and redemptive gravestones, where birds of the heavens can come to wash their feet [#19].

Canadian artist Gerard Pas [#20] takes the basic

[#17] Britt Wikström, *Woman*, bronze, 1984, Rotterdam —home of Inès and Calvin Seerveld

— NORMATIVE AESTHETICS —

[#18] Britt Wikström, *Noah's ark*, mosaics, in christian school in Netherlands

[#19] Britt Wikström, *Wim de Mol* gravestone, chiseled granite, 1983, Essenhof Cemetery, Dordrecht, The Netherlands

[#20] Gerard Pas, *Red-Blue Crutch Installation*, lacquer painted wood, 1986-87, London, Ontario

crutch, stigmatized by primary colors, through a contorting metamorphosis, as if the crutch going through the twelve stages of the cross is finally brought to its knees, transfigured by the imagination into a docile, balanced pyramid of expectant waiting. Another [#21] Pas watercolor goes boogie-woogie exuberant with color to celebrate an apotheosis of a trinity of crutches flying above a throne; Kandinsky-esque slivers of geometric figures are pulled loose into the vortex of an unseen power: this ascension or assumption of the crutch—he had polio as a child—in anticipation of the day when the lame shall indeed leap for joy.

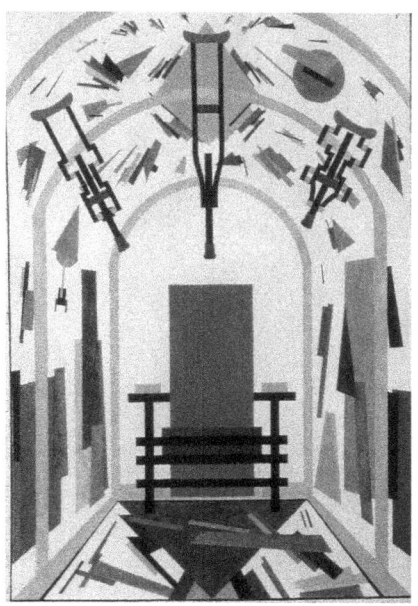

[#21] Gerard Pas, *Vision of Utopia*, watercolor, 1986

My few examples of nuanced knowledge provided by professional imaginators could continue for a long time. I purposely selected what is not spectacular, grandiose, but specimens of what I would call the results of christian imaginativity, art imbued with an awareness of the surd of sin, carrying a spirit of hopeful joy in anticipation of Christ's apocalyptic return and final redemption of God's creation. Christian art is not art with pious additions, or a testimony on the book or record jacket, but is simply art consecrated as God willed it to be creationally—faithful similation, edifying grasp of nuance, humbly walking and blowing bubbles with the Lord.

Those of us who are saints also engage in *sinful* imaginative acts. Those who fail to recognize Jesus Christ is the Lord of all life can be striking artists; but that does not imply they are anonymous Christians. What I have called **the halo of human imagination is a common trust of God's grace that a human can dedicate, default on, pervert, or mismanage**; the luster or halo is not a tongue of fire certifying the true faith of hearted obedience to the Lord.

What is important for us to resolve, I think, as we consider God's creation of humans with imaginativity is its **ordinary glory**, so that in the current climate of the recession of rationalism we not promote the

[#22] Karl Bucher, *Waiting Prisoners of War*, petrifying material, 1979, Red Cross Museum, Geneva, Switzerland

[#23] Joe Fafard, *The Pasture*, 1985, financial district downtown Toronto

inflation of imagination. **Imaginativity is not pivotal to human life, but it is integral to normal creatural well-being, shalom.** And it would be a disaster if those who have gone professional with their creational gift of imaginativity, or if we who want to support such professional artistic and poetic action, did not realize it is to be hallowed into feeding the little ones of God's people and anybody adrift in God's world, to feed them with grace notes of imaginativity kindred to the psalms: a lament of sculptured prisoners of war [#22] standing outside the new Red Cross Museum in Geneva, grouped disconsolately in nondescript robes, waiting and waiting, composed of a material that is gradually petrifying; or a petition of bronze cows [#23] ruminating on a minute piece of grass under a few shade trees in the downtown heart of Toronto's financial district, hoping God who spared Nineveh will have the humor to accept this offering of a concrete city.

And for those of us who are not professional imaginators, one could do worse than be found by the Lord returning to judge the living and the dead holding the hand of your grandchild, or an orphan, blowing bubbles, not as an emblem of *vanitas*, but as a miracle occasioning wonder in the next generation, a miracle God once taught Adam and Eve in the beginning. [

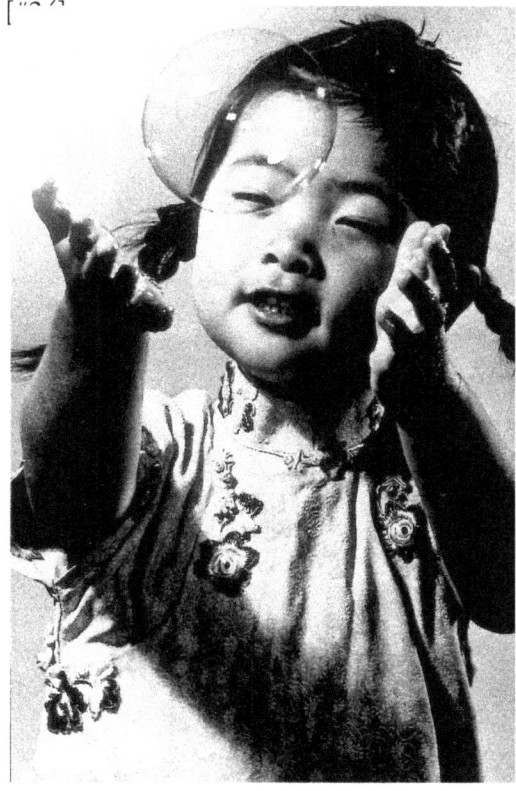

[#24] Gjon Mili, *Untitled* photograph,
n.d. ex Swiss magazine

Imaginativity

>Traditional philosophical uneasiness with imagining activity is documented. The reason adduced for the ontological homelessness of imagination is the inability of most philosophers to recognize the irreducible nature and function of imaginativity.
>
>Imagining is then distinguished from sense-perceiving, imaging, and conceptual activity. Imagining, it is proposed, is the reality of making-believe; and such human, as-if functioning can both (1) characterize human deeds as imaginative acts, and (2) be a latent or active functional moment within other kinds of human acts.
>
>Why God, creational ordinances, angels, and all earthly creatures can be imaginated is expounded, along with an analysis of such activity, its norm, and imaginative results (such as art). Remarks on relations of imagining to science and faith conclude the piece.

This brief paper attempts to stake out a reliable idea of imaginativity. First, pivotal errors of traditional reflection on "imagination" are interpreted. Second, I try to distinguish and describe imagining as an irreducible sort of bodily human activity. Then, from my ontological vantage point I sketch how the various categorial coordinates give a specific cosmological and historical setting to imaginative acts, events, and objects. Finally a few open-ended remarks will be offered on the important meaning of imaginativity and imaginative functioning for a full-orbed human life in God's world where Christ's Rule is acoming.

Traditional philosophical context

Imagining activity has often been disparaged by Western philosophers, as if imagination were a mental influenza.[1] Mature Plato codified in his dialogues a way of thinking that left all image-making activity disqualified. Both εἰκασία (fashioning a likeness of material objects—εἰκόνες, icons or models) and φαντασία (conjuring up imaginary appearances—φαντάσματα, illusions or mirages) are mimetic skills, in Plato's judg-

---

1 Edward S. Casey, *Imagining: A phenomenological study* (Bloomington: Indiana University Press, 1976), 4.

This essay originally appeared in *Faith and Philosophy* 4:1 (1987): 43–58.

— Normative Aesthetics —

ment, that deceive (τέχνη ἀπατητική). To image something is to make an artifact that seems to be what it isn't. A painterly image of a bed is comparable to the bells heard ringing in your head that are not there.[2] Both making images (ἐίδωλα) and lookalikes, and fancying imaginary things, says Plato, only have place in a just society if their products teach theistic polis morality to those who waste their time on them.[3]

Aristotle countered Plato's position because unlike Plato Aristotle trusted αἴσθησις to be true. Φαντασία for Aristotle was a sensitive ability that can rehearse sensational activity and carry on the production of images (φαντάσματα) even without external stimuli. In thinking animals φαντασία βουλευτική not only records phantasmic images of singular matters like acts of bravery, but human φαντασία is also active in forming image-patterns that aid the intellect in constructing concepts like "bravery." So Aristotle credits φαντασία with a pictorial, memorial character and with the function of mediating sensory and conceptual activity.[4] Image-forming becomes a very ordinary link in knowing activity. Thomas Aquinas substantially adopted Aristotle's position on imagination, even for prophetic knowledge (which does, however, take a special afflatus of God); only St. Paul's raptured intellection of God's essence lacked images.[5]

Kant recognized the normal integration of multiple sense impressions in cognitive acts, and attributed such schematic unifying activity to our imaging-power (*Einbildungskraft*). Human imaging-power is reproductive, he claimed, that is, reproduces images (*Vorstellungen*) of phenomena according to empirical laws of association. But human imaging-power is also productive and transcendental, says Kant; that is, imaging-power is apriori and guarantees that its synthesizing ability is constitutive for knowing experience.[6] Kant's most important contribution, however, comes in the *Kritik der Urteilskraft* (1790) where he develops the conception of productive *Einbildungskraft*. Productive imaging-power transcends natural affairs when it presents aesthetic ideas. Aesthetic ideas are mental pictures pregnant with so many thoughts that no concept or word can explain or express what so genially stimulates all our feelings and interacting cognitive faculties. Such productive imaging-power, says Kant, is playful, satisfying, creative, and generates the fine arts, but it no longer

---

2   Plato, *Sophista* 240a7–241e6, 263d6–266e2, and *Respublica* 507b2–511e5.
3   Plato, *Respublica* 606e1–607a9, and *Leges* 903b4–910e4.
4   Aristotle, *De Anima*, 427a16–429a9, 433a9–434a22.
5   Thomas Aquinas, *Summa Theologica* II–II q. 173, a.2–a.3, q. 175, a.3–a.4.
6   Immanuel Kant, *Kritik der reinen Vernunft*, A115–30.

affords us knowledge of reality.[7]

Coleridge is a solid figure among Romantic Idealists who followed Kant's lead without Kant's restrictions.[8] Although the systematics of Coleridge's map of human mental powers is open to dispute,[9] Coleridge clearly highlights three features he believes operate in the conjoined sense-understanding-reason experience of human creatures. (1) Primary imagination is a basic act of sustained, self-conscious perception of things. (2) Fancy is a mode of memory that is selective in its choice of timed and located sense impressions. (3) A secondary imagination is an essentially vital and transforming power that dissolves configurations in order to recreate, to idealize and unify . . . a synthetic and magical power that reveals itself in the reconciliation of opposite or discordant qualities.[10] It is this secondary (esemplastic) imagination-power as source of ideal, representative, and generic insights, where poetry and philosophy appear to coalesce,[11] which other thinkers like Schelling (*intellektuelle Anschauung*) were trying to identify too, as a supreme human act. Imagination for many secularized Romantic artists and poets as well as theorists comes close to being revelatory, certified *gnosis*.

Different current theologians who are fighting old-style, rationalistic dogmatics seem to latch onto the Romantic lead with imagination. Mennonite Gordon D. Kaufman recommends theological imagination as a way for us to be freed from the yoke of our sense-perceptional base and to relativize idolatrous attachments on earth. Man does not live by *phenomenal bread realities* alone; we humans live by "systems of symbols," a vision of life. And a continuing, critical, imaginative update on "God" will with "greater effectiveness orient contemporary and future human life."[12] The Roman catholic David Tracy avoids such a heterodoxical "inner light" theology of adjustment. But Tracy, citing Paul Ricoeur, ap-

---

7   Immanuel Kant, *Kritik der Urteilskraft*, #49.

8   Kant keeps genius subject to taste. "Der Geschmack ist, so wie die Urteilskraft überhaupt, die Disziplin (oder Zucht) des Genies, beschneidet diesem sehr die Flügel und macht es gesittet oder geschliffen" (*Kritik der Urteilskraft*, #50.2).

9   S. V. Pradhan challenges Jackson's ranging "primary imagination" with Reason, "Coleridge's 'Philocrisy' and his theory of Fancy and Secondary Imagination," *Studies in Romanticism* 13:3 (1974): 247–48 n.31. Lloyd Davies follows Jackson on this point, "Coleridge on the Deduction of the Imagination" (unpublished Interdisciplinary Seminar paper, Institute for Christian Studies, Toronto, 1984), 30.

10 Samuel Taylor Coleridge, *Biographia Literaria,* ed. J. Shawcross (Oxford: Clarendon Press, 1981), 1:202, 2:12.

11 Ibid. 2:19, 33–34.

12 Gordon D. Kaufman, *The Theological Imagination: Constructing the concept of God* (Philadelphia: Westminster Press, 1981), 12, 28–32, 71–75.

proves of imagination as the intensifying power needed within a text to make it classic and therefore, presto! the logos of an authentic moment of truth, no matter from what particular tradition the writing stems.[13] Tracy seems to trust an analogical imagination rather than the old-time reason of *philosophia perennis* to unite all corners into a conversation that will necessarily approach truth.

Most philosophers today credit human imaginative activity with much less promise. Edward Casey has made a careful attempt to give "imagining" its ontological due, rather than overrate it or leave it shuttlecocked in epistemological limbo. His phenomenological analysis details pairs of traits Casey thinks are essential to the (eidetic) structure of imagining. Imagining shows a surprising effortlessness; one has complete control of beginning and of terminating the process. Imaginings have a character of sheer, pellucid appearance based on self-contained delimitation. Imagining imputes pure possibility to the imaginatum and surrounds the imagined content and its mini-world of supposal with an imaginal margin that makes it intrinsically indeterminate.[14] "Imagining is entertaining oneself with what is purely possible," says Casey.[15] And he continues to isolate various modes of imagining acts with great precision from acts of perceiving, so that the autonomy of imagining comes into convincing focus. The problem, however, is that key questions as to why humans possess the remarkable power to initiate imagining and what imagining as a non-corrigible act means for the world of perception and action, which imagining "decommissions"—such problems are declared out of bounds.[16]

What has plagued Western philosophers in their attempts to come to conceptual grips with the reality of human imaginative activity is an over-simplified epistemological problematics based on various dichotomistic or bifurcated anthropologies. A "body-soul-spirit" conception of man translates into a "sense perception-understanding-noetic reason" partitioned theory of knowledge. Such schemes, whether hierarchically ordered or monistically enmeshed, tend to keep "imagination" ontologically homeless or a prime candidate for a category mistake.

The Platonic tradition treats imaginative activity as a *perceptual er-*

---

13 David Tracy, *The Analogical Imagination* (New York: Crossroad, 1981), 128, 149 n.96. Cf. Henry Venema, "Analogical Pluralism: An appraisal of David Tracy's 'The Analogical Imagination'" (unpublished Interdisciplinary Seminar paper, Institute for Christian Studies, Toronto, 1984), 10–12.
14 Casey, *Imagining*, 49–57, 68–70, 87–93, 96–101, 107–12.
15 Ibid. 119.
16 Ibid. 73, 189–91.

ror and therefore condemns images as illusions. The Aristotelian complex locates imaginative activity snugly within the workings of a sense based, complicated rationality and assigns it a modest, shadowy place close to memory; "imagining" is understood to be a constructive *imaging ability*. The fact that Kant comes to probe productive *Einbildungskraft* in the matrix of aesthetic judgment is significant. Although Kant denies outright any knowledge content to imaginative activity, Kant does, when he explains "imagining," point to the innovative and fanciful gift of "invention" long credited to poets and artists. The marks of *free play* and a world of *semblance (Schein) fashioned for lingering attention* hover around Kant's contribution to a sound idea on the nature of imagining. Romantic Idealist thinkers commit the error of conceiving imaginative activity to be a supralogical, *illuminating oracle of truth*. Casey's meticulous study succeeds with an almost antiseptic precision, when it distinguishes "imaging" from "imagining"; but Casey's analysis fails, I think, to differentiate (non-sensory) "imagining" from *"some form of conceptual intellection."*[17]

Imagining as an irreducible function

We would do well to identify "imagining" as a mode of human functioning that is irreducible, and to distinguish imagining from other kinds of human functioning, such as sense perceiving or image constructing or conceptual functioning. The confusion of imagining with sensing and imaging or concept-forming has obscured the specific, bona fide, and particular glory of imagining in a normal human life. The terminological confusion alone in common parlance,[18] along with the Platonic prejudice, has hurt attempts to give "imagining" a fair hearing.

Let us understand the "imagining" function of a man or woman to be the reality of making-believe. Sometimes that imaginative function of fancying or pretending stands out, and we can talk of imagining as an action. When children play bears, they make-believe they are bears. Such an imagining act is not an hallucination; children playing bears do not *see* themselves as bears. If a child were to sense-perceive his fellow playmates as bears, he or she would be suffering from a psychic disturbance, a delusion, because *imaginata* are simply not *sensa*.

The human functioning of "imagining" is also distinct from an "imaging" function. It is necessary to be clear about "images." A retinal

---

17 Casey himself notices the problem; cf. *Imagining*, 40–48, especially 43 n.8, and 227.
18 P. F. Strawson, "Imagination and Perception," in *Experience and Theory*, eds., Lawrence Foster and J. W. Swanson (London: Duckworth, 1970), 31, 53. Cf. also the earlier study by Gilbert Ryle, *The Concept of Mind* (New York: Barnes and Noble, 1949), 246–48, 256–58, 264–72.

image (*Abbild*) is a Gestalt formed on the sensitive retina or eardrum of somebody. An image proper (*Bild*) is a picture (remembered) or a tune running through one's head that is not being sensed at the time. Proper images and harkenings (*Bilder*) assume certain sense abilities but are constructions that do not depend upon and are not actual sense-perceived, retinal images (*Abbilder*). When someone muses in early spring and imagines that the returning birds in the trees are angels and the squirrels are demons, one can make-believe that that is so without imaging robins and cardinals to be angels. To pretend the two squirrels that munch my beloved strawberry plant to bits are minor devils is something different than imaging (afortiori, retinal-imaging) them to be visible devils. One might call the end result of such springtime imagining to be aural or visual *fictions,* to keep *imaginata* distinct from images (*Bilder*). Fictions may be the stronger if they are backed up by graphic images, and images may be more vivid if they have been earlier serviced by intense, retinal sights or eardrum sounds; but the fictions of whimsical tomfoolery embody unheard of and invisible subtleties that images (*Bilder*) lack and retinal images (*Abbilder*) may be incapable of. Pretended bears are not bear images. Playing bears opens up a world of virtuality that goes beyond the construction of images. "Imagining" is like mimicry: "imaging" is like making an imitation.

The human function of "imagining" is also different than a "concept-forming" function. Imaginative functioning does not show traits of thinking through a state of affairs or of accounting sufficiently for the identity of something. Imaginative functioning has an *as if* character and delights in ambiguity, hidden resemblances, concealed surprises. If I imagine myself to be Napoleon, I do not consider whether I be a good instantiation of a typical megalomaniac, evidencing the characteristics definitive of such a limited class. Rather, I amuse myself and perhaps others by assuming the guise of certain dictatorial powers and gestures. My imaginative act of pretending to be Napoleon, like playing bears, may suggest certain whimsical features to an observer who not only sees and thinks and follows the imaged mannerisms but also imagines along receptively with my make-believe. My imaginative act may help such a secondary imaginer come to know certain fine features often concealed in personalities who achieve the status to indulge their authoritarian whims. But "imagining" is not argumentative, "making a case." Imaginative functioning has the nature of oblique presentation (*Vorstellung*) and works on human consciousness with the hidden surprises that are characteristic of metaphor.

I do not wish to deny that every kind of human act harbors an imagining function within its peculiar confines, even if the imagining does not stand out. Human acts like speaking and thinking and believing and initiating corrective justice can be done with that moment of imaginativity actively enriching its performance, or without that quality showing. When the imagining function dominates and characterizes the very act in question as an imaginative act, as in playing bears or pretending to be Napoleon, analysis will show a very complex range of other human functions submerged within and colored by that imaginative act. Further, imaginative acts can sometimes be encapsulated, as it were, into habitats or settings that are not first of all imaginative operations, such as the liturgical ceremonies within a church worship activity or diplomatic maneuvers within negotiations between governments. All these complexities bear scrutiny and sorting out. But the first point needed to bring order into all the analysis is this: imagining is a function with an irreducible ontic structure. "Imagining" is not psychic or technoformative in nature, is not at core semantic or conceptual, is not essentially social or confessional.[19] The prime mode of creaturely existence that determines the nuclear kind of functioning we may call "imagining" is, as I see it, the aesthetic aspect of God's creatures.

Cosmic setting for functional imaginative reality
What is able to be imagined by human creatures?[20]

Imaginativable. In my judgment God, in so far as God is revealed in the Scriptures and disclosed in creaturely reality, is properly open to acts of our imagining. The biblical prophets and Christ's parables make-believe God the LORD is a judge (Genesis 18:25, Judges 11:27, Psalm 75:7), rock (1 Samuel 2:2, Isaiah 17:10, Psalm 95:1–2, 1 Corinthians 10:1–5), a nursing mother (Isaiah 49:13–17), husband (Hosea 2:7ff), bridegroom (Christ, Matthew 25:1–13), landlord-banker (Matthew

---

19 When a person says offhand, "I imagine you are trustworthy," it could mean various things. "I *think* you will reward trusting," "I *feel* you are okay," "My *social judgment* is that you are dependable," "I *believe* you are not deceptive," etc. Ordinary language is not always a good starting point for introducing the precision theoretical analysis requires. "Imagining" somebody to be trustworthy, strictly speaking now, would mean in the context of this essay: "I'll make-believe you are a reliable fellow . . . let me play the villain."

20 "Imaginativable" is a term that refers to anything extant that can be a real object of imagining activity. The "imaginativable" is not produced by or reducible to the subject's act of imagining.

25:14–30), and hen (Christ, Luke 13:31-35). It is entirely proper to imagine God to be like something we creatures are acquainted with. If the imagined comparison is biblically insightful, the fiction will provide a nuanced knowledge of God's almighty, redemptive Rule in our lives. The merciful sternness of the holy LORD, God's covenanted nurturing us from childhood on, God as betrothed lover, as brooding mother hen, as entruster of freedom-giving responsibility—such make-believe *Vorstellungen* with respect to God, by Augustine, Meister Eckhart, and countless poets and artists in varying grades of taste and wisdom throughout the ages, show that God is imaginativable. The fact that God is able to be imagined does not mean, however, either that God is an *imaginatum* or that God's imaginativability provides the inside track or corner on knowing God. Who God *is* creaturely *like* is but one way the revealing LORD is accessible to human nature.

God's rainbow of laws holding for creaturely kinds of things, in so far as discoverable in the world, are also open to Scripturally led imagining. God's ordinances are not subject to temporality because God's law-Word constitutes the very temporal limits of creatures, their ordered kinds of duration-to-the-end. Creatures are dated and change. God's ordering Word and Will, as God's self, neither ages nor is subject to change, but provides for the cosmic genesis and ordained passage of creatures in history. However, the psychic law that, for example, intimacy-with-another is not wholesomely possible without a person's first feeling sure of self-identity *can* be imaginatively caught by a whimsical author like Mark Twain and portrayed in *The Adventures of Tom Sawyer* (1876) in how Tom and Becky explore one another as girl and boy. Or the ethical law, for example, that broken troth blocks or destroys other facets of human life can be imaginatively investigated and prehended by a christian author, Alan Paton, and be presented in *Too Late the Phalarope* (1953). Such imaginative knowledge about the ways our on-going creaturely life is structured is very valuable, even though it is not the key to emotional health or the normative progression of a marriage.

Heavenly creatures and their ongoing ministrations, in so far as revealed by the Scriptures to human readers, can also be approached with imaginative attention. Christ in storytelling imagines how devils play at faking an exit only to return after the feint with vengeance (Luke 11:14–26). *The Screwtape Letters* (1942) represents devils in all their petty deviousness, and C. S. Lewis's christian imagining lightheartedly probes them and furnishes fine knowledge on temptations occasioned by real devils. One should note: although the fantasy world of gnomes and fairies is ontologically similar to the imaginative fabric of Goethe's *Faust* (1808–32) and Milton's *Paradise Lost* (1667) the realities for which *Snow White and the Seven Dwarfs* are the *imaginata* are childlike whims and industrial virtues, not devils, angels, and the abyss of human sin.

The bulk of what is imaginativable is to be found among earthly creatures and all their continual changes as the world suffers and moves onward, waiting for the redemption of our bodily human nature and the final coming of Jesus Christ (cf. Romans 8:19–23, 2 Thessalonians 1:3–10). The nuances[21] (= aesthetic object-functions) and suggestion-rich properties (aesthetic subject-functions) of primary states of affairs—things, acts, and events—can be captured by imagining subjects. All the relations of happenings and the multiple qualities of single creatures, groups, and institutional bondings given or becoming given in the world can be cast (*vorstellt*) in an imaginative light. Artefacts made by humans (for example, transportational devices) or animals (nests) or trees (fruit) or glaciers (aftermath of rock-strewn terrain), and their alterations, also can be approached imaginatively. It is the half visible and partly audible, quasi sensible and configurable, imaginativable glories of earthly creaturely reality that are the stuff musing fancies are made on. Such nuanceful matters are also the loci where artists gather in meaning.

Human imaginative act. When the imagining function of making-believe frames a certain human doing, we may call the activity an imaginative act. Artistic activity is an act of imaginativity par excellence, and assumes a measure of maturing skill to fix *as if* treatment of whatever one is busy with imaginatively in a medium that objectifies the nuanceful meaning that is fascinating the artist at the time. But ordinary joking and treasure-hunt adventures and playing games like pretending you are bears or Napoleon are all bona fide imagining acts, even though they may come and go with lightning speed in the course of one's pell-mell round of existence.

An imaginative act of anybody takes place in a full-bodied complement of human functionality. A person who is imaginatively focused in action normally depends upon a *fertile memory.* It is a working condition behind one's imagining activity that one's imaging ability be stocked with intuited awarenesses of striking past traits as well as futural glints of inter-

---

21 "Nuance" is a key term for me in describing that feature of reality that is peculiarly aesthetic. "Nuance" refers straightforwardly to whatever is partially hidden and playful ("ludic"), elusive like subtle variations and delicate shadings. A synonym of "nuancefulness" is "allusivity." Cf. my *Rainbows for the Fallen World: Aesthetic life and artistic task* (Toronto Tuppence Press, 1980), 49–52, 131–35.

esting matters all of which inhere in the present. One's gift for configured feelings and for ability to imitate or recall experienced images needs to be primed, as it were, to spill over into new constellations when one begins an imagining act.

An *empathetic sensitivity* is another underground function supportive of anybody's imagining activity. A flaccid sensibility drags down the fun of playing bears. But if one has developed a lively feeling power to sneak into crevices of hidden quirks waiting to be nuancefully felt (*Einfühlung*), then one's playing bears prospers. A free-wheeling association of ambiguities half-sensed and delightedly perceived percolates in one's consciousness and effectively gives buoyancy to any imagining activity.

The same is so for a person's basic physical and organic functionality: a kind of *impulsive vitality* and *spontaneous physicality* are corporeally necessary for imagining to flourish. A physically wasted person or elderly patient whose biophysical life processes as a whole are only marginal or severely malfunctioning will have trouble rising above such handicaps to be busy imaginatively. Muscle tone and healthy reflexes are normal preconditions for somebody to play bears.

Empathy, remembered imaging, impulsivity, and laughing spontaneity are *not imagining functions*. Empathy is a feeling, imaging is a formative function, impulsivity is organic, and a laugh in spontaneity is downright physical by nature. But empathy, imaging, impulsivity, and a concentrated physical spontaneity awaiting release are emotional, formative, organic, and physical functions of one's corporeal reality, deepened if you will, aesthetically. And such aesthetically impregnated and enriched emotional, formative, organic, and physical functionings are normally necessary (but not sufficient) conditions supporting anybody's ordinary imaginative action.

An imaginative act in which one pretends to be like something else or makes-believe squirrels are devils or a woman is a submarine probably comes to be in stages. It is difficult to discern exactly whether to count a person's active whimsicality as a state of simply being in "good spirits" prior to becoming imaginatively busy or read it as an early step that builds up to a full imaginative act. It may not make much difference. But whimsicality, a predisposition to laughter, and a demeanor brimming with fun, an attitude of playfulness, on the lookout for fanciful surprises: all such elementary aesthetic functionings—frolicking among nuances, so to speak—are constitutive moments within an imaginative act. The presence and coalescence of a mimic playfulness and fantasy are certainly critical in the becoming of an imaginative act. Playfulness and pretending *as if* may even be the minimal sine qua non, sufficient conditions for a given act to be qualified by an imagining function.

The singular, determinative feature of a human creature's imaginative act may be best described perhaps as a *similation of strange affairs*.[22] The core of being busy imaginatively is to be discovering resemblances of some odd-appropriate sort that remain allusive but compel attention and elliptically present metaphoric insight. Women whose vulnerable, bodily cavities give security, birth, and life to children can also be places of great strength and protection for their babies once outside in the world. An underwater submarine proceeds stealthily in dangerous water. If it must surface and raise its periscope, it does so warily. A human mother, a ponderous human Mother Earth, alarmed at the murder and destitution of countless children in the world, might rear up startled and vulnerable, rigid periscopic neck, adamant head, piercing eye, and look fixedly to see where her mighty limbs and massive care are needed. One is imagining about the earthy role of woman and the prospects of mortal danger for her offspring when one juxtaposes with intriguing ambiguity a mother earth figure and a periscope on guard. As a professional imaginator Henry [#25] Moore has also carved such a similation into a fiction composed of five meters of Travertine marble.

[#25] Henry Moore, *Reclining Figure*,
outside UNESCO Building in Paris, 1957-58

---

22 See note 7 on page 11.

The imaginative act of a human subject[23] is always situated and dated, circumstantial, within a personal life history, formed by a larger-than-individual tradition, set in a society with a cultural matrix of one spirit or another where cross-currents of historical retreat and development in all these many facets and more are constantly impinging upon what creatures do. Imagining acts admit of differences in quality. "My love is like a rose" is an inscription of a fiction that has less aesthetic staying power than the line "My luv is like a red, red rose." When imaginative acts are sturdy and rich, ranging widely and mature, they show coefficients of expressivity, wit, entertainment, irony, festivity, and many more (analogical) functions. When someone's imaginative attempt is thin, underdeveloped, or stillborn, the imagining reverts quite easily to what is trite, following the proper form but without the ludic spark. It is even possible for imagining acts to be denatured while the person carries on with it. A stunted imagining may stem from the fact that one's openness to imaginative activity was closed down by others, repressed or curtailed because imagining was considered to be an irrational or unredemptive waste of time. The anomaly is, however, that often zany people, neurotic, irreverent, socially maladjusted and skeptical, may still be richly endowed with imagining gifts.

God's calling for imaginativity. There is a creational law of God that holds for the human exercise of imaginativity, just as there are callings of God for other modes of functional activity. All the various creational ordinances spoken by God hold firm during changing times for the many different creatural subjects; each calling holds according to its kind. Any such *modal law* needs to be followed by a human subject who intends to be meaningful in that certain way of acting.[24]

For anybody to follow a modal law calling of God is a different matter than for one to be obedient in the directional Way of life or death.

---

23 Animals have an uncanny thought process, figuring out their survival, but they do not think out theories. Animals also sport about, and perhaps mimic a fellow creature (in a mating dance), but they do not narrate stories or write down metaphors. That is, animals may do animal thinking and animal imagining, but animals are not structured by selfhood and do not have the religious intentionality and responsibility that is inescapably at the heart of human acts.

24 "Modal law" is a technical term referring to the structural ordinances God has set for different kinds of activities, for example, a law for thinking or a law for doing what is just. "Modal laws" are not "natural" laws, but are understood to be our Creator's specific callings for creatures to be God's royal subjects. Cf. my chapter on "Dooyeweerd's Legacy for Aesthetics: Modal Law Theory," in *The Legacy of Herman Dooyeweerd* (University Press of America, 1985) {infra pp. 45–80}.

— Imaginativity —

The *command* of God, "Love me above everything—my Rule first !—and your neighbor as yourself" (Deuteronomy 6:4–7, Matthew 6:33–34, Romans 13:8–10) is put to the hearted human creature; and if man or woman has not been moved by the Holy Spirit to obey that directive, adopted in Jesus Christ by God's grace, that person remains sinfully headed toward the creatural end of death (Deuteronomy 30:11–20, Ephesians 2:9–10). So humans respond to creational ordinances basically in a godly or in a godless way, that is, with their heart open or closed to the direction of the Holy Spirit. Therefore it is possible for a human creature to be misdirectedly busy even if he or she follows the various modal law callings with brilliance.

The relation between God's directional command of love and God's various modal callings under which and within which we human subjects severally function is construed by the responsible human task of issuing *imperatives,* in order to disclose the way we may find obedient modal meaning. This is a foremost human office: to show what it means to love the Lord in this or that modal way, how to respond obediently as God's subject in following this or that kind of calling.

A possible way to formulate the (aesthetic) imperative for imagining functionality and imaginating activity of human creatures is this: note or present or perform the nuances there be playfully; present what a given state of affairs is like; transform dissimilars into a similative surprise; and do this as praise of God, with care for things, in winsome service to all and sundry.

Such an imperative for matters imaginative would be, I believe, if enacted by human subjects, a harbinger of blessing. The imperative holds for playing bears, for imagining bird songs are angel voices, for catching the nuance of a mother on submarine alert for her kids, for composing love songs with a Scottish burr, for the functioning of imagining wherever it isotopically lurks in the existential human makeup. This aesthetic imperative for all matters of imaginativity occurs in an interrelated mesh with many other imperatives for all the other kinds of callings we creatures have. And the imperatives relevant for callings diverse from imaginativity hold simultaneously on the person who for the nonce happens to be imaginating.

The particular law for imaginativity can be not met through ignorance or incapacity. Some people get carried away with the similitude and start to bite people when they play bears. Others miss the happy ingenuity of being compared to a submarine and are offended, as if their anatomy is under critique. Still another may question your biblical orthodoxy in comparing birds to angels because they miss the humorous play in the simile. Such offended, people-biting literalists do not know how to be imaginative.[25] In games they are called "poor sports." In daily concourse they may be dour, no-nonsense people who simply lack a lilt of joy to their life. They are not mean-spirited so much as void of make-believe; but unimaginative people often become serious kill-joys on the loose.

The particular calling of God for imaginativity can also be willfully violated. When people imagine and do it purposely without constraints, as if such activity were a law and domain to itself, autonomous, then imaginative activity becomes ugly and brutal in a self-preening sort of idolatry. The dandy who commits himself to live totally within imaginative splendor and regards unsophisticated folk as untouchables, such a usurpation by imagining activity of human life, which is subject to many other legitimate imperatives, brings with it a loveless quality of fevered, consuming preciosity that is both *raffiné* and effete. Whenever one indulges one's imaginative (or analytic or emotional or whatever) subjectivity not as a response to a cosmic calling but as a prerogative anchored in oneself, cultural ruin is at hand. The closed world of *haute couture* today, for example, is largely an expression ("suppression") of imagining in unrighteousness: exploitive, demeaning, ludicrous. The perversity of evil imagining and its curse upon creatures is not always the blatant lie of a cleverly tempting porno film that will destroy the play of erotic love and manipulate the flesh of victims; sometimes the imagining Lie is an insidious godlessness that induces one to enter an alluring labyrinth only to seal one up in a mesmerized ennui. Imaginative seduction is sinful and destructive as well as imagining rape.

Christians can posit mistaken imperatives for a given area of creation, such as imaginativity. Secular disbelievers in Jesus Christ can posit fairly correct imperatives for a given area of human activity. Even when theorists deny the existence of God's lawful callings as structured ways within which God commands an obedient response of praise and neighborly love, care and fruitful cultivating of the earth, anyone who recognizes, for example, that imaginativity has a nature of its own or some kind of identity, must and usually does fabricate an (ontological) rationale for imagining that meets the mark (whatever it is) or doesn't. In my judgment, even an old-fashioned positivist or a serious phenomenologist who intends merely to describe the marks which define pure cases of "imagining" is appealing to some kind of enduring order. That such order of

---

[25] For examples of this defect with respect to conversation, fairy tales, and one's confession of faith, cf. *Rainbows for the Fallen World*, 52–59.

interwoven, irreducible ways-of-being-there is God's structuring Word spoken in love for our creaturely good is an article of faith that shapes a biblically christian philosophical systematics.

Imaginata. The kind of entities that result from imaginating acts I called fictions. The distillate of brief, human imaginative acts may be fleeting imaginings, so fleeting or provisional that a conscious hold on certain prehended nuances, the *Vorstellung*, gets lost in the jumble of feelings, concepts, images, signs, concerns, and beliefs that are constantly in one's consciousness. But musings and fancies, similes and graphic metaphors—*imaginata*—deserve recognition of their distinct identity. A fiction is a nuanceful or aesthetic object in the way that concepts are analytic objects and words are semantic objects: results of human activity whose particular existence is defined by object-functionality. Concepts exist to be thought; words exist to be spoken; fictions exist to be imagined. It is so that *imaginata* are also thinkable and discussable, as well as (un)believable or copyrightable. But fictions, which are at core metaphoric similations, cannot be concept-straightened out or paraphrased exactly, tested as certitudes or exhausted as legal tender. Fictions are aesthetic modal objects in the press of life and embody their own peculiar kind of congealed knowledge and glory.

Artworks are a complicated sort of fiction in which the imaginative qualification has received crafted underpinnings in a medium that seems to provide a more independent entity-character to artworks than aesthetic objects enjoy. Artworks last beyond a circumstantial setting in ways that occasional *imaginata* do not. A discussion of such problems in the theory of artistry lies beyond the scope of this paper. It will also be important to test the thesis that while fictions easily subsume images and *sensa*, fictions do not depend upon semantic signs or distinct concepts for their integrity as fictions, because clarity and non-contradictory identifications dispel the penumbras of underexposed and overexposed hints and allusions fictions need.

Relational meaning of imaginativity

Just as language is not merely a convenient instrument for theoretical thinking but itself represents an important way humans exist historically in the world, each with a mother tongue, so imaginativity is not simply a quirk of the artistic personality that helps the artist write poetry, but is an important way men and women exist historically in the world. Our imaginating reality is not the center of human meaning, but imaginativity is as relatively fundamental in import for human life as our gift of speech. The world of music, literature, painting and sculpture, choreographic dance, architectural design, theatre, song, and much more artistry depends upon and is generated by the imaginating responsibility given to human nature, and affects everyone's livelihood with its presence and quality of specially constructed sight and sound fictions. But even before the world of artistry—which in our day is cruelly burdened by being split into an elitist tradition for the initiated and a pop art for the historically uninformed masses—there is the fund of *imaginata* into which each person enters in his or her time, the fund of *imaginata* that one alters and carries along unconsciously from day to day. The sort of *Vorstellungen* that inhabit us, the integrity and caliber of the "symbols" we subliminally live by, the versatility of our imagining functionality, and the exercised openness we have to the incredible wealth of imaginativables in the world (the aesthetic object-functions of non-human creaturely reality), all drastically shape the richness or poverty and texture of one's human disposition and well-being.

The imagining functional dimension to other kinds of human acts testifies of the relational meaning of imaginativity, its adverbial service one might call it. For example, thinking done imaginatively will thrive on suppositions, while thinking that lacks imaginativity will tend to shun the worth of probabilities. Edward Casey's analysis of "imagining-that," instead of defining imagining proper, is actually pointing to the imagining moment within thinking, a thinking common to modal logic, he says, and its projection of possible worlds, where contrary-to-fact distinctions are thought through and analytic postulates are made.[26] As-if thinking or hypothetic activity often sparks scientific exploration, and

---

26 Like Hans Vaihinger who dissociates "fiction" from "hypothesis" in *Philosophy of "As if"* (1911, translated by C. K. Ogden, London: Routledge & Kegan Paul, 1924, 81–95), Edward Casey differentiates "sheer supposing" from "hypothesizing" *(Imagining,* 48, 81, 114–116). The rationale of both Casey and Vaihinger, however, uses the criterion that fictions have *no relation to reality* ("sheer supposition"), while hypotheses are meant to be checked out against actual phenomenal facts. Such a position wrongly denies the fact that *realities!* are being imagined in leading to *imaginata.* Cf. pages 33–35 above. Kendall Walton's ingenious analysis of "fictional statements" and his proposal that "appreciators (of fictional worlds) are fictional" as well as "actual," in "How remote are fictional worlds from the real world?" *The Journal of Aesthetics and Art Criticism* 37:1 (1978): 20–21, is also troubled, I think, by the assumption that fictions lack real referents. Paul Ricoeur takes a different tack on "the referential values of metaphoric and, in general, symbolic expressions," in *Interpretation Theory: Discourse and the Surplus of Meaning* (Fort Worth: Texas Christian University Press, 1976), 25–44.

underlies much of what passes for "original" thinking. Polanyi's term for the function of a thinking act in touch with indeterminate reality is "intellectual passions," and thinking informed by intellectual passions selects facts that are "interesting," providing a valuable, heuristic service in scientific examination.[27] I too understand conceptual guessing and the important hunch in human life to be the imagining function within analytic activity. Without that functional dimension percolating in one's thinking, one's thinking will tend to lose play and become intellectually astigmatic, with blind spots, unable to identify what Maurice Cohen has called the "twilight zones" of reality that challenge conceptual activity to stay supple.[28] Arid thought happens when somebody (or even a school of philosophic thinkers) has let the imagining function within analysis atrophy.

When the imagining functional quality of one's confessional life goes limp, aberrations occur in creedal activity. Confession of what Allah has done for your nation, for example, may become fanatically doctrinaire, without a ripple of ambiguity. Or sacraments may virtually disappear from one's church worship and be considered formalities one is obligated to perform, for their teaching content or emotional effects, but not as an act intrinsic to the well-being of a communal confession.

When I *believe-that* "I am not my own but belong—body and soul, in life and in death—to my faithful Savior Jesus Christ" I am bodily testifying (*notitia*) of the faith worked in my heart by the Holy Spirit (*fiducia*) to whom I have wholeheartedly committed myself (*assensus*). When I deliberately *believe-in* the LORD revealed by the holy Scriptures, I am bodily testifying (*martyrion, testimonium*), directly recapitulatmg (modally) the faith rooting me centrally (*fiducia*) and to whose Giver I have entrusted myself (*assensus*). When the child of my body is ceremonially baptized in the name of the Father, the Son, and the Holy Spirit, I am *believing-how,* I am bodily confessing in a likeness (*symbolum*) the covenanted assurance of salvation from sin deeply convicting me by Grace (*fiducia*), and to what kind of Lord I have pledged my heart (*assensus*). Ritually showing I

---

27 Michael Polanyi, *Personal Knowledge: Towards a post-critical philosophy* [1958] (New York: Harper & Row, 1964), 134–36, 142–45, 150, 190.

28 Morris Raphael Cohen, *A Preface to Logic* (1944, New York: Meridian, 1956): ". . . there are elements of indetermination in the denotation of concepts. . . . the relative extent of illumined focal region and twilight or penumbral zone varies with different concepts" (80). "Metaphors may thus be viewed as expressing the vague and confused but primal perception of identity which subsequent processes of discrimination transform into the clear assertion of an identity or common element (or relation) which the two different things possess" (96).

"believe-how" the LORD deals with us creatures is a fully creedal act, ontologically possible because of the imagining functional dimension within the human credo. Sacramental and liturgical moments of confessional life find no substitute in piety, dogma, *koinonia,* sacrifice, prayer, or other features of a full-orbed, confessional profession of one's existential attachment to the true God or to any no-god. Without the imagining function at work in one's mode of belief, one's confessional edifying activity has lost a very subtle, constitutive element.

Much more could be said on the relational importance of imaginativity. At this juncture we can rest with the brief that imaginativity is the nucleus of an ontologically prime, functional aspect of reality. It makes historical and philosophically reforming sense to attribute the name "aesthetic" to such an irreducible mode of allusive reality—"making-believe." This "imagining" way of functioning and, upon occasion, of acting is an integral moment of our whole human existence *coram Deo.* We do well to accept the gift of imaginativity as an avenue for joy.

Dooyeweerd's Legacy for Aesthetics:
Modal Law Theory

Aesthetics as a special science

Dooyeweerd's legacy for aesthetic theory can be pinpointed by a footnote he added in 1953 to a passage written in 1935. First the passage:

> Logic, ethics, and aesthetics are generally considered as being parts of philosophy.* In addition, the concession is made that there must be room for a philosophy of the special sciences and for a general epistemology. But according to the generally held opinion, philosophy and science must remain separate, in order to insure the "objectivity" of the latter. When special sciences operate within their own sphere and employ their own scientific methods, they are to be considered as being independent of philosophy.

Then the footnote:

> *I can not agree with this opinion. Only the special *philosophy* of logic, ethics, and aesthetics does have this character. But, here too, philosophy permeates special scientific thought. (*NC* 1:545–46)

What Dooyeweerd has in mind here is his theory of modal law-structures, which, along with his theories of religion and faith, is another chief feature of his thought. Dooyeweerd contests an old-fashioned humanist thesis that a science like mathematics or physics does best on its own, free from philosophical interference. It is not true, says Dooyeweerd: every definite science has taken a philosophical stance on the limits of its field and how its conceptual results relate to other universes of discourse and knowledge. Mathematics is not merely mathematics any more than business is just business. Modern biological science has armed camps of mechanists and vitalists and holists, and they do philosophical war with one another (*New Critique of Theoretical Thought* [*NC*] 1:564–65)—why would they fight if biology is purely biology? Current positivists pretend the science of jurisprudence only deals with facts, but the positivist betrays a covert philosophical view of reality when he introduces jural facts

---

This essay originally appeared in *The Legacy of Herman Dooyeweerd*, ed. C. T. McIntire (New York: University Press of America, 1985), 41–79.

as "theoretical fictions" to be adjudicated, as if only psycho-physical realities are "facts" (*NC* 1:551–52).

Many thinkers do consider logic and ethics and aesthetics to be branches of philosophy—this is the opening quote from Dooyeweerd above—and presumably subject to philosophical whimsy. But here I disagree, says Dooyeweerd in the footnote. Logic, ethics, and aesthetics as specific disciplines will certainly have philosophical presuppositions; but what is important to realize is that logic and ethics and aesthetics are special sciences, each with its own irreducible terrain to map out, each science with acts and things and structural laws peculiar to its delimitable field. Aesthetics is a special science like economics, linguistics, physics, psychology, or whatever body of analysis that can cohere as a systematic investigation of reality brought into focus by some prime structuring feature (*NC* 1:565). Aesthetics is not a minor topic in philosophy proper, according to Dooyeweerd, even though that is the way aesthetics has been normally treated in North America. Aesthetics is meant to be a basic science with its own kind of integrity because there is an irreducible order of reality that demands special treatment as aesthetic reality, interwoven with all the other features of the universe.

To be sure, Dooyeweerd did not particularly have in mind the need to give aesthetics its own stamping ground. In volume one of his *New Critique of Theoretical Thought*, he argued that philosophy necessarily has presuppositions born out of one's religious faith-commitment and, further, that all immanentistic philosophy struggles with the basic antinomy of pitting part of creation as law *dialectically* against another part of creation as subject to the law (cf. also *Twilight of Western Thought* [*Twi*], 30–51). Dooyeweerd's concern in volume two was to develop a theory of functional modal law-structures that would explicate a nondialectical, seamless conception of the cosmic temporal order for creaturely subjects, an idea that he believed the biblical truth of God's creation generates. Dooyeweerd was intent upon finding a systematic way to achieve a true encompassing understanding of the interrelations of the proliferating special sciences. Within this setting of modal law theory, Dooyeweerd's thesis—practically no more than a casual assumption—that aesthetics is one of those special sciences was truly insightful.[1]

---

1 D. H. T. Vollenhoven, who was closely allied with Dooyeweerd in the formation of the philosophical community associated with the Free University of Amsterdam, also posited the irreducible nature of aesthetic reality and legitimated aesthetics as a special science; see his *Isagogè philosophiae* (1943) translated by John Kok (Sioux Center: Dordt College Press, 2005), 25–26. The thought may have been stimulated by Wilhelm Windelband's comments in "Normen und Naturgesetze" (1882) in *Präludien*

There had been fits and starts historically to identify a special terrain of investigation as "aesthetic." In 1735 Alexander Baumgarten initiated a discipline he called "aesthetics" by translating the age-old idea of Beauty into a concept of "perfection," which, when modifying sensate knowledge, produced poetry, as he saw it. "Aesthetics" then was conceived as a subordinate theory of perfect sensate knowing.[2] Although Immanuel Kant (1724–1804) began identifying "aesthetic" with sensation too, Kant's later attempt to mark off "aesthetic" as a distinct kind of human activity—"taste judgment"—located its character in the nondescript play of human cognitive faculties, which brims with thoughts not able to be captured in words.[3] Kant settled on a kind of uniting, favorable feeling of vague purposivity as the peculiar nature of "aesthetic" judgment.[4] C. W. F. Hegel (1770–1831) brought the long tradition of reflection on Beauty to a self-consciously sharp focus on art and, in effect, defined aesthetics as "philosophy of [fine] art."[5] Unfortunately, Hegel set the parameters for most aesthetic theory that followed his contribution.[6] Aesthetics remained a general theory, whether speculative or aggregative, about matters artistic.

Benedetto Croce (1866–1952) was among the first after Baumgarten and Kant who tried to give both a particular specificity and a scientific rigor to aesthetics as a science next to the other sciences of logic, economics, and ethics, each with its own defined terrain for attention. His formative volume, *Estetica come scienza dell'espressione e linguistica generale* (Aesthetics as science of expression and general linguistics) (1902), remained stuck, however, in an idealism that also elided art phenomena into an identification with (poetic) language.[7] Max Dessoir (1867–1947) tried

---

(Tubingen: Mohr, 1907), 291–92. See *NC* 2:239–41.

2 Alexander Gottlieb Baumgarten, *Meditationes philosophicae de nonnullis ad poema pertinentibus* (1735), par. 9, "Oratio sensitiva perfecta est POEMA. . ."; par. 115, "Philosophia poetica est per no. 9 scientia ad perfectionem dirigens orationem sensitivam." Cf. *Aesthetica* (1750), par. 1, 14.

3 See Immanuel Kant, *Kritik der reinen Vernunft* (1781), A21–22; altered in second edition (1787), B35–36. See also Immanuel Kant, *Kritik der Urteilskraft* (1790), par. 20, 44–45, 49. For commentary see Calvin C. Seerveld, *Rainbows for the Fallen World: Aesthetic life and artistic task* (Toronto: Tuppence, 1980), 115.

4 See Lambert Zuidervaart, "Kant's Critique of Beauty and Taste: Explorations into a Philosophical Aesthetics" (M. Phil. thesis, Institute for Christian Studies, 1975), 143–73.

5 G. W. F. Hegel, *Vorlesungen über die Aesthetik,* ed. Friedrich Bassenga, edition of 1842 Hotho publication (Weimar: Aufbau-Verlag, 1955), 1:13.

6 See Karel Kuypers, *Kants Kunsttheorie und die Einheit der Kritik der Urteilskraft* (Amsterdam: North-Holland, 1972), 157–58.

7 Benedetto Croce, "Filosofia del linguaggio e filosofia dell'arte sono la stessa cosa," in

to distinguish aesthetics carefully from art theory and to unite the relevant splinter of problems treated by psychology and cultural history and technical theory into a field organized properly by aesthetic categories.[8] But the *Zeitschrift für Aesthetik und Allgemeine Kunstwissenschaft*, which Dessoir initiated and edited (1906–39), remained a conglomeration of specialized studies in *Einfühlung* (empathy), epistemology, Japanese lacquers, the beauty of tragedy, and the like. Thomas Munro, founder of the American Society of Aesthetics (in 1942), wanted a "Scientific Method in Aesthetics" (1928) too.[9] But Munro's positivistic, empiricist bent left the "science" of aesthetics in the department of descriptive data, collections of art facts, and experimentally controlled responses to art facts. The encyclopedic *Philosophie der symbolischen Formen* (1923–29) by Ernst Cassirer, whose studies Dooyeweerd often cites,[10] did not treat aesthetics as a separate discipline; but Cassirer does give a perspective in cultural philosophy that seems to be congenial to a roster of varied sciences that do not need to be cut exactly on the "natural science" model.[11]

Now it was in the time of this ferment about whether aesthetics is a

---

Estetica come scienza dell'espressione e linguistica generale (Ban: Guis. Laterza & Figli, [1902] 1950), 156. See especially chapter 18, "Conclusione: Identità di linguistica ed estetica." Cf. Calvin G. Seerveld, *Benedetto Croce's Earlier Aesthetic Theories and Literary Criticism* (Kampen: Kok, 1958), 95–97.

8 Max Dessoir, *Aesthetik und allgemeine Kunstwissenschaft* (Stuttgart: Ferdinand Enke, 1906), xi–xii.

9 Thomas Munro, "Scientific Method in Aesthetics," in *Toward Science in Aesthetics* (New York: Liberal Arts, 1956), 3–150; in same volume see also "Aesthetics as a Science: Its Development in Europe and America" (1950).

10 See index on Cassirer, *NC* 4:24. Dooyeweerd criticizes Cassirer, however, for being controlled by the "science ideal" in his analysis of the development of the "Enlightenment" (e.g., *NC* 2:348f. n. 2).

11 Later Cassirer seems to gravitate toward a centering on art, almost as if artistic "symbolic form" activity typifies human nature more wholesomely than any other feature of human action. See Ernst Cassirer, *An Essay on Man: An introduction to a philosophy of human culture* [1944] (New York: Doubleday, Anchor Books, 1953), 41–44. See the papers of 1942–43 on "Language and Art" published posthumously in *Symbol, Myth, and Culture*, ed. D. P. Verene (New Haven: Yale University Press, 1979), 145–95. Cassirer's penetrating study *Zur Logik der Kulturwissenschaft* (Goteborg: Wettergren & Kerbers, 1942) deepens Dilthey's attempt to recognize not only the difference between "natural sciences" and the "humanities" but also the equal legitimacy of studies in both areas as "science." Dooyeweerd's distinction between "prelogical aspects" and "normative law-spheres" (*NC* 2:49, 118, 156 n.2, 335–36) struggles with the same problem and echoes, I think, albeit critically, the matter as it was formulated and left unresolved by Rickert and Windelband, who contrasted the areas of *Sollen* and *Sein*. For Dooyeweerd's critique see "Het juridisch causaliteitsprobleem in het licht der wetsidee." *Anti-revolutionaire Staatkunde* 2 (1928): 21–121.

science and a professional discipline of its own or not—of which Dooyeweerd as a nonspecialist in art theory or literary criticism was probably largely unaware—that Dooyeweerd challenged the religion-neutral autonomy of special sciences *and* proposed—en passant!—that aesthetics has the philosophical birthright to be granted the status of a special science. Dooyeweerd's legacy for aesthetics is this genial proposal, arising from his modal law theory, that aesthetics has a principle of integration that gives it bona fide limits and an irreducible field within the body of the sciences. Aesthetics is not to be just a subdivision of psychology, of semantics, or of societal theory; aesthetics is not the hobby of straight philosophers who like to use art for examples in their thinking. Aesthetics has its own rightful place and task to perform in the academy of systematic research, interpretation, and theoretical presentation of meaning. One could say, if one had an ounce of humor, that it is fruit of Dooyeweerd's whole philosophical vision that led him kindly to provide the orphan of aesthetics with a genuine home in the encyclopedia of the sciences (cf. James 1:27).[12]

Is the idea of "a special science," with its own kind of filtering analysis of things at large in the universe, a sound idea? Does it make any important difference in knowledge or curriculum whether economic science and political science are kept distinct? Is one's understanding of literature or sculpture harmed if the analytic concern of aesthetics is not differentiated from the analytic concern of linguistics? And what does "encyclopedia of the sciences" have to do with Christian scholarship? A reflective answer to such questions will disclose more deeply the genial insight of Dooyeweerd's legacy for aesthetics. The notion of "special science" can be examined from three vantage points: (1) a history of the problem of encyclopedia; (2) the multisided richness of ordinary human experience; and (3) the biblical perspective and Calvinian-Kuyperian vision directing Dooyeweerd's idea of special science.

Encyclopedia of the sciences

Dooyeweerd begins his *Encyclopaedie der rechtswetenschap* (Encyclopedia of jurisprudence)[13] exactly as Kuyper began his *Encyclopaedie der heilige*

---

12 See Calvin C. Seerveld, *A Turnabout in Aesthetics to Understanding* (Toronto: Institute for Christian Studies, 1974), 6–10 {infra pp. 235–240}.

13 Herman Dooyeweerd, *Encyclopaedie der rechtswetenschap* (Amsterdam: Free University of Amsterdam, Student Edition, 1946–68). This encyclopedia consists of several volumes of bound mimeographed materials from lectures Dooyeweerd gave at the Free University. They were issued as syllabi in various editions and arrangements from at least 1946 until 1968, although some parts came from the early thirties.

godgeleerdheid (Encyclopedia of sacred theology)[14]—with a review of the concept of "encyclopedia."

Ἐγκύκλιος παιδεία (encyclopedia) meant in Athens (400 BC) "the normal round of instruction" a freeborn Greek in the polis would undergo. Roman thinkers Vitruvius and Quintilian probably over-read the term to mean *orbis doctrinae*, "the circle of disciplines" (making up the universe of knowledge), because of what Aristotle did. He, without using the term "encyclopedia," had ordered almost all systematic knowledge (ἐπιστήμη) into physics (including kinetics, biology, psychology, mathematics), the "other" science (on first principles), practical science (including politicology, ethics, economics), and poietics (including rhetoric), with analytics as the propaedeutic, organizing instrument (ὄργανον). Patristic reflection considered the whole gamut of pagan scientific knowledge to be pieces of φιλοσοφία on which the new Christian γνῶσις (knowledge) rested—θεολογία; so φιλοσοφία became *ancilla theologiae*. Boethius (ca. AD 480–524), Casiodorus (ca. AD 490–ca. 585), and Isidore of Seville (ca. AD 560–636) gave a formulation for the *quadrivium* (arithmetic, geometry, musical theory, astronomy) and *trivium* (grammar, rhetoric, logic), which remained in force for centuries as the canon of liberal arts that any educated person would have studied. That pattern was altered slightly only when universities began to form in cities like Bologna, Paris, and Oxford in the 1100s and organized themselves into the four faculties of arts, medicine, law, and theology.

Dooyeweerd's point is that ever since Aristotle's ordering of the sciences, those in the West who busied themselves with general studies loosely followed Aristotle's compendium of knowledge without particularly questioning its teleological rationale. This fact holds true for the great scholastic philosophical theologians writing their summae too. Renaissance humanists, however, tried to unshackle particular studies from the Aristotelianized format topped by theology, and the emancipation of scientific studies that Galileo, Harvey, and others actually achieved against the constrictive authority of "the philosopher" was a happy fact by itself, says Dooyeweerd; but the eclectic, polyhistorical philology of literate humanists and the emerging, unrelated bodies of knowledge in astrophysics, calculus, and physiology boded ill for an integrated corpus of the arts and sciences. Francis Bacon's magnum opus, *Instauratio*

---

14 Abraham Kuyper, *Encyclopaedie der heilige godgeleerdheid* (1894) (Kampen: Kok, 1908), 1:1–45. This three-volume work was partially translated by J. Hendrik de Vries in 1898 and published with an introduction by Benjamin B. Warfield under the changed title, *Principles of Sacred Theology* (Grand Rapids: Eerdmans, 1963).

magna (The great instauration) of which two full parts appeared—*De dignitate et augmentis scientiarum* (On the dignity and advancement of scientific knowledge) (1605, 1623) and *Novum organum scientiarum* (A new instrument of theoretical thought) (1620)—and Reformed thinker Johann Alsted's enormous *Cursus philosophici encyclopedia* (Encyclopedia of the philosophical course of studies) (1620) still tried to incorporate all knowledge under a refurbished, Aristotelian schema; but the old center no longer held. Denis Diderot and Jean d'Alembert's edited *Encyclopédie, ou dictionnaire raisonné des sciences, des arts et des métiers, par une société de gens de lettres* (Encyclopedia, or a reasoned dictionary of the sciences, arts, and trades, for men and women of letters) (1751–72) capitulated and honestly arranged the collected knowledge about everything under the sun in an alphabetical, not systematic, order.[15]

This matter of "encyclopedia" is a genuinely philosophical problem also afflicting us in our times, says Dooyeweerd. A university seems to cohere today only by virtue of administrative glue. Despite Johann Gottlieb Fichte's *Grundlage der gesamten Wissenschaften* (Foundations of the entire corpus of sciences) (1794), "a science of science" (or "a theory of theory"), and despite Hegel's *Enzyklopadie der philosophischen Wissenschaften im Grundrisse* (A compendium of the encyclopedia of the philosophical sciences) (1817) that sought a unified, systematic principle to relate studies in "natural science" and "cultural science," "logic" and "societology," the acceptance of any overarching, interrelational structure for ordering human knowledge is taken to be uncritically dogmatic. Auguste Comte's *Cours de philosophie positive* (A treatise on positive philosophy) (1830–42) was instrumental in forming the positivist mind that "method" (understood as the accumulation of sociological, positive facts) is to be the up-front concern of a secular thinker who wants to insure unprejudiced meaning in scientific analysis. But, runs the thrust of Dooyeweerd's reflection, because the method of a given science and the method of scientific or philosophical theory as a whole are loaded with cosmological, anthropological, and ontological presuppositions, the problems of defining the method of a science, interrelating the sciences, ascertaining any grounding precedence among the sciences, and identifying principles of taxonomy and origination of newly formed sciences remain unavoidable

---

15 See Dooyeweerd, *Encyclopaedic der rechtswetenschap*. See also *NC* 1:528–41. It is significant that in the most recent *Encyclopedia of Philosophy* (New York: Macmillan, 1967) the extensive article on "Encyclopedia" (6:170–99), written by William Gerber, treats the term in the sense of a philosophical *dictionary*. Gerber remarks that in Johann H. Alsted's *Compendium lexici philosophici* "most of the material in it is not arranged alphabetically and is therefore difficult to follow" (6:1–76)!

if one believes knowable reality hangs together somehow and intends to analyze precisely this state of affairs. Dooyeweerd concludes that "encyclopedia" properly means the intrinsically systematic and interrelational coherence of sciences with different, definite identities.

Cigars in God's world of human experience
Lest anyone reproach the judgment, says Dooyeweerd, that a basic task of philosophy is the institution of an encyclopedia of the special sciences and a demonstration of how their meaning rests together on a focusing, religious Archimedean point and Ἀρχή going beyond the realm of temporal creatureliness (*NC* 1:545)—lest anyone reproach this judgment as speculatively a priori, says Dooyeweerd, let us simply take a look at ordinary experience.

I walk into a store to buy a box of cigars [#26].[16] If a jurist were watching, as a jurist, he would notice the rights and duties of buyer and

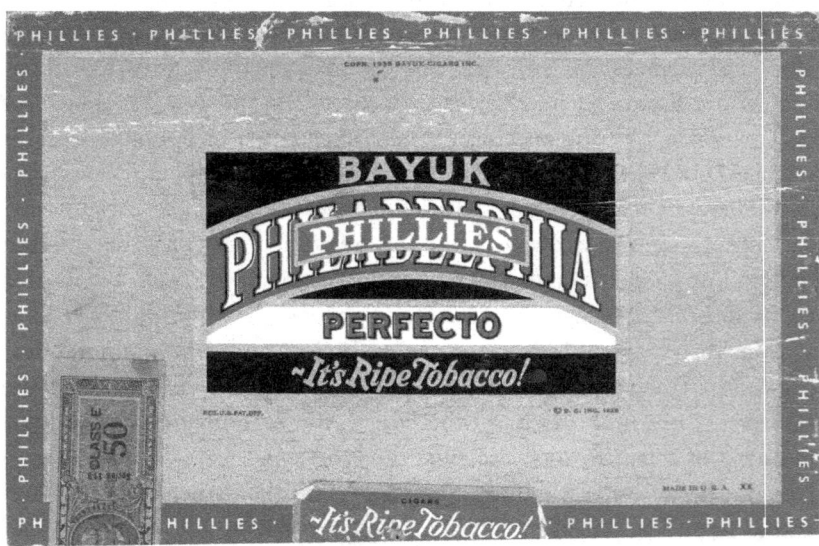

[#26] Cigar Box, *Phillies*

seller. An aesthetician will pay attention rather to the style of the activity, the gestures of the figures, perhaps the cut of their clothes and the interior design of the store. An economist will be interested primarily in the price and value of the cigars. A sociologist is concerned especially

---

16 Dooyeweerd is well-known among his students for this example, which he repeated with relish every year in the introductory seminar on jurisprudence at the Free University. See Herman Dooyeweerd, *Encyclopaedie der rechtswetenschap*.

with the mores of those in the shop, the customs of greetings and politesse, the neighborhood. A linguist might focus on the talk, its slang, correct speech forms, or inflection of dialect. An off-duty psychologist happening in would detect the emotions involved, the buyer's desire for a good smoke and the wish of the seller to please his customer. Although a physicist and mathematician do not usually examine the sale of cigars in their laboratory, such professionals could study the quantitative side of this business transaction, matters of inertia, velocity, size and number; after all, Dooyeweerd's buying cigars also falls into the realm of statistics.

The fact that the simple, concrete act of buying cigars really has such a rainbow of distinct sides to it, of possible interest to quite diverse professionals, is a remarkable given of our creaturely existence, says Dooyeweerd. Such a colorful range of facets holds somehow for every act, event, and thing in our lives. But what is even more fascinating is the built-in connection of these various aspects of an act. Suppose the invisible jurist noticed that the price paid by the buyer for this box of choice Havana cigars was a mere fifty cents. The jurist might wonder whether this exchange of goods and money was on the up-and-up, or the distribution of contraband to avoid governmental tax, or a payoff for illegal services. Immediately, every feature of the act is of jural concern to the jurist or lawyer: since the price was commercially not right, was the box of cigars a gift? reward? "protection money"? Was this neighborhood shop a storefront for a fence of smuggled luxury items? Was the wink of the buyer and shopkeeper's tug at his tie a covert sign of criminal agreement? Was the familiar brogue of the buyer and the elaborate style with which the box was wrapped and handed over an act to ward off suspicion that something illegal was happening? The jurist is not concerned with the emotions as such, but with whether and how the feelings of greed or fear or whatever complicate or mitigate the deed of these two persons which is controverting statute no. 1375 of the *Burgerlijk wetboek* (Code of civil law)—was there coercion or collusion? The jurist is interested in the movement of the box from the shopkeeper's shelf to the other person's briefcase not as an example of $F = ma$, but as evidence (secretly photographed by a CIA camera hidden in the ceiling over the counter) of a crime that will stand up in court as Exhibit A.

One could go on and on, about how buying and smoking cigars, whether illicit or legal, also has an aspect of passing interest to a professor of ethics—does the persistent nicotine stain on one's lungs received from smoking cigars constitute a willful (minor) mutilation of one's body and health and is, therefore, unethically destructive to a person? A jurist might want to tie into such reflection by possibly enacting a law forbidding sale of cigars to minors; for the common good, citizens should be old enough to know better before they engage in self-pollution. There is even a side to buying cigars that has affected the history of churches. The fact that Reformed Dutch piety set by Voetius (1588–1676) never banned cigars and *borreltjes* (gin cocktails) along with dancing and cardplaying has led many evangelical communions in North America, who regard all such practices as taboo, to judge the annual gatherings of the *Vereniging voor Calvinistische Wijsbegeerte* (Society for Calvinist Philosophy), for example, where cigar smoke rises so many feet thick above the heads of the members, as a witness to slack faith, maybe even a denial of 1 Corinthians 3:16–17.

The philosophical point Dooyeweerd is making is this: cigars in human life have myriad properties, qualities, and functional aspects (or modes), and all these rich strands of structuring reality are interwoven and hardly noticed by most of us in daily life. This actual richness of acts, events, and things is a creational a priori, however, holding for human consciousness, and can be disclosed, in Dooyeweerd's judgment, when specialized interests enter the scene and somebody in the office of jurist or psychologist, statistician, or researcher in linguistics—a theoretical scientist of some sort—looks for matters that particularly fit his or her focus for examination (*NC* 1:33–34). It is Dooyeweerd's thesis that this complex but unified fabric, which structures ordinary experience, needs to be recognized as ontically given, needs to be accounted for by philosophical endeavor, and may be accepted with thanks as an enduring hermeneutic for helping one understand happenings in history.

Abraham Kuyper's principle of sphere sovereignty
Dooyeweerd's entrée to this megaproject of theory—encyclopedia of the sciences, investigating the incredible, cohering richness of creatural existence—relates historically to a principle taught by Abraham Kuyper. In founding a university free from the state and free from the church—a Free University!—Kuyper enunciated in 1880 the biblically Christian confession of *souvereiniteit in eigen kring* (literally: A sovereignty for its own sphere, or sphere sovereignty). By this he meant that every circle of formative power in society has an authority proper to its own domain that is to be rightfully exercised by its leaders in direct responsibility to God.[17]

---

17 Kuyper introduced the Dutch phrase in the dedicatory speech by that name given at the opening of the Free University, *Souvereiniteit in eigen kring* (Amsterdam: Kruyt, 1880). These words have become a pregnant formulation of the insight and a veritable battle cry ever since. Following the principle of "a sovereignty for its

Kuyper proclaimed:

> Get it?! Not one bit of our thought-world is to be separated and hermetically sealed off from the other pieces of our conceptual universe. In fact, there is not to be a fingerprint speck of territory in our whole human life about which the Christ, who is sovereign over everything, is not calling out, "That belongs to me!"[18]

Kuyper's dynamic vision of sphere sovereignty under Christ was deeply formative upon Dooyeweerd. There is an extensive letter (15 May 1922) that Dooyeweerd wrote to the Dutch Minister of War, J. J. C. van Dijk, when he applied for the position of director at the Kuyper Institute in The Hague. In it Dooyeweerd, who was working in the Dutch government's Department of Labor at the time, analyzed the status quo of Calvinian societal research and then recapitulated two major Kuyperian themes when he announced what his priorities would be if he should get the job:

> Up to now we really have only piecemeal studies in the field of a Calvinian view of law and society. This is why the first task should be, it seems to me, to determine the method that will orient all our subsequent investigations. This method cannot be religion-neutral, but should be led by the principles set out so genially in Dr. Kuyper's developed theory of knowledge.... Once the method is set, then the primary work will be to subject the problem of "sovereignty"—the *foundational problem* of the whole Calvinian view of law and society—to a deep-going investigation.... I also see it as a definite advantage that the practical work in the Kuyper Institute will remain in close contact with theory. One-sided theoretical work can petrify into dried out abstraction if it misses contact with the pulse of life.[19]

---

own sphere," Christians of the Reformed tradition have been led to exercise communion of the saints outside the church door by establishing Christian schools, Christian colleges, a Christian political party (Anti-Revolutionaire Partij in the Netherlands, founded in 1879), a Christian labor union (Christian Labour Association of Canada, founded in 1952), Christian art workshop community and gallery (Patmos in Chicago and Toronto, 1969–79), and similar organizations.

For the connection between Kuyper and Dooyeweerd on sphere sovereignty see Albert M. Wolters, "The Intellectual Milieu of Herman Dooyeweerd," in *The Legacy of Herman Dooyeweerd: Reflections on critical philosophy in the Christian tradition*, ed. C. T. McIntire (Lanham: UPA, 1985), 1–19.

18 Abraham Kuyper, *Souvereiniteit in eigen kring*, 35 (my translation).

19 From a note appended to the letter of application Dooyeweerd sent to J. J. C. van Dijk (15 May 1922), quoted in G. Puchinger, "Dr. Herman Dooyeweerd," in *Perspectief: Feestbundel van de jongeren bij het vijfentwintigjarig bestaan van de Vereniging voor Calvinistische Wijsbegeerte* (Kampen: Kok, 1961), 49–51 (my translation). Kuyper, in the 1880 speech, emphasized that science (*wetenschap*) was also a life-sphere (*lev-*

Dooyeweerd's first article (1923) in the Kuyper Institute's popular journal dealt with the Calvinian principle of "a sovereignty for its own sphere" as the basic principle for statecraft.[20] This leading thought on the limited, responsible authority integral to a community in society—academic community, business community, family, church, state, or whatever—and the nonhierarchical interrelation proper to all kinds of communities within the whole of society was becoming a heuristic, methodological norm for Dooyeweerd's probing investigations.

> If one picks up a problem in a faulty way—if you faultily overreach from one universe of discourse and focus [*gezichtsveld*] into treating a different one with a view foreign to it, you are going to get confusion, or often worse, a kind of special pleading for one's own hobbyhorse [*beginselruiterij*].[21]

It was this germinal, Kuyperian idea of "a sovereignty for its own sphere," with its Calvinian ancestry,[22] that lay behind Dooyeweerd's imaginative formulation of a modal law theory.

Dooyeweerd very self-critically and gratefully acknowledges his debt to Kuyper, especially since Dooyeweerd was accused of threatening to bury the Reformational tradition with the first edition of his *De wijsbegeerte der wetsidee* (literally: A philosophy of the idea of law) published in 1935.[23] Kuyper in his Stone Lectures of 1898 at Princeton Univer-

---

enskring): "Wetenschap die wijs maakt. Uit het leven voor het leven. Eindigende in aanbidding van den alleenwijzen God!" (Scientific theory that makes one wise. That comes *out* of life and is *for* our life. That ends in being worship of the one and only all-wise God!) Kuyper, *Souvereiniteit in eigen kring*, 23.

20 Cited by Puchinger, "Dr. Herman Dooyeweerd," 53.

21 Quoted by Puchinger, "Dr. Herman Dooyeweerd," 99 (my translation).

22 See John Calvin, *Institutio Christianae religionis* (Institutes of the Christian Religion), IV.20.4. Martin Luther also broke with the idea of ecclesiastical hegemony, which had held big thinkers like Thomas Aquinas captive. But Luther's break with ecclesiastical hegemony did not have the positive appreciation for taking saintly command of "secular" political affairs, which Calvin showed. This fact is the reason why Dooyeweerd believed that a sense of Christian philosophy would probably need to rise out of a Calvinian milieu (*NC* 1:511–23).

23 See Valentine Hepp, *Dreigende deformatie* (Threatening deformation), 4 vols. (Kampen: Kok, 1936–37). It is ostensibly Hepp whom Dooyeweerd is answering in his article on "Kuyper's Wetenschapsleer" [1936], *Philosophia Reformata* 4 (1939): 193–94; cf. 198 n.2. Already in 1937 Dooyeweerd witnessed to the spiritual roots of his philosophical thinking in "Wat de wijsbegeerte der wetsidee aan Dr. Kuyper te danken heeft" *Reformatie* (29 September 1937). The most important, sustained, historical diagnosis in English of Dooyeweerd's roots is the careful, genial work by William Young, *Towards a Reformed Philosophy: The development of a protestant philosophy in Dutch Calvinistic thought since the time of Abraham Kuyper* (Franeker: Wever, 1952).

sity, wrote Dooyeweerd in 1939, leaves behind the traditional scholastic dichotomies that sometimes hinder his theoretical work and presents a powerfully biblical, Calvinian witness to God the Creator's sovereignty and God's varied ordinances for creation. Kuyper had written:

> Everything that has been created was, in its creation, furnished by God with an unchangeable law of its existence. And because God has fully ordained such laws and ordinances for all of life, therefore the Calvinist demands that all life be consecrated to His service, in strict obedience. . . Wherever man may stand, whatever he may do, to whatever he may apply his hand, in agriculture, in commerce, and in industry, or his mind, in the world of art, and science, he is, in whatsoever it may be, constantly standing before the face of his God, he is employed in the service of his God, he has strictly to obey his God, and above all, he has to aim at the glory of his God.[24]

Anybody, says Dooyeweerd,

> who has no more than even a half-baked acquaintance with the theory of modal law-spheres in the *Wijsbegeerte der wetsidee* will have to admit that the modal law-sphere theory is nothing but an inside, philosophically thinking-through and working-out of Kuyper's deeply religious and fully biblical conception of law-ordinance—the *Wijsbegeerte der wetsidee* explicates Kuyper's vision into a modal law-sphere theory as it makes its scientific-theoretical investigation into the structure of reality.[25]

All you need to do, writes Dooyeweerd, is read Kuyper's chapter on "Calvinism and Art" from his *Lectures on Calvinism* (1898):

> Our intellectual, ethical, religious, and aesthetic life each commands a sphere of its own. These spheres run parallel and do not allow the derivation of one from the other. It is the central emotion, the central impulse, and the central animation, in the mystical root of our being, which seeks to reveal itself to the outer world in this fourfold ramification. . . . If, however, it be asked how there can arise a unity of conception embracing these four domains, it constantly appears that in the finite this unity is only found at that point where it springs from the fountain of the Infinite. There is no unity in your thinking save by a well-ordered philosophical system, and there is no system of philosophy which does not ascend to the issues of the Infinite. . . . No unity in the revelation of art is conceivable, except by the art-inspiration of an Eternal Beautiful, which flows from the fountain of the Infinite. Hence no characteristic all-embracing art-style can arise except as a consequence of the peculiar impulse

---

24 Abraham Kuyper, "Calvinism and Religion," in *Lectures on Calvinism* (Grand Rapids: Eerdmans, 1961), 53.
25 Dooyeweerd, "Kuyper's wetenschapsleer," 217 (my translation).

from the Infinite that operates in our inmost being. And since this is the very privilege of Religion, over intellect, morality and art, that she alone effects the communion with the Infinite, in our self-consciousness, the call for a secular, all-embracing art-style, independent of any religious principle, is simply absurd.[26]

What immediately strikes a person reading this, says Dooyeweerd,

> is the pregnant thesis about the religious unity of the God-given law in its Source and central fullness of meaning. The idea of law-ordinance [*wetsidee*] runs quite parallel here with the conception of the human heart as the religious concentration point of all the temporal functions of its existence. So what follows from this [unity-in-diversity] is the mutual "sovereignty for its own sphere," the mutual, modal irreducibility of the diverse law-spheres expressly designated by name here in Kuyper.[27]

In this fertile conception of a Creator-ordained, providential world-order with temporally interwoven, mutually irreducible spheres of activity, Kuyper already had essentially the makings of a modal law-sphere theory. It was unfortunately a dichotomistic anthropology (of substantialized spirit and come-along body) and remnants of Logos-speculation, says Dooyeweerd, that hampered Kuyper from deepening the idea of "a sovereignty for its own sphere" into an encyclopedic theory of modal law-spheres. The Society for Calvinist Philosophy is trying to build, reformingly, on Kuyper's foundational vision.[28]

---

26 Abraham Kuyper, "Calvinism and Art," in *Lectures on Calvinism,* 150–51. It seems possible to me that Kuyper's idea here that religion "alone effects the communion with the Infinite, in our self-consciousness" is a source of the problem in Dooyeweerd about the so-called "supra-temporal heart." See the essays by James H. Olthuis and C. T. McIntire in *The Legacy of Herman Dooyeweerd.* See also John Vander Stelt's analysis of certain unreformed elements in Kuyper's pattern of thought, "Kuyper's Semi-mystical Conception," *Philosophia Reformata* 38 (1973): 182–87.

27 Dooyeweerd, "Kuyper's wetenschapsleer," 218 (my translation). Granted Dooyeweerd's apparent wobble on the "supra-temporality" of human selfhood, I still think there are good grounds for reading Dooyeweerd to mean here that the selfhooded subjectivity of the human is not lost in our many modal functions and is not dissolved in the unstoppable, continuous duration of time. Dooyeweerd means to say that the selfhooded subjectivity of every human is the gateway of religious unity humans have for knowing and living in Christ, directed toward the Sovereign Creator. The religious root ("den tijd transcendeerenden religieuzen wortel," *De Wijsbegeerte der Wetsidee* 1:471) in which selfhooded unity shares is *Christ.* Christ—and not the human heart!—is the Archimedean point, contrary to what Peter J. Steen seems to suggest in *The Structure of Herman Dooyeweerd's Thought* (Toronto: Wedge, 1983), 269. See *NC* 1:506 and 2:465, 473–74. See also note 55 below.

28 Dooyeweerd, "Kuyper's wetenschapsleer," 195, 225–27. Kuyper fell back into a fairly traditional and rough division of the sciences into five faculties: theology, law, medicine, natural science, and philological science (which included philosophy and his-

The nature of Christian theoretical activity

Dooyeweerd's connection with Kuyper and also with Calvin is made all the more clear when one realizes that the originating spark for these three figures was the fact that they had a common ear for the biblical revelation concerning the *kinds* of creatures God made, subject to God's will for their natures. The witness of Genesis 1 that the Lord made creatures after their kind, the eminent truth of Psalms 19, 119, 147, 148, and many more that God decreed laws for things, "an ordinance that the creatures do not overstep" (Psalm 148:6; my translation), and the New Testament truth that Christ's body is to be a unity of quite diverse tasks in life following the Lord's rule (Romans 12, 1 Corinthians 12): all this cumulative, biblically revealed truth moves one steeped in the Reformational, Calvinian tradition to respond with the confession and to catch the leading idea of God's protective, gracious, providing order for everything under the sun.

Occasionally, Dooyeweerd will explicitly cite the Scripture running behind the thoughts that direct his theoretical analysis, such as the truth of Psalm 139 lying behind the idea of "providential worldplan, which has its integral origin in the Sovereign Will of the Creator" (*NC* 1:174). But normally Dooyeweerd is not explicit: the basic scriptural *truth* dimension is present implicitly within the **Christian** philosophical *idea* that is shaping the conceptual *theory* that he is gradually assembling by way of the empirical analysis of the states of affairs he finds. It is my own judgment that this threefold distinction—truth, idea, theory—is a crucial one for rightly understanding the nature of the Christian scholarship that Dooyeweerd is attempting, and for grasping the tentative yet deadly serious spirit infusing his *theory* of modal law-spheres.[29] Dooyeweerd writes:

> To get one's thinking set by the true *a priori*, the first condition of all is to have the selfhooded one who is thinking *stand in* the Truth by a *hearted*

---

tory with linguistics). Cf. Kuyper, *Encyclopaedie der heilige godgeleerdheid* 2:132–61 (cited in note 14 above). Also *NC* 1:vi.

29 The sharp formulation of this threefold distinction is my own, but the matter is firmly present in Dooyeweerd's thought throughout. Dooyeweerd holds that a *transcendental idea* (a "limiting concept") serves as the real hypothesis for philosophical thought, that is, for the refined, *theoretical concepts* that articulate perceived distinctions. The *transcendental ideas* that limit philosophical thought also point toward *transcendent presupposita* (which for a Christian are biblically revealed *truth,* such as "the divine temporal world-order" and "Christ as the root and fullness of meaning of the cosmos"; cf. *NC* 1:506–8). *NC* 1:23–25, 86–88 and 2:44–46, 187–88. It is this very threefold distinction that makes clear how Dooyeweerd sets his own biblically directed theory off from Kantian and subsequent idealist theory that rests its "critique" of theoretical thought in *Ideas* (cf. esp. *NC* 1:88).

> acceptance of God's revelation. God's revelation enters our horizon of temporal existence only by way of our faith-functioning, which trusts fully in the *reliability* of God's Word. God is the Origin and Source of all Truth. Christ, as the complete revelation of God, is the full meaning of Truth. . . . So "standing in the Truth" directs also our subjective insight into the temporal horizon of our existence. (*De Wijsbegeerte der Wetsidee* 2:504; my translation)[30]

Dooyeweerd says this as he debates with the metaphysics of Thomas Aquinas (*NC* 1:179–85) because it lacks, in his judgment, a radically biblical rootage and integrality. What he means is: I believe the truth of Holy Scripture—that the Lord's creation cursed by sin is being redeemed through Jesus Christ along with those men, women, and children brought into the communion of his body by the Holy Spirit; I believe this truth is a real, convicting dynamic ("central ground-motive") that will bring "inner reformation of the theoretical vision of temporal reality" (*NC* 1:173, 176). In Dooyeweerd's words:

> The whole of my book is meant to give support to my fundamental thesis: it is precisely the perspectival structure of truth that grants surety that the Christian truth-idea *can* and *should* permeate scientific-theoretical thinking, root and branch. This idea of a genuinely *Christian* exercise of science and theory is utterly different from presenting an edifying faith-testimony that leaves the intrinsic practice of scientific-theoretical investigation really untouched.[31]

The theory of modal law-spheres is not Bible, Dooyeweerd is saying, but it is *Christian* theory, not just the theory of a Christian. The theory of modal law-spheres is meant to be conceptual *theory* (fallibly human, amendable, secondary reflection on experiential givens) that is infused by a holy sense of the central *truth* revealed by God in Jesus Christ and published in Scripture, and thereby led by *ideas* that are faith-formed translations of the truth and that as such bode wisdom for our theoretical, approximating knowledge of creaturely reality. For example,

> whoever denies "a sovereignty for its own sphere" of the societal communal relationships existing outside the church institution will—unless he or she accepts the organized hierarchical authority of the Roman catholic church communion—necessarily fall into a sectarianism that knows no bounds.[32]

---

30 I have translated the passage from the Dutch, honoring the italicized emphases of the original as well as making certain refinements. Cf. *NC* 2:572.

31 *WdW* 2:505; this passage, too, has been translated by me. Cf. *NC* 2:572.

32 Herman Dooyeweerd, "De strijd om het Schriftuurlijk karakter van de wijsbegeerte der wetsidee," *Mededelingen van de Vereniging voor Calvinistische Wijsbegeerte*, July

Or, if some thinker attempts to reduce one mode of meaning to another modal law-sphere,

> it must be distinctly understood that the abundance of meaning of creation is diminished by this subjective reduction. And perhaps without realizing what this procedure implies, one puts some temporal aspect of reality in the place of the religious fullness of meaning in Christ. (*NC* 2:36)

And Dooyeweerd could have added, quoting Kuyper, one might miss understanding that

> art is no fringe that is attached to the garment, and no amusement that is added to life, but a most serious power in our present existence. . . .[33]

This position on intrinsically Christian scholarship has been the core offense of Dooyeweerd to secular thinkers, but especially to many Christians who have been uncritical of the embedded categorial framework that schools their own analysis and judgments. Often such Christians have defensively attacked Dooyeweerd for not being biblically purebred in his philosophy. Dooyeweerd counters with a moving confession of the need to repudiate self-satisfaction on the part of Christians who confront secular thought (*NC* 1 :viii). Sin obfuscates insight again and again, and non-Christians have uncovered all kinds of things in God's world (*NC* 2:572); my critique of uncritical philosophical reflection and especially of synthetic Christian thinking, which compromises the wisdom that students and God's people need, says Dooyeweerd, is sharp because I am pleading with myself (*NC* 1 :viii).

But Dooyeweerd's scandalous thesis remains, and it is a mark of his genius: we can be blessed to work at and break through to "an inner reformation of philosophy" (*NC* 1:ix), even a Christian logic theory—why not?—God willing, if we think faithfully, reformingly together, over generations (*NC* 2:464–65).[34] It can become sheer vanity to reduce angels to

---

1950:3–6 (my translation). This article tried to explain why Dooyeweerd and Vollenhoven could not follow Klaas Schilder's movement to withdraw from the Gereformeerde Kerken in the Netherlands.

33 Kuyper, "Calvinism and Art," in *Lectures on Calvinism*, 151.

34 D. H. T. Vollenhoven made a start on theory of Christian logic in his *Logos en ratio* (Kampen: Kok, 1926), *De noodzakelijkheid eener christelijke logica* (Amsterdam: H. J. Paris, 1932), and *Hoofdlijnen der logica* (Kampen: Kok, 1948). N. T. van der Merwe carried the exploration further in his "Op weg na 'n christelike logika: 'n studie van enkele vraagstukke in die logika met besondere aandag aan D. H. Th. Vollenhoven se visie van 'n christelike logika" (Master's thesis, Potchefstroom University, 1958). Marinus Dirk Stafleu has impressively done something similar in the supposedly untouchable field of physics: *Time and Again: A Systematic Analysis of the Foundations of*

an academic problem; but it is a redemptive ministry to think through real problems, which face everybody, and to construct theories that may orient human consciousness in the way of shalom. The theory of modal law-spheres is a candidate Dooyeweerd puts forward as an analysis breaking the bread of life for thought. The theory of modal law-spheres is not presented as manna dropping straight out of heaven. But it is wholesome bread despite its impurities, and all interested Christian philosophers need to improve on its ingredients so that the Holy Spirit can multiply it to feed thousands of thinking students.

Modal law-sphere theory
It is not easy to make a simple statement of Dooyeweerd's modal law-sphere theory because he conceives systematic philosophy to be a web of mutually inseparably cohering themes. For example, simultaneously with the theory of the functional modes of existence as law-spheres, Dooyeweerd treats the theory of typical individuality structures and communal bonds holding for things. And these he explores with an awareness that one's transcendental categorial framework is determined by religious commitment, which is accompanied by an anthropological understanding that there is a central point of selfhood showing up in men and women who are irrevocably seeking ontic anchorage (*NC* 1:541–42). The intent of this essay, however, is not to repeat in outline all these theories, including the theory of modal law-spheres, which has been introduced many times before,[35] but to focus on how Dooyeweerd's theory of irre-

---

Physics (Toronto: Wedge, 1980).

35 In 1935 Dooyeweerd and Vollenhoven provisionally distinguished the following modal ways creaturely subjects were constituted: numerical, spatial, physical, organic, psychical, analytical, historical, lingual, social, economical, aesthetical, jural, ethical, pistic. See Vollenhoven, *Isagogé philosophiae,* 25–26, where Vollenhoven adds: "It is plain that there is a rich diversity in this first determinant [of being creaturely], and this rich abundance is perhaps even greater than we have seen so far." See notes 60 and 77 below.

Subsequent digests of the theory of modal law-spheres appear in various grades of completeness, clarity, and misrepresentation. Here follows a list of references: J. M. Spier, *Een inleiding tot de wijsbegeerte der wetsidee* [1939], trans. David H. Freeman, *An Introduction to Christian Philosophy* (Philadelphia: Presbyterian & Reformed, 1954), 31–122; K. J. Popma, *Inleiding in de wijsbegeerte* (Kampen: Snijder, 1951), 14–35; K. J. Popma, *Cursus ter inleiding in de wijsbegeerte der wetsidee* (Kampen: Vanden Berg, n.d.), 6–19; Michael Fr. J. Marlet, *Grundlinien der Kalvinistischen "Philosophie der Gesetzesidee" als Christlicher Transzendentalphilosophie* (Munich: Karl Zink, 1954), 48–52; Anna Louize Conradie, *The NeoCalvinistic Concept of Philosophy: A study in the problem of philosophic communication* (Natal: Natal University Press, 1960), 99–100; Vincent Brümmer, *Transcendental Criticism and Christian Philosophy: A presentation and evaluation of Herman Dooyeweerd's "Philosophy of the Cosmonomic Idea"*

ducible modal law-spheres presents a correction, challenge, and promise of blessing to the history of reflection on aesthetic realities.

For the sake of making a genuine legacy live for us, we do well to consider briefly: (1) a relevant historical tie-in with Nicolai Hartmann, (2) the particular, reformational philosophical features central to Dooyeweerd's position, and (3) a methodological problem in the modal law-sphere theory that can either unsettle or happily instigate ongoing reformation of this Christian theory in our generation.

Nicolai Hartmann's theory of strata of being

There is abundant evidence in the literature that this Christian theory of modal law-spheres is indeed a reformation of historical scholarship. One only need take a central dialogue of Plato, for example, the *Politeia* (Republic), to notice a developed theory on the different parts of the human soul. According to this Platonic dialogue, the λογιστικὸν (purely rational) and the ἐπιθυμητικὸν (driving-desiring) parts are structurally separate from each other as well as from a third, intermediate part known as the θυμοειδής (gutsy spirited). Each sector of soul activity has its respective ἀρετή (excellence or perfected power, virtue)—wisdom, courage, temperance—and each has its corresponding, ranking counterpart level of status in society—philosophic guardians, polis fighters (read "army"), the workers and tradespeople. In Plato's vision of human soul and society, the upper crust and the underdog portions of society, mirroring the microcosm of every soul, are simply the different, more or less coordinated ways things are set up, depending on Δίκη (justice).[36]

Aristotle's position on different facets of soul intersects with a commitment to an entelechaic bonding of matter (ὕλη) with superimposing form (μορφή). The result, at least in Περὶ Ψυχῆς (About the soul),[37] is a

---

(Franeker: Wever, 1961), 50–56; Ronald H. Nash, *Dooyeweerd and the Amsterdam Philosophy* (Grand Rapids: Zondervan, 1962), 39,57; L. Kalsbeek, *De wijsbegeerte der wetsidee: Proeve van een christelijke filosofie* [1970], ed. and trans. Bernard Zylstra and Josina Zylstra, *Contours of a Christian Philosophy: An introduction to Herman Dooyeweerd's thought* (Toronto: Wedge, 1975), 76–118; Hendrik J. van Eikema Hommes, *Inleiding tot de wijsbegeerte van Herman Dooyeweerd* (The Hague: Martinus Nijhoff, 1982), 33–73. I am afraid that Spier's early oversimplified popularization, and the inordinate amount of minute attention given to the "modal spheres" separated from their religious import often hypostatized into "modalities," misdirected the reception of Dooyeweerd's thought in the English-speaking world.

36 Plato, *Politeia,* 571a1–592b6.

37 Vollenhoven would note carefully how early Aristotle in *Physica* I, V–VI, showed a thoroughgoing interactionary monist conception of the ontic layers of reality. The Aristotle of *De Anima,* however, holds to a peculiarly inter-capsulated form of dual-

graduated, interlocked partitioning of the θρεπτική καὶ φυτική (growing-feeding) plant-soul formation of (ἄψυχον) body, which plant-soul in turn can be formed by αἰσθηική καὶ ὀρεκτική (sensing-longing) animal-soul formation, which may in turn be incorporated and activated by νοῦς παθητικὸς (a mental capacity) that can provide human composition to divine, contemplative theorizing.[38] Late Aristotle's strata of the physical, the vital, the sensitive, and the noetic present the strictly delineated and structurally differentiated ways of being certain things are, and, unlike Plato, Aristotle's conception views the hierarchy of ontic levels as purposefully interconnected. The higher layer depends upon the lower layer of being for its ability to be active, but the higher stratum of being is in principle independent for its character from the lower, more elemental kind of being.[39]

Such aporetic relations of diverse, autonomous substances and meshed connection, comparable to the schemata of Plato and Aristotle, carry on in various formats throughout the history of philosophy. Whether it be the several-in-one kingdom (ὑπόστασις) of Plotinus (AD 205–70) arranged in a circuit of processing (πρόοδος) and recurring (ἐπιστροφή),[40] or the logically speculative four divisions of φύσις (natural order) by John the Scot of Ireland (ca. AD 810–88) in *De divisione naturae* (On the division of nature),[41] theo-ontological cosmologies were formulated by thinkers who believed systematic completion was a requirement for a mature philosophy. When the cosmological problematics assumed a more epistemological focus, similar theories on how reality is structured continued. The monadological *harmonie préétablie* (preestablished harmony) of G. W. Leibniz (1646–1716) conceived a plenum of infinitesimally discernible force-centers that ranged by differential calculus from mechanical energy through grades of organic force, *l'appétit* (desire), *le sentiment* (feeling), memory, on to *l'esprit* (apperception), which harbors an abstracting think-ability operating by the laws of noncontradiction and sufficient reason.[42] Immanuel Kant's (1724–1804) *speculum mentis* (map of the mind) discerned *Empfindung* (sensation), *Rührung* (desire),

---

ism that Vollenhoven calls Monarchian dualism.
38 Aristotle, *De Anima*, 411b4–414a27, 429a9–429b4, 430a18–26.
39 For example, Aristotle, *De Anima*, 427b6–21. Cf. Nicolai Hartmann, "Die Anfange des Schichtungsgedankens in der Alten Philosophie" (1943), in *Kleinere Schriften* (Berlin; Walter de Gruyter, 1957), 2:181. Cf. also Henry I. Venema, "Aristotle and Imagination" (Seminar paper, Institute for Christian Studies, 1984), 3–11.
40 Plotinus, *Enneades* 1.6.6, 9; 5.5.3–6; 5.8.11–13.
41 See Hartmann, "Die Anfange des Schichtungsgedankens," 2:167.
42 For example, C. W. Leibniz, *Monadologie* (ca. 1714), par. 14–15, 19, 26–30.

Lust (pleasure), *Anschauungsform* (viewing-form), *Einbildungskraft* (imaging ability), *Verstand* (conceptual understanding), *Urteilskraft* (judgment-ability), and *Vernunft* (moral reasoning)—a veritable encyclopedia of ways human consciousness is busy, even though the principle of their teleological unity is one of uncertain locus and character.[43] But philosophical analysis seems by nature to be compelled to relate synthetically whatever it isolates for identification.

All these old-fashioned cosmological ontologies suffer, however, says Nicolai Hartmann (1882–1950), from the methodological mistake of the thinkers' supposedly intuiting the final substantial essence of things and then from this universal a priori deducing the metaphysical structures of the universe.[44] Even Kant's transcendental, housecleaning critique of a priori speculation presumed to get the basic ontological categories from an examination of the principles of our subjective, reasoning consciousness. But that's a mistake, says Hartmann, because knowledge goes beyond human consciousness; knowledge banks on the object, which is other than consciousness, and it is the sure detection of such real objects by a scientifically schooled consciousness (not a phenomenologically naive one) that will provide critical, nonspeculative ontological categories.[45] Earlier philosophers also touched on what one may call the strata of being *(Seinsschichten)* that actual objects disclose, but those thinkers hardly ever dealt with the strata with a critical, conscious sense of the discrete, statutory, determining character *(Gesetzlichkeit)* of the strata.[46] And the "old" philosophers tended to err either with materialist (upward) or a teleologist, monistic (downward) oversimplification. What we need, says Hartmann, is a "New Critique" and "new ways of ontology" that will be objectively valid.[47]

Since Hartmann's new ontology on the stratified structure of the world and Dooyeweerd's theory of modal law-spheres show certain similarities, it is instructive to note key features of Hartmann's conception and to compare them with Dooyeweerd's.[48]

---

43 Kant, *Kritik der reinen Vernunft* (1781), A94–130 and chapter ix in the second introduction to Kant, *Kritik der Urteilskraft* (1790).

44 Nicolai Hartmann, *Neue Wege der Ontologie* (Stuttgart: Kohlhammer, 1949), 8–9, 43–44. See comments on Dooyeweerd and Hartmann in Wolters, "Intellectual Milieu."

45 Hartmann, *Neue Wege,* 13–15, 17–18, 42–43, 107.

46 Hartmann, "Die Anfange des Schichtungsgedankens," 2:165, 179.

47 Hartmann, *Neue Wege,* 44–48.

48 For comments on Hartmann and Dooyeweerd see Wolters, "Intellectual Milieu." Dooyeweerd maintains (*NC* 2:51 n.3) that his theory of modal law-spheres, articulated in *Wijsbegeerte der wetsidee* (1935–36), antedated Nicolai Hartmann's *Schich-*

In forging a new concept of reality, says Hartmann, we need to reconceive the pure mode of being of the world structures and processes in terms of contextual *Realwirklichkeit* (*actual* reality) and circumstantial *Realmöglichkeit* (*real* possibility); that is, we need to let go of concepts of "entelechy" and "essential possibility" in order to face the being of becoming, to realize that becoming is a real form of being. Our philosophical task is to ascertain the kind of different forms becoming takes "according to the rungs or strata of the real" occurrence. We also do well to realize that time and individuality are more fundamental categories of true reality than "space" and "matter."[49]

The real world has a ladder of being, says Hartmann, whose four major rungs are the inorganic, the organic, the animal-psychic, and the supraindividual cultural (*Geistigen*)—with perhaps a few others, like the historical, that are substantially different—and each as a stratum with boundaries has a categorial homogeneity. There is also a hierarchy of particular, actual structures like inanimate things, organisms, animals, and humans, which the strata cut across. Only the human, society, and the historical process, however, embrace all four strata of being, which are ordered in such a way that the under layers of tiered reality are always included in the upper strata, but not the reverse.[50] There is also a whole raft of paired categories, such as unity and multiplicity, concord and discord, form and material, inner and outer, identity and difference, generality and individuality, and many more, that pervade all strata but take on different character according to the stratum. Reality is such that categories found in a substratum may recur in an upper stratum, but not the reverse. Categories novel to upper strata depend upon categories

---

tentheorie. That would be so if Hartmann's *Schichtenlehre* dated from *Der Aufbau der realen Welt: Grundlegung der allgemeinen Kategorienlehre* (1940) and from *Möglichkeit und Wirklichkeit* (1938) where Hartmann developed the ideas. But the *Schichtenlehre* is found already in *Grundzuge einer Metaphysik der Erkenntnis* (1921), and Dooyeweerd quotes this early Hartmann work in *Wijsbegeerte der wetsidee* (*NC* 4:87) and already in his inaugural address, *De Beteekenis der wetsidee* (1926). Dooyeweerd's early plea to Calvinists in Holland not to join the neo-Kantian way of doing philosophy was also early; cf. "Calvinisme contra Neo-Kantianisme," in *Tijdschrift voor wijsbegeerte* 20 (1926): 29–74. Because Dooyeweerd's scholarly orientation was biblically directed, in the neighborhood of Kuyper, and because Kuyper's philosophical problematics is quite close to that of Nicolai Hartmann (cf. John Vander Stelt, "Kuyper's Semi-mystical Conception"), Dooyeweerd may have found his renovation of whatever he learned from Hartmann to be but a tributary flowing into his own river. I use Hartmann's *Neue Wege der Ontologie* (1949) to draw the parallels since this text is a concise, mature formulation of Hartmann's extensive, ontological explorations.

49 Hartmann, *Neue Wege*, 22–25.
50 Ibid., 30, 35–41, 84–85.

from lower strata, and the more elemental categories are stronger because they are not dependent upon the upper ones. However, the autonomous novelty a category from an upper stratum enjoys guarantees its complete freedom: "freedom in dependence—there is no contradiction"; "freedom . . . in superiority over something else."⁵¹

Whether it be Nicolai Hartmann, whom Dooyeweerd was reading in the 1920s, along with Husserl, Heidegger, Max Scheler, Rickert, and others, or whether it be the whole history of Western philosophy, the point is that every thinker with systematic grit has tried to account for kinds of order that asked for human attention in our one given reality. Nicolai Hartmann faults others for "monistic" conflations and is prepared himself to "not scruple simply to accept the Cartesian dichotomy of the world into *cogitatio* [cognition] and *extensio* [extension] . . . a categorial difference of regions."⁵² Every philosopher finally makes his or her peace with some theory at odds with others, even though most thinkers would affirm with Hartmann:

> Phenomena do not let themselves be altered. A theory can only stand up if it accords with the phenomena. If the theory is in opposition to phenomena, then it is wrong.⁵³

Or, as Dooyeweerd puts it, probing more deeply:

> Structural states of affairs, as soon as they are discovered, force themselves upon everybody, and it does not make sense to deny them. It is the common task of all philosophic schools and trends to account for them in a philosophic way, that is to say in the light of a transcendental ground-Idea. They must learn from one another, even from fundamental mistakes made in the theoretical interpretations of the laws and the

---

51 Ibid., 53–54, 60–61, 69–72, 75–76, 102–4. The English translation by Reinhard C. Kuhn *(New Ways of Ontology* [Chicago: Henry Regnery, 1953], 95), renders page 76 of *Neue Wege* as follows:

Reflecting now that the "being stronger" of the lower categories as stated by the fundamental categorical law denotes ontological pre-eminence and superiority just as much as the "being higher" of the weaker categories, we come to see that stratification involves an interdigitation of two types of ontological pre-eminence and two types of superiority. They are echeloned according to the same order but in opposite directions. The ontological superiority of strength decreases with the corresponding gain in height. So the two types of superiority move, so to speak, along separate lines, coexisting with one another in the same order of ranks without disrupting its unity. The lower categories are superior only in strength. In structure, they are poorer. They leave it entirely undecided whether or not something is above them and even more so *what* is to be above them. They are indifferent toward everything higher. They do not produce it nor do they hinder it. But if something is above them, they support it. For it can exist only by resting upon them.

52 Hartmann, *Neue Wege*, 36, 45–47.

53 Ibid., 41.

> structural states of affairs founded in the temporal order of our cosmos. (*NC* 1:116–17)

Nobody has a corner on infallibility.

Reformational features of Dooyeweerd theory

But, then, how does Dooyeweerd's theory compare with the involved strata ontology of Nicolai Hartmann? Let us note certain features of Dooyeweerd's theory that indicate his reforming direction.

First, in Dooyeweerd's book, creaturely being is veritably meaning (*NC* 1:97 and 2:31). So the different ontic ways things are, the modes of meaning, present the different ordered-durational ways of existing, which encompass whatever concretely exists. These modal aspects of existent things are their creaturely defining moments of cosmic temporality. God's timing for creaturely things provides the warp and woof of both modal law (= *time-order*) and modal functioning durance (= factual *time-duration*), which indissolubly circumfuse everything (*NC* 1:24 and 2:3–4, 8).

Second, as far as the actual, enduring and changing, subjective functioning of things goes and the ongoing alteration of things, when something is taken as an object of certain specified activity by another creature, Dooyeweerd posits that these modes of meaning show both a mutual irreducibility and a veritably isotopic interpenetration of each other. Just as sunlight refracted by a prism shows up in a spectrum of brightly diverse colors, which are irreducible to each other yet glow through one another and really cohere as white light, so the different prime modes of meaning, which constitute the functioning of things, are a seamless mesh of enduring becoming and begoing (*NC* 1:101–2). "Color me rainbow," says every sweet pea flower, chip of quartz, family of turtles, and middle-aged man, not to speak of cigars. And the nucleus, so to speak, of every modal aspect of the factual temporal continuance making up things is iridescent with all the other ways of meaning. Sometimes the other analogical functional moments well up supportively ("retrocipatory") within its coloring fabric, other times they glint and reach for a mutational enrichment ("anticipatory") (*NC* 2:75–76; *Twi,* 7–11).[54] But no matter whether the mesh of ways a thing endures existentially gives evidence of a richly reinforced or a fairly impoverished functional matrix

---

54 Cf. also Herman Dooyeweerd, "De analogische grondbegrippen der vakwetenschappen en hun betrekking tot de structuur van den menschelijke ervaringshorizon," *Mededelingen* (Koninklijke Nederlandse Academie van Wetenschappen, afdeling Letterkunde), n.s. 17 (1954, no. 6): 171–92. This essay has been translated into English by Robert D. Knudsen as "The Analogical Concepts" (Mimeo, 1968).

of meaning, all the various modes of meaning that creaturely things are will show an interwoven whole.

Third, and most important, from Dooyeweerd's position, is the thesis about the law side to these colorful modes of meaning that constitute and hold for things. The modal laws have authority and give good, single, multisplendored direction for every creaturely thing because modal laws are prismatic variations of God's covenanting Word, which says, "Love me above all, respect and build up your neighbor as yourself, and take care of all the creatures I have entrusted you people with until I come back to perfect my rule of shalom" (see *Twi,* 8, 122–23). The multiple zones of meaning that creaturely things are, are all together the gift of God's timing (= "cosmic time"). God's gracious, good, ongoing temporal structuring of things for them is God's holy, creative will in operation. So every creature, indelibly stamped by the rainbow of God's will for its very temporal existence, is called upon to respond, after its kind, to its multifaceted, yet single-spoken, cosmonomic (= providential, ordinance-related, enduring) reality (*NC* 1:16, 101–2 and 2:74).

Fourth, God's Word for creatures—"praise! love! care! forever and ever"—became fully revealed in Jesus Christ, continues Dooyeweerd, referring to Ephesians 1:3–10 and Hebrews 1:1–4 (*NC* 2:563). So, as a matter of concrete fact—and here we necessarily step towards matters beyond but linked to the theory of modal law-spheres—both human experience and the meaning of every nonhuman creaturely thing entrusted to human ministry is brought together and reaches historically its God-intended meaning in Christ (*NC* 2:30). Just as human selfhood focuses referentially all one's diverse, concrete acts as diaconal obedience to the Lord or as exercises in vanity, so Christ's body relates and roots men and women, individual members of humankind, in the way of God-service and gives even those who spurn communion of the saints their grounds for meaning anything at all (*NC* 1:10–12, 97 and 2:418, 473–74; *Twi,* 120–21, 123–25).[55]

---

55 The important passage of *NC* 2:473–74 is not a good translation of the Dutch original. Here is my attempt:

> When our selfhood, insofar as its transcendent unity as religious root of our whole temporal existence is operative under the transcendental guidance of faith and is busy in the transcendental direction of time with theoretical intuition, then one becomes cosmologically self-conscious within the temporal togetherness and temporal meaning-diversity of all one's modal meaning-functions. It is not one or more modal functions of the human person, but at bottom it is the personality in the unity of its very religious root that is busy in knowing activity. This is so no matter whether the cosmological self-consciousness in the knowing activity is directed in Christ toward the true Origin of all things, the Sovereign Creator and Heavenly Father, or whether the person seeks oneself in the fallenness of sin and seeks the Origin in what is temporal. (*WdW* 2:408–9)

These four features of Dooyeweerd's theory are enough to demonstrate how a Christian reformation sets Dooyeweerd's theory of modal law-spheres off from Nicolai Hartmann and the received tradition of Western cosmology and metaphysics. The centuries-old philosophical witness to "chain of Being" is unequivocally rejected (*NC* 1:123 and 3:74), and the meaning of creaturehood—existing only by the living Word of God, the *ru'ah* (breath, spirit) of God's mouth (Psalm 33:6–9)[56]—is captured conceptually and thought through with the almost Heideggerian formula, "Things must not be, but mean." Also, the constant jostle in philosophical theories that pit the undeniable varieties of ways things are against one another, nominating transcendent features (like moral rationality) or picking scapegoats for our earthly troubles (like physical desire), is basically undone and overcome by the insightful recognition that *all* creaturely ways are good and are set to be a concert of integrally relative functions. Dooyeweerd's prism-refracted colors is a telling image in contrast to Nicolai Hartmann's "rungs of a ladder." Theoretical puzzles about the complexity of our creaturely glory remain, but Dooyeweerd's theory undercuts both a blindness to important differences and the imposition of a competitive hierarchy of priorities (*NC* 2:49–51, 76).[57]

An altogether singular idea, in my judgment, which marks the theory of modal law-spheres in its Christian wisdom drawn from a Reformed tradition, is the pivotal thought that the distinguishable, cosmic goings-on at large are to be understood as the gentle law of the Lord God (cf. *NC* 1:515–25). Both the "natural law" of perennial philosophy and the secularized philosophical assumption that "what is given, is just given—make heads and tails out of it" miss the radicality of God's gift in how anything structurally is. Dooyeweerd's theory relates the doings of us humans, including all our knowing, directly to the Lord's presence in our mundane existence. Once we discern that the law of noncontradiction (to be formu-

---

56 See the careful, sensitive, and imaginative account by Arie van Dijk, "Algemene beschouwing (Stoker-Brümmer)," in "Werkcollege systematische wijsbegeerte" [1965] (Mimeo, 1969), 44–52, under mentor H. van Riessen. Dooyeweerd's concept of "individuality-structure" is a substitute way of accounting for what Western philosophers, including especially Aquinas, try to approximate with the concept of "substance." See Herman Dooyeweerd, "De idee der individualiteitsstructuur en het Thomistisch substantiebegrip," *Philosophia Reformata* 8 (1943): 65–99; 9 (1944): 1–41; 10 (1945): 25–48; 11 (1946): 22–52. Also cf. Dooyeweerd's debate with Stoker in *NC* 3:61–76.

57 Hartmann does seem to allow for both "retrocipation" and "anticipation" of strata in other strata (*Neue Wege*, 71–72), but his emphasis is certainly upon what he believes is objectively valid: the higher strata are not included in the lower (*Neue Wege*, 40, 61–62).

lated, unlike Aristotle's canon, to admit of change)[58] is God's blessing for our acts of analysis, and once we discover that the law of syntactical clarity is God's blessing for our discourse, that is, once we realize that the creational laws we may uncover hold the Lord's direction for our creaturely well-being, then we will have made a philosophical start in outwitting the traditions of disbelief and hubris that entangle so many concepts of "human transcendence," "bare facts," and a host of skeptical *-isms*. There is redeeming humility and liberating knowledge in the proposition that human experience, including knowing God and one's self inhabiting the world, is "restricted and relativized *by* (but not at all *to*) our temporal cosmic existence" (*NC* 2:561). That's why, concludes Dooyeweerd:

> Christ, as the fullness of God's Revelation, *came into the flesh*; and for this reason also the Divine Word-revelation came to us in the temporal garb of human language [= the Scriptures]. (*NC* 2:561)

It is because of this confession of the compelling lordship of Jesus Christ and the necessity of scripturally directed learning, which surrounds and undergirds the theory of modal law-spheres, that I am led to think that Dooyeweerd and his English translators failed when they rendered *"Wijsbegeerte der wetsidee"* as "Philosophy of the cosmonomic *Idea*" (*NC* 1:93–96; italics mine). If there is any one matter central to this whole Christian philosophical endeavor, it is the rejection of Kantian and neo-Kantian rationalistic idealism, which allows a person to rest his or her conceptual burden in theoretical ideas (*NC* 1:96–99 and 2:187–88). Cosmological theory, epistemology, conception of the sciences, and much more, are indeed expressive of the core constellation of ideas that serve as a thinker's philosophically committed categorial framework. But the scandal of Dooyeweerd's philosophy—its dangerous, confrontational, and exciting thesis—is that this philosophical theory witnesses within theorizing to the truth of Jesus Christ as the alpha and omega of thinking and the only guarantee for the very meaning of things at large, and appeals in its theory of modal law-spheres to the truth of the Word of God visible in creation to which the Scriptures leads one whose heart has been opened. A more revealing English name for *De wijsbegeerte der wetsidee* (literally: A philosophy of the idea of *law*) might be "A philosophy of cosmonomic structure as the Lord God's Word" or, for short, "A philosophy of God's structuring Word."[59]

---

58 Cf. Vollenhoven, *De Noodzakelijkheid eener Christelijke logica*, 46–50.

59 Such a renaming might help put the Humpty-Dumpty together again that John Kraay has carefully parsed into pieces in his article "Successive Conceptions in the Development of the Christian Philosophy of Herman Dooyeweerd," *Philosophia Re-*

A methodological problem

Let there be no mistake: Dooyeweerd clearly affirms that his theory of modal law-spheres is a historically unfinished theory that is not infallible. Dooyeweerd writes:

> In fact the system of the law-spheres designed by us can never lay claim to material completion. A more penetrating examination may at any time bring new modal aspects of reality to the light not yet perceived before. And the discovery of new law-spheres will always require a revision and further development of our modal analyses.[60]

At the same time, Dooyeweerd maintains that when a philosophic thinker stands in the truth of God revealed in Jesus Christ, that thinker's analyses, first, will continue to witness to the horizon of modal law-spheres, which has "a constant determining character" for all the changing concrete facts extant, and, second, will be freed from absolutizing prejudices that hinder the necessary a priori insight into the modal horizon enabling

---

formata 44 (1979): 137–49 and 45 (1980): 1–46. It seems to me that Dooyeweerd's conception of the law-idea (ca. 1925) gathers existential poignance in his conception of the Archimedean point (ca. 1935–36), and is climaxed by his naming ground motive (ca. 1943) as the dynamic that gives the whole complex a historical formative power. That is, "*Wetsidee*" remains crucial for Dooyeweerd's thought, but "ground-motive" reminds us of the historical embeddedness of any and every philosophy.

60 *NC* 2:556. Dooyeweerd himself became convinced during the years between the 1935 Dutch edition and the 1953 English edition of *A New Critique of Theoretical Thought* that movement is a prime mode of creaturely things and is not to be confused with the physical aspect of entities, defined by "the energetic" (see note 35 above). "Movement" points in an original way to a kinematic mode of things (*NC* 2:97–100). So Dooyeweerd revised the theory. In 1960 I challenged the precision of Dooyeweerd's thoughts on a "modal meaning of history" when he talked of history "as such" (formative control) and history "at bottom" (as a struggle between the *civitas Dei* and *civitas terrena*). I proposed that we recognize "technical, formative control" as a mode of creaturely existence and understand "historical" as the more global "cultural unfolding of creation's secrets." See Calvin C. Seerveld, "Voor en uit de praktijk," *Correspondentiebladen van de Vereniging voor Calvinistische Wijsbegeerte* 24 (April 1960): 5–10. Several thinkers close to this philosophical categorial framework have found the suggestion helpful. For different comments on Dooyeweerd's historical aspect, see C. T. McIntire, "Dooyeweerd's Philosophy of History," in *The Legacy of Herman Dooyeweerd,* 81–117. In "Neurosis and Religion," in *Philosophy and Christianity: Philosophical essays dedicated to Professor Dr. Herman Dooyeweerd* (Amsterdam: North-Holland, 1965), 370, W. K. van Dijk suggested that "an oretic" mode between the biotic and psychic aspects of reality might be needed to explain human instinctive drives. This idea has not been followed up; see Arnold H. de Graaff, *Psychology: Sensitive openness and appropriate reactions* (Potchefstroom: Potchefstroom University for Christian Higher Education, 1980). There continues to be a ferment generated by the theory of modal law-spheres that attests to its theoretical fruitfulness. See notes 35 above and 77 below.

one to identify the limits of the special sciences (*NC* 2:556, 563, 572, 574). So there is a methodological problem: how does one fallibly discern what are truly the (modal) ways things are in God's created world?

Dooyeweerd develops his method for discerning the specific structure of a given modal law-aspect of a thing in polemic with Edmund Husserl (1859–1938) on *epochē* (bracketing) (*NC* 2:485–90) and with Max Scheler (1874–1928) on truth (*NC* 2:583–98). He probably wants to dissociate his own method of "insight" from their positions because he is aware that he does take his cue from phenomenology.[61] Dooyeweerd proposes to begin empirically with a scrupulously accurate, "unbiased" analysis, bracketing or suspending "all specific philosophical interpretation," of a modal nucleus of meaning, pointing out the nonoriginal character of analogical moments within that particular mode of meaning (*NC* 2:72, 74, 77). Such an attempt seems curiously like Husserl's demand to suspend all subjective activity except one's pure, cognitive act of *Wesensschau* (intuiting essence) to describe the *eidos* (structure) of phenomena. Not so, says Dooyeweerd. Husserl intends to black out ordinary experience and let a transcendental Kantian ego dictate absolutely what is essentially and permanently there (*NC* 2:489, 584). By contrast, Dooyeweerd's approach is to open himself up fully to the complex reality able to be experienced, investigate any precise moment of meaning in its most reduced, restricted state, and then tentatively formulate what "can be grasped only in an immediate intuition and never apart from its structural context of analogies" (*NC* 2:117, 129). [#27]

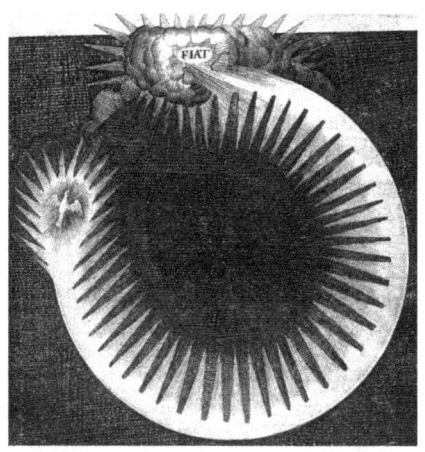

[#27] This is *not* how the theory of modal law-spheres came into being [Robert Fludd, *De tribus prioribus creationis diebus*, 1619]

It may be granted that Dooyeweerd's intention is different from that of Husserl (*NC* 2:73–74, 468 n.1) in that Dooyeweerd is intent upon

---

61 *NC* 1:v. Robert D. Knudsen characterized "Dooyeweerd's Philosophical Method" [1962] as "phenomenological," "transcendental," and, in a negative sense, "dialectical," in *Roots and Branches: The quest for meaning and truth in modern thought*, ed. Donald Knudsen (Grand Rapids, MI: Paideia Press, 2009), 327-349. Later Knudsen makes a precision and identifies Dooyeweerd's method as "empirical-transcendental," keeping it quite distinct from any "transcendent-metaphysical" method: "Transcendental Method in Dooyeweerd" [1979], in *Roots and Branches*, 301-309.

acclaiming the relativity and enmeshment of any prime aspect of reality and its independence from human consciousness; but Dooyeweerd's final court of appeal for discernment of a modal meaning-nucleus is *my insight* provided by "theoretical intuition" (*NC* 2:478–79), a very close analytic relative of Husserl's *Wesensschau* (*NC* 2:480, 483–84). Dooyeweerd provides elaborate criteria for double-checking and refining one's "grasp" or "limiting concept" of a given modal aspect.[62] But since a person's scientifically deepened insight is Dooyeweerd's ultimate criterion, there is not much room for dispute on the findings.

This methodological problem of ascertaining the various irreducible ways creatures exist is unavoidable I think. The difficulty is similar to the bind people experience when they waver between prescriptive definitions and makeshift empiricist approximations when trying to determine the nature of something: how does one fix and support what is fundamentally a basic choice about a nonanalytic affair? Besides, Dooyeweerd as a Christian thinker is consciously both thetical and self-critical; so he tends to be both certain and tentative (cf. *NC* 2:598 n.1). Again, in my judgment such a state of affairs is normal and needs to be recognized as inescapable whenever foundational philosophical matters are up for human decision. The fact that massive conceptual implications follow from such "intuited" decisions points up the responsibility of philosophical leadership.[63]

Theory of aesthetics

It is Dooyeweerd's considered judgment that "*harmony* in its original sense" is the nucleus of the aesthetic aspect of reality and the typifying, object-functional qualification of artworks (*NC* 2:128 and 3:117). Dooyeweerd uses the traditional term of "beauty," in the same breath, to describe the aesthetic object-function of "nature" (*NC* 2:139 and 3:114, 140). So it is very understandable that Hans Rookmaaker, learning from Dooyeweerd, popularized the idea that "beautiful harmony" (*de schone harmonie*) is the core concept for the nucleus of aesthetic order in the world.[64]

---

62 *NC* 1:69 and 2:486. In an unfinished paper "The Hermeneutic Problem of Modal Theory" (Mimeo, 1972) and a concept paper for seminar presentation on "The Methodology of Modal Theory" (Mimeo, 1973), Lambert Zuidervaart suggests that the various methodological procedures that Dooyeweerd uses for determining modal nuclei are as follows: intuitive insight, encyclopedic comparison, detection of antinomy, discovery of analogies, disclosure of object-functionality.

63 See Calvin G. Seerveld, "Methodological Problem of Definition," in *Rainbows for the Fallen World*, 105–9.

64 Hans Rookmaaker, "Ontwerp ener aesthetica op grondslag der wijsbegeerte der wets-

Dooyeweerd's exposition of "harmony" as the aesthetic mode of meaning is tied most tightly to features of "unity in multiplicity" and "nothing to excess," which are, in his thought, the mathematical and economic analogies within the aesthetic structure of meaning (*NC* 2:128, 347).

In fact, I think it would be fair to say that Dooyeweerd's idea of "harmony" is exegeted almost entirely in terms of frugality, sobriety, and simplicity, which he says the classicist aesthetics of Nicolas Boileau-Despréaux (1636–1711) rediscovered and posited but rigidified because it was guided by the humanistic ideal of science.[65] Dooyeweerd's correct polemic against a romantic idealist belief in artistic genius, which admits of no laws for individual aesthetic subjectivity (*NC* 2:128), is balanced by his critique of the classicist doctrine that finds the limits of art in linguistic and logical economy (*NC* 2:348). But Dooyeweerd's selection of Praxiteles' sculpture of Hermes for analysis of the nature and production of an artwork (*NC* 3:109–28) hints at the preference toward which his theory of "harmony" leans. Dooyeweerd's "harmony" is in line with the long, classical history of "beauty."

Plato, under the influence of Pythagoras, said the beautiful was marked by a whole integrality of working parts fitting together (πρέπε; cf. Aristotle's τάξις). However, this property of "design," as I understand it, is more appropriately regarded as a matter of enriched form than as that which peculiarly identifies what is "aesthetic." Augustine and many others considered the beautiful to be a matter of intermeshing *form* (*partium congruentia*), to which Aquinas added the note of "brilliance" (*claritas*). But even the quality of brilliance *quae visa placet* (which when seen delights), as I understand it, is better taken as the recognition of a quality corresponding to an aesthetically deepened *feeling*,[66] not as that which grasps a primary, irreducible "aesthetic" state of affairs.

Often the idea of "beauty" followed Plotinian theology and became a pancosmic order (*ordo, perfectio*) with intimations of transcendence. Dooyeweerd resolutely cuts off all such theological speculation around "beauty." In doing so, he offers a genuine reformation of even Abraham

---

idee," *Philophia Reformata* 11:3/4 (1946): 141–42.

65 *NC* 2:346–48. Dooyeweerd seems to be working from secondary sources here, using Heinrich von Stein's *Die Entstehung der neueren Aesthetik* (1886); and he makes the admission: "I will follow Cassirer's plan to show this aesthetic Idea from its strongest side, though indeed I see this strong side in a different light" (*NC* 2:346).

66 It is part of Kant's sweeping, integrative power of thought that prompted him to incorporate these age-old ideas of *form* and *feeling* (cf. also Susanne K. Langer!) as he probed the nature of "aesthetic" judgment with cognition-denying subjectivism. See note 4 above.

Kuyper, who still uncritically cited Anton Raphael Mengs (1728–79), Johann Joachim Winckelmann (1717–68), and Friedrich Wilhelm von Schelling (1775–1854) to back up his thought that Greek classical art revealed the divine ordinances for the beautiful and that art is the service of geniuses inspired by God to lead us up the scale of creational being to the ideal world.[67]

Dooyeweerd's "beauty" and "harmony," at its best, is closer to Plato's conception of beauty as συμμετρία (measured proportionality) and ἁπλότης (simple unity), genuinely kinetic and arithmetical analogies within aesthetic structure, as I understand them. Dooyeweerd's idea of "harmony" does not identify what is nuclearly aesthetic at all, but is an analogical concept denoting aesthetic proportionality or eurythmy. Proportionality, properly speaking, is originally a matter of weighted balance or regular rhythm, that is, a property of mathematical calculus, indeed present as a side of all creaturely reality. Dooyeweerd's designation of μηδὲν ἄγαν (not too much) as a sobering economic analogy within the aesthetic is also a mistaken naming of this same mathematical feature. Aesthetic economy, in my own judgment, is better conceived as a matter of "novelty" than as a matter of frugality or of logical simplicity reminiscent of Occam's razor.

It is so that Dooyeweerd's specific thoughts on aesthetic reality are underdeveloped, and his undefined concept of "harmony" resonates loosely with the major tradition of Western thought on a nondescript "beauty." Such a decidedly general "beauty" doctrine actually militates against the irreducible specificity of "aesthetic" reality that Dooyeweerd's genial theory of modal law-spheres demands.

One might mention a couple other tenets of Dooyeweerd's thought relevant to aesthetic theory that, like his concept of harmony, are concepts he picked up from elsewhere and left critically unreformed.

As one example: "Imagination" for Dooyeweerd is only a sensory function of psychic activity that can produce phantasms of merely intentional objectivity (*NC* 2:425–26 and 3:115). According to Dooyeweerd's scheme, the aesthetic "conception" of the artist's productive fantasy is

---

67 Abraham Kuyper, *Het calvinisme en de kunst* (Amsterdam: Wormser, 1888), 16, 63 n.23, 67 n.48, 70 n.53. Also, *De gemeene gratie* (On common grace) [1895–1901 in *De Heraut*], 3 vols. (Leiden: Donner, 1902–1905; 4th ed., Kampen: Kok, n.d.), 3:557. For an indepth correction of the standard idolization of classic Greek sculpture, showing how the ancient Greek mathematicistic view of artistic norms impeded the development of sculpture, see Dirk J. van den Berg, " 'n Kritiese besinning op die moontlike invloed van die vorm-materie grondmotief op die griekse beeldhoukuns" (Master's thesis, Potchefstroom University, 1972).

lodged in such sensory phantasms before the fancied intentional object is represented in a real, sensible thing like a painting on canvas or a marble sculpture (*NC* 3:113–16, 119–20). Although such a cumbersome description of artistic activity heads off both a copy-of-natural-object idea of artworks and a subjectivistic expressionism,[68] Dooyeweerd's analysis remains partial to the Neoidealistic notion of artistic production in which media are secondary to one's artistic activity.[69] Also, despite the important thesis that the "technical formative function" founds every bona fide artwork (*NC* 3:121–23, 125), Dooyeweerd lacks the concept of a *constructed image* that is neither a "sensory phantasm" nor a product of aesthetic fantasy. Much more clarity enters analysis on the formation of artworks when we distinguish retinal-images, nonsensory image-constructs, and bona fide aesthetic fictions.[70]

A second example: Dooyeweerd clearly differentiates analytic, lingual, and aesthetic ways of meaning among others (*NC* 2:224–25).

He describes the nuclear moment of the lingual aspect in terms of "symbolic signification," that is, the understanding of signs (*NC* 2:222). So for Dooyeweerd "symbol" is synonymous with "sign" in the sense that x stands arbitrarily and conventionally for y. He goes on to refer to an "abstract symbol" as that which "belongs to a rational system of signs" (*NC* 2:381). He can do this probably because he assumes that language rests on a logical sublayer.

A problem with this terminology and conception is that Dooyeweerd has opted against a tradition congenial to aesthetic theory that has reserved "symbolic" meaning precisely for that which is semantically

---

68 See Calvin G. Seerveld, *A Christian Critique of Art and Literature* [1963] (Sioux Center: Dordt College Press, 1995), 81–84.

69 Benedetto Croce is a prime example of counting media less than integral to art. Cf. "L'Intuizione pura e il carattere lirico dell'Arte" (1908), in *Problemi di estetica* (Ban: Gius. Laterza & Figli, 1949), 15–23 and "Brevario de Estetica" (1912), in *Nuovi saggi di estetica* (Ban: Gius. Laterza & Figli, 1948), 35–39. See Seerveld, *Benedetto Croce's Earlier Aesthetic Theories,* 93–95. Dooyeweerd's view of enkapsis tries to honor how the artist's "plastic aesthetic activity remains bound to the natural structure of his material" (*NC* 3:126) and how the "work of art itself, however, is not an aggregate, but an unbreakable *non-homogeneous whole*" (*NC* 3:124)! But the idealistic penchant shows through in such phrases as: "the marble cannot play a *constitutive* role in this artistic work" (*NC* 3:123); "To the artist the marble is important *solely* as a medium of expression" (*NC* 3:125; italics mine); "And this enkaptic relation is subject to the normative law requiring that in the inner structure of the work of art the marble can *only* function as a material for the expression of the artistic *conception*" (*NC* 3:126; italics mine).

70 See my "Imaginativity," *Faith and Philosophy.* See pages 31-33 above: "Imagining as an irreducible function."

and conceptually elusive. For example, Kant's conception of "symbol" as that which occasions much thought (yet is noncognitive!) but cannot be adequately pressed into either a definite concept or made intelligible by language[71] has led, in spite of the romantic idolatry it generated, to much fruitful awareness of "symbolic knowing activity." We may refer to the thought in aesthetics of Ernst Cassirer, Susanne K. Langer, Hans Georg Gadamer, and Paul Ricoeur.[72] "Symbol" in Dooyeweerd's setup becomes unserviceable for designating anything with "surplus meaning." His identification of symbol with sign is closer to the standard of G. W. Leibniz, Charles S. Peirce, and others who have telescoped semantic and analytic functioning into one another and leave aesthetic interests curiously on a sideline.[73]

Concluding comment:
prospects of the legacy for aesthetics

Dooyeweerd's living legacy for aesthetic theory lies in the systematic opening his philosophical framework makes for aesthetics as a special science, rather than in any of his specific analyses of beauty, artistic production, or a period of art. Dooyeweerd's general theory of modal law-spheres presents a format that saves aesthetics from elision into semiotics, sociology of art, metacriticism, or dismemberment. The theory of modal law-spheres introduces a whole set of categories, such as "aesthetic law," "relative aesthetic meaning" in a society filled with other related meanings, "kinds of art with enduring tasks," which frees aesthetic theory for a whole range of explorations not usually associated with it as a discipline.

Dooyeweerd's awareness of "aesthetic" subjectivity and "aesthetic"

---

71 Kant, *Kritik der Urteilskraft* (1781), par. 49.3, 7, 9; 59.3–4.

72 Ernst Cassirer, *The Philosophy of Symbolic Forms*, 3 vols. [1923–29], trans. Ralph Mannheim (New Haven: Yale University Press, 1955–57). Susanne K. Langer, *Philosophy in a New Key: A study in the symbolism of reason, rite, and art* (Cambridge: Harvard University Press, 1942) and *Feeling and Form* (New York: Scribner, 1953). Hans-Georg Gadamer, *Die Aktualität des Schönen* [1974] (Stuttgart: Philipp Reclam, 1977). Paul Ricoeur, *Interpretation Theory: Discourse and the surplus of meaning* (Fort Worth: Texas Christian University Press, 1976) and *The Rule of Metaphor: Multidisciplinary studies of the creation of meaning in language* [1975] (Toronto: University of Toronto Press, 1977).

73 Dooyeweerd certainly does not identify semantic with analytic modes of functioning, and his critique of Husserl's attempt to develop a *reine Bedeutungslehre* is that Husserl was busy with a "logicizing of the modal meaning of lingual signification" (*NC* 2:224–25). Semanticist P. A. Verburg also rejects most strongly this "error which has become fatal for linguistic theory. It started from Hobbes, Descartes, and Leibniz' rationalistic comparison, assimilation, and equation of words with arithmetical and metrical *symbols*" (P. A. Verburg, "Delosis and Clarity." in *Philosophy and Christianity*, 96).

acts as rich matters of primary "naive experience," basic to "artistic" activity as a more complicated kind of human subjectivity (*NC* 3:114), also opens up a whole vein of creaturely phenomena for analysis that has been left practically unexplored within aesthetics: the numerous depth dimensions of aesthetic activity such as play, fancy, adventure, entertainment, and festivity, for example, as well as taste.[74]

Dooyeweerd's theory of analogical aesthetic moments within other kinds of human activity prompts one to develop aesthetic theory in close proximity with other sciences since it is proposed that studies in empathy, probability, recreation, diplomacy, liturgy, among others, may be relevant for systematic aesthetic theory, although such phenomena properly belong first of all to psychology, logic, sociology, political science, and theology.

The prospects of Dooyeweerd's legacy for aesthetic theory are good, provided thinkers do not try to refine Dooyeweerd's actual, specific results and scholastically tie up the loose analytic ends.[75] Instead, thinkers should probe beyond his initial fragments in theory of aesthetics and concentrate upon pursuing some of his specific insights and generating new ones within the integrated, complex encyclopedia of knowledge he has fashioned. Many of Dooyeweerd's insightful, unfinished thoughts on aesthetic matters are worthy of specialized discussion, for example, on the relation of scores, performances, and artworks (*NC* 3:110) or on the intricate difference between encapsulated art ("bound art") and art-as-such ("free art") (*NC* 3:138–40).

My own intuition as to the nucleus of an irreducible aesthetic aspect of reality, backed up by scrutiny of various phenomena such as art, style, and imagining things, leads me to pose "allusivity" ("nuancefulness")

---

[74] See N. T. van der Merwe, "Aspekte van 'n funksionele beskouing van verbeelding en van 'n tipologie van teorieë oor die verbeelding," *Philosophia Reformata* 34:3/4 (1969): 147–78. See also Henry de Jong, Carroll Ann Goon, Michael Ophardt, Robert Rogers, and Calvin C. Seerveld, "Human Creatures at Play: Explorations in Christian Cultural Philosophy" (Mimeo, 1983). For Dirk van den Berg's involved account of elementary analogues within aesthetic structure, especially as it applies to artistic reality, see his "Aesthetic Extension and Related Elementary Concepts of Modal Aesthetics, Art-Theory and Hermeneutics," *Tydskrif vir christelike wetenskap* 14:3/4 (1978): 19–33 and 15:1/2 (1979): 1–47.

[75] Hans Rookmaaker's early article "Ontwerp ener aesthetica op grondslag der wijsbegeerte der wetsidee," *Philosophia Reformata* 11:3/4 (1946): 141–67 and 12:1 (1947): 1–35, was an important attempt to draw out implications of Dooyeweerd's specific ideas in the field of systematic aesthetics and as a general science of art (*algemene kunstwetenschap*), but the exercise proceeded without deep-going, philosophical critique of the basic notions. Rookmaaker himself in the 1960s lamented the abstract character of this early attempt.

as the core concept.⁷⁶ Dooyeweerd's notion of "[beautiful] harmony" then becomes simply an elementary mathematical analogue within the structural reality of original "allusivity." I am also convinced that Dooyeweerd's placement of aesthetic structure in the order of modal complexity needs reworking since aesthetic affairs are much more fundamental an underground in human experience than Dooyeweerd seems to admit.⁷⁷

And so one could begin to spend one's inheritance from Dooyeweerd. As long as one is willing to explore the foundations of modal aesthetic theory in the same diaconal and reforming spirit that Dooyeweerd's philosophy breathes, branching out with research into the encyclopedia of the arts,⁷⁸ the complexities of hermeneutics,⁷⁹ and the important problems of discerning and charting art historical development,⁸⁰ I think the gift Dooyeweerd has made to aesthetic theory almost en passant could indeed become a genuine blessing for those who need creational order and redemptive direction for their reflection on this vital but often neglected area of praise, joy, and caring in God's world.

---

76 See Calvin C. Seerveld, "Modal Aesthetics," in *Hearing and Doing: Philosophical essays dedicated to H. Evan Runner* (Toronto: Wedge, 1979), 263–94 and Seerveld, "Modal Aesthetic Theory, Preliminary Questions with an Opening Hypothesis," in *Rainbows for the Fallen World*, 104–37.

77 The order of complexity in the structured ways creatures are subject to God, which I have assumed for analysis since 1959, is as follows: numerical, spatial, kinematic, physical, organic, psychic, techno-formative, aesthetic, semantic, analytic, social, economic, jural, ethical, and confessional. See my "Skeleton to Philosophy 101" (Class syllabus, Trinity Christian College), 22–24, and also *Rainbows for the Fallen World*, 143. Hendrik Hart seems to support this realignment of modal order in *Understanding Our World: An integral ontology* (Washington, D.C.: University Press of America, 1984), 405 n.36; however, at present Hart names the aspect of allusivity "symbolic" (195) and tends to explain language in terms of analyticity. See notes 35, 60, and 73 above.

78 The spectrum I proposed in 1963 still looks feasible to me as a start; see *A Christian Critique of Art and Literature*, 83–84. Such an encyclopedia of the arts, as well as an encyclopedia of the special sciences, is not exhaustive and not prescriptive with prohibitions and taboos, precisely because it is not "eidetic" in a Husserlian sense. A modal law-sphere theory promises interrelational order and primary tasks to the varied arts.

79 See Calvin C. Seerveld, "Human Responses to Art: Good, Bad, and Indifferent" (1981), in *In the Fields of the Lord*, ed. Craig Bartholomew (Carlisle: Piquant, 2000), 316–329.

80 See Calvin C. Seerveld, "Towards a Cartographic Methodology for Art Historiography," *The Journal of Aesthetics and Art Criticism* 39 (1980): 143–54 {see *AH*: 61–78} and D. J. van den Berg, "'n Ondersoek na die estetiese en kunshistoriese probleme verbonde aan die sogenaamde moderne religieuse skilderkuns" (Ph.D. diss., University of the Orange Free State, 1984).

Joy, Style, and Aesthetic Imperatives, with the Biblical Meaning of Clothes and Games in the Christian Life

In this talk on AESTHETIC IMPERATIVES FOR NORTH AMERICAN LIFE TODAY I'd like to develop thoughts put forward in chapter 2 of *Rainbows for the Fallen World: Aesthetic life and artistic task*—the matter of "obedient aesthetic life." That means I want to get you thinking about the style to life that will be holy. I'm going to try to focus on certain specific features of human living that are a more neglected area in reflection on what we call the sanctified life, that response of thankfulness that characterizes human creatures saved from sin in Jesus Christ, who are being restored to communion with the Lord in their actual deeds. It has to do with clothes and games and taste.

I don't need to trouble you with the fact that I think lifestyle is a problem especially appropriate for philosophical aesthetic theory to tackle. But it is important to me to make clear that I believe style is a normative matter. The style to one's prayers or to one's meals is deadly or a blessing. The style to your courting a girl or a fellow, or simply your posture, is touched by shalom or led by a curse.

I'm not saying that the elect of God always stand or sit up ramrod straight and you can tell a reprobate by the slouch; and I'm not saying that dinner by candle light with iron-fired plateware makes cutting remarks impossible; but I do want to get out into the open that the style to our deeds needs to be redemptive. You may not as an adopted daughter or son of God simply pick up uncritically the style of work, the style of dress, the style of thinking and argument, the style of picking priorities or of giving leadership that happens to be historically current or presently successful. A popular style in bringing up kids, or in preaching, may be downright sinful; because **style is the response of human creatures on earth before the Lord in their calling to be aesthetic office-bearers**.

I want to explain that, but first let me tell you where I'm headed.

This popular lecture was given for the Institute for Christian Studies summer conference in 1984.

I intend to argue that to be an inveterate sourpuss is to be distinctively unchristian in style of behavior—it's wrong, not just undesirable. I also want to argue that a principled ascetic lifestyle denies the creaturely goodness God gave us to be festive with. And the main, encompassing point of this lecture is that **joy is the defining mark of full-fledged aesthetic obedience**. If the styleful moment to your playful caresses in bed, or to your acceptance of a corrective reprimand—if the style to your funeral is not knicked by joy, it falls short of giving glory to God in its style.

I believe the Scriptures tell us that there is to be a halo of holiness, of wisdom, around all our actions (Proverbs 1:7–9, Romans 12:1–2). I should like to claim that joy, rightly conceived, is the gift of God's blessing proper to the halo around the creaturely dimension of human life we may designate as "aesthetic," as the styleful side to our diamond-rich existence. And I believe this state of affairs holds true for us still today, after Auschwitz and after Hiroshima, during acid rain, wide-spread gluttony, and world-wide starvation, while living again the constant war of 1984.

Let me begin with Scripture and the mandate for joy, and then move on to talk about style and "aesthetic imperatives," before we pick up on concrete examples. This biblical, christian philosophical setting is crucial for not misunderstanding me, and for our growing together, I hope, in the consciousness of the heritage, promise, and surprises God has slipped into our make-up, so-to-speak, for us to explore reflectively and to exercise, rich with laughter.

Joy, as a mandate from Scripture, is a gift of the Holy Spirit

According to the Bible the kingdom of God is not a matter of doing what you know is permissible or of refraining from certain proscribed acts, but is the presence of right-doing, peace-making, and joy, thanks to the Holy Spirit (Romans 14:17; cf. Luke 17:20–21). Women and men who do not trample on the conscience of those who are weak believers but build up the other persons, fill out their discipleship, and are contagious with an expectant gladness to be alive in God's world: such women and men are serving Christ, says the Bible, making God happy, and passing the scrutiny of observant people (Romans 14:18; cf. Philippians 3:2–3).

Joy is, like the rain, a gift from the hand of God; but unlike the rain joy is a gift truly peculiar to God's children. Joy is a fruit of the Holy Spirit's historical activity in a believer's life that makes one alive to the sparkle of glory surrounding us creatures and eager for more exciting discoveries of amazing grace.

The Bible talks about joy especially when it describes happenings that overcome a person when you experience something's being found that was lost, the rescue of what was in danger, a fulfillment when there was lack, the sudden completion of something unfinished. Joy comes upon finding something valuable that was misplaced—retrieving a lost sheep (cf. Luke 15:3–10)—or realizing that the horror of war is now ended and the enemy is powerless to hurt you anymore (cf. Isaiah 9:2–7). Joy is in place at marriage, when your manhood or womanhood becomes filled in with a vow, or when your child is born, God's fruit in your womb, or when a good harvest of crops is being gathered in (cf. Deuteronomy 16:13–15). Joy rises particularly when there is surprise, when something good that has been concealed is uncovered and when a blessing that was in doubt becomes certain.

The fact that the Bible treats joy as the quality of experience that knows rescue and restoration as an act of the Lord can lead us to the wisdom of keeping joy distinct from pleasure. Joy always knows pleasure, I think, but pleasure— which is also a gift of God, an important and different kind of gift (cf. Ecclesiastes refrain, e.g., 5:18–20)—pleasure does not qualify as the dimension of joy. So, without asking for jargon-like precision yet trying to lead our thinking with christian care, I'm saying: "Joy" means rejoicing, jubilation, and is not a matter of simple "enjoyment" or satisfaction. The Greek philosophers and secularized persons tend to overlook this difference and reduce the possible differentiated experience of rejoicing to one of climactic pleasure, feeling mighty pleased. And in my book the reduction of joy to pleasure or the confusion of intense satisfaction with the special festivity of joy is an index of the kind of misdirected thinking that cheapens human life.

I want to add here that my working conception of "joy," primed by hearing Scripture, identifies joy, as distinct from other fruits of the Spirit such as gentleness and meekness: joy is fairly elemental to the christian life. Whoever comes to know salvation may be a long way from gentleness, meekness, temperance, understanding, and love-of-neighbor, but joy at having been saved, rescued, set right with God through the blood of Jesus Christ, can hardly be missing. Joy like faith will certainly grow stronger as the Holy Spirit gradually masters our whole corporeal existence in time, but joy is elemental to the life of the redeemed.

And if this is true, then it follows that strong piety without joy is strange. Hope without joy is subchristian. Faith in God without joy is impaired. Filial oh-so-dutiful care of one's relative or neighbor without joy, long-suffering patience without joy, "speaking the truth in love" without joy—and I'm not even mentioning church services, the 40–60 hour a week job, your *private* christian life: if there be no joy, one is a miserable follower of Jesus Christ, a poor witness to the indwelling of the Holy Spirit, grieving God, and not likely to pass the test of making those who scrutinize us "jealous" of our "heavenly citizenship" (cf. Romans 11:11, Philippians 3:20).

Joy, of course, will perspire through all the pores of a christian life. There should be trickles of joy in your thinking things through when you make plans for a trip. A soft note of gladness will lurk about the eyes in greeting friends, neighbors, or foreigners. But **joy finds its particular home**, I should like to contend, **in the style we develop**. Joy enters most easily and pervasively into our whole circle of activities—thinking, associating with people, paying debts, and the like. Joy finds its best, normal opening for filling in our ordinary life activities, you might say, in the characteristic way we suggest our meanings.

If you have a bad, weak style to your actions, it throttles the evidence of joy. I know, if a person is largely incompetent, uptight, sickly, or mismade, such a handicap usually—not always!—crimps rejoicing. But given a base of physical and emotional health and a measure of skill, people block a joyful life by disregarding the matter of style. Only when one's style-fulness is deeply opened up as a celebrative praise-response to the Lord can joy, I believe, flow freely through your creaturely veins, if its holy gift is indeed instilled in your heart.

Style is the way humans respond to God's ordinance for aesthetic life
Let me describe with two examples my understanding of "style" as a normal creaturely affair humans are bound to unfold one way or another, or try to suppress.

I know a family whose conversation is laced with references to current world events such as the stock market, what's playing in London and New York, why the current political trouble-spot materialized, and myriad interesting facts like the stage of rock sedimentation before Christ and the population of Tokyo. Meals are on a pick-up basis except in the evening at seven o'clock when it's a fairly formal dinner; you drink coffee after dessert in the sitting room out of pretty cups. Everybody has a responsible job and is industrious, but takes time to do sport or play bridge. Each one has opinions, but is polite; one is very cordial but a little reserved; there is always the breathing space of detachment in one's interests and commitments. The style as a whole is one of cultivated discretion. To be a classically educated gentleman and a woman of intelligent taste, aware of what's going on in the world, plays through all that their

— Joy, Style, and Aesthetic Imperatives —

family does, it's the style to their family way-of-life.

I know another family whose middle-sized kitchen is the hearth of the home. Married children and their off-spring gather there with the parents after the morning church service on Sunday for coffee and *iets lekkers*, without fail. They are an open-hearted folk, gregarious and hospitable, somewhat impulsive, unadorned, always busy during the week at good tasks. Meals are straightforward potatoes, gravy, vegetable, and a little piece of meat. Each one tends to be rather blunt—no offense—and has exaggerated loyalties to a baseball or hockey team, although one's real feelings are kept fairly private. TV has largely replaced reading, except for the Bible. There is a kind of matter-of-fact, wholesome, taking-for-granted, homespun style to the family life. To do an honest day's work to earn your keep—and a good night's sleep—is the style-quality of their routine, and even of special events.

Now there are a couple of things I'm after with this double description of different styles to daily life:

(1) This discernible yet elusive quality that pervades every activity as a kind of mixture of whim and breeding, which I've called "style," is something more durable than a "fashion" one may pick up for a while. Whatever term you use, there is a difference between the historically ingrained, abiding fabric of allusivity ("playfulness," if you will), which colors and gives a suggestion-rich contour to the meals, conversation, interactions of a certain family—between their family "style" and a "fashion" they may adopt, like putting a swimming pool in the backyard, or a bomb shelter, getting into cable TV, or going bonkers on diet-health foods. A fad may absorb all-consuming attention, but a fad does not have the quiet staying power of a style. A vogue, a "stylization," you could say, like a Lady Di haircut, is a catchy pattern that is briefly conventional. A fashion is culturally very important—although Christians in our secular day, I believe, will rightly, normally, be out of fashion—and if one were to appropriate the latest fad, one's lifestyle might become faddish. But fashion is of a different order and weight than the styleful dimension embedded in human activity, which surfaces in our actions to give them a definite, intimative, and imaginative cachet. Style is a worked-in aesthetic feature: fashion is a phenomenon of social decoration and is usually makeshift or experimental in usage.

(2) There is no one right model style for all families in all ages to adhere to. There is no secret paradigm of the perfect family style that has been passed on by oral tradition among the great saints of the church and

that I'm going to spill it now so you can wrap up your lifestyle problems tomorrow and then move on to another book to get your rationality paradigmatically straightened out. It's correct, those were two different styles of family life I sketched. A Marxist would label the first "educated uppercrust" and the second probably as "middle-class," and damn both of them for not being dispossessed proletarian families whose bearing must be one of perpetual revolution against the status quo. A certain brand of psychologists might analyze the one as introverted-thinking, Matthew-Arnold types, and the other as the extravert-intuitional manner, and then prognosticate what psychic cracks will show up once you delve behind this social armor (since "feelings" are the psychologists' business, and it's so that deep feelings are usually not above board in public). But my intent was neither prescriptive nor ulterior. I only wanted to hint that style, which has a discernible complexion and can be identified, maybe even catalogued some, is a complex business despite its unified focus, and is not simply "right" nor simply "wrong," but is relatively normative, like character, or like a species of flowers, or of weeds.

(3) Style is only one feature of our way-of-life. The slogan *le style c'est l'homme* ("Style is the essence of man") is wrong. Every sane person and every fairly integrated family has the makings of a style and also the larger, cohering network of multiple activities we call "way-of-life." Even people and institutions that have not articulated a *view*-of-life-and-the-world, a world-and-life-view, do have, as a matter of fact, a *way*-of-life in-the-world, a subconscious habit of activities beaten out in the press of daily life that marks their kind of whole integrity and that shows itself notably in crises. A people's way-of-life holds elements of style, a language, training, mores, temperament, mentality, and other kinds of matters kaleidoscopically together, and receives its over-all imprimatur from the faith-commitment underlying and leading the whole. But a way-of-life is not sacrosanct just because it is fundamentally shaped by a faith-commitment. Touch a person's way-of-life, alter a family's way-of-life, for good or ill, and you change quite drastically the exercise of their humanity. Now style is one feature, just one ingredient in a family or person's way-of–life. Style does not make or break a person, but the moment of style, I am convinced, is much more deeply implicated in the inhibitions or encouragement we know to live a full life of shalom before the face of the Lord than we usually give it credit for. A family, or fellowship you might say, that plays as well as prays together is more likely to stay together in the grace of the Lord.

Aesthetic imperatives
That leads me to explain "aesthetic imperatives," because style, while it is constituted and lived out largely subliminally, below the threshold of conscious attention, is set by us people in our office of caretaker of the Lord's garden, guardian of our fellows, worshipper of God self revealed in Jesus Christ, made known in the Scriptures, and witnessed to the faithful by the Holy Spirit loose on earth, so to speak, since Pentecost. Our style is *our* responsibility before the Lord; and if we bury our talent for stylefulness in the ground of disregard and adopt a mold that tends to prime us as snobs, as uncouth louts or cookie-cuttered stereotypes, instead of as sturdy or delicate vessels of joy, then we stand judged already, with a joyless lifetime and with possibly a vexed existence. God does not want us to be drab creatures—style is one of the good works for which we were created in Christ Jesus to walk around in (cf. Ephesians 2:9–10).

I believe the creaturely ways God laid down for us to be obedient within, oblige us to discern those various creational laws as God's will for our lives of service. The positive deeds we do in fulfilling God's call to be thoughtful, to keep promises, to be communicative, sensitive, imaginative, just, sociable, and the like: the concrete shape we give in deed to these many creaturely ways, I call issuing and enacting "imperatives."

The way I understand being a Christian—sharing in Christ's anointing—when I speak or think or use resources, I am not just "doing my own thing," but I am **in my speaking and thinking and resource-use** to be confessing Christ's Rule, presenting myself as a living thank-offering, breaking down the pet idols I sin with, trusting that the works of my speaking, thinking, and resource-using hands will be established by the Lord and follow us on to the new earth (cf. answer to the Heidelberg Catechism question 32; cf. Psalm 90:16–17, Revelation 14:13). When I speak christianly, that is, speak clearly and persuasively, assured of what is so, salted and peppered with a dash of attuned, pithy humor (cf. Colossians 4:5–6), I am saying, "Friend, speak likewise!" And when I think christianly, that is, make insightful distinctions that ring true with wisdom (cf. Proverbs 4:1–18), I am saying, "Fellows, think along correctively with a similar cloud of glory around our ideas, concepts, and analytic judgments." And when I use resources christianly, that is, show thrift, godly purpose, and generosity in the expense (cf. 1 Timothy 6:17–19), I am saying, "Neighbors, do this too in remembrance of our Lord's love for the creation he died to save from its travail" (Romans 8:19–23, John 3:16–17). That is, my deeds of whatever kind, as a follower of Jesus Christ, enjoin others communally to praise God (imperative), build up our neighbor (imperative), and keep the earth in truth (imperative) by speaking, thinking, and using things in some such way.

The same format and task holds, I believe, also for the specific area of human subject activity we know as being imaginative and becoming nuance-aware of things and events in God's world. Every creature, act, and happening is structured to have nuances. Whether that object-functional latency comes to the fore or not and is subject-activated by someone's apperceptive attention or not, I think that we do well to recognize that whole realm of nuances and nuancefulness—as the latent quality of something or as the potent nuancing moment in any activity—as "aesthetic." You can also refer to this order of creaturely existence as the "ludic" dimension of God's creation, where there's play in what's going on, subtleties, shadings that can tickle your fancy and make you smile. "Allusivity" is another term I've used to try to point to this specific reality that has its own irreducible character and is interpenetratingly present in our lives even when it does not give the defining character to what we are doing, as when we are "playing ball" or "fooling around."

Notice, I'm not talking art and "artistic" activity, even though artistry is closely related to "aesthetic" functioning. And I don't want to get into the philosophical problem right now of examining what precisely must take place for freewheeling aesthetic activity like imagining things, having fun, joking, and being surprised—what it takes to transform aesthetic activity into artistically structured acts like performing theatre, composing music, or making a painting on canvas that can hang on a wall. I would like to mention, in passing, that loose talk about what's beautiful can perhaps best be taken to mean that certain unusual nuances have been sighted; the moving mauve color-cloud-shadow-formation is so peculiarly impressive you can't crease it and put it in your pocket right away or wrap it up in a formula or a thought; its elusive quality of inscape is, well, "beautiful," or, if its nuanced mountainous glory is overwhelmingly huge, "sublime." But all I'm trying to make us aware of here in context is the fact that we are called as Christians to issue and enact aesthetic imperatives too. So, when I busy myself imaginatively as a Holy Spirit-filled child of God, that is, read things nuancefully, act frolicsome as a child, undertake adventures with great expectation, or celebrate something memorable—joyfully, then as saying, "My friend, let this kind of style kiss your workaday existence too."

A full-fledged aesthetic imperative might sound something like this: **Let there be suggestion-rich disclosure of nuanced creaturely reality, both within you and around you, people, so that your joy in the Lord may be**

— Joy, Style, and Aesthetic Imperatives —

filled full; otherwise, you will be condemned to the closure and death of the imaginativity with which God outfitted you as a hallelujah creature.

Now I'd like to explore simply a couple facets of such an aesthetic imperative for our lifestyle today in North America, but there are still two mistakes I should first try to head off in a few sentences before we reflect directly on clothes and on games.

"Style" has often meant to us in Western civilization putting-on-the-dog the way ritzy people do—expensive clothes on svelte bodies, affected accents and high-class education, a few antiques in the house, manicured hands, cigarette holders, and hauteur, the night-club act before night clubs were invaded by portly business men with expense accounts and overdressed wives. (I have no respect for such "style," even if watered down to a vestige of formal manners in which one seeks tatters of grandeur; they are the real people with "class" who can snatch compassionate, home-grown grace beyond the reach of fastidious "style.") If style meant sophistication, the aesthetic counterpart to analytic sophistry, God's folk should let "style" go to hell where it belongs, along with all the other idols of Renaissance-inspired Enlightenment. The style of democratized, Western "culchah" has killed its ten thousands of covenant children who have gotten a secular higher education, because the sheen of Humanist style within secular education stripped the biblical gears of their covenanted consciousness so they no longer could distinguish between a faux pas and sin, lies become "white"(!), and unlettered people living in the naiveté of tender-hearted love were considered to be "uncultured" VUPs, very unimportant persons. God's Word of Ephesians 4:17–5:21 is a stirring rejection of such Humanist style as one of insufferable, empty-headed vanity. I mention this just so we keep alert to the truth that we are treading on mine-filled ground when we discuss lifestyle.

The other thing to be wary of is raising our idiosyncrasies to the status of prescribed christian style. I'm smart enough to realize as a frustrated poet who has to make speeches for a living that the compacted density of my sentences in the drive to have something worth chewing on every fifty words is probably not the norm for the prose style of a lecture, and all the poetic, verbal play may profit the hearer absolutely nothing except the delightful sense of semantic vertigo if I stop before you fall down. If I finish off the festivity of being clothed, with a tie, it usually is of Irish wool and solid color or a soft plaid united by yellow. A favorite gift my Mother used to send me every Christmas was a box of carefully sharpened stubs of pencils, which made my miserly, stamp-collector heart glow at the salvage. What this adds up to, joined by my frugal wife, has been enough to give all of our children the style of street scavengers on their early morning paper routes. And I do believe garage sales can be sanctifying events when you move house and home, giving away the detritus of our lives to the happiness of bargain hunters (or punishing the greedy in kind). But I would not dare to think that my fishmonger lifestyle is the preferred conduit for saved people to know joy within.

However, aesthetic imperatives issued by parents, by teachers, by peers or disc jockeys, sports heroes, by the city you live in, or by a country town neighborhood on its inhabitants: the authority of the aesthetic imperatives postulated by leaders, the style that is set and is followed by many, easily assumes the power of what the Bible calls a "principality," a nondescript, categorial influence upon your life. This is so partly because one's style of life is so familiar you hardly notice it and partly because style materializes almost imperceptively and usually without having its consequences thought through, and certainly because style is a responsible human's elemental and casual answer, willy-nilly, to the Lord's call for aesthetic obedience. The control style exercises on the rest of our life is quietly profound. Your lifestyle tends to protect your faith-commitment, strengthen and enrich the quality of your daily, professional, and societal life at large; or the style to your life tends to dissipate the focus of our final, existential attachment to the Lord, and undermines the many other kinds of imperatives we embody historically. So despite the relative normativity of all lifestyles, in order to exorcize the curses of any ungodly style we may be cultivating we need prayerfully to consider: can we communally settle on certain directives for style that shall buoy those who intend to follow Jesus Christ to the bitter but triumphant and glorious end?

Clothing has a double ministry:
to protect privacy and to enhance our nuances
Clothes are a gift of God to men and women. **To be clothed is a mark of humanity.** Sea shells and lilies of the valley do not need clothes; and for animals, who are never naked, to be attired is usually an affront to any animal glory they may have left after being "housebroken."

Are not clothes a result of sin, and would not paradise have been a nudist colony?

Genesis 5:7 does not mean that husband and wife, since the fall, should have intercourse with the lights out and try to stay covered, since nakedness is always shameful; and Genesis 3:21 is not divine authorization for mink farms since, after all, God made the first fur coats. The point of the Bible about God's clothing Adam and Eve is that the Lord faithfully stayed close to the special creature made in God's image even in their sin and, from the very beginning of history, is busy protecting and redeeming our peculiar human glory, starting with actual clothes.

The Bible carries through on our being clothed in durable animal skins (rather than in makeshift, throwaway fig leaves) by reporting extensively on the splendid garments prepared for Aaron to don after he was ritually purified just prior to his being anointed with oil as high priest for God's folk (Exodus 28–29): the vestments certified that Aaron's official "naked purity" was covered over by the holy glory of God (cf. Exodus 39:27–31). Paul's idiom too on the Christian believers' wearing the armor of "salvation," "truth, and "righteousness" (Ephesians 6:10–20; cf. Proverbs 1:7–9, Isaiah 61:10–11) continues the whole "being clothed" perspective, and leads to reading about the day when the elect will be measured for fine linen robes as they appear before the throne of the victorious Lamb (cf. Revelation 7:9–17, 19:1–10). That is, along with the rich, biblical literary way of revealing that we men and women need to be clothed with the Holy Spirit (cf. Judges 6:34, Romans 8:1–11), protectively enhanced, reclothed with Spirit-glory in our lifetime if we would indeed that our mortal corporeality be clothed-over with immortality (2 Corinthians 5:1–10): along with that biblical truth is the corollary that there's more to clothing than keeping warm. Clothing is an act of God's grace to refurbish our lost glory.

If that is so, then clothing becomes a God-given opportunity to cut our aesthetic teeth on. Imagine! clothing is a blessing intended for us to show we are sons and daughters of God. Cotton plants and flax, the wool and skins of animals, are at our disposal for us to enhance our bodily nuances while protecting ourselves from evil. We are called to be dressed in ways that set off the color of our skin, the demeanor of our person, the lineaments of a homely face, the curves of our bodily sexuality, the dedication of our lives, the shape and strength of shoulder, arm, or leg, with a style that will not arrest attention prizing itself but reflect that you are corporeally a good-looking, godly man or boy and a glorious girl or woman of God.

Let me elaborate a minute on this christian idea of **the double ministry of clothes: to protect and to enhance our human nature**.

> You probably could only surmise how funny my family thinks it is for me to talk about clothes, since I seem to treat apparel as a utility, with as little attention and expense as possible so long as it's kept in time-saving, running order. And maybe I do have

an unopened-up clothing praxis, although I find great relief in not being anxious about what to wear tomorrow, and my thanks to God and God's people go much deeper than believing there will always be kind folk who give away used clothes that are not completely worn out to Good Will Industries, if I really need something: I have the necessaries of life, including clean clothes (as Ecclesiastes 9:7–10 puts it), and am free to enjoy life with my wife and to work hard tending one of God's flowers—theory. So I'm just following my christian theoretical nose on clothes. . . .

It's significant that Christ mentions clothing in the same breath when he said our heavenly Father knows we need food and drink for life, but don't chase it down the way godless people do (Matthew 6:1–5). God knows we need habitational shelter and a sense of safety too (cf. Psalm 121). I think those spell out the most basic needs to sustain human life: to be free from hunger, thirst, fear, buffeting cold and heat and predatory animals, *and* free from the exposure of nakedness. Clothes protect you against the elements, thistles and insects, but especially against other people who to show off their powerful selves might wish to invade and violate the privacy we human creatures know. Whenever you are illegitimately stripped as a captive, it is utterly demeaning; robbed of your clothes, naked, it takes just a cruel or coldly erotic look to rape you of your self-respect or force you to dehumanize yourself and act brazen like a creature without the depth of shame. The minimum grace in clothes is the defensive covering they afford for us in our glorious but vulnerable nakedness.

It's the other ministry of clothing, however, I wanted to highlight: to bring out and share our nuances. **To be dressed is more than to be clothed.** The destitute are closed off from exercising fully this range of the aesthetic calling to be dressed, just as those who are emotionally distressed need to be calmed down first before they can learn richer feelings of sympathy for others. But then people are able, thanks to God, to accept clothing as a positive opportunity to spread joy—from the bright-colored ribbon in the hair to sash around the waist or the gay little feather stuck in a senior citizen's derby—it would be evil to repress that opportunity as if it were letting the devil get his foot in your door. Why should the human glory God gave us be hid under a bushel basket (cf. Matthew 5:14–16)? And the injunction to "rejoice with those rejoicing and weep with those weeping" (Romans 12:15–16) means that a believer should enter into the full gamut of happy and sorrowful experiences among the congregated faithful with whom he or she worships; it does not mean you should visit the sick appearing grim, or not have three shirts (so you can change one for variety and give one away) so long as there are people on earth without any shirts on their backs. Scripture asks us to be not one with the frenetic, worldly fashion of gaudy luxury but also to be not conformed to the somber sadness, to the monotonic drone and blank stereo-typicality flooding our disenchanted, technocracked society. Our aesthetic mission is to remain colorful, to please God with style made "new," packed with a joy for all seasons (cf. Romans 12:1–2), You don't cure the sin of condoning aesthetes by turning into a self-righteous kill-joy who with a guilty conscience goes around giving nuance-aware followers of Christ an anaesthetic needle of dour woe (cf. 1 Timothy 4:1–10).

I'll not repeat what I wrote in *Rainbows* (70–72, 180–82)about killjoys and cultural eunuchs, but let me add a couple of suggestions on the problems of redeeming clothing,

There is a line between making (or buying), wearing, and caring for a well-cut suit, supportive underwear, a lovely dress, or a warm, rest-giving sweater, that makes it aesthetically obedient dress and not having it become a vain pre-occupation. The line between obedient dress and disobedient clothing is not drawn necessarily, I think, by the expense or by the amount of attention it has taken (although time and money are relevant factors): it depends on the spirited way the clothing is conceived and borne—do the garments remain allusively functional, soft-pedaling their enrichment of your corporeal presence, or do they put you on display and show-off themselves, like a costume? It's the difference between being (prayerfully) stylefully clad and being "dressed-to-kill," as the expression goes. And some of the very same articles of clothing could be redeemed dress or unredeemed—how does that sound?—because while "clothes make the man or woman" it's also true that "the man or the woman makes the clothes"; and it's the whole operation of being dressed that counts in context. So you can't superficially say, "ankle-length dress is in God's kingdom," and "Stovepipe pants you have to snake into belong to the devil": you have to test the spirit of the styled clothing and dress wearing—it may be indiscernible on occasion—but the religion difference does become evident, especially if clothes are offensive dress because all that he or she is as a person is a clothes rack and wants to be packaged-to-sell in the crowd.

> Six miles above the ground in an Air Canada jet once I was making conversation with a very distinguished, smartly dressed gentleman who I found out was a vice-president in some cosmetics firm. "Oh," I said naively, "have you decided on what

lotions we'll buy next year?" He looked at me with a disbelieving grimace. He was flying back from a high-level, executive council meeting of the firm in New York City where they had just decided on their line of soaps and deodorants for fifteen years from then. Ever since, I really have preferred to smell sweaty, and whenever on the packed subway a wave of onions and garlic perfume engulfs me, I think, "Good for you, fellow; don't let any high-priced executive in New York City fifteen years ago tell you how to smell"; and I drink in the reek christianly! before I have to push my way out to get some air.

This is the background to why anything stylish (fashionable) is suspect to me, clothes or cosmetics. There are so few christian tailors in positions of cultural authority, and I don't trust the reigning couturiers. Just because it's cheap and off-the-rack does not make the piece normative clothing. Since Christ died to save our clothes too, set clothing free! we should be humorfully wary lest we adorn ourselves in secular costumes and have unwittingly joined a masquerade party headed in the wrong direction.

Many of us probably realize that high heels are unrighteous shoes because of the abnormal, body-wrenching position they manipulate a woman into who, granted, may be eye-popping elegant high-heeling it along a sidewalk in a short dress, like a stork doing classical ballet pirouettes. Many of us probably realize that shirts made out of solid plastic fiber, like nylon, are unfair to temples of the Holy Spirit, since the plastic cloth prohibits the pores of your skin from breathing, even though it's drip-dry and wrinkle-free. A few of us might find it mildly interesting that padded-shoulders were introduced by Henry VIII to counterbalance his belly, and we might be willing to discuss, over coffee, the ethics of wigs older waitresses need to wear to get better tips, whether that's an imaginative exegesis of 1 Corinthians 11:2–16 on the "clothing" of hair or a capitulation to our youthist culture and the male leer. But most of us, at least those over 30, I suppose, think clothing is a less pressing cultural arena for christian concern than politics, the draft, and nuclear fall-out, and accordingly dress humdrum conservative or feel most comfortable in the old hippie uniform of cotton jeans. Yet I'm beginning to wonder—hence the "consciousness raising"—after observing punk dress closely in London, England, recently: there are more ways to die than one.

Have you ever known the menace of being in company with those who wear unisexed, black leather jackets studded with shining metal knobs worn proudly like medals, a hardened, angry parody of the honored colonel with a stiff upper lip back from his India campaign for the British Empire, now sported by veterans of the Sex Pistols War and "White Riot" clashes? Hair tortured and war-painted into red, green, violet tufts, like straw, coiffured to be explicitly disheveled? Their women sport the sexy same in meshed stocking and pinched shoes or florescent balloon pants and riding boots or the briefest of tightest skirts, with dog collars for necklaces, long chains with padlocks and razor blades about the throat or waist, trophies, as it were, of future scalps. Thin-lipped mouths set hard, eyes painted exaggeratedly exotic, blue and blackened, street-wise, underworldly tough. I could only feel it all on with a terrible sadness, helpless in my faded polyester pants and short-sleeved shirt from Sears to reach out, stymied before such flamboyant, self-mutilating, self-dishonoring clothing. And the clothing mask had become their very skin; the costume was the ritualistic gang uniform of harnessed, militant anarchy dedicated without compromise to the kamikaze shock and overthrow of every established order. Their clothing testified vividly that they were the ungrateful dead, still walking around on the prowl in the 80s, as lethal as unexploded bullets. It was a sermon in clothes that showed what is at stake in the war of being dressed: the style of life or the style of death.

How then shall we dress? to stay alive and proffer life to our neighbor rather than just muddle through?

I know the Bible says a woman who waits upon the Lord remains beloved even if her looks go (Proverbs 31:30). I know that Christ prefers a man who hopes in God's mercy rather than in somebody with a show of strong leg (cf. Psalm 147:10–11). But it's a cop-out to say we should be "clothed" in humility and righteousness (1 Peter 5:5, 1 Thessalonians 5:3) and don't bother your head so about dress: we need deeds of humble and righteous clothing! Otherwise that song about "love" is mouthwash. It really does mean, doesn't it, "They'll know we are Christians by our . . . dress" and games and taste and style—love in action!

Christian dress that is aesthetically obedient will not be uniforms, but will encourage an imaginative variety of becoming clothing within the community, with homespun novelty perhaps, and be primed to recapture nuancefully the sense of different occasions, since we do indeed joy in the diversity of creation (rather than cater to wearing the same jeans or business suit to the office, to church, to the playground, probably even to bed).

The good news of Christ's Rule over all nations should give us Christians who dress the insight and grit somehow to renew in hybrid our folk tradition of clothes too—the Spanish mantilla, the Scots kilt, the Indian sarong, Eskimo mukluk, the Slavic embroidered tunic, Dutch wooden shoes: not as a badge of ethnic courage and race nor as a tourist item, but as a liberated, rooted contribution of hope—even if it seems quaint to the poor souls who have lost their roots—a fleeting allusion in our attire celebrating the pied beauty, better, the many-splendored joy schnorkeling in us resurrected people of the new creation.

If clothing bodies is an aesthetic opportunity to be dressed, in the very basic human matter of covering our bodily selves, then clothes are necessarily very integral to our style of life and the quotient and quality of joy we provide others. Games are a different sort of aesthetic affair; but because anything aesthetic lodges very fundamentally in our human make-up—at least the way my anthropological theory goes—games, too, fill a very elemental human need God created. That one plays games, and what games you play how, whether a man or a woman plays unconsciously out of a holy faith in Christ's certain Rule (cf. Romans 14:23) or whether you reject game-playing on principle or out-of-hand as a waste of time—something for kids, maybe—or whether you've been sucked into the secular brand of pay-for-play: however you respond to the creaturely aesthetic call to play games deeply affects the style-quality of your life (in which your underlying faith-commitment comes through) and the whole functional strength you build. (Those who are habitually slack in apparel might recoup certain aesthetic fiber and potential if they are game for play—God made us amazingly intricate creatures with all sorts of built-in, life-saving features for the times when we slip up on certain obediences....)

The Nature of Games
Games are like complex toys that people who know how and will obey the rules of the game can enter, for the time being, as players. You are a whole, real person really there at the checkerboard, but you are all there focused to be playing. Playing is one way a person can actually act for a while, and games ask to be played—that's all. You unlock the meaning of a game by playing it, period.

Lots of people are not satisfied with this explanation. It's like asking mountain climbers why they climb mountains and then come down again and be told, "Because they're there!" But why, what's a game for? Why play games? What's it do for you?

> I was argued into joining the high-school track team by a secular coach who said, "If you're going to become a minister, and

> you've run the distance like Gil Dodds, and won the mile in a couple meets, young people will listen to your sermons better."
>
> But that wouldn't hold for tiddlywinks champion or hide-and-seek, would it?

Is "playing games" redeeming the time for grown-ups? Have you never heard as a child: "Go play somewhere else!" (sotto voce) Nuisance! Don't you know this is an adult world for working here?

Because games are much bigger than any one person, structured by a communal faith-perspective, societal milieu, historical circumstances and level of cultural complexity, anthropologists can examine the fact that Eskimo children play games of physical skill taking memory-attention rather than those of chance and strategy, and interpret it in terms of shamanism, clan-orientation toward subsistence congruent with the policy of nurturing the young to do one's best but not at the expense of others. The games of Iroquois Indians in years past, where I grew up on Long Island, were more athletic contests and tied closely to rites invoking rain or ceremonial dances for the blessing of fertility—things out of human hands—and so sometimes the games lost their ludic qualification and become "terminal" contests like the prayer service for rain Elijah once attended on Mount Carmel (cf. 1 Kings 18).

> Mississippi Choctaw Indians hated witches, but they allowed them at matches of stickball games to out hex the other side's witch. That's the historical background to cheerleaders today. Cheerleaders are secular witches, with show biz and sex thrown in, to manipulate the "spirit" for our side.
>
> The only christian cheerleader I've ever seen was a short, stocky Calvin College fellow—I don't know his name anymore—in 1948 who could walk out to the middle of the basketball court at the old Burton Street gym at the right time-out and pound the floor with his fists—no legs and cancan routine, no antics, nothing—just kneel and pound the floor with his fists, and you became a yelling maniac—

Social scientists too have studied games and playgrounds and noted that as more playthings like slides and "monkey bars" were placed there you saved on expensive playground directors, because the more play equipment in the park the more physical exercise among the children and the less social contact, and conflict. And developmental psychologists can tell you what games are best for what age, to the month, for developing your child into a good North American character—when to move from "peek-a-boo-baby" to knocking-down-blocks to playing-house, watching Bugs Bunny cartoons (before age 8 is best) on to puzzles, charades, games with written rules and team sports—because games do build character, of a Darwinian sort or another. Psychoanalysts also use games, watching you play through one-way-looking-glass mirrors to diagnose neuroses, and will tell you confidently that youth play "King on the Hill' to blow off steam and inflate their egos.

> I noticed that when we Institute Senior Members grew too old to play the ritual soccer match at retreats, with threat of injury and crutches, our verbal arguments heated up. There's just not the same kick in volleyball as you have in soccer.

People play games, as another theory has it, to simulate the problems they'll have in later life, the better to cope with them: you play dolls in anticipation of being a mother; if you take to games with dice, you'll do very well later on in the North American business world—

Enough. It's so that the games people play, like the clothes one wears—sneakers, step-in loafers, laced shoes—can be read to detect other things.

> I'm willing to believe that informal games are germinated in a non-competitive society, and that a rise in highly formal games, boxes with instructions, selling for $15.95, corresponds with a growth in popularity of rightist political opinion in a country. I balk, though, when a teacher is fired for pushing "Ring-around-the-rosey" in a kindergarten class, as if it were a Communist plot to instill revolutionary ideas ("Ashes, ashes, all—fall—down")!

And games do generally help one discharge surplus energy, aggressive and otherwise. Games do exercise competencies in non-threatening situations—one's strength, agility to eat watermelon, vocabulary, memory, invention, decisiveness, and so on. Games do normally enlarge one's feelings, unless you suffer repeatedly from being a "poor loser." But I'm not willing to leave games hostage to Durkheimian anthropology, pragmatistic social engineering, or Freudian psychoanalysis. Not just because of a general, godless disorientation and what seems to me to be resulting lopsided, special-pleading theories of play, but specifically because (1) games need to be recognized first of all as properly aesthetic matters and not as a front or means to an end of non-play activities, and (2) playing games needs to be reconceived, I think, as God-service for mature people rather than as something particularly childish, remedial, or a middle-class luxury.

Behind the untold variations in games of the world, its many cultures, and despite the grievously denatured form most games probably reach us in today, because of their contextualization by our secularized post-Christian civilization, I believe there is an ontic gift of God, an ordinance of the Lord for "playfulness" (cf. *Rainbows*, 52–54), that makes games possible as a channel of grace and as an avenue of service.

A game is organized play. That's the difference between "Tag" and a prank, "Dominoes" and horseplay. Giving your children names is primarily an aesthetic act too, I think, but it is not a game, even though it is playful, imaginative (one hopes), and meant to bring your daughter or son an unpressured, joyful calling card. Games always have rules and usually demand some skill of its players, more than is required, for example, to play in a sand box. That's why it's often said that babies and children play; older children play games. Games thrive on uncertainty, and usually involve some kind of guessing on what to do next. Every player strives to reach the end or goal of the game first. A great thing about games is that, if you're not "IT" or not the first person who says, "Rover, red rover, I dare you to come over," everybody, technically, begins even, and that's so every time you start the game again, so that children can occasionally win over their parents, and the stronger may lose to the weaker, thanks especially to the wonderful unexpected that always goes with a real game—the ground was uneven for that particular croquet shot, her first card was an ace of spades, you read the word "guano" in your novel last week before the Scrabble game when you happened to get those letters and they fit the square for the triple word count. . . .

The glory of games: invitation to the Haha! Erlebnis

So? What's so good about a game? God said, "Let there be . . . games, and he saw that they were good"? God said, "Let my people go, pharaoh . . . to play games"?!

It's very tempting to moralize the meaning of games and say something like: "Games can help Christians take themselves less seriously, you can learn to relax and lose; they are pleasant exercises in humility." Or, "Games are a foretaste of heaven and true humanity where we will be totally free from duties, drudgery, and real evil; so enjoy them when you can, don't be a work-righteous Calvinist." But I think that tack is wrong, is built on a covert natural theology of play or humor, and misses the glory of games.

The glory of a game lies in its objective invitation to the haha! Erlebnis. (The so-called Aha! Erlebnis refers to the moment of lived insight when you catch on to something—Aha! Well, let's call the lived experience of continuing smiling, subliminal laughter-percolating, and bubbling frolicsomeness to be "the Haha! Erlebnis.") A game is structured for nothing so much as to elicit the haha! Erlebnis from boys and girls, women and men, who submit themselves to its gentle yoke. The haha! Erlebnis happens in playing a game *not* because you as a person are *released* from sensing, thinking, and being obliged to your "Bridge" partner, released from keeping your wits about you what "fruit" you are in the "Fruit Basket Upset" game as you calculate how to get next to the girl you like who is sitting next to an "apple," but she's a "peach" and you're a "lemon"—some of my game experience is a bit dated: you experience what the game is for, the haha! Erlebnis, not by jumping out of your ordinary skin and numerous responsibilities but by *focusing* all the ways you are and your human responsibilities *playfully*. And the exhilarating haha! comes from fully living to the hilt the imagining world of consciousness games provide and build solely out of fantasy and fun. The glory of a game it is to wake you up as a person to being imaginatively active in which the "acting," the mimicry, the making-believe, remains low-key-merged in the mesh of you awaiting actual new surprises.

A game to its player is very close to what Wonderland was for Alice. While your playmates turn ropes for you in "Jumping rope" and you recite limericks like:

> All in together, girls / dressed like the weather, girls
> When you count to six / you must do the splits— / 1 2 3 4 5 6!

While jumping up and down, the muted illusion of being a prima donna or queen titillates you most cheerfully during your turn. You play the hunter and the hunted with shivers of expectation and tables-turned in "Kick-the-can"; you're tickled pink at being a veritable private edition of Webster's dictionary when you guess an unusual word in "Probe" or "Scrabble"; there's thrill to masterminding a concealed rook attack behind a pawn maneuver in chess. . . . That is, when you are wholly busy, thoroughly humanly absorbed in a game as a game, from "Kitty-in-the-corner" to "Chinese checkers" and from "Backgammon" to "Bocce," you feel jovial, think favorably about all and sundry and nothing fixed in particular, act congenial, puny in verbal connections, noticing unimportant details with interest, turning all your combinatorial dexterity happily toward winning the elusive prize of the game, which is imaginary!

> That's why a "real" prize tends to spoil a game, be an intrusion that dampens the universe of having fun. That's also why an em-

barrassing rather than an imaginative forfeit in a game is even more cruel and out of taste.

If it's right, a game puts you on all-aesthetic alert. Games set you up for the haha! Erlebnis. And discovering in a lived way—*not thinking about it* as we are doing now—discovering the aesthetic way our playful God (cf. Proverbs 8:22–31) created us to be is an amazingly good use of time.

> The only thing I know to compare it to is the discovery of reading. I couldn't cite one precisely dated moment when I realized the Holy Spirit had locked me permanently safe in the Lord's grip—I could relate several vivid experiences of it to you. But I do know exactly where I lay sprawled between the kitchen and the living room in my childhood home and have a vivid image of the lighting and people movement at the time when precisely at ten minutes past six o'clock on Saturday evening, 5 September 1936, as I was following the large print in a book before me, perusing it on the floor, suddenly I discovered I could read, "I can read! I can read!" I hollered, and ran to my mother doing the dishes in the kitchen, and she had to stop and listen to me haltingly read.

A game focuses you, normally more quietly, yourself, depending on age and health perhaps, more bemused than electrified, to an ongoing haha! sense of creatureliness and God's rich blessing of surprise.

For some people, like long-term convalescents, the aged lonely, or feeble persons in rest homes whose families have left them behind, the only time they're likely to meet a bona fide surprise is in a game. Playing checkers with a sick child or with an old, forgotten man who can't see or hear so well anymore, may indeed be acting as a channel of God's love, offering a true cup of cold water in Christ's name, letting him be imaginatively useful (which is different than "imagine he's useful,"), acting as if he's in command again, jumping your king, necessarily taking initiative in response to your feinted attacks, possibly sparking joy through such allusive human functioning.

> I have mixed thoughts about games in our cursed, secular prisons. The horrible state of our penal institutions corrupts playing a game even before it starts, makes a game impossibly grotesque, an abomination like forcing somebody in pain to laugh. The only perverse aesthetic activity that can breathe in our prisons, I'm afraid, is baiting the guards, one another, and riots.

> There will be no games in hell. No crossword puzzles either, not even "canasta." Hell will be a *complete* waste of time. Total ennui. No surprise conceivable—you can't even wait for Godot there.

It is important to say right here, however, that playing games does not necessarily convert you into a playful person, no more than wearing clothes necessarily finds you dressed up. You can play games so seriously hard, even without the compulsiveness to win, that you kill its game character. I do believe it's possible to nurture playfulness with game-playing, especially home-made games, roughhousing, and story-telling (cf. *Rainbows*, 54–59), but even a relatively normative game can be debased by its players. Further, if playing games is not crowned, suffused, made interrelated, relative to the rest of your life activity by a quiet or exuberant, celebrative joy in the Lord for this gift of haha! life thanks to the Holy Spirit, then playing games will run away with you, just as dress that misses being a servant of joy under Christ's Rule slips toward ugly, glittering vanity. In fact, a given game can be cultured evil.

> In my judgment dice do not violate a believer's gladness in the providence of God; but in a game context dice are simply a handy way to bring play on play-in-reality to the fore. I willingly admit, however: on rainy days my younger brother and I as boys would play "Monopoly," and it always ended in fights. My mother came to hate the game even though she didn't forbid it, and I remember her saying once, "That game must be of the devil!" She probably was right—although that judgment probably exonerates me too much as the brother older by three years.

And playing games may become so joyless that the players are turned into bored mercenaries or assassins of God's good, playful reality while going through the play motions, as in gambling and perhaps as in most arenas of professional sports today. The playing of games that is not God-service sooner or later in our secular world voids its aesthetic promise and becomes cultic worship of Mammon. The resulting non-sportive engagements parasite off the creaturely reality of play and games. That is why we like to watch them in all their fascinating unpredictability! But actually the game of game has gone dead; and it is very sobering to imagine that the dazzling spectacles of enormously skilled teams of gladiators one may view throughout the whole world are historically in line with those dreadful, "playful" events years ago when they fed Christians to the lions. But now the Christians who as humans God made for playing sit in the stands as cash-paying "fans."

How then shall we play games to bear life instead of death and pseudo joy? Should we still play . . . games, if it's culturally today like the times of Noah (cf. Matthew 24:37–41)?

I believe that so long as there be God-given creatures like water and dirt and toys, preferably home-made, to awaken us as grown people or as younger ones to the rich nuances of our Lord's creation: kites that beckon us to appreciate the wiggle of wind and the tug of air currents, a seashore with mud to ooze through your toes and waves to tantalize us into laughing at God's slap of wetness, and miraculous sand that can take on the imaginative dimensions of castle and moat—so long we should praise our playful God for such haha! experiences as comforting gift indeed worth sanctifying with thankful fun. So long as there are swings to reveal existentially what "ludic" means, and "leap-frog" for sharing the bony crevices of our backs, and bikes for "Slow-bicycle races," horseshoes, balls, frisbees and boomerangs to throw, hobbies, potato sacks in which to fall over one another in: so long as the Lord gives us the occasions we should indeed redeem those times by swinging for God, leap-frogging in the communion of the saints, making merry with the debris of Western civilization as our rightful booty, because God loves seeing God's people play joyfully before God's face on the earth. That's one of the reasons Christ died and was resurrected: that the believing style of life might hold a shared, playful-joyful note (cf. refrain of Ecclesiastes, Isaiah 9:2–7, Psalms 146–150, Galatians 5).

The best games for the most enriched play, I suspect, will not be those that one can become more and more skilled at, sharpening the competitive edge, but rather those games that stretch one's imaginativity the most elastically, and games that most generously spread surprises around, to those who are ennui-stricken ("the players who have everything") or to those who need to be reintroduced to joy because they are too fearful even to laugh after the persecution suffered. Games that lean toward bonding younger and older generations in good fun, that tickle smiles to the face of those who have been wasted, that cement friendships because of the playing time you remember afterwards that was as holy as good prayer: these are the kinds of games to be invented by us imaginative saints as we play, keeping a lookout for Christ's awaited return.

Whether a renewed sense of redeemed game-playing would spur a wave of amateur artistry among God's people as a stepped-up witness servicing a deeper nuance-awareness in our perceptions, I do not know.

Whether a new consciousness of the glory of play-in-holy-joy and its power as pretheoretical, pre-verbal good news might reform the workaholics in the kingdom of God, who can tell?—

Reality check: Is it time to play games?
By this time you realize I am tempting you all to a style of christian life that takes a deep, mature biblical faith, a full faith that is worthy of the exceptionally rich love of our playful Creator God (cf. Psalm 104), worthy of the staggering, sorrowful but sure outreach of our Lord Jesus Christ (cf. Colossians 1:9–23, 2:1–3:4), and the demanding-enabling, ebullient leadership of the Holy Spirit (cf. Proverbs 8, John 16:5–15). Because I pray hard that all these thoughts will be a temptation you will count as a joy to have weathered in your life and will absorb with a refining wisdom that shall help us become the striking examples James mentions, of creatures receiving and responding to and with the good gifts . . . of clothes and games and aesthetic life at large that our heavenly Father does provide for us (cf. James 2: 2–27), I want to close with a three-point challenge on the matter of style—working within the perspective that all human life is religion in operation.

(1) Our cultural times are bad, and the reigning style of life in North America that constitutively, silently, and therefore most effectively, weights the media—that means the TV and newspapers in your christian home—the reigning style of life that weights the media, thought patterns, and public opinion of society its way, I believe, will get worse. I don't just mean the Blue Jays will start to play such professional, hard-nosed baseball their franchise will become as lucrative and corrupted as those in the boxing world, or that the punk and junk aesthetic imperative will become more blatant and prevalent. I mean that the dominant lifestyle will become so technocratically good you won't be able to see it's bad. For example: secular industry has made better and better plastic spray against rust and more and more deadly pesticides against bugs: when you've got a perfect, poisonous plastic in which to protect your treasure, it's hard to hear the Bible say your heart may be treasuring the wrong things (cf. Matthew 6:19–24). Just so: our lifestyle may become such a satisfying escape and insurance against the very frenetic pace and metal efficiency of technical perfection that the style itself demands to exist, that it becomes almost impossible to hear the Bible say that hedonism, even democratically wholesome and respectable hedonism, is a style for the damned antichrists (cf. Ephesians 3:15–41, 1 John 2:18–29).

If you people were to mistake my proclamation that it is obedience on the part of God's people to claim his gifts and promises of joyful play and festive dress even in evil times, if the Lord provides: if, because we can make do with the money we have, show the Protestant work ethic and guts to hold a job even with a lot of unemployment and financial uncertainty, and put on a little bit of cultural dog now and then, if you hear me say "nice clothes?" "fun and games" "style?"—Man, where were these aestheticians earlier on, to salve our Calvinistic guilt-feelings!—and then adopt the most normative going style touched up a bit under the formula of "for the glory of God," then my neck gets the millstone (cf. Luke 17:1–2) but lamentably we sink together. Old time "Christian Humanism" is not a vital Reformational christian life.

(2) An ascetic looks like a saint today because the cultural market place is so corrupt. A Christian who is an ascetic, that is, who for the love of God, after counting the costs of following Jesus Christ with one's cross in tow, cuts out of his or her life attractive creaturely affairs that might compromise the purity of loving God and therefore lead to evil (cf. Luke 14:25–35): a God-loving ascetic is an aesthetic scandal. An ascetic would never play "Spin-the-bottle," gladly! missing such fun. Personally I feel at home with a christian ascetic because you know where you stand: their whole, untiring, tiresome life of denying themselves things always drives you back to the heart of the matter—are you wholly free solely to love God (cf. 1 Corinthians 7:1–11:1)? A principled ascetic Christian is also not fooled by "Freude schöner Götterfunken, Tochter aus Elysium," and knows by faith—not by sight or hearing, of course—that joy to the world, if it is not Jesus Christ-centered, is either the Holy Spirit spilling some drops, like rain, to fertilize the unbeliever into becoming jealous of holy life in Christ, or is ersatz, fake joy, parasitic. Not all those who disbelieve Christ is the Lord have a punk style to their life, but those whose style is mail order from Dior or whatever indeed boast a style living on borrowed time. But there is more than one way to go to hell.

Asceticism, however, is as vain a philosophical tradition as hedonism (cf. Acts 17:16–21), and mixed in with the christian faith is bad news, especially when holy men or women who were not covetous and knew how to live unadorned lives long ago with warmth and pleasure! have been appropriated as godlike models of penny-pinching sanctity. A christianized asceticism tends to make virtue out of sins of omission, confuses sanctification with redemption, and therefore cannot shuck a Pharisaic yeast of ordering life negatively in an attempt to be sinless, while the overriding thrust of the Bible says to order your life, saved by Christ, positively in an attempt to be obedient . . . in every thing, so that "fleeing sin" is swallowed up in "doing good works" with joy (cf. e.g., 1 Samuel 15:22–23, Psalm 100, Isaiah 1:10–20, Micah 6:6–8, Matthew 6:16–18, Romans 6:1–11, 2 Timothy 2:14–26, Hebrews 10:1–10). Asceticism would burden the christian life with denying part of our human nature: it's better not to be married, it's better not to dress up, it's better not to eat and drink and be merry—as if it's better for women and men, as it were, to act like angels. A disciple of Christ who swallows asceticism misses certain essential fine points in reading the Bible: use the world, says Paul *as if* you could let it go (1 Corinthians 7:29–31); nobody lets any creaturely good things go for the sake of Christ, for the sake of the Good News, says the Lord, without getting it all back a hundredfold *now*! *in these days* along with persecutions (Matthew 10:23–31). And too often in history, the amalgamation of asceticism and confessing Christ, beside crimping lifestyle aprioni to one of no-frills austerity, has offended many little ones into believing God is a kill-joy. And that is a blasphemous lie! Our covenanting God sacrificed God's Son in history to save God's people, and that was no joke; but our heavenly Father also plays catch with us, in the ministry of the Holy Spirit.

(3) North American life is in great need today of biblical direction. I have touched on only one aspect of creaturely life where that need can be picked up and served by able-bodied Christians in the tradition of the Reformation and Evangelical Christianity, along with many others who have not bowed the knee to Baal (cf. 1 Kings 19:1–18). Despite our history of relatively underdeveloped reflection and praxis in this area of style and thus with a certain vulnerability in giving informed leadership, I believe we should try. Many humanists are noting with dismay how the consummate virtuosity in aesthetic matters today seems to go paired with a vulgarization of style and undeep cultural life at large. Critical humanists are going to be giving more and more attention to "play"—recreation and leisure activities—I think, in calling for richer quality of life. They will be appealing, at bottom, to the restorative power of God-created creatureliness without reference to the Redeeming Creator. I believe there will be no real rescue in that; a richer quality of life that is not "christian," contextualized by honoring Christ's name in the deed (*not in vain verbiage*), is not, I believe, the kind of "good works" God in Christ has troubled God self about (cf. again Ephesians 2:8–10). Christians with a biblicist tradition, fed up with the show of aesthetic luxury and vulgarity all around us and inhibited by guilty consciences (cf. 1 Timothy 4:1–10), will be inclined, I think, just to tighten their cultural belt another notch or two as the apocalypse nears, and restrict their acts of mercy to remedial

— Joy, Style, and Aesthetic Imperatives —

ones, healing, teaching, and preaching to be ready for the judgment coming—they would not like to be caught playing when Christ returns. But precisely that is maybe what we could learn to offer to the world: what a blessing it would be to be able, amid the holocaust of when *Christ* wraps things up, to be playing "Blind-man's-bluff" at a family reunion, putting a pair of clean socks on a stranger whose feet are naked, visiting the zoo with a friend, or telling a christian joke to an unbeliever, as a way of making God's will known to our neighbors.

The Bible does not call us to an economics of simplicity, but to a thrift of being stewardly, or still better, to be generous husbands of creaturely resources (cf. Luke 16:1–13, 1 Timothy 5:17–19); and we are not called to a poverty-stricken style of life nor to a wealthy one, but to a deeper, aesthetically deepened lifestyle, that is, for me, joyfully playful. And this particular call, the aesthetic imperatives we are to give obedient flesh and blood to, are not another raft of laws to get bogged down under, but is our gladsome task to wear the wedding garment of joy the Lord tenders us creatures invited to his party (cf. Matthew 22:1–14). The Lord will always prepare a table for us in the presence of our enemies (Psalm 23), but will we have the style to respond by eating and drinking what he provides, carefree, with the enemies looking on? Will we have the aesthetic stamina to sing a Phrygian modal lament of anguished praise when we have to use our hung-up harps on the willows in Babylon (cf. Psalm 137)? That is, it will take a tremendously strong faith *and* a holy imagination for us to offer the aesthetic fishhook of joy to our neighbor in the days ahead; but I believe the Lord will smile and use it gladly to catch unbelieving men and women, to unnerve the hardened disbelievers, and to strengthen the weak knees of God's children.

Professor Sytze Zuidema once told me a christian joke, without knowing it. Zuidema told me the story of how he with a few others nearing death after long deprivation in the Japanese concentration camp in Indonesia on a certain day had gotten together a bribed jigger of wine and diluted it with stolen water to celebrate one last Lord's Supper before they died. "Now that was a quietly joyful event," he said. The next day, instead of dying, they were set free by the Allied forces. Years later, still suffering from black-outs and broken nerves from the wartime ordeal, which killed him finally when he was 69, Zuidema said to me on a certain day, with a childlike boast, "Finally I have my revenge on the Japanese! My book has been translated into the Japanese language!" It was his moving book on "Prayer."

That's a christian joke. I pray that our game-playing and clothes-wearing and joyous style of life will prepare us with the grace to reach that deep, when necessary, to present even our suffering with aesthetic obedience to the Lord. Such comic relief, I dare say, is like a sweet-smelling perfume to the God from whom all blessings flow. And such aesthetic activity gives the devil fits, because then the devil knows he's lost even the last laugh on earth, haha!

Glossary

aesthetic (adj.) an irreducible ordinance God laid down for creatures to follow, a creaturely dimension with ludic structure, one way we exist characterized by nuancefulness; a window on joy.
aesthetics (n.) a theory of what is "aesthetic."
aesthete (n.) a person who swallows the whole of life as if it were only aesthetic and chokes on the impossibility of doing so; a prig.
anaesthetic (adj.) insensitive to, obtuse.
ascetic (adj.) given to (self-)denial and abstaining from things, positively negative.
imaginativity (n.) a God-given capability human creatures have to be allusive, to imagine, to be imaginative.
ludic (adj.) (Lat. *ludo*, I play) "ludicrous" without the *r* factor, i.e., playful.
allusive (adj.) just playing around with, imaginative, nuanceful.
elusive (adj.) playing hard to get, baffling.
illusive (adj.) playing tricks on you, deceptive.
nuance (n.) subtle variation, a delicate shading.
style (n.) the allusive, playful, imaginative fabric consistently showing up in someone or some groups' activities.
play (v.) to be engaged in one basic sort of possible aesthetic activity.
game (n.) an aesthetic object or event, like a complex toy, that you activate by becoming a player; organized play.
Haha! Erlebnis (n.) an experience characterized by surprise and subterranean laughter.

Relevant Readings

Ager, Lynn Price. "The Reflection of Cultural Values in Eskimo Children's Games," *AASP* (Proceedings of the annual meetings of the Association for the Anthropological Study of Play) 1 (1975): 92–98.
Bernard, Mergen. "Playgrounds and Playground Equipment, 1885–1925: Defining play in urban America," *AASP* 4 (1978): 198–206.
Bowman, Jorn R. "The Organization of Spontaneous Adult Social Play," *AASP* 3 (1977): 239–50.
Campbell, Chris. "Thinking Play Seriously," *Dialogue* (March 1979): 41–45.
"Dance and the Christian Life," Jack Westerhof, reporter for study committee, in *1980 Acts of Synod: Christian Reformed Church* (Grand Rapids: CRC

Board of Publications, 1980), 448–66.
Duthie, J. H. "Athletics: The ritual of a technological society," *AASP* 4 (1978): 91–98.
Kline, Meredith G. *Images of the Spirit* (Grand Rapids: Baker, 1980).
Koyzis, David. "Principalities and Powers." Institute for Christian Studies (ICS) study paper for Biblical Prolegomena seminar, 1979. Typescript, 13 pages.
Morrison-Sereda, Wendy. "Rookmaaker on Play." ICS study paper for seminar in Systematic Aesthetics, December 1978. Typescript, 15 pages.
Richardson, Jane and A. L. Kröber. "Three Centuries of Women's Dress Fashions: A quantitative analysis," *Anthropological Records* 5:2 (1940): 111–53.
Ridderbos, Simon J. *De Theologische Cultuurbeschouwing van Abraham Kuyper* (Kampen: Kok, 1947).
Rookmaaker, Hans R. *Kunst en Amusement* (1962), translated as "Art and Entertainment," in *The Creative Gift, Dürer, Dada and Desolation Row: The complete works of Hans R. Rookmaaker*, vol. 3 (Carlisle: Piquant, 2002), 3–131.
———. "Kunst en Levensstijl," in *Vier Glazen: Gedenkboek 1886–1961* (Delft: Societas Studiosorum Reformatorum, 1961), 325–338.
Rijnsdorp, Cornelis. *Aan de Driesprong van Kunst, Wetenschap en Religie* (Baarn: Bosch en Keuning, 1964).
Salter, Michael A. "Play in Ritual: A ethnohistorical overview of native North America," *AASP* 4 (1978): 70–84.
Schrotenboer, Paul G. *Man in God's World: The biblical idea of office* (Grand Rapids: International Reformed Bulletin, 1967).
Seerveld, Calvin. "A Cloud of Witnesses and a New Generation" (1978), in *In the Fields of the Lord: A Calvin Seerveld reader*, ed. Craig Bartholomew (Carlisle: Piquant; and Toronto: Tuppence Press, 2000), 209–234.
———. "Nudism," "Innocence," "Modesty," in *Baker's Dictionary of Christian Ethics*, editor Carl F. Henry (Grand Rapids: Baker, 1973).
Smit, Meijer C. *Cultuur en Heil* (1959), translated as "Culture and Salvation," in *Toward a Christian Conception of History*, edited and translated by H. D. Morton and H. Van Dyke (Lanham: University Press of America, 2002), 260–80.
Sutton-Smith, Brian. "Towards an Anthropology of Play," *AASP* 2 (1976): 222–32.
Sypher, Wylie. "Foreword" to *Rococo to Cubism in Art and Literature: Transformations in style* (New York: Random House Vintage, 1960), xvii–xxvi.
Vertès, Marcel. *Art and Fashion* (London: Studio Publications, 1944).
Vander Hoeven, Johan. Lectures 14–16 on "Marx and Marxism," held at the Institute for Christian Studies, Toronto, 1978.
Von Meyenfeldt, Fritz H. *De Christelijke Levenswandel* (Wageningen: Zomer en Keunings, 1957).

ORDINARY AESTHETIC LIFE:
HUMOR, TASTES AND "TAKING A BREAK"

Hi, my name is Cal. I'm a workaholic. I feel good when I've put in a solid 15 hour day. I love the work at my desk reading books, imagining, thinking things through, and trying to write down discoveries and insights.

I used to work through nights, fairly regularly too, under the pressure to teach classes as well as make public speeches. If you were into a topic and got something going and stuck with it, at a certain point the endorphins would kick in, you got a high, the writer's block would break, and it would be exhilarating! to work through the quiet reaches of the night, scratching ink onto paper, sitting carefully on your chair, as Thomas Edison did, so the lactic acid would not build up in the muscles and make you tired.

My Dutch-born wife had the character, patience, humor, and love to admonish me but still be supportive.

"You live such an anti-social life!" someone once told me to my face, "locked away in your study, no telephone."

"But the whole world of evil tempts me in the books I read," [#28] was the reply I thought up afterwards; "the monstrous demons who attacked St. Anthony also crowd my desk, and I do faith-battle with them day in, night out. Secluded study deals in reality and relationships too. . ."

[#28] Study desk with books

My idea of the best vacation has been to go alone for two weeks to do research on a new topic, spend 10 AM to 6 PM in the Warburg library (University of London, England), and attend the theatre every night, especially the excellent off-

---

This popular lecture was given for the Institute for Christian Studies summer conference in 1999.

beat fringe theatre held above pubs, and then sleep soundly on the floor of a friend's downtown city apartment (no costs). —A sweet refreshing intensity that unites my Calvinian work conscience, an ascetic bent to frugality, and a vigorous desire for quality artistic experience, and after two weeks leaves me entirely refreshed.

Introduction
After that truncated workaholic confession, let me read you a brief, telling story from the Bible (Mark 6:30–34):

> The apostles came back together to Jesus and reported to him all the stuff they had done and how much they had taught.
>
> Jesus said to them, "Well, why don't you come away by yourselves to a place without people and rest for a little while." There were so many folk coming and going, the apostles didn't even have enough time/leisure (*eukairoun*) to eat.
>
> So they went away in the boat to a place without people, all by themselves.
>
> But a lot of folk saw them take off and found out where they were going, ran there on foot from all the towns around, and got there before the persons in the boat did.
>
> As Jesus disembarked, he saw the big crowd of people and was moved with tenderness for them, because they were like sheep who didn't have a shepherd. So Jesus began (again) to teach them many things. . . .

My topic is ordinary aesthetic life—how to conceive and practice this gift to us from God in a fruitful way in our generation.

I have begun this way so that you realize what my historical, existential bias is: an unreformed workaholic is talking to you about "taking a break," struggling to have holy Scripture conform my life to love for God and neighbor.

Just because my professional task is philosophical theory does not mean I am out of touch with the reality of the Bible's footnote on leisure, or with practical creatural matters like humor and imaginativity, which I mean to examine as constitutive of the lifestyle and the preferential taste one has adopted. What I am talking about—"aesthetic life"—is as untheoretically concrete as how many square feet your home or apartment has, so crucial for leisure. If I can prompt us to self-critical, edifying reflection together on these actual states of affairs, we will be moving toward redeeming the time, I dare say (cf. Colossians 4:5–6).

A whole tin-can picture of human nature

First, I want to sketch for you more of the whole picture so you can orient yourself on precisely what we are dealing with, before I say it would be normative for the Institute for Christian Studies (ICS) to have an Institute song, as well as a logo, and if you don't have your kids' or grandchildren's drawings stuck up on the fridge, you should be ashamed of your grand-parental selves. So let me begin with a tin-can model of a full-orbed human creature.

God made us whole, corporeal human creatures with an enduring identity that functions in many different ways. (I always diagram humans with solid tin-can modesty to emphasize that we besouled bodies are not made up of parts, and to nip in the bud any Humanistic pride in our responsible grandeur in creation.) [D#1] We are physically based, alive with a measure of health, a sensitive creature with feelings, able to develop skills, to imagine, speak, think, and interact with other human creatures. Every human spends and saves things, holds loyalties one judges important, can be friendly, and prays under your breath to God or sometimes to various idols. Everybody also normally moves, can't help but be located somewhere, and there is just so much of you flesh and blood. Every human is also inescapably neighborhooded (not shown on this diagram) and a fellow creature with animals, plants, and mountains.

To pray is different than being friendly; to think is different than to speak; to feel is not the same as breathing: but all these different ways a person is created/born with are inter-penetratingly present. You can be physically handicapped, underdeveloped in skills, sport a fertile imagination, be poor in possessions, and rich in friends; and every which way you be colors somehow all the other ways you are there—everybody is of one piece in his or her societal circumstances. Naturally you don't always hit on all cylinders: after a late social night out, you may show up at church on Sunday morning over-compensatingly pious but health-wise a little sleepy.

Every human, in this philosophical perspective, is primed to be filled with the Holy Spirit, which does battle with that black sludge of Sin resident in us bodied creatures ever since Eve and Adam fell historically into disobedience toward God. If the Holy Spirit does indeed grip your heart and aligns your will with God's ordinances for human deeds, then gradually all the ways you were created are meant to come to a maturity of holiness (cf. Matthew 5:46–48), no matter whether you be tone-deaf, are outgoing, stutter, be a whiz at mechanics, or are a difficult personality. But the LORD does want us to become developing, full-orbed humans

— Normative Aesthetics —

Diagram #1: A christian tin-can model of the human creature

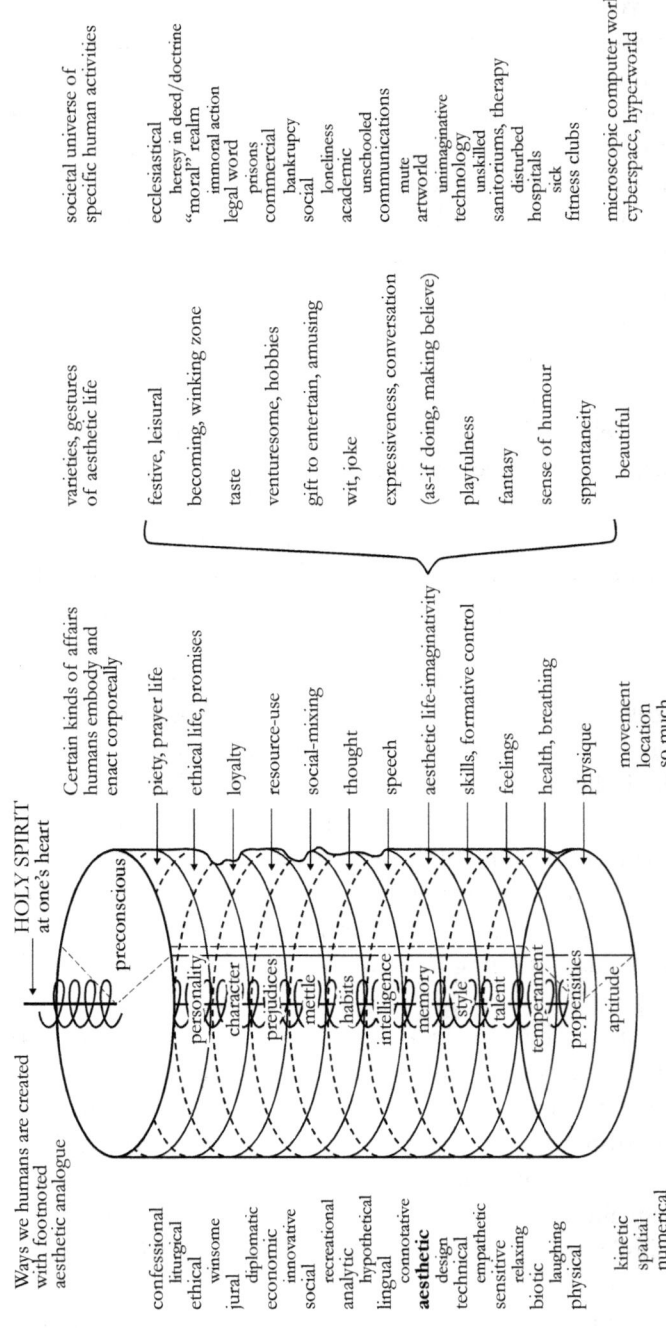

who respond to God's many-splendored world all these worthwhile ways we were created to experience shalom.

Our cultural setting:
two distortions detrimental to usual aesthetic life

Now why would anybody today hold a three-day conference for ordinary believing people on aesthetic life, looking at and listening to art and understanding popular culture, when there is so much political evil, economic greed, marriage and family breakdowns, urban crime, shootings in schools, more and more neurotic persons using drugs on the streets and on the job, sensational violence in the media, overworked nurses in the hospitals, bickering trivia and power politics in the churchworld? If you want to contribute to the biblical reformation of society in God's world, why go to art? to imagination?

To set up the rationale for paying attention to the redemption of human aesthetic life, let me draw a schematic picture of the two kinds of humans who distort our full tin-can humanity, and then struggle briefly, as a workaholic, to make biblical sense of leisure.

(1) The North American cultural air we breathe is dominated, I'll say, by a thorough-going spirit of commercialistic technocratic Pragmatism. By giving what I think is one of the most powerful principalities of our age that name helps me to understand how this invisible force tends to reduce men, women, and children to consumers. The managers of global corporations conceive human beings to be shopper-buyers of things that will make one's life easier, more comfortable. Human nature is squished down, you could say, into a creature whose tin-can corporeality is stream-lined to that of an instrumental physical repository [D#2].

Diagram #2: Technocratic man/woman/child (cf. *Wired* or *Glamour* magazines)

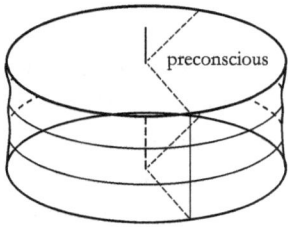

technical qualification: instrumentality
                sensitive
                organic
physicality with quantifiable moveable location

The most important thing about you is to be a means to the end of More goods. Humans are driven to live in the fast lane of prosperity, privilege, and power, in transit to a greater measure of whatever we are after.

— Normative Aesthetics —

Best Buy flyers boldly advertising the latest gadgets you need for your computer set at sales prices, if you act now! epitomize locally what saturates globally the consciousness of everybody who counts in the world today. The credit card is the universal passport: it provides instant gratification without your actually paying for it yet. The technocratized consumer, like a bona fide pragmatist, always lives only on credit, because you can always make future adjustments to what didn't work well or give adequate satisfaction.

My interest lies in the reduction to human nature that such technocratic consumption effects: one's creed becomes "I believe that the new must replace the old"—planned obsolescence; efficiency is made the standard for ethical activity—does it get the job done?; loyalty extends to "scratch my back, and I'll scratch yours"; "economical" means it's cheap; social intercourse is cashed into crashing the club that leads to your career advancement; thinking and speaking are geared to maximum profit, while artistic or literary imagination is severely discounted next to figuring out what is best to do next.

I'm not saying everybody consequently lives out this protean spirit of Mammon; but I am saying that transnational global business corporations, which mediate such technocratic commercialism, furnish the insistent drumbeat of world culture that is insinuating itself into our and our children's consciousness and daily walk. And what happens to those in God's world who do or don't dance to this drumbeat of "time means money and what money can buy"?

(2) The other kind of distortion to our full tin-can humanity that I want to depict is a conception I'll call Agent no. 666. It's the kind of human, William Butler Yeats described (and approved of) in his poem "Sailing to Byzantium":

> Consume my heart away; sick with desire
> And fastened to a dying animal.

These folk value their rational moral soul like a precious stone and consider their animal nature below the belt an embarrassment. [D#3] A person has to feed the body, keep it tethered, under strict control, so you can give quality time to the higher things in life. After all, as poet Robert Browning said, "What's a heaven for?" but to yearn for, prepare for, contemplate.

There is a long history of proponents for this take on human nature as a combination of angel and beast: ancient Greek philosopher Plato, Hellenistic stoics and cynics the apostle Paul knew (see Acts 17:16–21, Philippians 3:2–3), various medieval mystics, enclaves of modern Spiri-

Diagram #3: Agents no. 666: men, women, youth (cf. Yeats' poem)

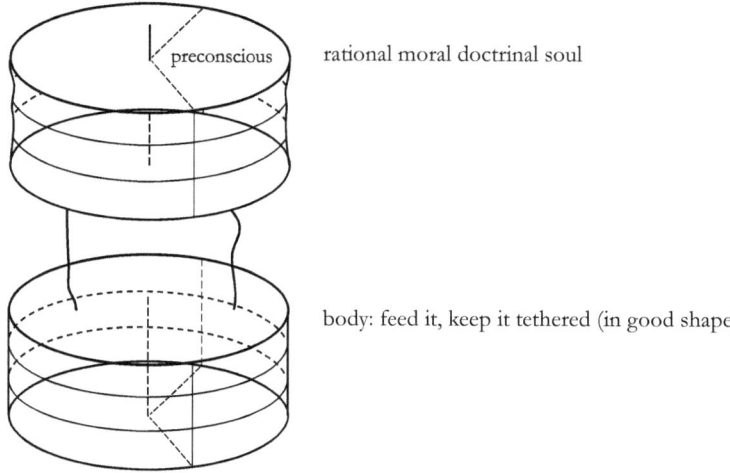

tualists who sold all their worldly belongings to go wait on a mountaintop for the apocalypse, Buddhist monks.... There are many cults today who make this split-level option of humanity attractive for business executives, movie stars, middle-class people who tire of the consumerist technocratic rat-race, because the otherworldly, often Idealistic spirit of such "New Age" cells helps one think to escape the rampant technical materialistic treadmill—you have time for TM, friendships, group loyalty, a green economy, and your basic elemental needs are taken care of. Leonard (*Suzanne*) Cohen has recently converted to be an absolutely subservient disciple of a Zen *rashi* in Southern California (*Globe and Mail,* 1 May 1999, C1,C6).

My interest is especially with the christianized variety of this piecemeal humanity, which normally dedicates an extraordinarily high priority to concerns in church, family, and moral issues in the nation, doing one's job dutifully; that is, it is focused on orthopraxis, attended also by a reasoned-out, doctrinal orthodoxy. Such folk do not disparage one's physical baggage, but give no-frills attention to emotions, diet, and physical fitness. These good people look like saints next to the self-indulgent, capitalist Consumer model, but Scripture has harsh words for spiritual, moral, rational people who have "the form of godliness but repudiate the power of piety" (2 Timothy 3:5), that is, who look right but harbor a selfish or deceptive spirit. Such people the Bible calls anti-christlike (1 John 2:18–22) because their lily-white facade covers up a deep denial that God's son Jesus Christ must utterly humble you to abide by the

Lord's just judgment, mercy, and faithfulness (cf. Matthew 23:23–27).

Important to my analysis is that Agent no. 666 can be Pharisee or Sadducee, politically Far Right, conservatist Fundamentalists, or leftish intellectual Liberal activists who have all the right answers for what ails society. False piety comes in very different stripes, and each person must look to oneself rather than judge the other's heart, for we are all prone to self-righteousness.

The point of delineating the human turned Consumer, which blankets our culture, and humanity in Agent no. 666 dress, which is a perennial problem in christian circles, is that neither has a good place for aesthetic life. Imagining is made a means for making money or considered a distraction. Art is used for conspicuous consumption by the fast-track professional crowd, and ignored or misused by traditional "spiritual" people, or perhaps, at best, embraced as reminders of "Precious Moments" of bliss.

Nobody can get out of God's world or jump out of your human skin; so willy-nilly you are gifted with aesthetic life to live. We can, however, pervert our human responses to the Lord God's blessings, or leave certain callings to rot in a napkin in a hole in the ground (see Luke 19:11–27) because we're too busy with other things. Even if we would-be Reformers in the contemporary computerized world have a full-orbed perspective of our human nature, we are not immune, it seems to me, in our faith tradition gone evangelistic, to the temptation to neglect or then idolize or be non-plussed by what's the relative good of aesthetic activity in a life of obedience to the Lord who is acoming . . . to judge not only the militaristic nations of the world and the dithering churches in Western civilization, but also the art in Yorkville Toronto galleries (cf. Revelation 18:21–24), and to inquire about our personal lackluster vocabulary (cf. Matthew 12:33–36, Ephesians 5:3–5, Revelation 20:12).

Leisure as celebrative aesthetic time.

First, a refractory note about leisure.

I have difficulty accepting the idea that leisure is timeout, time-off, "free" time. Because temporality defines our creatural existence, no time in my life is ever "extra." I still believe what I said 40 years ago in teaching Philosophy 101 at Trinity Christian College: **when you truly give your time to someone, it is your very self you give**. One's time is never neutrally empty but is always being either redeemed or wasted.

I recognize that "taking a break" can be redemptive. After God spent regular time creating the universe and everything in it, the Lord God "took a break," says Exodus 31:17 as commentary upon Genesis 2:2–3, "and was refreshed" (in Hebrew: took a long deep breath), celebrating what had been completed. After Jesus heard that Baptizer John had been beheaded by Herod and the severed head was presented on a platter to the dancing girl to give to her mother, "Jesus took a break from there," it says, "and went by boat to a deserted place all by himself" (Matthew 14:13)[1] to rest, pull himself together, to recover from such a barbarous, jolting atrocity. And the LORD God specifically told God's people to give a sabbath rest to their children, slaves, domestic livestock, and any visiting guests, so they would all remember the exhilaration of the release of captive Israel from Egyptian slavery (Deuteronomy 5:12–15). No other people gets a break from daily toil, says the LORD: restful sabbath celebration is a mark of the Covenantal LORD's special election of you people to anticipate a permanent period of spending time with God, neighbor, and land in peace (Hebrews 4:9–11), uninterrupted by telemarketers.

So too today I accept and enjoy the festive time to celebrate with your children and others the happy conclusion of a strenuous project of work, even as God originally did. I accept and cherish God's gift of recovery time, to get away from "everybody" (except my wife): in my telephoneless study, walking in sturdy shoes with a friend on the Bruce Trail, or as *flâneur* in London, England, or in a foreign language-speaking city full of surprises. I also gratefully accept the LORD's extraordinary blessing of sabbath—even if as workaholic I sinfully do not always enjoy it—a kind of forgiven time, where there is time to spare (no obligations), as wonderfully uplifting and restorative as the *mirabilium* of deep sleep. I hear and would obey Psalm 46:10, which might best be colloquially translated: "Take a break![2] (you serious Reformational worker), let it go! and experience that I God am the One who is in control of the nations, and in charge of the earth"—*you*, take a break!

But what I think the Scriptures reject—this is open naturally to your objections and correction—is the notion that what humans want is absence of work, do-nothing time, pure leisure where you can do whatever you please: then we shall be happy. That ancient pagan Greek idea of elitist leisure (σχολή) void of manual labor was synthesized to meditative contemplation of God or Beauty or of "universal realities and their sustaining reasons" (Pieper),[3] and still later converted by European 1700–

---

[1] The Mark 6:30–34 passage referenced above also follows the beheading of Baptizer John.

[2] The Septuagint (LXX) uses σχολάσατε.

[3] Josef Pieper. *Art and Contemplation* (1980/1990), 27. Pieper is a disarming exegete

1800s Capitalistic industrialism sweatshop drudgery into begrudged/coveted "vacations" "free from work." That view of leisure burdens human nature with pie-in-the-sky illusions, I think, and falsifies the celebrative time, the sabbatical rest, as well as the recovery time Scripture hints is normal for you to take when a loved one untimely dies of cancer or a colleague is decapitated. But such good pauses are not "leisure" or "a vacation"!

We need to be aware, I think, that when Henry Ford in 1914 adopted the technique of a moving conveyor belt in his Michigan automotive plants along with the then handsome salary of the $5 day,[4] Ford set in motion a work-system that prizes and instrumentalizes "leisure." Work-breaks and vacations get fine-tuned into what helps you work harder, produce more, and is a module in the pay scale. Such a pragmatistic denaturing of human work blocks out, in my judgment, any deep-going reform of the assembly line setup, which grinds humans down into technical gears of a machine. Vacations are simply commodities about which you bargain, and the year of jubilee becomes "40 and Out!"

I have also begun to think God's faithful people have too often been sold a 666 version of Sabbath rest, where it was proscribed what you should not do and prescribed what you ought to do on the Lord's Day with a stickling, kill-joy spirit that was thoroughly legalistic even if the requirements were only transmitted orally. Then the idea also creeps in that two worship services + church society meetings + works of mercy add up to a way to avoid secularization of the Day of rest (if not quietly build up extra credits for heaven)—precisely what Isaiah 1:10–31, Amos 5:1–6:7, and Zechariah 7 excoriate!

I've been learning about the Sabbath from the Seventh Day Adventists I've become close to, entering with them into the wonderful relaxing richness of this day set aside for a friendly Bible study (worldwide on the same passage), a worship service expectant of Christ's coming back soon, followed by a congregational potluck (vegetarian) meal and then partying activity! It's almost like an ICS Conference Sunday, restoring the holiday God wants in the holy day: preaching celebration, joyful music, and festive communion! Jesus apparently thought the sabbath was the best time to perform miracles! which made the Agents no. 666 of his day grind their teeth.

---

and subscriber to Aristotle's dictum, which I believe is wrong: "Happiness is thought to depend on leisure; for we work busily so we may have leisure, and we make war so we may live in peace" (*Nichomachaen Ethics* X, 7 1177b4–6).

4 Juliet B. Schor. *The Overworked American: The unexpected decline of leisure* (1991), 60–66.

A biblical conception of leisure for me is that ample time becomes a coefficient of one's daily work activity. In the gospel story I read, the apostles, through the pressure of their kingdom work, did not have enough time to sit down for a meal; "Let's take a break," said Jesus. When you have enough time in what you are humanly doing, you have leisure. When there is time for you to move around in unpremeditatedly, you experience leisure. When it is possible for you to enter into an unexpected opportunity that arises, you are blessed with leisure.

The Pragmatistic culture and Agent no. 666 mentality squeeze leisure out of ordinary daily life. Since the LORD God created human life to be a joyful response to the LORD's mercy and instituted sabbath rest in history to mark completion of tasks and liberation from captivities, and to demonstrate the prospect of everlasting life that is peaceful, leisure belongs to redeemed human life in this age. That's the place where a more wholesome consciousness of aesthetic life may be serviceable, to offset the debilitating strictures of the technocratized and six-six-sixtyized blight on our humanity in God's world.

Postscript: Work in my father's fish store, reading books over the years as a student, preparing breakfast as a parent, and thinking hard long hours in the study has usually been leisural, not hurried, except for the curse of deadlines. Thank God, on the new earth there will be no deadlines for anybody—imagine! Our deeds, as Psalm 1 puts it, will always bear fruit on time. That's why, for me, a great Sunday is to have a good exegetical sermon finished beforehand, and then you drive out early morning on the 401 highway almost devoid of traffic as sunlight brightens up the distant horizon with lovely stillness; you bring God's gentle direction, firm hope, and rest to weary people in the pew who bear so many burdens (cf. Matthew 11:28–30), sweating through your underclothes till they become like wet dishrags, and then return home to shower, share a meal, and take repose—a foretaste of the redeemed life to come. One might even put Proverbs 5 into practice on a Sunday afternoon: get carried away with your wife's breasts, Scripture unashamedly says (Proverbs 5:15–23), let your erotic caresses intoxicate one another. . . . This is a day of sabbath rest in God's eyes?

So far I've sketched what I think are the basics of a biblically sound perspective on a whole tin-can human creature, where it is assumed that good creatural realities like praying, sleeping, eating, thinking, defecating, are God's gifts we may receive with thanksgiving (1 Timothy 4:1–4), or treat as adiaphora (neutrals), violate, overindulge, or open up with joy. Then I tried to situate us in technocratic Babylon and to make us be wary of the insidious Agent no. 666 distortion to our humanity. Finally, I explored and wanted to reconceive leisure as a sabbatical touch to our working daily lives: leisure as the celebrative aesthetic life moment to our existence.

I don't want to repeat here chapter 2 in *Rainbows for the Fallen World* (1980) or what I wrote in the previous chapter on play and games; so I intend to focus my attention on the matters of humor and taste as concrete varieties of aesthetic life, imaginativity, and then make a reflective comment on style—particularly on lifestyle, which becomes a disposition in one's makeup after so many years of aesthetic life activity practiced whichever way you do.

Humor as vital imaginative activity
Something is funny, let's say, when there is an incongruity that suddenly becomes apparent to somebody, though usually not to the person or event that is funny.

Howard Rienstra once described to me how in the old days Dr. H. Evan Runner would mow the grass of his lawn. He would stand motionless, upright behind the hand-push mower at one end of the lawn, suddenly cock his head to the side, scrutinize the line and lay of the grass he needed to shear off, go upright again, and then hurriedly, with tiny steps, quickly scoot down the length of the row. Then turning around at the end, upright again, pause, cock the head sidewise the other way, peer down the lane just traversed, curious, triumphant as it were, if it were flawless, and then do the whole routine again. It looked like a wound-up marionette, or a scene out of *Alice in Wonderland*: a brilliant mind in tenuous contact with a lowly piece of machinery that somehow were not both in the same universe. (It's probably good that Dr. Runner never learned to drive a car!)

Normally there is no point to something that's funny, as there is a point to a joke—it's just humorous, that's all, and induces a chuckle in those who perceive the disparity. Clowns by make-up exaggerate grimaces and wear over-tall hats or flapping shoes to be funny. When men or women dress to appear younger or more exotic than they really are, it becomes borderline comical—I'm not saying this is bad!—to those who see the covert wish but also sense the discrepancy: it's like the fun kids have to play "dress-up," but in reverse. What's funny is usually circumstantial, a basic matter of eccentricity that leans toward fantasy, banks on spontaneity, but does not depend on words, as wit does. To find something funny does take aesthetic awareness, I believe, a nuance-"sensitivity," because the humorous while palpable is not exactly visible, it exists in the cracks of what's there, so to speak.

Laughter is a biophysical human act as crying is a biophysical human act, but human laughter is not just a vegetative human process like vomiting, coughing, or sneezing, anymore than human crying is simply dripping or leaking water. Laughing is more like blushing. Laughing has an aesthetic component built-in to its muscular movement and release of tension, and stretches such vital corporeal action to carry an imaginative note, even when you are being tickled. To laugh with somebody or to laugh at something takes imagination, I think, although the actual act of laughing is a biophysical act.

Now, as I understand it, a readiness to laugh or smile is foundational, propadeutic, you could say, to "a sense of humor," because humor is an intransitive imaginative human activity at the elemental level of one's vital, organic gut reaction to funny realities. So humor is important to human health. If you remain blind to what's funny in God's world and have difficulty laughing, you're in bad shape. I'm not saying you have to be a humorous character, "the class clown" or the like, but if very little in life tickles your funny bone, you are a sorry person, in my judgment.

To have a propensity to perceive and to appreciate what is humorous, serves a person well, helps a community or societal grouping to be more fully human.

I remember Canadian Reformed pastor François Kouwenhoven who at a certain tense moment in ICS history, when the Association for Reformed Scientific Studies (ARSS) was making what it thought was an important policy decision in a fiery members' meeting at the Unionville Conference barn in 1964, I think it was—lots of people speaking fiercely, impassioned against one another—went up to the podium, got the mike to speak, and said, "Listen to me. I've been a minister for 20 years. I can please everybody—"

The whole crowd of people laughed (together), the anger was defused by this light self-deprecating introduction to his tempered counsel; he had the aesthetic insight to see how disproportionate all the heated rhetoric was, about whether or not people had to have a certifying sponsor to be a member of the ARSS. Good humor has a way of disarming conflicts, pin-pricking pomposity, reviving defeated people as if with smelling salts, freshening a stultifying atmosphere with the airwick of merriment. A sense of humor can help you not take yourself too seriously, forestalling steps into pride.

It's true: humor can be evil-spirited. The old Greek sophist Gorgias had a diabolical policy: treat your opponent's seriousness as if he is joking, and treat your opponent's joking as if he be serious.[5] It ruins your opponent with laughter every time. Gorgias's recipe for sly rhetorical ridicule is sometimes used in aggressive power plays at committee meetings.

Holy spirited humor, however, will be gentle, I believe, in noticing how something is too rigid or how pretending to meet a norm has failed. There is always a forbearing *mea culpa* ("It's my fault too.") note cheerfully admitted in redemptive humor, nursing the incongruous defect back into its relative/related human place (cf. 1 Thessalonians 2:7, 2 Timothy 2:20–26, James 3:13–18).

Sometimes I'll put a smile into a sermon, which is ruined when somebody in the fourth pew guffaws loudly, treating a mental wink as if it were the punch line of a standup comic. So humor is regularly taken amiss or completely missed, because humor corrects what is inflated or wrong by itself imaginatively transgressing, as it were, certain carefully laid plans or priorities. This is also why the aesthetic activity of humor often helps pry open a human nature closed down to technocratic instrumentality or held captive in the airless room of legalistic piousness. Humor can aerate what is stifling, and oxygenate tired blood, but it may offend those who are anaesthetically present.

How can one develop a sense of humor and let the sunshine of holy funniness shine into your daily life, bathe your family, and even relax the church?

Not by reading the joke books, I think, based on the several I perused, which are usually aimed at sacred cows, muckrake authority, or angle for laughs by being risqué. You could regularly read *Charlie Brown* comics, and show Nick Park videos to your children, like "Creature Comforts" with *Wallace and Grommet*—that might help.

A good way to develop a normative sense of humor is (a) to become biophysically fit so you have healthy muscle tone and are ready to laugh, (b) become emotionally secure so you don't settle for a defensive temperament, and (c) you learn to do something well—play an instrument, cordially answer the telephone, learn a lot about fish, stand on your head, anything—so you have one area of skill where you rightly stand out: these matters are the abc's, the preparatory infrastructure, you might say, that facilitate a person's developing the playful demeanor one needs to be ready for the humorous.

---

5   Gorgias, fragment B12, in *Die Fragmente der Vorsokratiker,* eds. Hermann Diels and Walther Kranz (Berlin: Weidmannsche Verlagsbuchhandlung, 1952), 2:303.

Then, of course, one must exercise your budding humorous aesthetic life activity: plan at least one surprise every two months for your children, spouse, or friend; do something harmlessly zany yourself once a year, perhaps where nobody knows you; concoct an occasional "practical joke" on somebody that does not isolate the person but honors their foible or peculiarity.

When I was speaking at an ICS/AACS/ARSS conference out west in Banff, Alberta, with Professor Van Riessen in 1962, he wanted so badly to see a bear outdoors. It was the last night before the conference ended the next morning, and Van Riessen had just finished his lecture, when a couple conference organizers rushed in and told him to come quick, there was a bear outside in the woods. So they quickly went out, and led him carefully to the woods. "It's a white bear," they told the trusting Van Riessen. Sure enough, there in the dark was this large white shape lumbering about. They crept closer and a little closer in the darkness. Suddenly there was this terrible Rarrrh! from the bear. Van Riessen and the two guides turned and ran for their lives.

Later, when Henk van Riessen found out it was two conferees under a couple of big white bed sheets, no one laughed harder than he did. When situated humor is shared, its memory unites persons, edifies and solidifies friendships, with an amazing resonance that compares well to weeping or praying with someone together.

Varieties of aesthetic life

I also want to comment briefly on the range of human aesthetic life as I understand it, and note for you how the moment of aesthetic life operates in our human makeup and infiltrates our many other kinds of activities (as suggested by diagram #1). Then I will treat the prickly matter of aesthetic taste, and finish by making a comment on lifestyle.

Aesthetic life is that zone of human existence in God's world where we are subject to the LORD's ordinance for being imaginative, for responding playfully to the quirks and quarks, the wonderful nuances all around us, which are gifts of God, grist for shalom. Aesthetic life activity, for example, a sense of humor, is not pivotal to our well-being, as a faith-commitment in Jesus Christ is pivotal, but imaginativity is integral to a normal human life and, to my mind, relatively basic to reaching a human maturity that functions normally on all its cylinders.

Notice the order of complexity this anthropological theory assumes in diagram #1.

If you have overwhelming health problems, like advanced cancer in your body, I've noticed, your world virtually shuts down to a regimen of blood analysis, chemotherapy, radiation, experimental drugs, and pain; prayer and friends may be rays of light breaking into the prison of biophysical concern, but many ordinary activities can be simply blocked out by the wall of pain. If you have a severe neurosis that incapacitates you from holding a job, hinders you from mixing socially, or having friends, your world is blighted. If you are an unskilled laborer, not schooled in reading, speaking well, or thinking things through, that untrained state may inhibit your assuming certain leadership positions in society, or you overcompensate and try to do them anyhow, unprepared for their complexity. Likewise, if you are unimaginative, can't take a joke, are unable to envisage different possibilities than those that stare you in the face: even if you are a skilled technician, have robust emotions, and are physically sound, not overweight, the reach of your life will be restricted, lack color and discovery, and likely result in a scrunched-down, narrow-minded, rather humdrum, unimaginative life.

The way God structured our humanity is not in some exceptionless lock-step bind. But there is an ontic order of prerequisites and supplementarity, I think, to how we are made that is worth finding out, so we can check out one's weak spots and remedy what needs shoring up. It's fairly well accepted that art therapy and role-playing therapy helps psychically disturbed patients work through trauma more unifiedly than the traditional, highly lingual-analytic psychoanalysis. Exercising wholesome imaginative activities seems to free up a person's distorted feelings so they can be lifted up and over the blockage and be re-formed in a better emotional alignment. If that is true, it would seem wise to me that we humans give concerted, not to say "programmatic" attention to exercising imaginative activity in our daily lives, especially in our schools, but also in Reformational movements, before you have to engage aesthetic life (for example, humor, role-playing make-believe) and aesthetic time (leisure) as remedial therapy.

That does not mean that disciples of Christ who are dedicated to enacting justice for the helpless, securing dignified work for the unemployed, helping families become centers of love rather than enclaves of abuse, seeking to maintain christian doctrine in the church that is soundly biblical, should now also have to take fooling around seriously. Aesthetic life is recalcitrant to solemn resolutions. Imaginativity does not let itself be manhandled, but responds best to subtle coaxing, exemplification, apprenticeship, actually experiencing the joy of making-believe, and doing as-if this-is-that, which I consider to be the core of imagining.

All I can do as theorist is raise your consciousness to realize that we humans do well to look for opportunities to be playful, venturesome, fanciful, entertaining—these are varieties of aesthetic life. Give time to picking out piquant words (cf. Colossians 4:6) to express your judgments, and know that being witty can be a way to love your neighbor, fulfilling the law of Christ (Romans 13:10). To wear becoming clothes, to share a festive meal, to notice how beautiful are the soft skin patterns of a poisonous viper: all these features of aesthetic life activity are possible and enriching, thanks to the LORD God's winks of grace.

And if we descendents of the Reformation faith tradition take time to plant flowers and watch them grow, reserve a place in our busy lives to read and tell imaginative stories to our children and grandchildren, hold extended candlelight tête-à-tête conversations with guests at a meal: such exercises of one's aesthetic life capabilities tends to rub off on or seep into our other responsibilities, give aesthetic color to the lines of what we do non-aesthetically.

For example, if we color imaginatively our moves to get justice done, they are apt to be diplomatically persuasive rather than sheer strong-arm, a count-heads-and-vote approach to lobbying. If aesthetic life inhabits our economic policies, they will show innovative flair rather than a barebones, get-as-much-as-you-can, winner-take-all attitude. Our promise-life will bear a winsome quality rather than be plain dutiful; church worship can become liturgically suggestion-rich rather than just helter-skelter or unimaginative. There will indeed be a recreational note to socials instead of the stilted "It's our turn to have them over," and so on.

The infusion of aesthetic life into our non-aesthetically qualified activities does not happen automatically, and to have imaginativity in all you do is not necessarily redemptive. But if the aesthetic life component of your humanity is happily percolating and breathes a holy spirit, the aesthetic life enrichment of your prayers, governance, love caresses, interaction with other people, spending money, or whatever, is bound to carry along the nuancing discipline of joy to be afoot in God's incredible world. And that is a valuable gift in our troubled day.

(Aesthetic) taste: its nature, multiple normative contours

Aesthetic taste is complicated to talk about because of its elitist history, which assumes "taste" is epitomized by the charming Renaissance courtier, a gallant fop at Louis XV's court, or David Hume's essays and Whiggish suavity, Oxford-educated Edwardian gentlemen and ladies; all of-which are disposed of by the beer-drinking TV-addicted North

American sportsman as snobbery, an affected "culchah"—let's talk about who's going to win the Stanley Cup next year, not Picasso.[6] Yet practically everybody has used at one time or another the stupid line, as clinching defense for the color of your socks or the cluttered decor of your living room, "You can't dispute about taste!" But disputes about aesthetic taste are constant, often heated, always irritating. Why? if everybody is a pope on taste—the beer-drinker, the wine sipper, as well as the Pepsi crowd?

Aesthetic taste for me is the practice, resident in a person, of imaginatively judging which contrasting nuances comport with equanimity. **Your taste is your aesthetic conscience!** Your taste in clothes, in men, in radio stations or magazines, in diction, in entertainment, is your final aesthetic court of appeal. Taste is the state of where your imaginative prejudices are at (and everybody has prejudices, aesthetic presuppositions, even if it's a blank mind). So if someone questions your taste in dress, they are saying, "You're prejudiced!" When someone challenges your remarks in a public meeting as having been in poor taste, they are stepping on your aesthetic conscience and saying, "You lack discrimination." So it feels like an affront, because it is! a putdown of your judgment-ability in matters aesthetic—not "artistic"—but juraesthetic (to use jargon): you and your comment didn't come through in an imaginative way that was meant to do justice, to hold in ranked suspension opposite subtleties—speaking the truth in love, saving somebody's face, differing on difficulties, trying to move the discussion forward. You should have been more imaginative in how you said it—

Aesthetic taste is learned. Taste depends a lot on your background: on whether you were born in Paris, Florida, or Thunder Bay, on whether you were allowed to put both applesauce and ketchup together on your potatoes as a child or not, on whether you were brought up on sweets or olives and pickles, or if you were middleclass. Taste changes with the company you keep. One's aesthetic conscience can be dulled, sharpened, or re-educated too. If you always thought a certain red and purple clashed, after you've seen enough Matisse paintings, you may develop a taste for it. If you always thought a hymn like "I walk through the garden alone / while the dew is still on the roses" was tastelessly oozing sentimentality but saw once how it quieted a dying saint, you might loosen your imaginative boundaries to tolerate it grudgingly near the margins of your hymnological approval.

That is, your subliminal criteria for aesthetic judgment of what is

---

6 Cf. William David Romanowski, chapters 3 and 12 in *Pop Culture Wars: Religion and the role of entertainment in American life* (1996).

suitable in daily life are always in process, like your waistline. A person's aesthetic taste too can be anorexic, bulimic, frigid, promiscuous, lackadaisical, rebellious, or need to be weeded. There is no *Robert's Rules of Taste*, which sets the universal standard. But are certain aesthetic tastes more equal than others?

There are various ways to be anti-normative when it comes to aesthetic taste. For example, it seemed to me that the Southern Gentlemanly taste for resolving disputes in certain christian circles in Mississippi in the late '50s was to keep up frontal appearances like peaches and cream but take care of things with a stiletto once the other fellow turned his back. However, while up in Canada in the late '60s in certain christian circles it seemed to me the immigrant Dutch male way to handle disputes was to hit you flush in the face while you were looking and then expect you to haul off a responding blow. Neither tactic displays much imaginative justice, I think, not the affable ruthless settling of scores nor the brutish rudeness.

It also seems clear to me that there are certainly many normative ways to show good taste, for example, in war memorials. Zadkine's *De verwoeste stad* (1951) in Rotterdam's harbor, with gaping wound for its heart and lungs, and contorted limbs begging for the destruction to stop, as well as the utterly different black-granite slabs of Maya Ying Lin's Vietnam Memorial (1982) in Washington, D.C., with so many names chiseled there they seem nameless who were killed: both somehow catch the despondent meaningless waste modern war inexorably brings.

A less philosophical problem than the reality of multiple aesthetic life normativities, but a problem that poses serious threat to the shalom of christian communities in North America, I think, is the matter of mass taste. I don't mean the quality of TV shows, the songs played by disc jockeys on the radio, or the popularity of Hollywood cinema released worldwide—that's Bill Romanowski's call (and I support his brief to take what I would call encapsulated entertainment art to be as significant as what rests in the Louvre and MOMA). My concern is the fact that "aesthetic taste" has become big business. Powerful blockbuster media advertising imposes a common denominator taste on our lives in household appliances and in "weekend" activities. And despite the ruse of niche marketing, it practically consolidates lowbrow, highbrow, and middle-brow taste to be the same in everything from cars to perfume to sports goods, whether we buy from GAP, Eatons, Byways, or E-bay: the technocratic commodification of aesthetic taste blankets us public with an insidious standardization as to what is fashionable. The tastemakers marked by 666 are not far behind, but promote a more nostalgic conformity.

What's worrisome about the monolithic market-driven forces aiming to shape the taste of everyone to the same—and they know well the price of every man and woman—is that one's taste is liable to end up not being one's own, but a prefabbed shell that confines what you can grow into; such that individual variation to the ruling taste becomes almost futile.

A "christian" aesthetic taste will not be so regimented, in my judgment, and a person's taste is not made redemptive by lining it within "moral" rules or by giving it doctrinal specifications. **The creatural norm for human taste which pleases God is this: any nuance decision that engenders thankful imaginativity within a community.**

I'll give three examples:

(1) Walking to church on a Sunday morning with our eldest daughter in the '70s, I remarked on the bright, loud colors in her skirt. "Is that the right dress for church?" I asked. Anya replied, "You always told us to dress for God. God likes colors!" And I envisioned God looking down from heaven smiling at our daughter's taste, taking pity on me in my worn, dull grey suit.

(2) I was invited alone to say goodbye to my dying colleague Bernard Zylstra with Josine in his hospital room (1986). When the time came for me to go, with some effort the emaciated Bernie got himself sitting upright in the bed to shake my hand goodbye. It carried the shadow of that magisterial gesture characteristic of his manner, which often infuriated more democratized people because of its regal bearing. But it was a poignant moment for me to see how important it was to him to make his final farewell this side of the grave not lying prostrate but tastefully sitting up.

(3) My professor Vollenhoven was unexpectedly attacked in a public written forum by a very close friend with quite unjust, wild, slanderous accusations. When Vollenhoven was told he should forthwith set the matter straight, Vollenhoven declined. "Hij heeft het zo moeilijk," he said (He has such a difficult life). As Sietze Buning would say, Vollenhoven's tasteful reply had class.[7]

I hope the development of our communal christian taste will encourage an idiosyncratic bent that is not pixilated, and bear a specific Reformational grit that is open-endedly "catholic," while not trying to be universal. If a holy spirit breathes life into our aesthetic taste, the refined

---

7   Sietze Buning, *Class and Style*, 13–28.

experience will not become precious or turn crude, but foster a versatile, colorful imaginative cachet to our own various life activities and bring bouquets of imaginative enrichment to the life and lives of our neighbors.

Lifestyle: its aesthetic nature and godly calling in our way-of-life
My concluding note about "style" will be pointed, brief, and aimed at starting reflective discussion.

I do not mean by "style" being stylish, the way Sietze Buning uses the term "style," meaning hoity-toity, just as by "taste" I do not accept the casually received designation of taste as "an elitist refinement." By style I mean the imaginative fabric consistently showing up in someone or some group's activity. Your lifestyle is the sedimentation of how you have been and keep on living your aesthetic life, in all its various features. Your style of life depends upon and is constituted by your on-going brand of humor, how playful you normally are or are not, your gift to entertain, hobby predilections or lack of them, the shape of your taste, the kind of festivity to your partying, the leisural quality to your work and the like. Style is the ingrained contour of all the subliminal decisions you make in working out your aesthetic life. One's lifestyle is always in process but also always does have a certain slant to it, a direction—godly, ungodly, mixed-godly—and a particular density—discrete, bumptious, matter-of-fact, eccentric. . . . Lifestyle does not catch all of you but is as relatively important to your whole integral tin-can human make-up as other dispositions, like your temperament, intelligence, character, or personality.

To repeat a couple sentences from my 1984 lecture: If we bury our talent for stylefulness in the ground of disregard and adopt a mould that tends to prime us as snobs, as uncouth louts, or cookie-cuttered stereotypes, instead of as sturdy or delicate vessels of joy, then we stand judged already, with a joyless lifetime and with possibly a vexed existence. God does not want us to be drab creatures. Style is one of the good works for which we were created in Christ Jesus to walk around in (cf. Ephesians 2:8–10).

Two final remarks to consider: (1) Different lifestyles can be obedient to the LORD of aesthetic life. Jesus said as much when he reported on the Agent 666 killjoy mentality of his day, those who said, Baptizer John was demonic because of his ascetic lifestyle, and Nazarite Jesus was a glutton and drunkard because he liked wine and stood for dancing and flute-playing. Jesus said both the sober-minded style of life emphasizing repentance and the joyful gospel style of life bringing a forgiven thankfulness to the fore: both can reveal the wisdom of God (Luke 7:18–35 / Matthew

11:2–19). We need to think about that: both an Amish/Mennonite rural lifestyle and an evangelical-Reformational urban culture-engaging lifestyle can make God happy.

But Christ's biblically revealed truth does not give carte blanche to anyone. The Dutch Reformed Groninger farmer and the Manitoban Ukrainian catholic farmer-father whose lifestyles had no place for Henk Krijger and William Kurelek as boys to draw pictures, it seems to me, lack the wideness of God's grace for aesthetic life. And any educated aesthete whose hybrid cultural nature is humanistically indistinguishable as to whether his or her lifestyle be wheat or tares in God's world would have difficulty claiming to be one of Christ's disciples. God does not ask us to straitjacket human aesthetic life, but the Lord calls us to a holy imaginative freedom (cf. Galatians 5:1, 13–24) to explore the myriad good ways we may obediently color our lives and all its wrinkles in love for others.

(2) Lifestyle is closer to the bone of our faith than the worldview we may have. It has gradually become fashionable in christian circles to talk about the importance of having a Scripturally directed worldview. That's true, but it is not the whole biblical story. One's way-of-life underlies and undergirds—or is out of joint with!—one's adopted worldview (and one's philosophy, if you develop one).[8] A person's way-of-life, in one's lifestyle, discloses corporeally how you stand before God, among God's people, and with your neighbors, in a most deep-going way. Tell me what a man laughs at, and without judging the heart, I'll have a sound litmus reading on the caliber of his faith-commitment, no matter what the worldview be he says he holds.

Lifestyle, the worked-in pattern of your aesthetic life activity, is not small potatoes. We must not let our technocracked culture or the current Sadducee and Pharisee temptations in us squeeze out of us or denature the good little gift of homespun imaginativity the LORD created for us to breathe in and out. And it is okay?—a workaholic talking to himself—to spend a whole hour thinking about leisure, humor, aesthetic taste, making-believe, while, if not Rome, Toronto, and Grand Rapids are burning, Freetown, Sierra Leone, and Belgrade, East Timor, urban ghettoes everywhere are smoldering with open hatreds . . . and you spend time thinking about aesthetic life?!

Yes. Jan Disselkoen's e-mail "Jottings" will tell you that children of God in the worst settings emit sparks of joy that make you cry thankfully, and be ashamed of our frenetic, unaesthetically hurried fix-it mentality.

---

8 Cf. my "Philosophy as Schooled Memory" (1982) in *In the Fields of the Lord: A Calvin Seerveld reader*, 84–89.

Paul Marshall once told me of his walking above and around, looking down at a shanty town in South Africa from a hillside knoll in the early '90s, hearing fragments of a haunting, happy melody floating quietly over its sad terrain, which seemed to be voiced here, fade out, and again be picked up over there by others further on: sharing aesthetic life does not depend on prosperity.

When busy professor Bill Rowe, Reformational chair of the Jesuit philosophy department at Scranton University, Pennsylvania, finds the leisure to take guitar lessons with his young son, that is not small potatoes either. Jesus Christ enjoyed an extravagant christening of perfume on the eve of his crucifixion (Mark 14:1–11)—an aesthetic life experience the apostles at the time wrongly thought much too costly and totally out of place. Even Almighty God took a break, says Scripture, to walk in the garden during the early evening breezes, to hold conversation with Eve and Adam (Genesis 3:8–19)—

That's probably in the back of my workaholic mind when around midnight, when good people should be in bed, my wife Inès and I, since we don't have a dog, often walk each other around the block, a kind of aesthetic kiss in the dark under the stars—a workaholic practicing for life on the new earth. Luke's unusual beatitude says, "You are blessed if you (toil and weep) now, because later on you shall truly laugh!" (Luke 6:21) A quiet evening walk hand-in-hand is good practice for holy laughter later.

Or, like the story Harry Boer, who recently went to be with Jesus himself, told me about an elderly woman in The Netherlands who lay on her death bed, extended family gathered all around. She asked for a final *borreltje*; for everyone a round. So everybody was poured a thimbleful of that gut-searing Dutch gin called *Jenever*. As the ancient matriarch managed to get the drink up to her lips, almost like at *avondmal*, she said, "Op de Heer Jezus!" swallowed, and died (Cheers for Jesus!). That quality of aesthetic life is worth nurturing in our busy days of service to the Lord if we would understand and make known to one another the glory of God's shalom.

Glossary

aesthetic (adj.) one way we women and men are created to live, in response to an irreducible ordinance God laid down for creatures to follow, namely, to be imaginative.

humor [sense of] (n.) a vital level of imaginative activity in a person that notices what is funny in God's world and sometimes participates in human antics.

imaginativity (n.) a God-given capability human creatures have to be allusive, to make-believe, to do as-if.

leisural (adj.) the quality of having ample time to engage in surprises; celebrative aesthetic life time.

style, lifestyle (n.) the consistent imaginative fabric a person or group shows in making aesthetic decisions; one's aesthetic disposition.

taste [aesthetic] (n.) the practice of holding richly contrasting nuances justly together, with equanimity; your aesthetic conscience.

Selected Bibliography

Bayles, Martha. "Theory, Snobbery, and Agony of Popular Culture," *Chronicle of Higher Education*. 6 June 1997, B4–B5.

Chaplin, Adrienne and Hilary Brand. *Art and Soul: Signposts for Christians in the arts* (Carlisle: Solway, 1999).

Clark, Kenneth (presenter). "What is Good Taste?" seen by three million people on 1 December 1958. Unpaginated 14 pages of text. Associated Television Ltd.

Heintzman, Paul, Glen E. van Andel, Thomas L. Visker, eds. *Christianity and Leisure: Issues in a pluralistic society.* revised edition (Sioux Center: Dordt College Press, 2006).

Lynes, Russell. *The Tastemakers: The shaping of an American popular taste* (New York: Dover, 1980).

Monro, David H. *Argument of Laughter* (1951) (Notre Dame, IN: University of Notre Dame Press, 1963).

Pirandello, Luigi. *L'umorismo* (1960), translated by Antonio Illiano and Daniel P. Testa as *On Humor* (Chapel Hill: University of North Carolina Press, 1974).

Plessner, Helmuth. *Lachen und Weinen: eine Untersuchung nach den Grenzen menschlichen Verhalten,* translated by James Spencer Churchill and Marjorie Grene as *Laughing and Crying: A study of the limits of human behavior* (Evanston: Northwestern University Press, 1970).

Popma, Sytse U. *Geloof en humor* (Kampen: Kok, 1946).

Romanowski, William D. *Pop Culture Wars: Religion and the role of entertainment in American life* (Downers Grove: InterVarsity, 1996).

Rookmaaker, Hans R. "Kunst en Levensstijl," in *Vier Glazen: Gedenkboek 1886–1961* (Delft: Societas Studiosorum Reformatorum, 1961), 325–338.

Starkey, Mike. *Born to Shop* (Eastbourne: Monarch, 1989).

———. *Fashion and Style* (Crowborough: Monarch, 1995).

Schor, Juliet B. *The Overworked American: The unexpected decline of leisure* (New York: Basic Books, 1991).

Vander Hoeven, Johan. *Als Denken Gaat Dansen: Van Hegel tot heden* (Amsterdam: Vrije Universiteit, 1998).

Wiersma, Stanley. *Sietze Buning: Style and class* (Orange City: Middleburg Press, 1982).

BOTH MORE AND LESS THAN A MATTER OF TASTE

I believe taste has relevance for the quality of daily life. I also think taste is both more and less than a matter of taste as it has been conceived in the Western tradition. Therefore I will recall our philosophical inheritance on the topic in order to re-locate where the antinomy of taste has been found. Then I should like to connect taste more closely with the idea of "the sublime," as it emerged in the 1700s. I will suggest, much too briefly, that this connection has promise for reinvesting our analysis of the nature and meaning of taste as an aesthetic reality. The connection of taste with the sublime will also help to reorientate discussion on the deserved relevance and authority of taste.

As Gadamer (32) points out, the worldly-wise Jesuit Baltasar Gracián y Morales began to differentiate and identify taste as the mark of *el discreto,* whose protean *despejo* (charm) counted for everything. His man of taste is able to give and take a hint, is skilled at putting people into a good humor, and intuitively knows when something is ripe to harvest its opportunity.[1] Gracián had read the 1634 Spanish translation of Nicholas Faret's *L'honnête homme ou l'art de plaire la Cour* (Paris, 1630). It advised the uninitiated on how one needed to comport oneself in the circles of Louis XIII. So the conception of the specific quality of taste in Western civilization was generated in terms of the compleat courtier.

Johan Huizinga (1919: 87–113) traces Castiglione's ideal of courtly Renaissance society back through the code of chivalry to the καλοκἀγαθία of Socrates. And it makes good historical sense to find the background or, one could say, the underground of taste in τὸ πρέπον, that quality of fittingness or suitability that Socrates posited as the crux of good-beautiful functioning. A human lives well, fittingly, if he or she is virtuous (=professionally excellent) and shows equanimity, whether it be in defining

---

[1] Gracián, *Oráculo Manual y Arte de Prudencia.* Par. 39, 65, 77, 127. 233. Also see Karl Borinski, *Baltasar Gracian und die Hofliteratur in Deutschland* (Halle: Niemeyer, 1894), 41, 47–8.

This essay, first delivered as a lecture at the Rand Afrikaans University in South Africa in May 1992, appeared in *Acta Academia* 25:4 (1993): 1–12.

piety or in taking the polis hemlock. Such is the ancestry of the man and woman of taste.

There is more to the genesis of what becomes a Western understanding of taste than Socrates. One needs to mention at least Aristotle's φρόνησις, Cicero's *decorum*, Augustine's *aptum,* and the *prudentia* of Thomas Aquinas, if one wants a measure of insight into the pedigree—the chromosomic code, as it were—of taste when it surfaces in Gracián. An account of the fluctuating ideas of taste from Boileau through Addison to Hogarth would reinforce the point that whether taste was propounded in terms of royal privilege, rococo whimsy, neoclassical line or, later on, the wild Romantic ideal, all disputants and cultural leaders counted on taste as having a structure of discriminating refinement. However such breeding was concretely spelled out, they all believed that taste was a feature of human life that deserved everyone's responsible attention if one wished life to be lived and normed humanly.

The historical plot grows dense when rationalistic philosophers enter the fray. Instead of understanding taste as a quality of commanding decency to which humans aspire, they turn it into an epistemological problem. Then taste becomes an anomaly, because the kind of knowledge taste purports to involve is not clear and distinct, and certainly lacks compelling, analytic necessity. To qualify as knowledge, taste would need rational grounds and a reasonable standard.

In Leibniz's calculus of human faculties taste comes closest to a native instinct formed by convention that perceives with acute clarity what is indistinguishable, like the roar of the ocean one is approaching. It makes no sense, says Leibniz, to demand of human taste that it explain or give a rationale for what one is tastefully so sensitive to and tests so minutely. Taste is an affair of perceiving fused-together excellencies (*les perceptions confusés*), and is not at all something conceptual or non-contradictorily precise and argued.[2]

Baumgarten tried to locate taste as a subordinate form of thinking, a sensate knowing he named "aesthetic," or "thinking beautifully."[3] Like the British empiricists who followed his lead, Baumgarten valued sensation for knowledge, and then tried to factor out "perfect" sensation as that human activity which is peculiarly "poetic". When sensed impressions that are internally reproduced are particularly vivid as affecting

---

2 Letter of Leibniz to Coste, in *Die Philosophischen Schriften,* ed. Karl J. Gerhardt (Berlin, 1887), 3: 430–1. Also, cf. *Nouveaux essais sur l'entendement humain* (1714), II, par 54.

3 *Aesthetica* (1750), par 1.

images (vivid means "clear" but not "distinct"), then one's felt perception has that special coefficient of being "aesthetic."[4] Hutcheson worked with such taste as an "internal sense,"[5] but the rigorous subjectivism, compounded by a partial-individualism, which sets the problematics for Hutcheson's reflection on taste, led to conceptual trouble: there is no possibility of having bad taste.

David Hume had also held this "skeptical" view, but by 1757 he was altering his earlier "common sense" position,[6] and in matters of taste appealed to the standard of a universal human sentiment, common to human nature "and nearly, if not entirely, the same in all men" (Hume, 17, par. 23). Taste is by nature a tender and delicate sympathy for beauty and a fine antipathy for deformity, said Hume, and the self-guarantee of taste-sentiment to be just is defeasible only if a given individual is crude, inexperienced, prejudiced, or suffers from poor judgment.[7]

But there is a telltale hesitancy in Hume's elegant phrases treating of "the Standard (singular!) of Taste," which is "*nearly*, if not entirely, *the same* in all men*,*" and which appears to enjoy "an entire *or a considerable* uniformity of sentiment among men" (my emphasis). The slight caveat both hides and introduces a vexing problem. Hume affects an argued standard for taste; but in reality he has simply elevated his own brand of Enlightenment tolerance and Whiggish suavity to the preferred criterion of taste, also for Hottentots and Puritans.

Robert Ginsberg has shown by an exhaustive analysis of the style of Hume's essay that the hesitancies in the text are anything but philosophical blurs (Ginsberg: 200, 211, 215, 220, 228, 231–3). As an eloquent literary critical theorist, Hume is certifying the societal dimension of taste,

---

4   Baumgarten, *Meditationes philosophicae de nonnullis ad poema pertinentibus* (1735), par 15, 29.

5   *An Inquiry into the Origin of our Ideas of Beauty and Virtue* (1729), Treatise I, sect. 1, 6.

6   In "The Sceptic" of 1742, Hume (125) endorses the thought that "beauty, properly speaking, lies not in the poem, but in the sentiment or taste of the reader. And where a man has no such delicacy of temper as to make him feel this sentiment, he must be ignorant of the beauty, though possessed of the science and understanding of an angel." In the 1757 essay Hume cites the "common sense" opinion that "Beauty is no quality in things themselves; it exists merely in the mind which contemplates them; and each mind perceives a different beauty"; but Hume later states that the "common sense" thesis should be modified (Hume: 6–7; par. 7 is followed by the "But" par. 8).

7   Hume: 8–17, 19; par. 10, 12, 16–7, 21–2, 27–8. That is, taste for the later Hume, as I read him, is an establishment feeling to which every normal human being has practical access. Only if one's taste is out of the common line and held to religiously, obstinately, does one forfeit the assumption of one's individual being and peculiar circumstances into the validating generality possible to every one's taste.

its proleptic norming character, and the *dégagé* flair associated with taste since Gracián. As it happens, British thinkers from Shaftesbury through Burke to Adam Smith downplay the role of knowledge in this complex feeling, and have valued taste for its social grace, as a kind of urbane solvent in which morality congenially melts into mores, and sophisticated mores, whether Augustan or Edwardian, then dominate society and humanity with the well-disposed intentions and self-evident truth and normativity assumed by any ruling ideology. Yet the significant and, I think, confusing historical development in the conception of taste that took place with Hume is the shift in attention away from the service of taste in human society to a presumed debate about its criterion, which debate one is led to believe is settled by weighty reasons (cf. Brunet: 698, 858–61).

Kant, in his way, accentuated this shift and turned the matter of taste into one of *taste-judgments*. Kant's transcendental critique of taste (1790) acted as a watershed for serious reflection on the nature of taste, because Kant assimilated the history of the various ideas on taste and still advanced its cause as something purebred, as a peculiarly aesthetic reality. Taste has the defining structure, said Kant, of a disinterested, non-cognitive, good-naturedly tolerant, refined favoring (*Gunst*) of what is beautiful. Taste is based on feeling; it may be pregnant with multiple thoughts (*ästhetische Ideen*). Taste is propadeutic to morality and at the heart of human nature. But its constitution as a playfully musing, public delight in what is formally purposive or ideally sublime, said Kant, is preconceptual and simply not susceptible to being caught in the straitjacket of words. Taste is essentially intransitive, a lingering and pleasantly whiling away activity of creative imagining *(Einbildungskraft . . . schöpferisch)* that displays our human freedom par excellence. Taste does, however, involve all of one's cognitive faculties, and is a judging decision.[8]

So Kant bites the philosophical bullet and denies knowledge-character to taste, thus stripping taste of any connection with factual phenomena. Yet Kant still honors taste as the lynchpin of an enlightened, cultural humanity.[9] Taste is pressed by Kant into the format of a (reflective) aesthetic judgment *(das Vermögen der Beurteilung)* that needs to be defended and acquitted before the bar of reasoned argument.[10]

---

8 *Kritik der Urteilskraft*, par. 5, 9, 12, 15.4, 16.2, 17.6, 22, 29 GR.10, 49, 59.
9 Ibid., par. 60.2,4 and 83.6.
10 When Paul Menzer (1952:111, 116–8) documents the teleological matrix of thinking that situated Kant's finishing his second critique, he notes that until 7 March 1788 Kant referred to a forth-coming *Kritik der Urteilskraft*. Kant long planned to consider taste (more rigorously than he had in the 1764 *Beobachtungen*) but he had

This is so because Reason, for Kant, is the final arbiter of human normativity and because taste has come to function as the unifying pivot of his whole ontological-anthropological philosophical systematics and is identified at bottom with judgment-ability (*Urteilskraft*). Hence Kant dutifully frames what has become the traditional antinomy of taste:

> Taste-judgments are not disputable,
> but taste-judgments made do claim universal assent from those who differ.

To shorten a longer story, let me state my critical proposal in adumbrative form.

I propose we do not follow the lead of our rationalistic philosophers who narrowed down the matter of taste to a problem of whether and how taste-judgments can be objectively grounded. Rather, let us re-examine the primary reality of taste and face a basic cultural antinomy taste entails, one that philosophical aestheticians have neglected: do the reality of poor taste and better taste and the historical relativity of taste prove that the limits of good taste are an ideological imposition?

Since Hegel's fundamental decision to restrict aesthetics to the theory of art carried the day,[11] "taste-judgments" became art-specific and were important within the framework of art critique and art history, or they faded into discussions of *Einfühlung* and problems of ordinary "value theory." "Taste" itself dropped out of professional analytic sight. But taste later rose to prominence, if not notoriety, one could say, as the practice of an elite who wanted daily life itself to be an artwork. There was the Victorian dandy who outrageously flaunted aristocratic advantage and whimsy— leisure, learning, travel, mondanité—in the face of grim industrialization and the urban pauperization of thousands of unfortunates. And it is to the dilemma of this state of affairs that I should like to direct attention.

Does taste by nature demand privilege? Is there any way to avoid the hauteur of the fop, prig, and snob towards which the pursuit of taste seems to gravitate? If so, would one then forfeit the call to refinement of one's human imaginative capabilities? Would one then just settle back, in principle, and join the "anything goes" crowd, immortalized in our democratic society by Duane Hanson as the American tourists doing Europe by bus in the '60s? [#29]. If one denies an "artistocratic" edge to

---

not thought through using taste as a bridge between Nature end Freedom, relating *Kritik der reinen Vernunft* and *Kritik der praktischen Vernunft*. Only in the *second* introduction to the *Kritik der Urteilskraft* does *the* connecting role of *Urteilskraft* between *Verstand* and *Vernunft* become explicit.

11 See Hegel 1955, 1:13–4 and Kuypers 1972: l55–8.

[#29] Duane Hanson, *The Tourists*, 1970

taste, its burr of calling one to meet an aesthetic norm, does one then not condone the uncouth life or promote a nondescript quality of life that aesthetically muddles through?

Perhaps we need not follow Bourdieu's (1979: 569–78) indictment of Kant's critique of taste-judgment as an uncritical attempt to legitimate the social-climbing aspirations of a bourgeois intelligentsia. Still, Gadamer (1972: 32, cf. Bourdieu 1979: 12) is probably too quick in dissociating taste from "class," since *Bildung* (education, breeding) is also deeply conditioned by one's parentage and home. However, the fact that societal and historical forces inevitably condition the formation of one's taste existentially does not settle the root antinomy that either one accepts a norm for taste that is ideologically imposed by someone, or one freely abdicates caring for the aesthetic quality of public life.

Although I cannot present a complete brief for resolving this cultural antinomy, I will conclude my remarks by sketching a way to go, and say why, with a final illustration.

The Enlightenment conception of the sublime, notably in Burke (1757)—awed human notice of what is dangerously impressive in nature[12]—was historically important, because this new conception of the "sublime" ended the monopoly of "harmonious beauty" in defining what was coming to be called "aesthetic." Subsequent Neoclassical attempts to regularize the sublime, and Romantic Idealistic moves through bad deist theology to increase the awful obscurity of sublimity,[13] unfortunately made the concept unfruitful. "Sublimity" unraveled into the grotesque and the horrific. However, from my viewpoint, in treating the sublime as he did, Burke was grappling with the reality we do well to identify as taste: an imaginative human capability to regard richly contrasting nuances with equanimity.

I should not like to promote as the epitome of taste the dumb gaze of some young blade making the Grand Tour, standing rapt on a precipice before an Alpine panorama. Human taste concerns itself with "lower-case sublimities," if you will, microscopic refinements, and not only or first of all with the contrasts of telescopic grandeur. Taste is a human disposition that both generates and notices subtle refinements. Taste is a lived experiencing (*Erleben*) of both extraordinary and subliminal nuances that ask for minute attention in a kind of ranked suspension. Taste is a developing proclivity for funding such deftly correlated subtleties, so that one imaginatively embraces and introduces the surprise of such weighted, winsome, discriminated complexities. For example, taste is appropriately called into action not only before muted or exotic color combinations, or in the presence of trenchant word choice, but also in being diplomatic in carrying out administrative decisions or in saying what is imaginatively apropos at the bedside of a dying person.

---

12 Edmund Burke, *A Philosophical Enquiry into the Origin of our Ideas of the Sublime and Beautiful*, Part I, sections 17–18.

13 For example, while Schelling practically conflates sublimity and beauty, he holds that the aesthetic production by the artistic genius resolves the deepest contradictions of human nature in "Gefühl einer unendlichen Harmonie." Cf part VI of *System des transzendentalen Idealismus* (1800), in Schelling 1967, especially 7: 616-23.

If we approach the nature and meaning of taste along the avenue of the "sublime" as conceived in the 1700s, we will have grounds for limiting its kind of authority as well as for appraising its particular relevance. The experience of the sublime was not thought to be so central as to be definitive of human life, but was promoted as a way to deepen human awareness of self and world. Just so, taste would not need to stand for the resplendent dignity of cultured humanity. It could be valued more modestly as an interlinear or supervening quality within modes of human activity, a quality which contributes the spice of imaginativity to these activities. It was accepted that human "passion" before the sublime, or the absence of such a response, need not be corrected by argument, or be declared an affair of (im)morality. Similarly, taste need not depend for its validity upon back-up argumentation or be found universally binding on others. Taste could come to be valued and judged on the climate of imaginativity it engenders in the community where the given taste obtains.

Our philosophical inheritance testifies to the normative push within taste. As Godlovitch (1981: 543) puts it, why should anyone become upset if pronouncements of taste were only statements that one has something today like a bout of the flu? The call for humans to be tasteful is not an elitist or ideological imposition, however, if (1) the refinement expected is defined open-endedly as "bringing crevices and nuances of meaning imaginatively to the fore," and if (2) a plurality of normed tastes is taken to be normal, and the authority of taste is agreed to be communal and suasive, never universal or simply individual.[14]

Much of Kant's critical analysis of taste-judgment illuminates the matter of taste itself,[15] but we would be wise to honor Bertram Jessup's (1961: 55–6) insight enunciated more than thirty years ago that avoids confusing taste and taste-judgments; actual taste precedes and sanctions taste-judgments; taste comprises a decision on what is aesthetically normative, while taste-judgments are secondary and reflective confirmation (and I would add, never falsifications) of taste.

In Adorno's view, "the concept of taste is itself outmoded."[16] While

---

[14] In her analysis of the pleasures of taste, Eva Schaper's end remarks reinforce my conclusion here; but I am not certain she has absolved Kant from failing in his well-meant attempt to keep "aesthetic experience" distinct from "a species of pleasure" (Schaper, 54–56).

[15] For example, Kant notes the relevance of knowing historical examples of normativity as an antidote to crudity (*Kritik der Urteilskraft*, par. 32.5), and remarks that the fact of antinomies in taste-judgments force us humans to face the problem of some kind of normativity (*Kritik der Uteilskraft*, 57.9).

[16] Theodore W. Adorno, "Über den Fetischcharakter in der Musik und die Regression

— Both More and Less Than a Matter of Taste —

that judgment rightly catches the serious, almost chthonic power of money and cupidity in our civilization, so ruinous for human taste, I think Adorno overstates the problem and renders genuine reform hopeless. Taste is always historically relative, relatively subject to its norm. Although no outcome today is certain, we can still encourage contemporary representatives of non-dominant tastes, in common cause against what regresses towards the crude, the fastidious, the vain, or the vulgar. We can exercise normative aesthetic activity without dictating a monolithic fashion. That calls for tasteful, imaginative deed more than for argument.

To illustrate my suggestion I refer you to Zadkine's war memorial for Rotterdam [#30], which Hitler without warning bombed the heart out of one fine day in May 1940, to force the capitulation of the defenseless country. Most war memorials tend towards obelisks for the dead patriots, severe busts of heroes, and stolid monuments that would prove it was not all worth nothing. Zadkine's taste is different. He presents a broken torso with a gaping hole, writhing on massive legs, with huge lumbering arms raised like those of a Moses pleading in protest to God in the skies from which the devastation came. It reminds survivors and may even stir the naive to imagine the crushing, tortured, wasted humanity that modern technocratic war both conceals and metes out. The taste of those who commission war memorials is less than it takes for a human solution to political peace. But the war memorials of a country (think of what is in Paris, Berlin, Moscow, Washington DC, Ottawa) are more than innocent statues or constructions. Depending upon the taste for the horrors of war that

[#30] Zadkine, *De verweoeste stad*, 1951-53

des Hörens," in *Zeitschrift für Sozialforschung* 7 (1938): 321–355; 321.

these works of human hands embody, there hangs a subtle, eloquent tale of a certain quality of life, which moves its people and leaders. Taste is both more and less than a matter of taste.

Selected Bibliography

Adorno, Theodor W. "Über den Fetischcharakter in der Musik und die Regression des Hörens," *Zeitschrift für Socialforschung* 7 (1938):321–355. (Available in English as "On the Fetish Character in Music and the Regression of Listening," in *The Essential Frankfurt School Reader*, eds. A. Arato and E. Gebhardt (Oxford: Blackwell, 1978), 270–299.

Borinski, Karl. *Baltasar Gracián und die Hofliteratur in Deutschland* (Halle: Max Niemeyer, 1894).

Bourdieu, Pierre. *La distinction: critique sociale du jugement* (Paris: Les Editions de Minuit, 1979).

Brunet, Olivier. *Philosophie et esthétique chez David Hume* (Paris: Librairie A-G Nizet, 1965).

Gadamer, Hans-Georg. *Wahrheit und Methode*, 3 A. (Tübingen: Mohr/Siebeck, 1972).

Ginsberg, Robert. "The Literary Structure and Strategy of Hume's Essay on the Standard of Taste," in *The Philosopher as Writer*, ed. Robert Ginsberg (Cranbury: Susquehanna University Press, 1985), 199–223.

Godlovitch, Stanley. "A Matter of Taste," *Dialogue* 20:3 (1981): 530–537.

Hegel, Georg W.F. *Vorlesungen über die Ästhetik*, ed. F. Bassenga (Frankfurt am Main: Europäische Verlagsanstalt, 1955).

Huizinga, Johann. *The Waning of the Middle Ages* (New York: Doubleday Anchor, 1954).

Hume, David. *Of the Standard of Taste and other Essays*, ed. John W. Lenz (New York: Library of Liberal Arts, 1965).

Jessup, Bertram. "Taste and Judgment in Aesthetic Experience," *Journal of Aesthetics and Art Criticism* 19:3 (1961): 55–60.

Kuypers, Karl. *Kants Kunsttheorie und die Einheit der Kritik der Urteilskraft* (Amsterdam: North-Holland, 1952).

Menzer, Paul. *Kants Ästhetik in ihrer Entwicklung* (Berlin: Abhandlungen der Deutschen Akademie der Wissenschaften, 1952).

Schaper, Eva. "The Pleasures of Taste," in *Pleasure, Preference and Value: Studies in philosophical aesthetics* (Cambridge University Press, 1983), 39–56.

Schelling, Friedrich W. *Ausgewählte Werke*, Bd. 7 (Darmstadt: Wissenschaftliche Buchgesellschaft, 1967).

CHRISTIAN AESTHETIC BREAD FOR THE WORLD

It is a biblical faith position that followers of the Christ should give away the bread they bake freely (Ecclesiastes 11:1–16, Matthew 5:38–42), rather than try to force your neighbor to accept it. Maybe the others only eat cake, or hardboiled arguments. If the neighbors, however, need and ask for nutritious bread, we rich Christians are called by God to provide wholesome food for thought as well as bellies, says Scripture, with a gentleness, respect for the stranger, and with a sound, self-critical consciousness that may involve our getting hurt ourselves (1 Peter 3:13–17).

Since the reality all creatures inhabit is God's world, the body of Christ on earth is deeply convinced that the good news of the Rule of the Lord coming is universe-wide. So we dated/located earthenware pots with this gospel (cf. 2 Corinthians 4:1–10) do not have to pretend to be a group of some kind of Stoic cosmopolitan Pan-humanists with the final all-encompassing answer. A Taoist may feel compelled to identify with the in-and-out breathing of the whole universe and affirm what is known to all beings. A hardcore Pragmatist may be wont to pontificate on how a neutral Techno-Science is on the verge of "final solutions" for the socio-economic, politico-cultural ills on our hands. But my thoughts in this chapter can be content to be only those of a Euro-American Christian born in 1930, grateful for being ingrained in a Dutch-Calvinian faith tradition of life and reflection who, while at home in Canada, is committed to bake redemptive theoretical aesthetic bread for the world at large. I do not have to be a Renaissance *uomo universale* ("universal man").

There will still be a tinge of σκάνδαλον—offense—to my or anyone's particular contribution if it be truly framed from a biblical perspective and bear a holy spirit, because philosophical analysis worthy of Christ's name claims to provide insight, as fallibly faithful as possible, on what God wills to be done on earth (cf. Romans 12:1–2), even though such injunctions will not receive the consensus of humanity.[1] Aesthetic theory,

---

1 Sander Griffioen (1994:19–21) carefully agrees with Nicholas Rescher, that "univer-

This essay originally appeared in *Philosophia Reformata* 66:2 (2001): 155–177.

too, like artistic praxis, political negotiations, economic transactions, media theory, or whatever concerted human activity is being enacted, needs to be spilling a flask of healing perfume over the worn feet of one's distant or nearby neighbors, a deed of love that surprises God by bearing up the other fellow's burdens. Such neighborly love gets hateful people with established authority angry (cf. Mark 14:3–9, Galatians 5:25–6:2).

I realize that christian philosophical thinking, as well as praxis of the institutional Church, has been woefully compromised in history because our theorizing, as well as our crusades and prayers for victorious colonializing armies, has broken God's command and adulterated the truth with our own fixated human privileges (cf. Matthew 15:1–9).[2] Yet I want to offer a few thoughts for edifying discussion on that zone of human life characterized by imaginativity: making music, story-telling, casting bronze snakes (cf. Numbers 21:1–9) or scarabs, composing paintings in the sand, singing laments (cf. 2 Samuel 1:17–27), acting out plays; that is, the creatural realm conducive to make-believe, which affords children and grownups everywhere in every age (sometimes even academics) the gift of ordinary (tearful) joy.

Reformational christian assumptions

There are a few basic assumptions I make, peculiar to the Reformational strain of the historic christian faith that focus and set up my systematic exploration in philosophical aesthetics.

(1) The body of Christ in God's world, busy in responding to the building of God's kingdom coming, as a community of saints, is centered in but not restricted to the rightly creedal, confessional church institution. Therefore, the christian faith is neither privatized nor ecclesiasti-

---

sal" does not demand "consensus." One can dissociate the claim to universality for one's judgment (somewhat like Kant's *ästhetische Urteilskraft*) from needing to pursue an actual consensus that would purport to evidence universality of knowledge.

Trinh T. Minh-ha says (11–12) that committed writing (like Sartre's *engagés* [intentional] essays) is not imperialistic propaganda if one just makes one's stand known instead of advocating one's cause.

Causing a ruckus (σκανδαλίζεται) or cleverly tripping up someonwe is not what God wants (2 Corinthians 11:29, Matthew 18:6–19). The σκάνδαλον (affront) of gospel truth is that it cuts to death those who let its wisdom go hang (Luke 2:34–33, 1 Peter 2:6–8, 1 Corinthians 1:18–25).

2 Tzevtan Todorov's comment (1991) on Frantz (*Wretched of the Earth*, 1961) Fanon is instructive, however, for anyone who damns "Western values" so absolutely that he pulls out his knife: "en voulant ne pas faire comme l'Europe, ils ont fait comme la pire partie de l'Europe" (94) ["in wishing not to do as the Europeans do, they have acted like the worst part of European culture"].

cized, but is considered responsibly free to fund in public the communal cultivation of tasks that may form a (minority) christian culture—not a churchly culture. Hence one avoids, for example, the tension of a dialectical "theology of the arts" and instead works at constructing "a christian philosophical aesthetics" where confessional dogmatics or clerics do not have the last word.[3]

(2) A human person's faith or ultimate trust in whatever one takes to be God and the spirit ("ethos")[4] that infuses and drives one's work are pivotal factors in the meaning of whatever cultural fruit is produced. Therefore, "culture wars" between popular and elite artworlds, for example, or the struggle for diverse ethnic cultures to survive, and even the battle between "Western civilization" and the "Oriental" way of life, are important but relative to the real war between the *civitas Dei* (the city of God) and *civitates mundi* (the worldly communities/cities). Our philosophical analysis must not be sidetracked by secondary polemics, however fashionable they be. In my judgment the cultural repression under various "religious Fundamentalisms" today (evangelical Christian or Muslim) and the cultural disintegration in force throughout the world, thanks to the skepsis or nihilism native to "the Force" of Secularism, point us to the most critical problem amid all the other kinds of diversionary turmoil.

(3) The cosmological theory of mutually irreducible and interpenetrating modes of meaning, structuring creatural existence, formulated by Dooyeweerd, gives wonderful, flexible analytic precision to the rainbow of ways the LORD God Creator hugs us creatures.[5] The complex rich meaning and integrality of daily earthly life is affirmed, and specific

---

3   "Theology" can be a weasel term. For my careful distinction between "biblical theology," which necessarily underlies a christian philosophy and theoretical aesthetics, and the specialized study of "dogmatic theology" proper to the institutional church, see my *Why Should a University Exist?* (Pusan: Kosin University Press, 2000), 26–30 {see *CE*: 45–46}.

4   Sander Griffioen suggests (1994: 11) the identification of "spirit" and "ethos," along with *mentalité* [mentality], perhaps to avoid confusing the devious "principalities" Scripture mentions with the German Romantic monolithic *Zeitgeist* [Spirit of the age].

5   G. C. Berkouwer showed in *De Voorzienigheid Gods* (Kampen: Kok, 1950) how the biblical idea of "providence" mutated into a form of deistic fate if one lost the element of God's providing nearness in the concept of "providence." I say "hug" here to try to prevent a similar fatal slip in reading "modal law" as a kind of "natural law" theory, rather than as the hugging providence of the LORD God. No one as yet has picked up my thought (1985:59–62 {supra pp. 68–71}) about renaming the *Wijsbegeerte der Wetsidee* in English, "A philosophy of God's structuring Word."

features of creation like the sensitive, imaginative, and economic areas, often ill favored by philosophers, are credited with bona fide ontic status; thereby this Reformational philosophical theory commissions and ferments a genuine encyclopedia of special scientific investigations. Genial about modal law theory is how it precludes any desirability for a vague "spirituality": instead, things like diet, fashion, and handling money are considered to be terrain for holy or profane activities.

(4) Vollenhoven's cartographic methodology for plotting and tracking historical changes in multiple philosophical visions, succeeding period dynamics, and definite contributions made to our common reflection by even the most misguided thinkers, has a genial, biblical simplicity to it: salient features of God's gracious world will be noticed and exegeted by every human under the sun; the wise historian remembers traces of similarities and differences as human endeavors in philosophy, artistry, cultural theory, ruling tribes and nations, or whatever, both unfold and pile up behind us,[6] so that he or she can become wise in discerning human strategies to serve or outwit God (cf. Ecclesiastes 7:29). Because Vollenhoven's historiographic categories prehend the LORD's structured world with antennae tuned to a biblical wavelength, couched in cosmological and ontological as well as anthropological terms,[7] Vollenhoven's in-depth categories are not Eurocentric: the tenets of Chuang-tzu and Tao Te Ching can be educationally ranged on a par beside mythologizing archaic Greek Orphic figures, and later European thinkers like Agrippa von Nettesheim and Foucault. Vollenhoven's christian approach would help anyone, including Near-Eastern Muslim scholars, to understand Ibn Arabi's mystical Sufi Islam faith as he tries to trump the Averroistic legalism of *Qur'an* clerics with a gnostic commitment to imagination, not unlike that of Böhme, Swedenborg, Solovyov, and Rudolf Steiner—there is nothing new under the sun! except what the Holy Spirit makes everlasting.[8]

---

6 Cf. Walter Benjamin, "Über den Begriff der Geschichte," Thesis IX (1939), *Gesammelte Schriften*, ed. Rolf Tiedemann and Hermann Schweppenhäuser (Frankfurt a.M.: Suhrkamp, 1985), I: 693.

7 Cf. my "Biblical Wisdom underneath Vollenhoven's Categories for Philosophical Historiography," *Philosophia Reformata* 38 (1973): 127–43 {see *AH*: 1–22}.

8 Cf. my article "'Mythologizing Philosophy' as Historiographic Category," in *Myth and Interdisciplinary Studies*, eds. M. Clasquin, J.D. Ferreira-Ross, D. Marais, R. Sadonosky (Pretoria: University of South Africa, 1993), 28–48 {see *CE*: 343–58}. Henry Corbin remarks about the "isomorphisms" to be noted between Christian and Muslim mystics "when, unbeknownst to them, a pre-established harmony gathers all those 'esoterics' fraternally in the same temple of Light. . ." (93).

The objection to Vollenhoven's "pigeon-holing" complex philosophies misun-

What time it is

The technocratic pace of both the McWorld standardization managed by transnational corporate Mammon, and a centrifugal swirl of incredibly disparate, partisan interests and outlandish, unstable cultural experiments, which seem to indicate our World Highrise Maelstrom has no center (cf. W.B, Yeats, "The Second Coming"): it all can induce in society a suppressed state of vertigo, if one takes the time to notice what is happening. I am daring to suggest, however, that after several generations of Reformational christian reflection, because of its biblical orientation, we have a working framework that is not stuck in "the Western philosophical tradition," but has enough heteronomic (Bakhtin's *vnenakhodimost*, exotopic) leverage to point whoever has ears to hear toward a way of shalom rather than toward (conceptual) waste and violence.[9]

That is true, credo, especially for our—let's call it by its right name—"postChristian" age. I do not mean there are no Christians and the Church is passé, but Christendom is in default—our colonializing sin has apparently outshouted our earlier missionary voice. The massive Babylonic secularity that now dominates world culture has all the anti-Christ trappings of well-spoken christian virtues. Secularism is not pagan: secularism has gone "through" the Western christian synthesis and rejected the amalgam, so the postChristian simulacra that fill our media have a smooth, hard-hearted corrosive virulence. The enviable Western "progress" in living standards built on the subjugation of other peoples (somewhat like the ancient Egyptian and Greek civilizations) is narrow-minded, selfish, a false glitter, conveniently outfitted with selective amnesia, like a cultural Alzheimer's disease.

It is time for educated, affluent children of the living God revealed

---

derstands his problem-historical methodology, which is deeply concessive toward all manner of thinkers from a radically christian standpoint: every slanted philosophy, from whatever "bad" neighborhood it operates, is wrestling with God's world and cannot help but uncover matters God's children may also need to notice and realign within our own servant (not "master"!) narrative being written.

9   In closing his inaugural address at the Institute for Christian Studies Al Wolters seems to agree that Kuyper, Vollenhoven, and Dooyeweerd were not "simply a product of their times" (16–17), but earlier on he seems to say that all of us who work in philosophy are always "*tradition-bound*" (5, 8–9, his italics) and must work "along the grain of history" to bend it and move in another direction.

   It seems to me that behind the Greco-Roman European tradition and all other thought traditions lies God's limiting creational order. If a communion of saintly thinkers can be spired by Scripture to be critical of the thought tradition we are immersed in, why can that same generation not take its directional beginnings from the special God-breathed biblical writings, and go against the grain of history?

in Jesus Christ to humble ourselves to listen to what suppressed voices of the world are saying, whether they be women, ancient saints, misjudged strangers, or enemies, so that we may learn how to translate any saving wisdom we know to fit the needs of the neighbors in trouble. You do not say, for example, "Columbus discovered America," once you have heard the Aztec Moctezuma, who organized human sacrifices and knew cruelty to the core, say, "The Spaniards invaded our continent!" and in the next two generations 70 million natives died under European "governance."[10] The injured, it is true, are not therefore saints. And though women are half the population and Black is indeed beautiful, neither gender nor race, like neither economic class nor hate, can serve as Archimedean point for culture without becoming a pernicious ISM that dislocates and destroys others. Despite our track record, however, a radically biblical christian faith can still proffer hope, even for philosophical orientation, when we carefully, self-critically listen to others so that our contribution not be glib.

Systematic cast to philosophical aesthetics

If we distinguish the LORD's central command to humans, "Love me with a whole-hearted obedience," from God's rainbow of creational (modal) ordinances, which structurally limit the varied aspects of creatural existence and need to be followed if the creatures would be kept meaningful, then we have the conceptual wherewithal to relate to God's grace the cornucopia of norms simultaneously holding for creatures, without demonizing human error or criminalizing sinfulness. When humans posit or propose what God's ordinance means for an area of creatural life, you get a norm.[11] Norms are fallible directives and injunctions on what God's will be for certain creatural responses [#31]. Misformulation of norms

---

10 Cf. Tzevtan Todorov, 1991/1995 (Fr. 141–142,185–186/Eng. 99–100,138).

11 It is a Vollenhovian insight that humans have the special task to articulate what God's central command of "love me above all and your neighbor as yourself" means for human action within the creatural laws that order our existence. Such human positivations, "posited formulations" of would-be, God-obedient action, I call here "norms."

Thomas Aquinas dealt with this problem too. Aquinas distinguished such particular human designations from *lex aeterna* (eternal law), *lex naturalis* (natural law), and supervening *lex divina* (divine law), as *leges humanae* (human positive laws). In Aquinas' perspective, unlike Vollenhoven's thought, *leges humanae* are posited by *ratio*, which participates in the eternal reason of God, and therefore naturally tend to align themselves with natural law (cf. especially *Summa Theologica*, I–II, qq. 90–95). Vollenhoven, however, conceives that such human "norms" are inherently subjected to being directed by a human heart filled with God's holy grace and/or misdirected by sin.

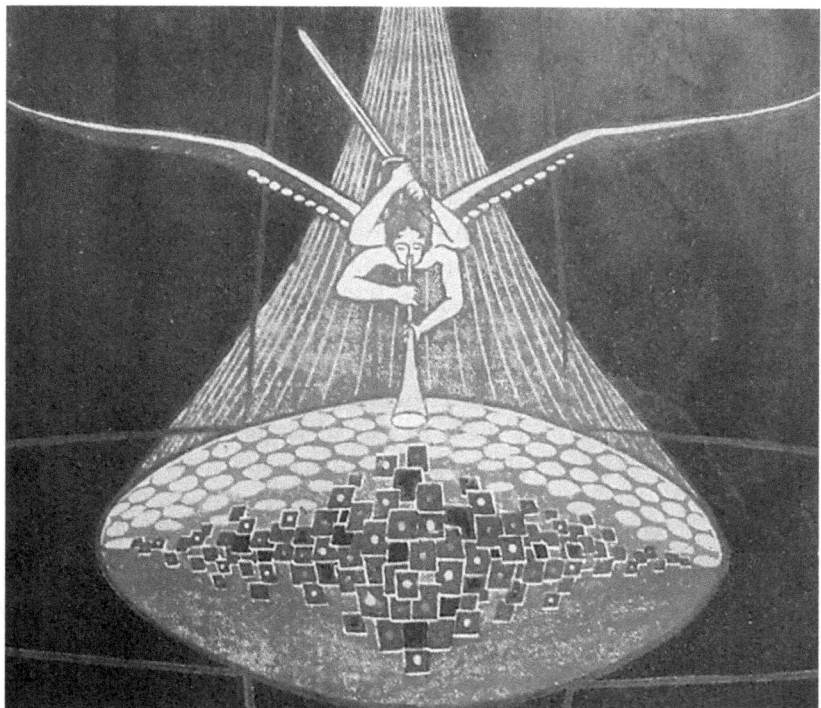
[#31] Ed Hagedorn *At the sounding of the trumpet*, 1972

and violation of a norm still happen within God's ordinantial bounds. Sometimes godless persons figure out better than saints positing norms how to think or speak or trade meaningfully.

There seems to be more room to be sinful, without quick retribution, the more complex the creatural mode of activity be: to pollute the atmosphere allows less room for error than to fake confession of one's faith; to be stunted emotionally through abuse happens quicker than to become socially disabled by repression. The more normative a specific injunction be, the more wholesome are the orderly contours of wisdom for people following along in that creatural zone. Because of the multiple ways norms can be historically posited and exercised, or disregarded, all within God's world, it is important to remember, without going relativistic, that there are plural ways to live normative lives, and there are even traces of humanity in inhuman deeds.

My attempt to reform the Western philosophical tradition on BEAUTY as the norm for good living[12] and sound art is to posit instead that the

---

12 Socrates' τό εὖ ζῆν (to live well) (*Crito* 48b5–6), and Alexander Gottlieb Baumgarten's *cogitandi pulchre* (thinking beautifully) (*Aesthetica*, 1750, par. 1).

nuclear moment of what has come to be called "aesthetic" is *ludicity*—that a playfulness that assumes vital, sensitive formative ability is at the core of imaginativity.[13] The norm for the imaginative side of experiential life is, "Be allusive!": "fool around" in the connotations of your speech, in the conjectural dimension of your thinking, within the diplomatic element of your just-doing, be a trifle flirtational in keeping troth with your neighbor. When imaginative functioning is at its zenith, a quality of celebrative festivity fills the event.

When an aesthetic quality predominates in a person's action, and one has the trained facility to produce an artifact or performance embodying such refined subtlety, then the product or event has entered the field of decorative crafted artisanry or, eventually, the symbolific region of (fine) artistry-as-such. In careful jargon one could say that the "beautiful" is simply the most elementary, and therefore pervasive, mathematical analogue of parabolic harmony within the essential obliquity of given (object-functioning aesthetic) nuances or (subject-functioning) imaginative activity [D#4].

Diagram #4: *Hunched suggestions on the richness of aesthetic functions ordered along lines of modal grades of complexity*

anti-normative aberrations which kill joy	normative functional analogues affording joy
pretentious, show-off	festive, awful, wonderful, amazing, marvelous
repulsive, horrific	ugly, grotesque, monstrous, elegant, pathetic
terrifying, tasteless, flagrant, insipid	tragic, ironic, fearsome
extravagant, uninteresting	novel, odd, rare, interesting, fantastic
boring, tiresome, tedious	entertaining
inane, undistinguished, blatant	puzzling, caricaturing
verbose, clichégenic	expressive
IMAGINATIVITY ALLUSIVITY	**LUDICITY [INVENTION]**
hackneyed, trite, monotonous	comical
unpleasant	fanciful, picturesque, charming
stillborn, vapid, jejeune	funny, vivacious, humorous
forced	spontaneous
dull	inscape, splendor
amorphous	concinnity
at random	beautiful harmony

A normative aesthetic ambiguity to art

What happens when one revamps the aesthetic/artistic norm and dares to posit that in the beginning God said, "Be allusive!" rather than "Be beautiful!"?

---

13 Cf. my "Imaginativity" in *Faith and Philosophy* 4:1 (January 1987): 43–58 {supra pp. 27–44}.

For one matter, the reconceived and reformed norm challenges the Western tradition, which has identified the glory of God's creatures with just a specific facet of creation and idolized "proportional harmony" to be the norm for good art.

The proud equilibrium sculpted for the ancient Greek god of the sea, Poseidon, or the unbowed equanimity of Sophocles' Oedipus blinding himself to confess τἀμὰ γὰρ κακὰ ("The evil is mine!") to accept and bear as fated; and the impeccably chaste composition of Renaissance Raphael's *St. Celia*—not a line out of place, the primary colors quietly filling the foreground and whole painting with simplicity: from my viewpoint (granting that "beautiful" is the most elemental mathematical feature of aesthetic reality), this ancient Greek Western monumental Beauty constricts the world of meaning that it allows to be shown to an order that is calculated to disallow the possibility of mercy and forgiveness. And Raphael's exquisite Renaissance Beauty has absorbed the wheel of torture in his painterly treatment of St. Celia as if pain be unreal in the eternal reward of beatitude—such ideal "beauty" is other-worldly, distortional! a whitewash of historical evil.

My notion of aesthetic normativity, which downplays the "beautiful" element of parabolic proportion, is also ready to recognize Western artistry that is manifestly not beautiful: the artistry of Grünewald's *Isenheimer altarpiece* is beyond question, but the distorted picture of the Savior's death—the awful contortions of rigor mortis, ugly wound in a flogged cadaver of putrefactive color—is formally intent upon being deformed, just as Grünewald's demonic shapes of grotesque monsters torturing St. Anthony cannot be said "to delight the eye." The art of late Goya's "black paintings" minimize too any note of "beautiful harmony," eclipsed by the bold excess of awkward, horrific shapes that jostle any viewer into wondering about the permanently equivocal insight of such gruesome art, presenting the cannibalistic depravity of pretending "justice is the might of the stronger."[14]

Much Western "Romantic" painterly art, like Füseli's *The Nightmare* (1782) and Gericault's *Raft of Medusa* (1817), or Victor Hugo's *Notre Dame of Paris* (1831), at this time in Europe is hard to rhyme with

---

14 Thrasymachus maintained this doctrine of "Might makes right" in Plato's *Respublica*, book 1. The terrible, chaotic state of political life in Spain after Napoleon's invasion in 1808 until the restoration of Bourbon King Ferdinand VII in 1823 was filled with suppression and persecutions that operated with Thrasymachan impunity. During these years Goya did his series of aquatint-engravings on *Los desastres de la guerra* (Disasters of war) (c. 1808–1814, unpublished until 1863), followed by the "black paintings" (c. 1820–22).

"Beauty," except in some perverse redefinition of the term, as happens when systematicians following Hegel write volumes trying to justify, let's say, the pathetic demise of Shakespeare's mad King Lear or the piled up corpses at the end of a Senecan tragedy as being "*schön*" (beautiful).[15] No, powerful art, like the contemporary Australian christian Warren Breninger's [#32] *Gates of Prayer* (1993–2008), can be better approached as a grim play on the anguish of pursed lips and clenched teeth as a synecdoche for Job's bootless cries to God for answers!

Although one could comment "beautiful" about the playful markings on most well-crafted utensils, when one is faced with a 1500s image of a Persian manuscript, to ask whether it be beautiful is the wrong question. One needs to figure out to what does the configuration allude? Of what meaning is it symbolic? Once one knows you must not read the piece from a "Western" perspective as mimetic representation, but see the image in an ancient Persian manuscript as if from a height vertically down to a mandala able to occasion a theophanous event in which you become veritably present in the Muslim paradise, then one begins to

---

15 Johannes Volkelt mentions Christian Hermann Weisse, Friedrich Vischer, Moritz Carriÿegre, Theodor Lipps, and others in whose writings "das Schöne tritt uns sofort als der alleinige Gegenstand des Ästhetik entgegen" (1:78) ("the Beautiful immediately faces us as the exclusive Gegenstand of aesthetics").

Hegel thought that ancient Greek tragedy always reached the unity (*Einheit*) of reconciliation (*Versöhnung*): "Die wahre Entwicklung besteht nur in dem Aufheben der Gegensätze als *Gegensätze,* in der Versöhnung der Mächte des Handelns, die sich in ihrem Konflikte wechselweise zu negieren streben. Nur dann ist nicht das Unglück und Leiden, sondern die Befriedigung des Geistes das letzte, insofern erst bei solchem Ende die Notwendigkeit dessen, was den Individuen geschieht, als absolute Vernünftigkeit erscheinen kann, und das Gemüt wahrhaft sittlich beruhigt ist: erschüttert durch das Los der Helden, versöhnt in der Sache. Nun wenn man diese Einsicht festhält, lässt die alte Tragödie begreifen" (G.W.F. Hegel, *Ästhetik,* ed. Hothos/Bassenge [Frankfurt a.M.: Europäische Verlagsanstalt, 1965], 2:566. ("The true development of dramatic tragedy consists simply in the annulment of opposites *as opposites,* that is, in the reconciliation of the acting powers which strive themselves reciprocally to annihilate each other in their conflict. Only then can the absolute rationality of what happens to the individuals show up rather than the misfortune and suffering: only when the necessary finality of what happens satisfies our consciousness can our disposition be truly brought morally to rest. Only then are we who are shocked by the fate of the heroes reconciled to what actually takes place. So, when one holds onto this insight of reconciled opposites, then the ancient tragedies let themselves be understood.")

Hegel also posited that Shakespeare gives us "die schönsten Beispiele" (the most beautiful examples) of characters who consistently bring destruction onto themselves, so that "Dies Weh, aber, das uns [Zuschauer] befällt, ist eine nur schmerzliche Versöhnung, eine *unglückliche Seligheit* im Unglück" (Ibid. 2:581). ("This sorrow, which delights us viewers, is a kind of sorrowfully touched reconciliation, an unhappy blessedness in the misfortune.")

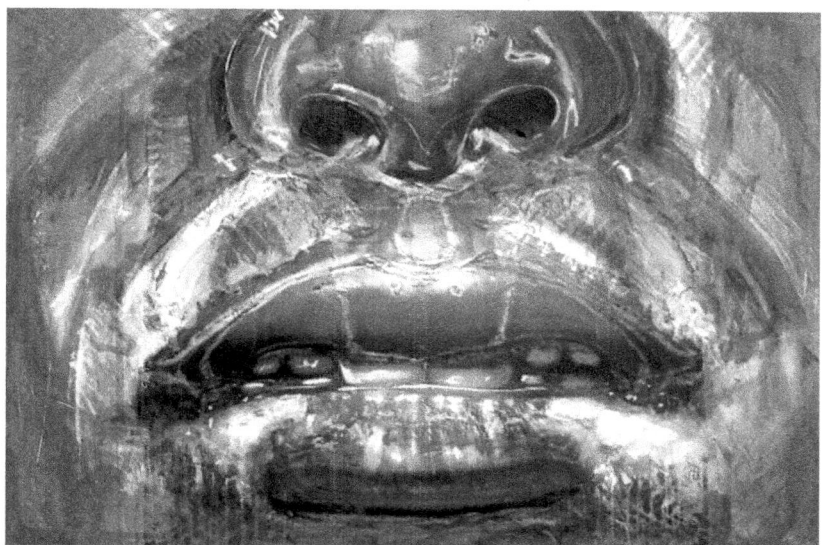

[#32] Warren Breninger, *Gates of Prayers*, 1993-2008 [detail]

enter into the artifact's meaning.

To say that an Australian bushman's dream painting has a beautiful pattern is quite peripheral to reading its aerial-view itinerary of a landscape. And certain African tribal masks are purposely ugly artifacts, because the dreaded supernatural reality they invoke in the ritual dance overshadows any jot of balanced symmetry within the distortion the artisan fashions to elicit what threatens and bodes evil.[16] Canadian Northwest coastal Kwakiutl Indian huge gift chests and masks used by the chief dancing at a grand potlatch ceremony are also conceived and made not to be "beautiful," but to attest to the legendary fierce animal-power and mystery in the pedigree of the tribe. So the exquisite, extravagant wooden Raven dance masks are scary imaginative tributes to the majesty and cunning of the Ur-Mighty source of Kwakiutl hunter-provider ingenuity.

Salvaging theoretical aesthetics

I am assuming that by understanding the defining quality of artistry, one will have an entrée for grasping the nature of God's "aesthetic" ordinance for creatural reality, just as by probing the defining quality of human theory, one gains insight into the nature of "analytic" creatural reality, which forms the conceptual background to scientific theory in the same

---

16 Picasso's idiosyncratic expropriation of formal features from (poor) examples of African masks he had access to in 1907, thrived momentarily on the imaginative reach of this nonWestern, not-beautiful, carved workmanship, but deracinated the African animist-embedded, enculturated meaning.

way that aesthetic imaginative reality is the watershed for making art.

By suggesting that "allusivity" is more sound for doing justice to the symbolific character of Western as well as non-Western craft and art, I am proposing at least two things for philosophical aesthetics: (1) The Platonic idea and theology of Beauty, canonized by Thomas Aquinas in terms of perfection, proportioned harmony, and splendor,[17] is a reductionistic theory of "the aesthetic," which at best is forced to treat Western art that is not formally beautiful as anomalies, and to think that much non-Western artisanry and art at best are strange curiosities, since they transgress the norm of beauty held by this logocentric position. (2) The concept of "ugly" or "grotesque" is not an "unenlightened" gesture or a passing moment like dissonance to be resolved by a beautiful chordal harmony: "ugly," "grotesque," "tragic" are bona fide, deepened normative features of imaginative perception able to explore subtleties of troubled meaning far beyond the reach of "beautiful harmony."

Historical support for my thesis can be found in the significant break with the tyranny of Beauty in the Western philosophical tradition attempted by Edmund Burke's approval of "the sublime," which "though contrary to the beautiful" is capable of producing in the observer "a sort of delightful horror," astonishment, and awe,[18] that is worthy! for an English gentleman to experience on the Grand Tour, as he surveys the amazing expanse of Alpine wonders safely ensconced on a dangerous precipice. Immanuel Kant gave theoretical (rather than Burke's psychological) legitimation to the sublime as part and parcel of an aesthetic judgment that, when one is impressed by the gigantic and colossal (Egyptian pyramids, St. Peter's edifice in Rome) or what is terrible (War), lets one's imaginative faculty, unlimited by one's sensing sensibilities,[19] respect what is awe-full. Then one's aesthetic taste, says Kant, anticipates

---

17 *Summa theologica* I, q. 39 a.8 resp: "*Species* autem, sive *pulchritudo*, habet similitudinem cum propriis Filii. Nam ad pulchritudinem tria requiruntur. Primo quidem, integritas sive perfectio: quae enim diminuta sunt, hoc ipso turpia sunt. Et debita proportio sive consonantia. Et iterum claritas: unde quae habent colorem nitidum, pulchra esse dicuntur." ("A model form or beauty has similarities with properties of the Son of God. Three matters are requisite for beauty: First of all, a certain wholeness or perfection, since ugly matters consist in those which show lack or loss; then second, proportionality or harmony; and finally splendor—that is why things that have brilliant color are said to be beautiful.")

18 *A Philosophical Enquiry in the Origin of Our Ideas of the Sublime and Beautiful* (1757), Part IV, sect. 7 and 24.

19 ". . . unsere Einbildungskraft in ihrer ganzen Grenzlosigkeit," *Kritik der Urteilskraft* (1790), Sect. 26, par. 13. (". . . our imagining-power in its utter limitlessness.")

our supersensible human religious destiny of living a moral life.[20]

Let it be granted that historical philosophical recognition of "the sublime" downgraded "the beautiful" in a subjectivistic philosophical climate that made normativity itself a moot problem. But it is a mistake to identify "beautiful" and "normative" in general, since beauty can be seductive,[21] and artistic beauty can be wicked (for example, Goya's *Maya desnuda*). The puzzling, freckled, quantitative proportionality the beautiful affords is good, and only becomes oppressive when its inbred Pythagorean harmony presumes to be the controlling, limiting concept for imaginative reality.[22] Correct about recognition of the sublime as an enriched aesthetic property of things and a corresponding complicated imaginative appreciation of such dumbfounding matters as the prodigious, the grotesque, and the tragic, is that "the sublime" recoups the medieval valuation of monsters.

Monsters *(martikhora, cynocephali,* cyclops) had been projected by ancient pagan writers as powerful mythical realities antagonistic to humans. Already before the time of the Hippocratic canon, because its seizures were deemed inhuman, the scary epileptic fit was popularly known as ἱερὴ νόσος (sacred disease).[23] However, monsters, often shown on the margins of medieval biblical manuscripts, were not considered necessarily *contra naturam* (against nature), demonic, or morally reprehensible, but as evidence that there are God-given realities *supra naturam* (beyond nature), beyond human reason.[24] Scotus Eriugena recognized the monstrous as a way to liberate us human creatures from the pride of thinking

---

20 *Kritik der Urteilskraft,* sect. 25–29.
21 Genesis 3:6.
22 Although Volkelt sometimes treats "aesthetic" as synonymous with "artistic" (1:77) and casts the whole area of "the aesthetic" into what he calls its "psychological nature," his ruminations support my analysis: "Das Wort 'schön' ist für gewisse besondere Gestaltungen des Ästhetischen aufzusparen. . . . Das ganze Gebiet des Ästhetischen unter der 'Schönheit' zusammenzufassen, ist wider das Sprachgefühl. Wer wird—um nur gewisse äußerste Fälle aufzuführen—das furchtbare Erhabene, das grauenhaft Tragische, das karikaturartig Komischem, das wild Humoristische als 'schön' bezeichnen!" (1:78) ("The term 'beautiful' is to be reserved for only certain special configurations of 'the aesthetic.' To comprise the whole field of the aesthetic under the concept of 'beauty' is counter-intuitive to the feel of language. Who will identify—to bring up only certain extreme cases—the fearfully sublime, the dreadfully tragic, the caricaturing comical, the wildly humorous, as 'beautiful!'").
23 Temkin (3–9, 83–100). Plato thought the name "sacred disease" was a good name (*Timaios,* 85b1–2), because the convulsions were caused, he thought, by disturbing motions in the human head, which is the most divine part of us humans.
24 "There are more things in heaven and earth, Horatio, / than are dreamt of in your philosophy" (Shakespeare, *Hamlet,* I,v).

we can understand everything, including invisible and divine realities; so the monstrous was conjugated as an anagogic, uplifting matter.²⁵ Ambroise Paré (1510–1590), chief surgeon of Charles IX, said, "*Les causes des monstres sont plusieurs. La première est la gloire de Dieu*" ("The causes of monsters are many. The foremost cause is the glory of God.") (4).²⁶

My philosophical proposal is more modest in scope: the sublimity of the grotesque and the monstrous is an intriguing opening for our human consciousness, which is affronted by such disturbing phenomena: these "sublimities" are an occasion for us to respond imaginatively in kind to their nuances of mismatched disparity. Do you have ample enough imagination to rest with (*Gunst*) the rub of what is a mighty misfit as a clue to meaning worth wrestling with? For me "the ugly" is closely allied to "the tragic."²⁷ "Ugly" is not the failure of "beautiful," but is a nuanced reality that discloses an exuberant playful imaginativity begging for

---

25 A secularized remnant of this belief is found in the usual contract clause negotiated by insurance companies, that they will not pay damages for earthquakes and most catastrophic "acts of God."

26 For his teratological authority Paré cites John 9, to back up the first cause of monsters (5). Pare continues his listing of causes: "La seconde, son [God's] ire. . . . La cinquiesme, l'imagination," up to "La treiziesme, par les Démons ou Diables" ("The second cause is God's anger. . . The fifth, the imagination . . . the thirteenth, caused by demons or devils") (4).

In a 1579 edition of *Des Monstres et prodiges* (Of Monsters and Prodigies), discussing earthquakes, whirlpools, and natural disasters, Paré reports: "D'avantage les eaux se sont si étrangement et prodigieusement débordées que l'an 1530, la mer se déborda tellement en Hollande et Zélande que toute l'ile çuila était noyée, et toutes les villes et villages furent rendus navigables par longue espace de temps" (150 n.) ("To add more: the waters flooded so unnaturally and prodigiously in the year 1530, the sea overflowed Holland and Zeeland so much that the whole island was veritably deluged—for a long period of time you could only reach many cities and villages by boat"). Paré comments: ". . .en cela Dieu se monstre incompréhensible comme en toutes ses œuvres" (150) (". . .in this event God showed God self to be incomprehensible, as in all of God's great deeds").

Wittkouwer comments about the reception of such thoughts by Rationalists: "While the Augustinian conception had made the monsters acceptable to the Middle Ages . . . while the later Middle Ages had seen in them similes of human qualities, now in the century of humanism the pagan fear of the monster as a foreboding of evil returns. We are faced with the curious paradox that the superstitious Middle Ages pleaded in a broadminded spirit for the monsters as belonging to God's inexplicable plan of the world, while the 'enlightened' period of humanism returned to Varro's '*contra naturam*' [contrary to nature] and regarded them as creations of God's wrath to foreshadow extraordinary events" (185).

27 In jargon one could conjecture that "the tragic" is a jural analogue within the aesthetic, while "the grotesque," "monstrous," and "the ugly," are ethical analogues within the aesthetic facet of reality.

a gracious, curious acceptance of the incongruities, ironies, or brokenness it intimates. Unless "ugly" be taken loosely to mean what is unpleasant or anti-normative in general,[28] "ugly" matters. (Because I think terminological precision is required,) "ugly" describes a very interesting nuance of implacable distortion that bespeaks suffering and demands a charitable, intimate imagining to touch its troubled meaning.[29] It may even take a redemptive imaginative eye to find the quotient of joy hidden in the folds of what is ugly—hunchback, anything disfigured, shameful, or hideous realities.[30]

It should be mentioned that much non-Western art appears content with "the beautiful" because, I think, for example, Rabindranath Tagore's (1861–1941) representative teachings tend to blend polar opposites into a universal harmony that basks in the Brahman doctrine of blissful truth. A Muslim ethos too favors geometrical simplicity for the site of Paradise [#33] and the abstract designs of flat plant motifs and arabesques in carpets. It seems as if a pacific, contemplative mood here upholds a conception of καλοκἀγαθός (the good-beautiful quality favored by Socrates in Plato's dialogues) over the imaginative inventions of its Buddhist and Muslim artisans and artists, which is consonant with such a theological merger of good-and-beautiful that has also ruled Western imaginative praxis for centuries. The cleft between "East" and "West" is perhaps less sharp in this cultural area than ignorance and prejudice have led us to believe.

Anti-normative aesthetic/artistic activity

If we reform the approach of our philosophical aesthetics to think that "beautiful" is low-grade allusivity and "ugly" is a high-grade imaginative nuance, what in God's world would be anti-normative in the playful,

---

28 Usually, says Volkert (2:562–69) "Das Hässliche ist nichts weiter als die Zusammenfassung des ästhetische Misswertigen, des Widerästhetischen" (562) ("Ugly is taken to be nothing more than the summation of aesthetic disvalues, that is, what is contra-aesthetic").

29 As Jauss has argued, thanks to the incarnation of Jesus Christ, which turned Platonic idolatry of Beauty upside-down, it was a christian innovation, quite different from the pagan Greek orientation, to acknowledge that Satan, hell (cf. Dante's vivid *Inferno,* 28:118–142, peopled with headless human creatures bitterly remembering the good old earthly days, versus Homer's powerless "shades" in Hades), the passion of Christ, and martyrdom, are evil realities, not just (early Augustine's) *privatio boni* (privation of good).

30 Victor Hugo approximated this truth when he wrote, "Le beau n'a qu'un type; le laid en a mille" ("The beautiful has only one form; the ugly has a thousand possibilities") (207).

[#33] Taj Mahal, India, 1632-53

aesthetic zone of life and making art?

Just as there is more than one way to go to hell, paved with good intentions, there are several ways to miss being normative in different (modal) fields of human action. An illogical mistake of contradiction is different from deceptive discourse that houses a lie to mislead. An unethical slip is different than a low moral blow, which still pales next to a deliberate betrayal of troth by disclosing confidentiality in public. And the differences are important to recognize, not to obtain a complete roster of offences so one can mete out exact penalties, but to honor the relativity of anti-normative human activity so as to avoid relativism or the curse of treating every human error with a *fatwa* (sacred prescription to destroy), while at the same time knowing clearly what is wholesome aesthetic/artistic bread for the world, and not pseudo-beautiful stones.

Subaesthetic activity does not measure up well to the ludic norm: it was not quite an imaginative flower arrangement; the funeral eulogy was not entirely well-spoken. Unimaginative people can be rather dull, closed down to the joy of flair in other modes of one's activity, somewhat obtuse. Art that lacks a full-bodied aesthetic normativity will be patent, mediocre, hackneyed, trite. The painterly sunset will be formulaic, the harmonic progression obvious, and the plotted happy ending not unexpected.

Para-esthetic activity goes imaginatively overboard: the flamboyant eccentric is one who dresses to be noticed in the crowd; his or her manner tends to be histrionic. Hyperimaginative people are the aesthetes, overly refined, perhaps fastidious, blatant about their playfulness. Dada art exemplifies this excess of imaginativity, which overturns the playful factor of symbolification into a riot: automatism, chance, and whimsicality run amok. Instead of making music with a grand piano, John Cage has it hacked to pieces with an ax before the expectant audience, turning a prim bourgeois concert into a one act guerilla theatre event. Yves Klein [#34] used nude women as paint brushes before a jaded Parisian audience, while clothed male cellists lined up against a wall played classical music: meretricious art, in my judgment, which is precisely what André Breton advocated: *la beauté convulsée* (convulsive beauty)!

[#34] Yves Klein, *Anthropometries of the Blue Period*, Paris event, 1960

Anaesthetic activity subverts ludicity and persists in pretending to be interesting when it isn't: the verbal report of their vacation droned on and on, cliché after cliché, awash in trivia; the sermon was stillborn, all jots and tittles, without a whisper of playfulness, putting you soundly to sleep. Hypo-imaginative people are boring persons who drill away tirelessly repeating the same old stuff; under-imaginative people curse life with banality, the ability to reduce what is wonderful or strange to the overly familiar.

Kitsch is an anaesthetic because it kills surprise, neuters subtlety, and wraps its devotees in an unreal world of untrammeled comfortableness devoid, as Milan Kundera says, of the possibility of shit.[31] Logical positivism aimed to shave philosophy back to parsing protocol sentences, which would reduce philosophical activity meant for wisdom to utter banality. Andy Warhol (1928–1987) specialized in banality: from his six-hour film of a sleeping man (*Sleep,* 1963) and an eight-hour film of the face of the New York Empire State Building (*Empire,* 1964); to the anti-art serigraph repetitions of *Jackie* (1965), erasing any meaning to the image except its appearance;[32] on to the campy chatter and nonsense of *The Philosophy of Andy Warhol (from A to B and Back Again)* (New York: Harcourt Brace Jovanovich, 1975): Warhol epitomizes, in my judgment, anaesthetic banality with a fraudulent gloss contrived to induce a kind of obsessive, hypnotic trance that is literally worthless.

Anti-aesthetic activity tries to erase the playful imaginative factor in human life: the parent ridiculed as "sissy" the young boy's desire to draw fantastic pictures with a pencil and to mess with watercolor paints; the demanding, exhaustive regimen of graduate study in medicine or law allows no quality time in the education to be playful. Anti-imaginative people are kill-joys who, because of the sanitized, authoritarian system they strictly implement or because of personal *ressentiment,* rancor, at their own frustrated attempts to breathe joy, seem to take perverse pleasure in exterminating any ludic bubbles in life, as if they made a person HIV positive.

Anti-aesthetic artistic activity not only produces anti-art, as does anaesthetic activity, but tries with premeditation—ridiculous as it may sound—to preclude art-making. Marcel Duchamp's "readymades," by the artist's indifferent anaesthetic fiat (with the collusion of the curatorial guardians of the artworld), annihilate with cheap grace the artistic enterprise of symbolifying meaning as itself unnecessary. Iannis Xenakis

---

31 *The Unbearable Lightness of Being* (New York: Harper & Row, 1984), Part VI, sect. 5.

32 "L'esthétique du banal, c'est l'esthétique de l'absolue subjectivité d'une subjectivité sans sujet qui est aussi une objectivité sans objet. . . . Image ou énoncé, le banal dit seulement qu'il est ce qu'il paraît" (Sami-Ali, 74, 77) ("The aesthetic of the banal is the aesthetic of absolute subjectivity, of a subjectivity without subject that is simultaneously an objectivity without object. Whether it be an image or an utterance, the banal says only that it is what it appears to be").

invented six xylophonic instruments called "sixxens," none of whose 19 unequally distributed pitches could ever form a harmonic unison; when his *Pleiade* (1979) was performed on the sixxens in Toronto the sounds forced you to cover your ears because of the pain it produced: anti-music music. The two-year world museum tour of Cindy Sherman's large color photographs, which are meant to hold up a feminist mirror to parody the male gaze at magazine horizontal centerfolds, also would parody the exploitation of women's bodies by pornography. So Sherman dares to forge a montage of mutilated, disembodied male and female genitalia and rubber body parts so that the amputated would-be erotic objects, reduced to a stare, repulse your view: visual art at which you wish to close your eyes.[33]

The overall question behind the reflections in this article has been this: How can we as the body of Christ respond to the crass technocratic Commercialism dominating the earth and, given the Church's sad participation in the historical oppression of so many peoples of the world, comport ourselves as a believable voice in the cacophonous chorus of cultures today?

With respect to the limited area of aesthetic life and artistic task, which theoretical aesthetics examines, the thrust of my remarks has been God's ordered world and sin are no respecter of persons or of a person's creedal, tribal or national, gendered, or ethnic cultural background. If our philosophical aesthetics, dated and located in the Reformational christian faith tradition, approximates more normatively today the goodness of ludicity/allusivity as God's aesthetic will for creatural subject- and object-functioning in our common history of the earth and its inhabitants, then such ideas and insights will be a service for developing the gift of joy in human lives anywhere in God's world, and for constructing nuanced compassionate judgments on what fails to follow the aesthetic norm or tries with hardened heart to annihilate God's ordinantial claims, whether it be the monotony of Asian bodhisattva, the plethora of Maria images in seicento Italy, or the interminable squares of Josef Albers made-in-USA. We may need to learn, by more intently listening to our neighbors, how to phrase our contribu-

---

33 The standard philosophical analysis of "ugly" by Rosenkranz, which grasps the ugly as "das Negativ-Schöne" (the negative-beautiful), never lets it be more than a transient foil for (a quasi-Hegelian incorporated) more complex Beauty. David Estrada, however, seems to recognize a "fealdad radical" (a radical ugliness) that immobilizes imaginativity and "the transformative power of art" (722, 737). I call such sights and sounds not "ugly" but kill-joy phenomena.

tion in language still somewhat strange to us.

If I were to compare breaking the aesthetic/artistic bread of life to peoples at home (Euro-American) or in the uttermost parts of the earth (where there are no McDonalds or Disney movies), we Europeans, I think, will have the hardest time being imaginatively obedient to God in our own standardized backyard, because it is harder to be authentically Christian in a post-christian culture than in a Buddhist, animist, Muslim, or Confucian land where a disciple of Jesus Christ sticks out like a sore thumb. We philosophically trained people may also need to consider the fact that artistry mediates between cultures and continues to respect the ethnic diversity more, I dare say, than the mold of a scientific theory, which seems to weave and cut all the cloth on the same logical

[#35] Sadao Watanabe, *Anointing at Bethany*, 1991

loom. If philosophical discussion of matters aesthetic could normally be accompanied by artistic offerings from the different continents, would that imaginative artistic component not make a significant difference in our consciousness of the problems and opportunities we face interculturally in God's world?

A modest way to demonstrate the shalom of an aesthetics that does not just play on the one-string instrument of Beauty would be to explore (as I have started to do by broaching a different approach to the phenomenon of "ugly") the many modal analogues of ludicity: the comical,[34] novelty, the festive, ironic, the fanciful and entertaining, emblems and spontaneity. Also, we need to cast our net more widely—ready with a dove-and-snake policy (Matthew 10:16) to import as well as export sights and sounds—in honoring the allusive meaning of Muslim calligraphic ornamentation and Sadao Watanabe's delicate depiction of Mary washing Jesus' feet [#35], in calling the shots on the kitsch of Victorian Bouguereau's objectification of woman for lust, next to the Hindu artistry of copulating couples shamelessly consecrated at their High places, championing human fertility as practically identical to that of vegetation.

We need a doxological aesthetics that helps us look deeper than the media broo-haha does at museum art pieces like Canadian Jan Sterbak's Vanitas—Flesh dress for an Albino Anorectic (1988) [#36], which sews raw flank steaks into a bloody modish dress, which, like Lazarus, after four days begins to stink, disclosing a deep truth about our civilization. A Reformational philosophical aesthetics will also encourage the imaginatively gifted among us to practice the σκάνδαλον (stumbling block) of translating the bittersweet hope

[#36] Jan Sterbak, *Vanitas—Flesh dress for an Albino Anorectic*, 1988

---

34 Cf. my "God's Ordinance for Artistry and Hogarth's 'wanton chace,'" in *Marginal Resistance: Essays dedicated to John C. Vander Stelt*, ed. John H. Kok (Sioux Center: Dordt College Press, 2001), 311–336 {see *AH*: 197–221}.

of faith in the Lord's coming into ordinary jewels like a greeting card by Joyce Recker, where the ripped paper shapes of burnished gold and brown furnish a restful, trustworthy background for the dark *Shadows passing* (1992), it is called, as we wait through our tears for the laughter of Rouault's *Sarah* (1956), promised to the faithful of all tribes and nations, says Scripture, at the final resurrection Day (Isaiah 60–62, Revelation 19:1–10).

Bibliography

Adams, Robert M. *Bad Mouth: Fugitive papers on the dark side* (Berkeley: University of California Press, 1977).

Aschenbrenner, Karl. *The Concepts of Value: Foundations of value theory* (Dordrecht: Reidel, 1971).

Begley, Wayne E. "The Myth of the Taj Mahal and a New Theory of Its Symbolic Meaning," *The Art Bulletin* 61 (1979): 7–37.

Bell, Quentin. *Bad Art* (London: Chatto & Windus, 1989).

Bouchez, Madeleine. *Ennui de Sénèque à Moravia* (Paris: Bordas, 1973).

Carroll, David. *Paraesthetics: Foucault, Lyotard, Derrida* (London: Meuthen, 1987).

Carvill, Barbara and David I. Smith. *The Gift of the Stranger: Faith, hospitality, and foreign language learning* (Grand Rapids: Eerdmans, 2000).

Corbin, Henry. *Alone with the Alone: Creative imagination in the Sufism of Ibn Arabi*, translated by Ralph Manheim (Princeton, NJ: Princeton University Press, 1998).

Dengerink-Chaplin, Adrienne and Hilary Brand, *Art and Soul: Signposts for Christians in the arts* (Carlisle: Solway, 1999).

Dieckmann, Herbert. "Das Abscheuliche und Schreckliche in der Kunsttheorie des 18. Jahrhunderts," *Die Nicht Mehr Schönen Kunst: Grenzphänomene des Ästhetischen*, ed. H.R. Jauss (München: Wilhelm Fink, 1968), 271–317.

Estrada-Herrero, David. *Estética* (Barcelona: Editorial Herder, 1988).

Fisher, Philip. *Wonder, the Rainbow, and the Aesthetics of Rare Experiences* (Cambridge: Harvard University Press, 1998).

Funk, Holger. *Ästhetik des Hässlichen: Beiträge zum Verständnis negativer Ausdrucksformen im 19. Jahrhundert* (Berlin: Agora Verlag, 1983).

Gowens, Allen. *The Unchanging Arts: New forms for the traditional functions of art in society* (New York: J.B. Lippincott, 1971).

Griffioen, Sander. "Is a Pluralist Ethos Possible?" *Philosophia Reformata* 59:1 (1994): 11–25.

———. "Kleine typologie van pluraliteit," in *Pluralism: Cultuurfilosofische beschouwingen*, eds. Theo de Boer and Sander Griffioen (Amsterdam: Boom, 1995), 204–226.

Hugo, Victor. *Préface du Cromwell*, ed. Maurice Souriau (Paris: Société Française d'Imprimerie et de Librairie, n.d.).

Huyssen, Andreas. *After the Great Divide: Modernism, mass culture, postmodernism*

(Bloomington: Indiana University Press, 1986).

Jauss, Hans Robert. "Die Klassische und die Christliche Rechtfertigung des Hässlichen in Mittelalterlicher Literatur," *Die Nicht Mehr Schönen Kunst: Grenzphänomene des Ästhetischen,* ed. H.R. Jauss (München: Wilhelm Fink Verlag, 1968), 143–168.

Klapwijk, Jacob. "Pluralism of Norms and Values: On the claim and reception of the universal," *Philosophia Reformata* 59:2 (1994): 158–192.

De kunst van het leven: De cultuuruitdaging van de 21e eeuw, eds. Jan Peter Balkenende, Roel Kuiper, and Leen La Rivière (Rotterdam: CNV-Kunstenbond, 2000).

Leuthold, Steven. *Indigenous Aesthetics: Native art, media, and identity* (Austin: University of Texas, 1998).

Minh-ha, Trinh T. *Woman, Native, Other: Writing postcoloniality and feminism* (Bloomington: Indiana University Press, 1989).

Misrahi, Robert. *Les actes de la joie: fonder, aimer, agir* (Paris: Presses Universitaires de France, 1987).

Owens, Craig. "The Discourse of Others: Feminists and postmodernism" (1983) in *Postmodern Culture,* ed. Hal Foster (London: Pluto, 1987), 57–82.

Paré, Ambroise. *Des Monstres et Prodiges,* ed. Jean Céard (Genève: Librairie Droz, 1971).

Rosenkranz, Karl. *Ästhetik des Hässlichen,* unchanged reproduction of the original Königsberg 1853 edition, introduction by Wolfhart Henckmann (Darmstadt: Wissenschaftliches Buchgesellschaft, 1973), and Leipzig: Reclam, 1990, with postword by Dieter Kliche, "Pathologie des Schönen: Die Ästhetik des Hässlichen von Karl Rosenkranz," 301–427.

Sami-Ali. *Le banal* (Paris: Gallimard, 1980).

Seerveld, Calvin. "Both More and Less than a Matter of Taste," *Acta Academia* 25:4 (1993): 1–12 {supra pp. 135–144}.

———. "Dooyeweerd's Idea of 'Historical Development': Christian respect for cultural diversity," in *Westminster Theological Journal,* Festschrift issue for Robert Knudsen, 58 (1996): 41–61 {see *CE*: 211–244}.

———. "Dooyeweerd's Legacy for Aesthetics: Modal law theory," *The Legacy of Herman Dooyeweerd,* ed. C.T. McIntire (Lanham: University Press of America, 1985), 41–79 {supra pp. 45–80}.

———. "On Identity and Aesthetic Voice of the Culturally Displaced," in *Towards an Ethics of Community: Negotiations of difference in a pluralist society,* ed. James H. Olthuis (Waterloo: Wilfrid Laurier University Press, 2000), 200–216 {see *RA*: 29–45}.

———. "The Necessity of Christian Public Artistry," in *The Arts, Community, and Cultural Democracy*, eds. Lambert Zuidervaart and Henry Luttikhuizen (New York: St. Martin's Press, 2000), 83–107 {see *RA*: 1–28}.

Spacks, Patricia Meyer. *Boredom: The literary history of a state of mind* (University of Chicago Press, 1995).

Temkin, Owsei. *The Falling Sickness: A history of epilepsy from the Greeks to the beginnings of modern neurology* (Baltimore: Johns Hopkins Press, 1945).

Todorov, Tzvetan. *Les Morales de l'histoire* (Paris: Bernard Grasset, 1991); translated Alyson Waters, *The Morals of History* (Minneapolis: University of Minnesota Press, 1995).

———. *Nous et les autres: La Réflexion française sur la diversité humaine* (Paris: Editions du Seuil, 1989); translated Catherine Porter, *On Human Diversity: Nationalism, racism, and exoticism in French thought* (Cambridge: Harvard University Press, 1993).

Van Damme, Wilfried. *A Comparative Analysis Concerning Beauty and Ugliness in Sub-Sahara Africa* (Gent: Africana Gandensia, 1987).

Van den Berg, Dirk. "Coping with Art Historical Diversity in Methodological Terms," *Acta Academia* 22:1 (1989): 35–52.

Volkelt, Johannes. *System der Esthetik* (München: C.H. Beck'sche Verlagsbuchhandlung), vol. 1 (1905), vol. 2 (1910), vol. 3 (1914).

Williams, David. *Deformed Discourse: The function of the monster in mediaeval thought and literature* (Montreal and Kingston: McGill & Queens University Press, 1996).

Wittkower, Rudolf. "Marvels of the East: A study in the history of monsters," *Journal of the Warburg and Courtauld Institute* 5 (1942): 159–197.

Wolters, Albert. *Our Place in the Philosophical Tradition* (Toronto: Institute for Christian Studies, 1975).

Zijderveld, Anton C. *On clichés: The supersedure of meaning by function in modernity* (London: Routledge & Kegan Paul, 1979).

The Place for Imaginative Grit and Everlasting Art in God's World

Maybe I am old enough to begin by telling a personal story.

When I was first teaching philosophy at Trinity Christian College in Chicago (1959) I worked hard at developing, from a biblically led world-and-life vision, a christian philosophical perspective—with enough exact jargon to give students a redemptive headache—so that the categorial framework I presented would help them be critical of ideas, policies, and practices they met that did not honor the Lord Jesus Christ's Way of doing things. And then we would go on to study the philosophy of Plato, Aristotle, Augustine, Thomas Aquinas, Descartes, John Locke, Kant, Husserl, John Dewey, Heidegger. . . .

A colleague visited me in my study at home. During our conversation he said, "If you are so critical of Western philosophy, culture, and its art, why do you have all these books around you?" and he gestured to the thousand or so books of philosophy, theology, literature, drama, and art surrounding us as we drank coffee.

"To make me more obedient to the Lord, God willing, by noting the blind spots in my neighbors' brilliant cultivation of God's world." I probably did not say it quite so succinctly, but that is what I meant.[1]

Many years later in the National Gallery of Art in London, England, I watched a single grown man viewing Velasquez' famous painting [#37].

---

1 For a developed conception of this position on how a follower of Christ may interact with extant culture, see my article on "Antiquity Transumed and the Reformational Tradition," *In the Phrygian Mode: Neo-Calvinism, antiquity and the lamentations of reformed philosophy*, ed. Robert Sweetman (Toronto: Institute for Christian Studies and University Press of America, 2007), especially pp. 254–259 {see *AH*: 106–110}. Johan Stellingwerff's remark on Vollenhoven's approach indicates the same stance: "Het genot dat zijn kennis hem schonk, bestond niet zozeer uit de geestelijke omgang met de filosofen, als wel uit het peilen van hun filosofie, uit het gebruik daarvan voor zijn eigen inzicht en uit de verrijking van zijn inzicht ten dienste van anderen." *D.H. Th. Vollenhoven [1892–1978] Reformator der Wijsbegeerte* (Baarn: Ten Have, 1992), 235.

This lecture was given for the Paideia Centre at Redeemer University College in January 2009.

— Normative Aesthetics —

He stood rapt, mesmerized by the cool, almost tactile erotic beauty of the unclothed woman pictured with her back to the viewer, drawing one in; but the long languorous body painted was so impeccably cool, distanced yet perceptionally real. The man was oblivious of anything else in the room, unusually empty of others, as I watched him. Two young female guards at the door were silently laughing at his absorbed preoccupation.

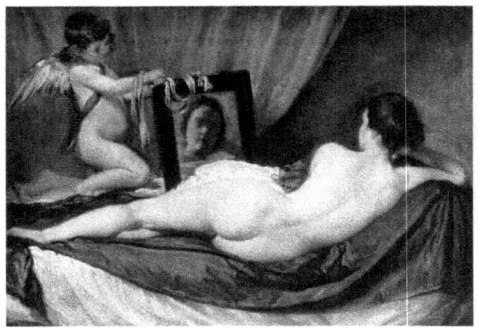

[#37] Velasquez, *Rokeby Venus*, 1651

The fellow probably did not know the title was, "The toiletry of Venus," the goddess of sensuous love. You needed a title like that at the corseted court of King Philip IV in those days of Velasquez, you might say, even as the favorite court painter, so as not to get into trouble with the Spanish Inquisition.

What do you think? Can you look at this painting as a young male, and still honestly pray the Lord's prayer, "Lead us not into temptation"?

My wife and I visited Egypt a week before the Seven Day War with Israel in 1967, and saw the huge Abu Simbal Colossi [#38] at the cut-into-the-rock temple of Ramses II (1292–1225 BC, 10 meters high). It helped you realize the Pharaoh whom Moses and Aaron confronted, recorded in the Bible, was considered a god (divine!) by the Egyptians of those days. These colossal statues are idols, exquisitely chiseled tributes to false gods people believed in and served.

Later the ancient Greeks followed suit by practically deifying humans who won competitions [#39] at the Games dedicated to the gods who they believed hung out at Mount Olympus. You may consider this an artwork, but the old Greeks conceived this mathematically bal-

[#38] *Abu Simbal Colossi*, temple of Ramses II, 1292-1225 BC

anced perfected imitation of a naked Olympic champion in the neighborhood of ἀγάλματα (replicas of a god to be worshipped).² The Olympic mortals were treated only as demigods, and put up in the best Greek hotel for a year after winning the discus throw. Nowadays clothed Olympian winners are immortalized on the pedestal for only the length of their national anthem, although the spinoff on commercial endorsements can amount to a considerable pile of dollars.

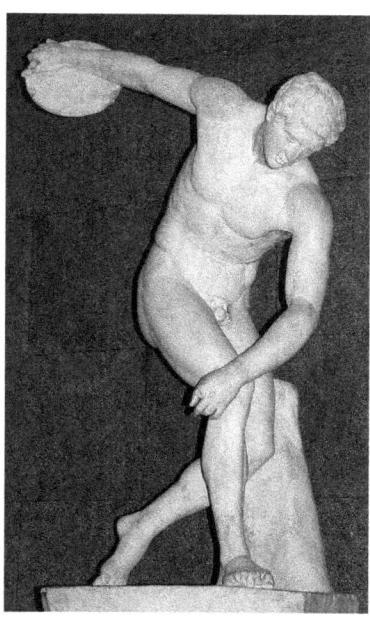

[#39] Myron, *Discobolus*, c. 470 BC

What do you think? When Protestants took over Roman Catholic church buildings in the Netherlands in the 1600s [#40] and smashed off the faces of statues of saints—"Idols have no place in a house of worshipping the true God!"—was that action wrong? And is fame legit, or is it actually a Trojan horse in someone's life?

Maybe you students saw the incredible shot of a person leaping to his death from the 90th floor of one of the New York World Trade Center towers on 11 September 2001 AD rather than be incinerated alive in burn-

[#40] Utrecht Cathedral side chapel, smashed in 1600s

ing airplane fuel. You are probably too young to know about surviving the Nazi concentration camps,³ but look at this memorial sculpture by Glid Nandor [#41] outside Dachau, which portrays against the open blue sky the tangled remains of prisoners struggling to flee from the

---

2 Cf. Dirk van den Berg, *'N Kritiese Besinning op die Moontlike Invloed van die Vorm-Materie Grondmotief op die Griekse Beeldhoukuns* (Bloemfontein: Potchefstroomse Universiteit, 1972, Diss), 169–170, 181 n.18.

3 Cf. Carl D. Tuyl, *Stories and Sermons of Survival: Meeting God in the wilderness* (Baltimore: Publish America, 2006).

— Normative Aesthetics —

gassing chambers, who were caught and electrocuted in the barbed wire perimeter fence keeping them captive. Does this say anything to you about what you could/should do for your life's work in God's world?

[#41] Glid Nandor, Dachau Memorial, 1960

When Mennonite Käthe Kollwitz, sidelined by Hitler's administration, etched [#42] an inconsolable mother with her child who has just died, aching to reabsorb the very fruit of her womb back into her body to give it life again: when you see this, are you doing anything to prepare yourself for reaching out to speak comfort or to touch with grace such suffering of your neighbor?

[#42] Käthe Kollwitz, *Woman with dead child*, 1903

Good artists can detect nuances of meaning in creatural existence people may have overlooked, neglected, or suppressed. Good artists always have a certain committed point of view and a spirit, also frequently astigmatism. The artists often over-expose or underrate the glory of the naked human body, the price of skilled achievement, the evil of suffering. Good artists can also be bad people, tough to live with. But some Christians wrongly think you can live a God-fearing life without artistry and imagination of any sort. . . .

What I plan to do here is present an overview sketch of what makes humans tick, briefly characterize our current cultural milieu, posit what being christian students entails, as I understand it, and then talk about how the place of imaginative grit and enduring artistry in God's world enter into and matter in **our mission for life: heralding the royal Rule of Jesus Christ, the coming of the Kingdom of God.**[4]

<u>A clay jar model of human creatures</u>. Our world is a created theatre of God.[5] Once upon a time the Almighty LORD God said, "Let there be stones like stars and mountains, plants like trees and flowers, creepy-crawly animals, fish and birds, and man and woman who will cultivate the earth and make artifacts like houses, cooked meals, and clothes." God saw this setup was very good, and said, "Let all these **kinds** of creatures be there to praise me, serve the co-creatural neighbors, and take the time to bear good fruit." But the first woman and man, Eve and Adam, thumbed their noses at God, and the punishing curse of Sin began, like a cosmic virus, to lay waste things in God's world.

The LORD God continued to provide limiting order for creatures, like gravity, genetic codes, emotional breaking points, and protective institutional hugs like families, cities, markets, ruling bodies, places to pray. And the LORD promised to run a red thread through history from Abel, Noah, Abraham, David, Ruth, through God's own Son Jesus Christ as mediator, to fashion a people of God fallibly obedient to the end when Christ will return in glory mercifully to judge all peoples and brusquely wipe away the tears of God's adopted children.[6]

---

4 Cf. Mark 1:14–15, Matthew 13, Luke 4:16–30, John 3:17, Acts 1:3.
5 Cf. John Calvin, *Institutes of the Christian Religion*, I, vi, 2.
6 Cf. Genesis 1–3, 12:1–3; Exodus 34:6–7; Psalms 19 and 89; Matthew 25:31–46; Revelation 19,21–22.

With that backdrop I'd like you to consider a Scripturally led conception of us human creatures as clay jars called to be vessels of God's Holy Spirit [D#5], for disclosing the glory of God by enacting historically the royal Rule of Jesus Christ in all the different kinds of ways we exist.[7] We humans can be pious or impious, which is different from being friendly or unfriendly, which is different from being loyal or disloyal, thrifty or spendthrift. Everybody is sociable or not so sociable, which is quite different from being thoughtful or scatterbrained, talkative or taciturn,

Diagram #5: A clay jar model of human creaturely consciousness.

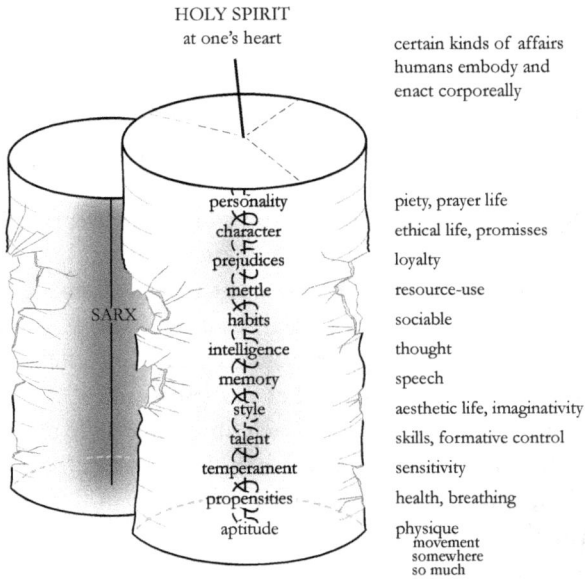

imaginative or unimaginative. And such corporeal kinds of human activity are different from being skillful or incompetent, sensitive or insensitive, vigorous or invalidic, physically fit or overweight. But everybody human, I would contend, is all these different kinds of ways as well as being so big, somewhere, and moveable.

How a person is one-of-these corporeal ways can significantly affect how one operates in the other ways we be, all of which are simultaneously current, in force. If he unexpectedly drops you as a close friend, it is bound to trouble you emotionally. If you have a toothache, it is liable to bother your thinking in preparation for the exam. And once one has too much alcohol coursing through one's veins, one's body may close down

---

7 Cf. 2 Corinthians 4:1–15, especially v. 7; 1 Corinthians 6:12–20, especially vv. 19–20.

somewhat and function on only a couple of basic vomiting cylinders, without the skill to drive a car.

Further, any human clay jar, female or male, whatever ethnic color you be, anytime BC or AD, anyplace—Mumbai, New York, or Toronto—every human clay jar is formed with the built-in propensity to respond at heart to the Creator God who made us in God's image. Humans cannot help but be structurally prompted, as it were, by a focusing invisible axis to the corporeal circumference, to offer whatever we do . . . to Something!—to the true God, to fake gods, to "Humanity"—Whatever. Every human deep down, unlike stones, plants, and animals, is built to be self-consciously, even self-*un*consciously willing, willy-nilly! to function for some final purpose or other. As Bob Dylan sang, "Ya gotta serve Somebody!" And if you don't at heart truly serve Jesus Christ's redemptive ministry, a proud vanity can't help but materialize, because we humans are extraordinary creatures.

I can't mention everything right now that fills out this whole systematic picture of the human place and task in God's wide world. But let me stipple in a few matters: (1) The multiple, irreducibly different ways we humans function can be fallibly distinguished upon examining our human make-up, but in daily life we act corporeally as a seamless whole, even if we are somewhat out-of-joint sometimes. A human act is like a beam of white light, which upon refraction you can see has a rainbow of colors.[8] A person praying in public might sound well-spoken, but upon reflection one might discover it was "just" formulaic, uneconomically wordy, emotionally cheap, and possibly insincere. Human deeds are normally characterized as being discernible, qualified acts of thinking or speaking, digesting or loving by caressing, confessing your beliefs or spending money, but **every kind of specific act is colored by all the intra-penetrating other ways we exist too, at different stages of maturation.**

(2) Because humans often quietly "serve Somebody" in their normal pattern of daily life, some become aware of the integrating perspective within which they carry on their doings, and articulate it as their "world-and-life vision," which gives contours to one's actions.[9] Although it takes even deeper self-reflection, some humans admit to what spirit drives them on—the ideal of fashioning a utopia, the spirit of "does it work?!" or the deep motivation to be astutely tentative rather than be

---

8 This metaphor was used by Herman Dooyeweerd to describe how the varied lawful limits that hold for creatures can be phenomenologically analyzed, although the cosmos of entities functions in all these ways simultaneously, imperceptibly, as an unbroken whole. Cf. *In the Twilight of Western Thought* (1960), 6–9, 13–14, 120–128.

9 Cf. "Philosophy as Schooled Memory," *In the Fields of the Lord*, 84–89.

overly sure. **Which spirit underlies and drives one's actions is awfully critical, even more important to human well-being,** I think, **than one's world-and-life vision.**

(3) Our human deeds take place today in a society where certain differentiated institutions, which have been historically formed and misformed over the ages, impinge upon our human lives [D#6]: families (extended, nuclear, legally prescribed), nation states (or tribal rule in certain geographic areas) with police, prisons, and armies, schools (elementary, secondary, universities, tutors), neighborhoods (village, cities, megalopolis), communions of faith (Christian church, Jewish synagogue, Muslim mosque, Hindu ashram, Humanist lodge), trade centers of commerce (markets, industries, banks), media (radio, newspapers, TV, internet), artistic networks (museum, art galleries, expositions), hospitals, sanatoria, spas, and fitness clubs. . . .

Diagram #6: Societal institutions

And every institution, says a Christian, has its particular, proper in-house responsibilities **and** outside-the-house, so to speak, obligations toward the other institutions, of which all humans may be members. For example, the legal government must ensure that the banks act justly in commercial transactions, and hospitals must not become businesses and turn patients into customers, or you deform sickness into a commodity (although hospitals in society need to pay bills and fair wages to nurses and medical doctors too.) That is, **my and your human deeds are imbricated in a very complex, complicated societal mesh of institutional cares and particular concerns.**[10]

(4) Humans who are committed to follow in the footsteps of Jesus Christ as a Holy Spirited communion of sinful, repentant saints live as faithfully as they can in the certain eschatonic hope of Jesus Christ's return to earth to finish off reconciling the world of creatures back to the LORD God self (2 Corinthians 5:16–21). In this earth world, which belongs to God, that is **the crux of history: the coming of Jesus Christ's Rule. We humans who bear and betray God's image are called to participate glocally** (global **and** local) **in the blessing of such an on-going redemptive ministry.**

<u>**Our convoluted cultural dynamics today**</u>**. Given with creatural nature is to be dated and located.** So we are students and mentors situated for the time being at Redeemer University College in Ancaster, bedroom community of Hamilton, Ontario, Canada, North America. And what time is it? culturally speaking. Do I dare suggest what time it is *Anno Domini* before the eschaton of Christ's unknown return like a thief in the night (1 Thessalonians 5:1–11)?

The fact that many now designate our times as CE, Common Era, rather than BCE, Before the Common Era, hints that we seem to be in a post-christian period. The birth, death, and resurrection of Jesus Christ, BC and AD, is no longer taken to be the turning point of world history. And the centuries of hybrid Christian Humanism of Western civilization is often considered nowadays as a kind of hangover we should get rid of. The superb writer, atheist modern philosopher Betrand Russell (1872–1970) had still gone to Sunday School as a boy, and knew firsthand what he could make fun of. But many bright young sharp-shooting thinkers today miss such a Bible-aware background. And the pell-mell tempo of

---

10 Abraham Kuyper germinates this idea in his lecture, *Souvereiniteit in eigen kring: Rede ter inwijding van de Vrije Universiteit* (Amsterdam: Kruyt: 1880): "Al deze kringen nu grijpen met de tanden hunner raderen in elkaar, en juist door dat 'op elkaar werken' en 'in elkaar schuiven' van deze kringen ontstaat het rijke, veelzijdige, veelvormige menschenleven. . ." (12). Dooyeweerd develops the idea with a very involved description of different types of structured groupings in society and their "encaptic interlacements" in *A New Critique of Theoretical Thought*, translated by H. de Jongste (Amsterdam: H. J. Paris, 1936/1957), 3:168–191, 627–639. For a clear exposition of "societal connections" in humankind, cf. John H. Kok, *Patterns of the Western Mind*, rev. ed. (Sioux Center: Dordt College Press, 1998), 242–247.

our technocratized media is so insistent, ubiquitous, and time-consuming, it tends to crowd out taking-your-time to remember, and induces a cultural amnesia, belying the reality that the past always is somehow **in** the present, even if you don't know it.

Rather than try to characterize our times with what seems to me to be a one-dimensional, vague, and unhelpful term like "postmodern"[11] I should like to suggest that there are a number of world-and-life visions currently held by people **and** a swirl of several competing dynamic spirits, several antagonistic authoritative, what the Bible calls, principalities and powers (ἀρχαί, ἐξουσίαι) in force in world cultural activity—in politics, business, academics, artistry, confessing faiths—different conflicting driving forces leading what people do and have done to them.

I'll first mention sketchily **a few concurrent world-and-life-visions:**

C: one mentality holds that there is nothing new under the sun; so maintain the status quo of order, an everlasting equilibrium—don't rock the boat, enjoy the ride [ETERNAL FIXED ORDER];

B: another vision holds that the sky is the limit for change, and we should be on the cutting edge of innovation world without end [EVERLASTING PROGRESSIVE CHANGE];

A: there is another world-and-life vision that finds that the changing world needs reënchantment, retrenchment of processes somewhat mythically [ISSUES ARE REPEATING]; and there is

D: a christian pattern of vision that sees our reality to be a God be-wonderable cosmos of provident grace with Jesus Christ's royal Rule still acoming [TIMED LIMITED GOD-RESPONSIVE TASKS];[12]

E: as well as others. . . .

A dozen or so of such world-and-life visions, orienting perspectives, are held by people today, and have been **operative throughout history in**

---

11 Richard Kearney's good book, *The Wake of Imagination* (London: Hutchinson, 1988), unfortunately schematizes history into "premodern," "modern," and "postmodern" narratives, as if the "modern" somehow is the center of historical gravity. Kearney's schema tends to skew realization of what is pre-christian pagan thought and what is a post-christian continuum of loss and distortion that a Humanist secularization brings to the fore. K. A. Bril notes how Vollenhoven's partition of the history of philosophy correctly pivots changes around BC/AD and so understands the basic periods to depend upon how human cultural activities respond to the gospel of Jesus Christ's Royal Rule—Kornelis A. Bril, *Vollenhoven's Problem-Historical Method: Introduction and Explorations* (Sioux Center: Dordt College Press, 2005), 93–98.

12 This TIME LIMITED GOD-RESPONSIVE TASKS (my formulation) perspective is articulated in Craig Bartholomew and Michael Goheen, *Living at the Crossroads: An introduction to Christian worldview* (2008).

all cultures.

What distinguishes our period of history, however, is **the welter of dynamic spirits**[13] that drive human cultural production no matter what world-and-life vision you happen to hold [D#7]. To give a name to what I think is

(1) one of the dominant motivating powers (δυνάμεις) behind and underneath much leadership in all areas of human action today is "PRAGMATISM": the total drive to do what works, because what works is right!

(2) A quite different spirit but as wholly all-consuming, particularly in academic circles, is ZETETIC AGNOSTICISM,[14] the relentlessly rigorous compulsion to be permanently searching but never finding anything ultimately certain, unwilling to settle down with a ποῦ στῶ, dedicated to drifting, because everything is iterable, could be otherwise.

(3) There are communities still driven by FUNDAMENTALISTIC NEO-IDEALISM: the mania to go-for-broke to establish a perfect world, because "what's a heaven for?" (Browning) except to achieve it, even if it costs you your life.

(4) Another demanding Spirit at work in our day, possibly without a lot of PR, is the Holy Spirit: God's spirit of comforting wisdom, which bides its time but firmly edifies, redemptively sanctifies, infuses people with a patient working HEALING HOPE for shalom;

(5) Another alternative spirit option ready to make converts today,

---

13 My attempt to take this biblical revelation of δυνάμεις seriously (as does Walter Wink in *Unmasking the Powers: The invisible forces that determine human existence*) must not be misinterpreted as a Hegelian Zeitgeist. With Hegel's Universalistic philosophical approach *Zeitgeist* became a single blanketing "Spirit-of-the-Age" phase of a dialectical progress of World Consciousness. Foucault's conception of *episteme* has a similar totalizing force to determine the temper of an age, although the changes in *episteme* for him have no progressive logic. Thomas Kuhn's idea of "paradigm" seems to designate more a dominant "worldview" than the dynamics of a period. Dooyeweerd recognizes a succession of four basic "religious ground-motives," but does not pursue their nature (cf. *In the Twilight of Western Thought*, 39–52; Rousas John Rushdoony makes an important precision on Dooyeweerd's "motives" in his "Introduction" to *Twilight*, p. xv). Vollenhoven carefully distinguishes *tijdstrooming* from the systematic conception of a philosopher's thought pattern, but leaves the ontic status of "timestream" undetermined. Bril exposits Vollenhoven's *tijdstroom* as having to do with "the place of the law" (69), "a mega-trend" (80), "the question of good and evil" (85). For my attempt to distinguish and relate recurrent world-and-life visions and dynamic periods, which do not recur, cf. "Toward a Cartographic Methodology for Art Historiography," in *The Journal of Aesthetics and Art Criticism* 39:2 (1980), especially pp. 147–149 {see *AH*: 74–76}. The important point here is that there is the "possibility of more than one Zeitgeist per culture" (Jim Collins, *Uncommon Cultures: Popular culture and post-modernism* (New York: Routledge, 1989), 115.

14 "Zetetic" is a bonafide English word meaning "seeking."

Diagram #7: Dynamic spirits

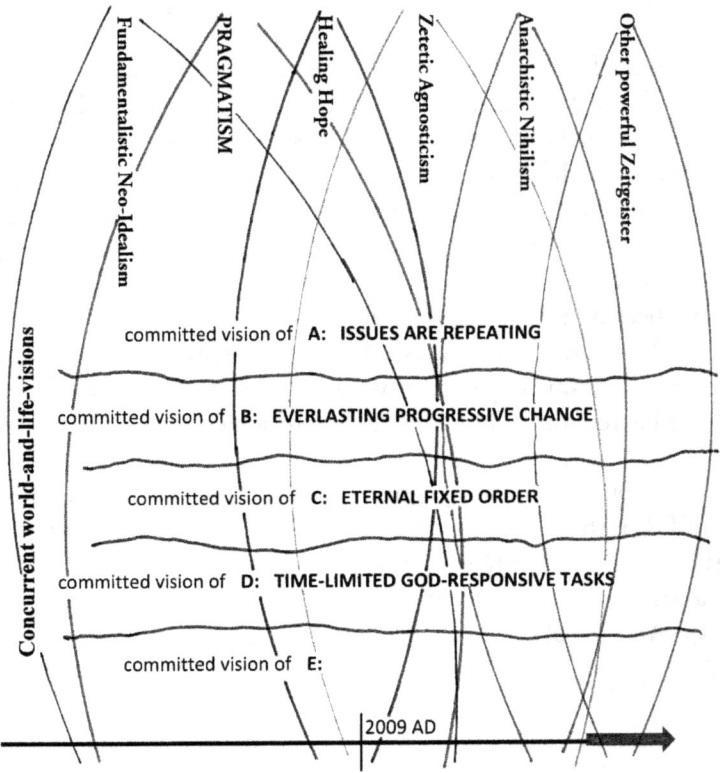

especially in the artworld, one might call ANARCHISTIC NIHILISM: the commitment to be fixedly transgressive in deed, because any norm is intrinsically restrictive, an affront to human sovereignty; so, slash and burn as you will.

(6) More ἀρχαί. . . .

That is, as I understand what time it is today in God's world, we humans live and move and have our meaning amid **a legion of overlapping, mutually antagonistic principalities and powers, which mysteriously fill people with commitment, form communions of not only adherents but advocates for what they will live and die for, and can drive people with differing world-and-life-visions.**

The destructive principalities seeking whom they may devour often incarnate themselves in institutional bodies, and camouflage themselves as angels of light (2 Corinthians 11:14)—"Spend! spend! God will send!

... prosperity to everybody! (... who has a credit card). These uncanny malicious Dominions and Powers (δυνάμεις) become embedded in the very marrow of society; the Evil becomes systemic, hidden, so nobody in particular seems to be responsible ... for the Militaristic policy of preemptive strikes and dropping bombs on civilians ... for the Consumeristic praxis of no down-payment, no interest until next year, immediate possession of the newest techno-communication device ... for the common Exhibitionist program of avant garde transgressive artwork in process, or don't expect to get into the gallery.... Once evil principalities are societally in force, embedded institutionally, their pushing people to extremes affects normality, so the working of the Holy Spirit's healing hope in human cultural life activity seems rather timid and impotent.

University-college schooling. Well, here we are at Redeemer University College in Ancaster as students and profs, situated with a dozen *Zeitgeister* tornadoes surrounding us, ready to suck you up into one or another turbulence, since any old consensus (or metanarrative) has been shredded to pieces. God's sun faithfully shows its face every day, and God's trees shed their leaves to wait out winter time to give birth to new leaves come spring, and God's Canadian Shield under the Bruce Trail is still praising the LORD despite pollution by firmly getting older. What are you doing spending life time here?

To be brief I'll say what I think is the crux of what a body of Holy Spirited students in Canada, 2009 AD, should best be doing, and you can question me later to fill out and correct the picture.

To have the twenty year old's leisure and borrowed money to study intensely in a center of learning under the mentorship of an older generation of scholars who form a community with a common christian world-and-life vision and a glocal perspective—aware of the whole world as well as local responsibilities—is an enormous privilege. Once you are 30/35 years old and have found or are struggling to find your tentative place in society, it will be much more difficult for you to be in full-time service of learning to think, speak, imagine, and develop basic skills.

To be a bona fide member of an academic institution today here, in my judgment, asks you to throw yourself wholly into **thinking through** facets of God's creation and the history of human deeds, good and bad, and into learning to **read and speak languages**—if you don't know French in bilingual Canada, or Spanish in the Americas, Dutch (in which Redeemer's faith-thought heritage is embodied), German to access rigorous scholarship, Chinese to be opened up to a civilization overtaking the American era, do you realize how restricted one's ability is to practice genuine, full-fledged hospitality? to be truly welcoming to strangers foreign to the English Koiné?[15]

A college is an institution where surprises should be constitutive to its offerings, where both staff and student body are encouraged to **imagine possibilities** of innovation **and** conservation, because a memory stocked with images, voices, ideas, remembered failures, is fertile ground for finding new/renewed wholesome steps to take in many fields of endeavor. An academic institution is the proper place to learn the **discipline** of dissection in a biology lab, or regulated deep thorax breathing in a voice class.

A student naturally is a full-orbed clay jar of flesh-and-blood, so you are busy physically, socially, ethically, prayerfully too; but **as a student** you are to be focused especially on being trained to think, speak, and imagine what has been and is going on in God's world.

A christian academic institution is not a Church, is not a for-profit business, is not a place of entertainment and for finding a spouse, or a hospital, even though Redeemer should root you deeply in parsing and hearing God's Spirit-breathed Word—why not learn Greek and Hebrew so you can read the Bible more slowly!?—and you may gain employable knowledge, have a lot of fun and find a life-long partner, and can receive therapeutic counseling if needed on the side. But a christian academic institution worth its salt, in my judgment, is primarily to be **a monastic training ground, an intense apprenticeship at a crossroads, a preparation engaged in communal temptation—training, testing (πειρασμός)—in exorcism!** Your saintly profs, as I understand it—this is Paul Klee's portrait of your profs, *Le Savant*, 1933 [#43]—are helping you learn how to exorcise the seductive, evil spirits out of the texts of Aristotle and Foucault, John Locke and Trudeau, Simone Weil and Phyllis Tribble, John Stuart Mill and John Maynard Keynes, Eisenstein and American musicals—not as a witch-hunt, but in order sadly and excitedly to learn what in God's world these gifted fellow humans have noticed cross-eyed, wrong-spirited, that we followers of Christ need to pay attention to so we can posit what indeed is to be done.

When I sit solitary in my basement study trying to become wise, hemmed in by all the books with notes, images, and music [#44], I some-

---

15 Cf. Barbara Carvill and David I. Smith, *The Gift of the Stranger: Faith, hospitality, and foreign language learning* (Grand Rapids: Eerdmans, 2000).

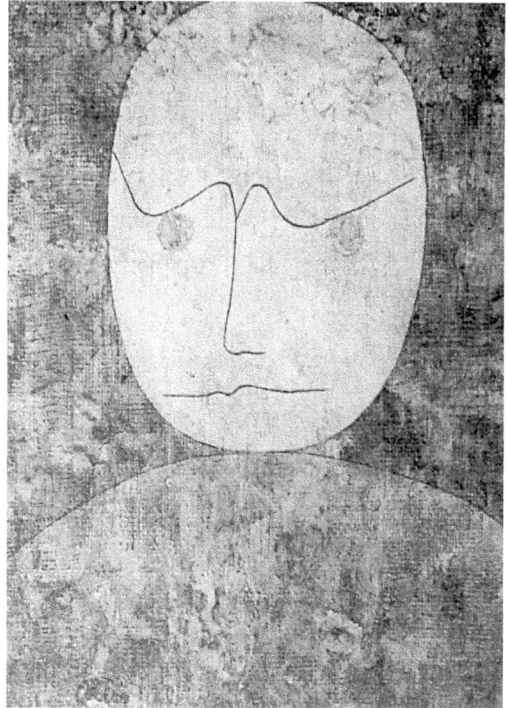

[#43] Paul Klee, *La Savant*, 1933

[#44] Hemmed in by books (2006)

times feel like St. Anthony being tempted by demons [#45], because many of those writers are smarter than I am, and words can seduce and kill you too. That's why a communion of disciplined scholarly saints is normative for a disciple of Christ, to help you get up when you fall down (Ecclesiastes 4:9–12). College is privileged leisure time to be rooted in God's written, incarnated and creational Word [regenerate], to discover your particular gifts [speciate], and to take the time slowly to prepare for enriched, discerning human service [diaconate],[16] the way God schooled Moses for forty years in the Midian desert before he faced Pharaoh and had to lead the obstinate tribes of Israelites to a promised land.

University studying is **practice learning time** in your life, the best time to make mistakes in judgment, because they are only "academic" errors, which your profs will help you straighten out. You can indeed be misformed by schooling, twisted crooked in your mentality, or catch an elitist intellectualistic virus at college. That's why a truly redemptive schooling is a great blessing. Christians should not act as if they themselves have all the knowledge and have house-cleaned their consciousness from all wicked inclinations, because then, as Christ's parable intimates, you become a sitting duck to have seven times as many **self-righteous** demons take over your life (cf. Luke 11:14–26). Now is the time to practice, experiment in a communion of repentant saints what is going on in yourself but also all around you.

Would your education [#46] change if your buildings looked like this [#47] educational institution?

Matt Cupido's fine murals [#48] testify of God's faithfulness in the vegetation and water the Psalms celebrate, so basic to all life on earth. But could Redeemer maybe make place for more murals?

It is the custom at the Rands Afrikaans Universiteit in Johannesburg to give each graduating class a wall to image their reflection before leaving; the next year the following graduates paint over the same wall to show their reflection, like this comment on their extra-!curricular activities, plus a vivid comment in the upper right corner [#49] on the wars America engages in or precipitates, where the stars of the USA flag become crosses and the Statue of Liberty becomes a hangman.

Would that be a good project at Redeemer? The graduating Seniors strike a committee, receive a back wall of the cafeteria, some acrylic paint,

---

16 Cf. my "Glocal Culture as Redemptive Gambit" in *That the World May Believe: Essays on mission and unity in honour of George Vandervelde*, eds. Michael W. Goheen and Margaret O'Gara (Lanham: University Press of America, 2006), especially 55–59. Also cf. "Cities as a Place for Public Artworks: A glocal approach" {see *RA*: 233–261}.

[#45] Matthias Grünewald, *Temptation of St. Anthony*, 1510-1515, oil on panel

— Normative Aesthetics —

[#46] Redeemer University College, Ancaster (2012)

[#47] Ontario College of Art and Design, Toronto (2007)

[#48] Matt Cupido, Psalm mural
Redeemer University College, Ancaster

[#49] Rands Afrikaans Universiteit student mural, 1992 [detail]

to fashion their redemptive, glocal artistic memorial as a christian Canadian university college student body? to show with what kind of vision and decisions you have approached your mission while **in** college?

Schooling imaginativity and aesthetic life. If we move now to think and talk about aesthetic life activity of humans, it is important to realize **imagining is not restricted to artists**. Art-makers do not have a corner on aesthetic activity just because they become professional imaginators. When a mother or father dandles and coos at their newborn baby, they are acting aesthetically, **as if** their little one is holding a conversation with them. When you play hop-scotch and **pretend** certain squares on the sidewalk are fatal to step on, you are busy with imagining activity. To play chess, tell jokes, collect postage stamps [#50], flirt, make a lovely flower arrangement, you are definitely acting aesthetically. **Making-believe, as-iffing, pretending, fooling around, is not *artistic* activity**, in my book, **but is basic normal *aesthetic* activity—imaginativity at work—which activity is usually submerged in all the other ways we solid human clay jars function too**, even when it does not come to the fore as in playing games.

[#50] Block of $8 Canadian Bear postage stamps

A speaker weak in imaginativity will be boring, with a diction void of connotations. A thinker strong in imagining will propose interesting hypotheses. A judge with an underdeveloped aesthetic life component will tend to be legalistic, and a politician void of much imaginativity will likely be undiplomatic. That is, the aesthetic life moment inherent in the more complicated ways we humans act provides a footnote bubble of joy in such serious acts. And when the imaginative coefficient is active in heightening one's feelings, the person is empathetically sensitive to others in all kinds of matters. Laughter is ludo-physical action, and relaxing in a sweaty intramural basketball contest invigorates your organic processes aesthetically (see D#1 - page 114). My favorite glass-cutter artisan, for repairing house windows broken by our children playing ball in the backyard, always measured the glass with great precision, and then cut it with a flourish, with aesthetic flair.[17]

So, in my philosophical perspective, aesthetic life activity, imaginativity, is intrinsic to human nature and lies in wait to provide invigorating grit, bounce, surprise, to every way we function. Biophysical activity is a bottom line to our human existence. If you can't breathe air and lack food and drink for too long, you expire. More basic to humans than aesthetic life, I think, is to be free from fear, to have emotional cohesion, a sensitive stability. But the human need for protective habitation and clothing reaches toward aesthetic implementation. **Imagination**, I am trying to posit, is not a luxury for elite individuals with time on their hands, but **is fairly elemental in our make-up, residual**, without which or if poorly exercised leaves you handicapped, liable to a drab and cheerless human existence.

Imaginative subjectivity is nuance-aware. The technical term for "nuance" is aesthetic object-function. All God's creatures have nuances; maybe even devils and angels do since they have different names in the Bible. A stone can wink with a glint as well as be an economically precious object. A flower [#51] being gentled by wind in the garden or meadow has inscape. Most animals are fantastic!—God surely had a lot of fun creating [#52] their features. And women and men have myriad subtleties to their lives. When a person cries, weeps, if you can't imaginatively perceive that, in William Blake's words, "A tear is an intellectual thing," and treat it as

---

17 Food service advice from a consultant to chefs at fine restaurants—G. Ian Jameson, "Pathway to the future," in *Food Service Hospitality: Canada's hospitality business magazine* (September 2008): 62: "Customers expect global products to still have some local flair. . . . Customers don't just want their food to taste and look good, they want an experience when eating it. . . . they want to be able to taste the open field that a cow has been grazing in before it ended up in their meal."

if the person just be leaking water, I feel sorry for you. If you do not realize that a shy person may be tremendously courageous, **you** may just be obtuse to an important nuance in your neighbor's behavior. We're not yet talking art, but I am diagnosing the underlying fundamental reality of aesthetic life, of being imaginative as a human, and describing how closed down you are to God's world if your aesthetic life is stunted, dysfunctional, or repressed.[18]

[#51] Flower of Paradise, South Africa

[#52] Walrus

College years are prime time to develop your aesthetic life, because this academic hiatus, when you can work/study like crazy without earning money for it, is a good time to read fiction, view artwork, listen to music—redeeming the time by giving fiber to your aesthetic life, charging your imaginative batteries. Quality artwork, when talked and thought about, playfully confronted and taken in, can provoke, exercise, and deepen a person's aesthetic life. You can do this outside academic circles too, but the college schooling focus of study, somewhat like a greenhouse in cold weather, like a "hothouse," affords a special concentrated time and place to learn an edifying

---

18 My careful definition of "artistic" as something distinct but related to "aesthetic" activity would be something like this: Aesthetic activity becomes artistic activity when the aesthetic endeavor develops and conjoins the complementary skillful ability to form media into objects/events that have their derivative entitary and eventful existence imaginatively qualified. Artworks are symbolical (metaphorically defined) objectifications of certain nuanced meaning perceived and executed by the amateur/professional imagining person. Artistic reception needed for unlocking the flavor of artworks depends upon the persons' responses being informed and focused by imaginative/aesthetic activity.

response to artwork.

Let's try it for a minute, to give an example.

So far as I know, nobody knows what this painting [#53] means, or even who actually painted it in the story-telling 1800s of Europe. Does it fantasize an heroic Alpine rescue of a damsel in distress? Is this the final rapturous dream of a falling mountain climber before he takes up lodging in the heavenly palaces in the background blue sky? Why is her yellow hair so long? The little branch the fellow is clinging to is not real, is it? Could you make up a story that led to this preposterous predicament?

Here is a Christ figure [#54], is my hunch, hanging crucified without a cross, strung up, but stigmatized with the usual five bloody spots. Why is the figure composed of Bibles!? The wires make you suspect tor-

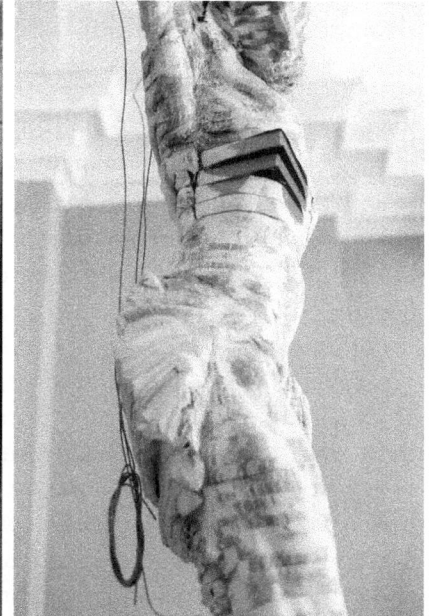

[#53] Alpine disaster or rescue?　　　　[#54] Wim Botha, *Bible Christ*

ture, and the fallen head says the person is dead. Why are the black hard covers of the Bibles and tight bright red pages protruding from where the heartbeat would be, while the rear of the figure is unseemly unraveling into disheveled blank pages?

Maybe you have seen reproductions of Rodin's [#55] *Le Baiser* (1886), carved in hard, cold white marble. Does this kiss seem Romantically "ideal" to you, that is, unreal? What happens to Rodin's nuanced message and to the spirit of the piece when it is parodied by Jeff Koon, posing a live naked woman and man in the same posture? Cruel, pre-emptive kitsch.

Or, finally, an old Dutch painting from the 1630s [see #4]: a partly eaten pastry, an overturned dish, a pewter carafe, a wine glass half full, and a peeled lemon drying out. Art critic Hans Rookmaaker once told me he wanted someday to show Billy Graham around the fabulous *Rijksmuseum* in Amsterdam, walk up to this painting, and tell Billy Graham this is the most christian painting in the whole art museum! Why could that be, do you think?

[#55] Rodin, *Le Baiser*, 1886

If you are willing to play along, looking at painterly artworks, remembering and comparing sculptural images, holding free-wheeling discussions of a play you and your friends experienced but did not quite get, guessing what a puzzling artwork means with somebody who knows a little more art history than you do, that exercise can get the imaginative juices flowing.

Immanuel Kant's third *Critique*, on judgments of human "taste," got close to the playful, pre-analytic apperceptive nature of aesthetic life activity;[19] but Kant missed out on grasping that **imaginative human activity does provide knowledge: fine, nuanced knowledge** often hard to put in words, difficult to size up in thought, but deeply enriching a person's awareness and prehension of subtleties all around, like the shelf life of lemons as a visual metaphor on the mortality of us aging humans also drying out. Such basic imaginative attention can be developed and schooled by learning to appreciate artistry, because normative artwork is defined by the quality of imaginativity, submitting to God's ordinance for allusivity.

The generational task of making art that lasts. I have emphasized the integral place of **aesthetic** life in our human lives because a mediocre or robust imaginativity permeates every way we function, **and** without

---

19 Cf. especially the third moment of taste judgments in *Kritik der Urteilskraft*, par. 10–17.

subjective imaginative reception, art objects will fall flat and seem odd superfluous luxuries, instead of prompts to elicit and build up the aesthetic ingredient in our many non-aesthetic ways of living a daily human life. So, if Redeemer University College honestly commits to preparing and training **professional imaginators**—studio artists, music performers, song writers, actors and theatre dramatists, film editors, not to mention literary writers and poets (a small college cannot do everything) in its over-all curriculum, sustained study needs to be given to art history, art critique, and art theory too, because even those who are not gifted with the native talent and gumption to try to put bread on the table with their artwork, need to be readied to form a communal setting which makes professional christian artistry a viable option for one's life work.

Art historians learn to test the spirit (1 John 3:1) of artistry and how the spirits change from 1600s AD Netherlands [#56] to 1700s France [#57] to contemporary First Nations Canadian [#58], and detect what percolates in the nuanced meaning, goes lost and gets found in each different located—Dutch Reformation, French rococo, First Nations sadly hopeful—period. **Art critics** learn to sniff out the slant an artist takes [#59], how sharp or askew is the vision in which [#60] the artist makes his or her allusive contribution, tracking the scope [#61] of vision in which the artist operates—Iconic unchanging patriotism, an Idyllic awareness of relationships, myopic preoccupation with color definition.

Art viewers, prospective patrons, learn to notice what art is worth returning to again and again [#62], since you are attracted right away but sense there are deeper folds of meaning to discover in the modulated colors, mysterious brightness, and dark shadows. Training in **art theory** helps a student structure the panoply of problems connected to making art in society, so you get an idea of the complexity, that there is no one simple solution to all the tensions and troubles we face to have artists bring their offerings of shalom. Maybe it will take a few generations as a communion of saints to approximate a more normal role for artistry in the post-christian culture. So those who set university policy and who tempt students to take up making art, commenting on art, tracing the contribution of artwork historically to human life, need to count the costs and set priorities so nobody be deceived as to what is at stake.[20]

It is a mistake, I think, to pit engagement with art-as-such in the abstract against other pressing concerns, arguing that translating the gospel of John into the Tiv language, or stopping the cholera epidemic in Zimbabwe, trumps becoming aesthetically obedient here or in Africa. Yes,

---

20 Luke 14:25–35; cf. also Matthew 18:1–6.

— Normative Aesthetics —

[#56] Johannes Vermeer, *Delft*, c. 1661-1663

[#57] François Boucher, *Madame Pompadour*, c. 1750

— The Place for Imaginative Grit and Everlasting Art —

[#58] Anonymous First Nations Canadian carver,
Hewn face with tears

[#59] Leutze, *Washington Crossing the Delaware*, 1851

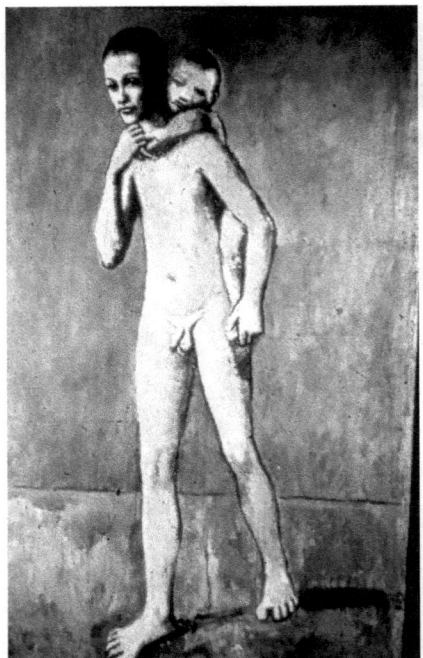

[#60] Picasso, *Two brothers*, 1905

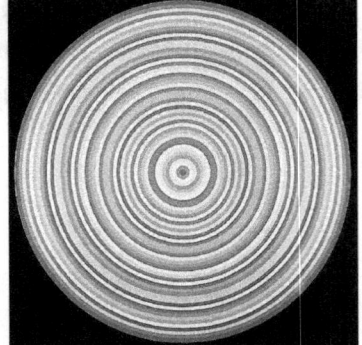

[#61] Claude Tousignant, *Accelerator Chromatiques*, 1968

[#62] Rembrandt, *Self Portrait*, 1659 [detail]

you don't give trumpet lessons to a fellow dying of thirst. But I noticed when I once visited persons in a desolate shanty town outside Potchefstroom in South Africa (1994) a remarkable [#63] carpet of green grass leading up to the one communal outhouse amid the numberless huts of corrugated tin and rough boards and the dusty stone-cobbled blowing dirt, **as if** this "rest room" deserved special attention not only for sanitation but also the touch of inviting festive decoration—aesthetic life quality was operational.

My conscience condemns me for the thousands of children dying of malnutrition and preventable malaria in distant places, but I also am aware of the ten thousands of youth dying from formulaic meretricious songs. When I took a course at York University a couple of years ago on "How to write pop songs," the prof made convincing what a good melody is (e.g., *Greensleeves*), and how overwhelmingly poor so many melodies on CHUM radio were, but with powerful audio production, so listeners are deceived and cheapened, musically anaestheticized. Along with fighting injustices at home and abroad we must not forget to do

— The Place for Imaginative Grit and Everlasting Art —

[#63] Top City shanty town outhouse, South Africa (1994)

right in aesthetic/artistic matters too, to point out, for example, that the large Dundas square in Toronto, meant to become a joyful park-like piazza gathering place with fountains, has been smothered by the clutter of huge, repetitive blinking billboard signs 7/24 [#64] for corporate advertising, turning the place into a marketing venue. There is more than one way to be killed: commercialistic **anaestheticized** places can have the forlorn mark of a Las Vegas virtual cemetery.

Once upon a time long ago artisanry and artistry were practiced within the sheath of liturgical rituals: a dance mask [#65] to augur well for the hunt, an altarpiece [#66] to locate a sacred place that presents a real transsubstaniated taste of heaven. Eastern emperors, Western rulers [#67], and Southern Incan or African chiefs assumed the prerogative of being honored with artistic treasures. European barons and the New World American tycoons got into the *nouveau riche* custom of showing off their culchah with purchased masterpieces (which later could be donated to a museum for a tax write-off).

And then leading artists of our Western culture rebelled and decided to make art only for art's sake [#68], let the public be damned! and the public included the church, kings and queens, the big shots, and especially the middle-class who wanted nice pictures to complement their vacations and match their over-stuffed living room furniture. **Avant garde art was born: artistry with an anti-societal chip** [#69] **on its shoulder.**

–197–

— NORMATIVE AESTHETICS —

[#64] Dundas Square, downtown Toronto (2010)

[#65] Kwakiutl, Henry Hunt (1973)

[#66] Matthias Grünewald, *Isenheim Altarpiece*, 1506-1515

[#67] Marcus Aurelius on horse, Rome

— Normative Aesthetics —

[#68] Whistler, *Nocturne in Black and Gold*, 1874

[#69] Aubrey Beardsley, *The Peacock Skirt*, 1892

[#70] Paul Klee, *Dancing girl*, 1940

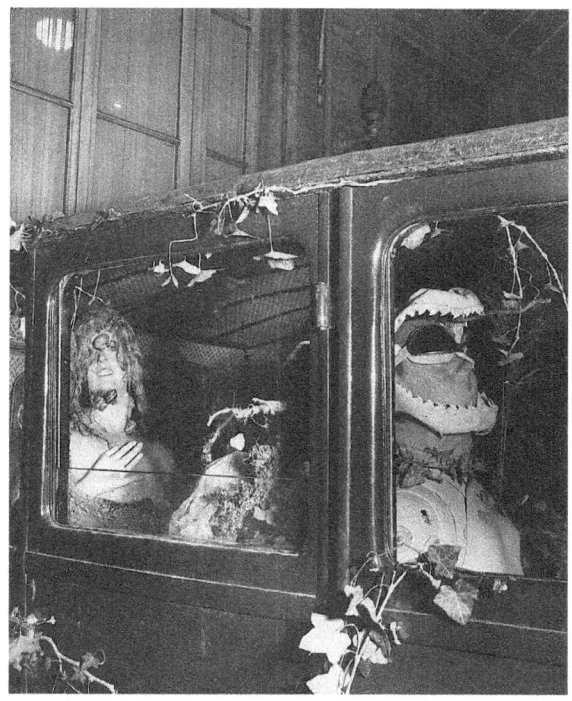

[#71] Salvador Dali, *Rainy Taxi*, 1938

And avant garde art flourished because art-as-such [#70], **art recognized to have its own task and excellence itself in society—building up human imaginativity—is proper,** although in the European Positivistic historical last quarter of the 1800s AD in which this differentiation took place, its confining, off-putting, transferred elitism was funded by a coterie of the wealthy like Peggy Guggenheim, with her own New York City art museum, and oil magnate J. Paul Getty.

Art musea tell this story of artistry quite well, because when your artwork was curated for exposition in a museum early on, your handiwork was certified as the real art goods. Art in the early art musea, you could say, was practically "sanctified," since musea served as Humanist churches, where "the elect" were gathered in somewhat chronological order to be purely viewed, if not adored, "as-such." Anti-social artists like the "Dada" group (Switzerland, 1916–1918) tried to make outrageous art pieces [#71]—like Dali's *Rainy Taxi* (1938)—that would **not** be acceptable in a museum institution, those mausoleums! But pragmatistic musea curators adopted such aesthetic jokes as bona fide artworks, and therefore co-opted the revolutionaries.

So art musea began to collect more than time-honored treasures of dead white males, and began to canonize experimental pieces of imaginative skill. Today zetetic agnostic spirited curatorial staff, who are skeptical of any certain, definite cut-off criterion for art, promote "visual culture" as the locus for professional attention. Such a move tends to meltdown art musea to collections of cultural artifacts, blurring the distinction, let's say, between the Art Gallery of Ontario and the Royal Ontario Museum. And it's true, every artifact has aesthetic object-functions that can be focused upon by the beholders' eyes. Artists who disliked the antiseptic sterilization of artworks on a white wall opted in the '70s for site specific art, which cannot fit within museum walls [#72]. Art institutions, comparable to financial institutions, are quietly having a meltdown too—the *Tate Modern* in London, England, organizes its art holdings in de-located and un-dated **thematic** fashion. What counts as bona fide art is really up for grabs today.

There are a couple of ways people are struggling with the bricolage and disarray the artworld finds itself in these days. A good old standard praxis is to instrumentalize art: make art useful! Beatify your political dictator [#73]. Art is a weapon, said the Communist theorists, to topple the corrupt moneybag Capitalists. No, use art to save people, say certain Christians; then art is useful and worth the time—an eye-catching tract [#74],

— The Place for Imaginative Grit and Everlasting Art —

[#72] Robert Smithson, *Spiral Jetty*, Utah, 1970

a church cantata, or banner for Lent. "Can you sell it!?" says another; "Is your art marketable, like a Scandinavian style of furniture? or can you design an attractive website? Then your art is useful and integrated with earning your keep."

And I agree on the relevance of what I call "incapsulated art," "double-duty artistry," where bona fide artwork is joined and bound to a non-aesthetic task, like advertising art or monuments or liturgical church art. Good **advertising art must obey two norms: aesthetic allusivity and economic stewardship** [#75]. If the art is superb but the ad pushes to make one covetous of a luxury, it fails its double obligation; or, if it promotes obtaining resources people need but is an imaginative dud, the advertising art fails its double duty. The same way with the commemorative art of **monuments**: both the aesthetic norm of suggestion-rich subtlety **and** the political norm of doing justice in what is remembered must both be met. That's why national war monuments are so touchy: celebrating victory [#76] and killing courage [#77] a bit too obviously instead of letting the agony, failure, and shame of the mutual murder in war [#78] seep slowly into your consciousness is a difficult choice and double task to navigate.

"Incapsulated art," that is, willingly slipping art "as-art-itself" into an "other-than-aesthetic" deed capsule, is indeed "useful." But it is important to me to affirm that art-as-such like sculpture, painterly artworks, a

— Normative Aesthetics —

[#73] Vladimir A. Serov, *The Delegates from the Village Visiting Lenin*, 1950

[#74] Baker Press kitsch tract

— The Place for Imaginative Grit and Everlasting Art —

[#75] Maiden form bra advertisement, 1960s

[#76] *Arc de triomphe*, Paris (1806-1836)

[#77] Frederick Hart, *The Three Soldiers*, 1984, commemorating the Vietnam War

[#78] Maya Lin, *Vietnam Veterans Memorial Wall*, 1982

concert of songs, a theatre piece coming across the boards, a novel, is **not** good-for-nothing, are **not** not useful, are **not** divorced from everyday, workaday life, but have an integral place and crucial role in our being human. In fact, to have art trigger the imaginative, playful side of our lives is deeply "practical," even though today it is very difficult to make a living wage as professional artist, and many in the public only find it "useful" if art is bound to the capsule of entertainment.

There is also an other major way secularized post-Christians and also many Christians in the last while have found for art to be important to human existence: art, it is professed, provides intimations of transcendence. Art naturally lifts one above the mundane, and is therefore pregnant with spirituality. So art is a gateway to the numinous, to an almost "out of the body" experience, as it were, an experience somehow of God or of divine presence.

I do not believe this about art. I realize the transcendent gambit is well-intentioned and comes out of a long, well-established tradition, a Neo-Platonic "natural theology" conceptional framework, often allied with a sacramental, not to say, sacerdotal turn to worship, tied into devotion to Beauty as the penultimate step before facing the Holy.[21] But I find such an approach confusing, making art mostly a sensible step-ladder to rise above up to mental, maybe ecstatic contemplation and veneration of God-in-general, assuming the benefit of activating this universal common spirituality to escape our more trivial preoccupations. In its explicitly christian versions this project evidences a penchant to funnel the work of art through the institutional church.

I just mention this option posed by theologians of quite different frames of mind,[22] and wish to close now by summing up a few mis-

---

21 Genial proponents of this approach are Gerardus van der Leeuw, *Wegen en Grenzen: De verhouding van religie en kunst* (Amsterdam: H. J. Paris, 1955), translated by David E. Greene, as *Sacred and Profane Beauty: The holy in art* (New York: Holt, Rinehart and Winston, 1963), and Nathan A. Scott, Jr. editor of *The New Orpheus: Essays toward a Christian poetic* (New York: Sheed and Ward, 1964).

22 For example, Jacques Maritain, *Creative Intuition in Art and Poetry* (New York: Meridian, 1954); Frank Burch Brown, *Good Taste, Bad Taste, and Christian Taste: Aesthetics in religious life* (Oxford University Press, 2000); Elaine Scarry, *On Beauty and Being Just* (Princeton University Press, 1999); David Bentley Hart, *The Beauty of the Infinite* (Grand Rapids: Eerdmans, 2003); Wilson Yates, "The Theology and Arts Legacy" (giving background also to the Society for the Arts in Religious and Theological Studies [SARTS] sprung from a Lilly Endowment in 2003), in *Arts, Theology and the Church: New intersections,* eds. Kimberly Vrudny and Wilson Yates (Cleveland: Pilgrim Press, 2005), 1–28.

sional theses resulting from the christian philosophical aesthetics I have too quickly sketched.

(1) **Prepare here at Redeemer University College for the long haul** not to transcend the tornadoes mess of our circumstances but **to redirect redemptively whatever you in community put your hand to in God's world.**

To me that injunction means: don't be in a hurry, but root yourself firmly deep in God's written Word so you hear and trust that following Jesus Christ by caring for God's creatures and loving neighbors is indeed what alone will last (cf. Romans 12, Galatians 5:1–6:2). Scripture needs to speak to you at your centering, focusing heart, so the Holy Spirit radiates through all the way you be there as a human creature. And if you have the gifts to be artistic, don't try to be generically "spiritual," but weep with those who are weeping and laugh along with those who are smiling. My impression is that God's people need coaching in psalm laments in our times more than they need "praise teams."

Unfortunately Abraham Kuyper strayed into this outlook too, misled by Schelling and Winckelmann, in a rector's address at the Vrije Universiteit, 20 October 1888 (Amsterdam: Wormser, 1888): "Oefening baart nimmer kunst. Kunst wordt alleen uit God geboren. En al wat oefening en inspanning vermag, is slechts een minder maken van de beletselen, die het opvlammen van de goddelijke vonk in den kunstenaar tegenhouden" (16).

"Natuurlijk moet hier met Winckelmanns Neoplatonisme rekening gehouden, en is zijn poging om met begrippen te opereeren, niet geslaagd; maar het **goddelijke** in het schoon en in de kunst greep deze zeldzaam fijne aestheticus toch met geniale helderheid" (70 n.53). In his famed Stone lectures Kuyper also says wrongly, in my judgment, because his thinking about art is confused with "beauty theology": ". . . if you confess that the world once was beautiful, that by the curse has become undone, and by a final catastrophe is to pass to its full state of glory, excelling even the beautiful of paradise, then art has the mystical task of reminding us in its productions of the beautiful that was lost and of anticipating its perfect coming luster. Now this . . . is the Calvinistic confession" (*Lectures on Calvinism* [Grand Rapids: Eerdmans, 1931], 155).

For my early entry into this problematics, see *Rainbows for the Fallen World* (Toronto: Tuppence Press, 1980/2005), 121–125. While William A. Dyrness' fine, sturdy book on *Visual Faith: Art, theology, and worship in dialogue* (Grand Rapids: Baker, 2001) dances close to SARTS now and then, he makes a very careful, important correction to Urs von Balthasar's approach and the "incarnational" apologetic and rationale for art making: "Perhaps, then, in starting with the incarnation rather than with creation, or even with God, the story of the interaction between God and his work may be slightly misread" (91). Adrienne Chaplin provides a sound airing to problems related to beauty in her "Beauty Transfigured," in *It was Good: Making art to the glory of God*, rev. ed. by Ned Bustard (Baltimore: Square Halo, 2006), 33–50.

Canadian Gerald Folkerts' "Head over heels" series [#79] portrays the beaten face and worn out shoes or sore feet of "street people"; the artist sits down beside them with his painterly art and compassionately gives the outcasts company. Australian Warren Breninger repaints [#80] photographed paintings he begins with and re-photographs the repainted photographed paintings in his "Resurrection of the living and the dead, Series II" (2008) which gives the hollow-eyed face with the tilted head of an expiring martyr and the woman's bruised shoulder cavity a media-indistinct, distanced, screened tenderness the unfortunates need in a woman's shelter.

[#79] Gerald Folkerts, *Ralph*, 2005

[#80] Warren Breninger, *Resurrection of the Living and the Dead, Series II, No 1*, 2008

(2) **Be grateful for the specific art-as-such task, which can provide nuanced knowledge for us humans.** Studying art is not just for art majors, because learning how to respond well to artworks—theatre, songs, short stories, painterly art—develops the infrastructure of your corporeal consciousness. Imagining is elemental to one's life, and like broken underground sewer pipes and weakened bridges or potholed roads, if your imaginativity is flaccid, unattended, "out-of-order," or, God forbid, stillborn, you are severely handicapped in your response and witness to God's glory and your following in Jesus Christ's footsteps. Other sides of your life can go brittle, and without exercising nuanced perception you may become simple-minded.[23]

British Peter Smith's wood engraving [#81] entitled "Fallen Tree" (1989) is a requiem for a massive living plant creature of God felled by a tempest, now being man-handled by a chain saw to clean up debris in the park: so, look again, viewer, before you too rest sadly, heavily in peace. South African Andries Botha presents [#82] a man face down drowned in flood waves of Zulu-thatched grass while the upper half of a

---

23 Exceptional autistic children, persons unschooled in art who are attuned to animals and fauna, underprivileged people impressed by hardships, can be vividly sensitive with aesthetic insight; so artistry is a schooled way to develop imaginativity, which can be deadly if it becomes snobbish.

[#81] Peter S. Smith, *Fallen Tree*, 1989

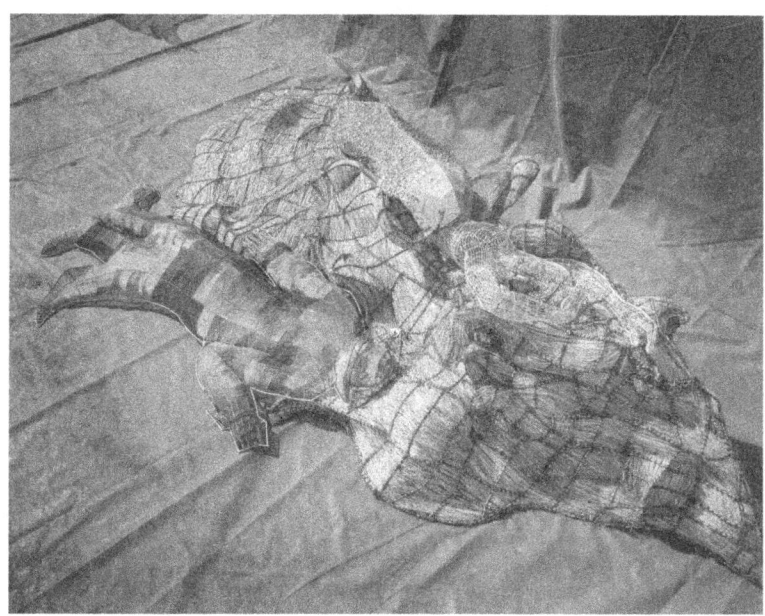

[#82] Andries Botha, *Baptism for the fallen...and those taken darkly*, 1991

wire woman figure emerges like a Jonah from a shiny fish sculpted out of bottle caps. Entitled "Baptism for the fallen . . . and those taken darkly" (1991) this installation plays with the reality that one person dies and a second person miraculously survives when it comes to apartheid life **and** being "taken" by the faith water of baptism, which sets you apart, the living and the dead.

[#83] Dayton Castleman, *The End of the Tunnel*, 2005

[#84] Dayton Castleman 2

— The Place for Imaginative Grit and Everlasting Art —

American Dayton Castleman witnesses in an old God-forsaken stone penitentiary outside Philadelphia with a very red thick steel pipe that threads its way up and down corridors [#83] and through walls surfacing out into the prison exercise yard where it finally scales the impossible wall [#84]: once over on the other side the red pipe (not a silver lining!) multiplies into a seven-fold set of organ pipes [#85] heralding a "Hallelujah!" freedom chorus! This site specific art piece is called "The End of the Tunnel" (2005) and epitomizes for me the christian mission of artwork: in **public**—not inside a church—publically focusing attention obliquely upon the surd of sin and the curse of punishment in our human lives while simultaneously instilling the promise of joy for which one may hope. Similarly Dutch Britt Wikström's bronze sculpture *Caritas* (2006) placed in the cancer ward waiting room at the University of Chicago hospital: the weak patient being helped on with his coat [#86] quietly turns to thank with wonder a friend who would perform such a little/momentous kind gesture of love. This kind of art, which breathes the persevering, healing hope of God's Holy Spirit, will last forever, I believe, as a living testimony of God's saving grace in us mortal vessels (Ecclesiastes 3:10–15).

[#85] Dayton Castleman 3

[#86] Britt Wikström, *Caritas*, 2006

(3) **Faithfully giveaway your gifts together and expect blessing upon**

–213–

your faulty diaconal work (Ecclesiastes 11:1–6).

I am very thankful to be here today because I am old enough to be your academic grandfather, since some of your profs were once my students, and it is best to have at least three generations of face-to-face contact, I think, to keep the collective memory of a world-and-life vision intact and pliable. If your student generation can come to trust, live into, and own the christian worldview distilled in *Living at the Crossroads* and presented by this conference at Redeemer, 2009 AD, then you don't have to start over from scratch, but can enter into a living Reformational christian faith-thought tradition that recognizes the encyclopedic, relative interrelated place of **all** fields of learning for service to God and neighbor, including aesthetic life and artistry. Join this communion with your questions? since we must beware of becoming parochial, in-grown, ideological, and keep in mind that the multigrain cultural bread we bake is formed to feed neighbors in a three-generational context worldwide, not to serve ourselves stale cake.

If you have the talent to make art like Toronto-based Joyce Recker's [see #14] *Murmurs of the heart* (1994), for God's sake, do it. And let its enigmatic wind-and-water smoothed stone mysteriously suspended over a nest of thatched wood chips, protected by a rib cage of sharp-pointed, purple-heart wood strips, help you imagine a lighted cathedral poised with the fragile egg/hard rock of an offering: such is human life before God. And if you cannot make art, remember we need counselors of imaginativity: youth leaders who specialize in joyous interactive fun games, journalists to write reviews of art gallery shows, musea curators able to turn their aloof treasures into a graphics library for education, and ordinary people informed and motivated to place artworks in their homes, in their worship environs, but especially in schools and public places.

French Georges Rouault's [#87] *Sarah* is for me a beacon of hopeful art-as-such. Rouault knew how to paint without judgment and with consummate mercy the brutalized shame of [see #8] *les filles des joie* who wandered the streets of Paris trying to survive. Our artists should not be blind to such misery either. Then maybe we will mature as an artistic faith community and have the seasoning to understand *Sarah,* whose name is associated with incredulous but deeply thankful "Isaac" laughter,[24] as we bravely smile through the tears of our days in anticipation of meeting the Christ returning soon at the crossroads we inhabit.

---

24 Genesis 18:1–5, 21:1–8, especially v. 6.

— The Place for Imaginative Grit and Everlasting Art —

[#87] Georges Rouault, *Sarah*, 1956

Background reading

Assmann, Jan. "Collective Memory and Cultural Identity," translated by John Czaplicka, in *New German Critique* 65 (Spring–Summer 1995): 125–133.
Baptist Reflections on Christianity and the Arts: Learning from beauty. A tribute to William L. Hendricks (Lewiston: Mellon, 1997).
Bartholomew, Craig and Thorsten Moritz, eds. *Christ and Consumerism: Critical reflections on the spirit of our age* (Carlisle: Pater Noster, 2000).
Bartholomew, Craig and Gideon Strauss, eds. *In the Fields of the Lord: A Calvin Seerveld reader* (Carlisle: Piquant, 2000).

Bernier, Christine. *L'Art au Musée: De l'œuvre à l'institution* (Paris: L'Harmattan, 2002).

Bogart, Michele H. *The Politics of Urban Beauty: New York and its Art Commission* (Chicago: University of Chicago Press, 2006).

Brown, Frank Burch. "How Important are the Arts, Theologically?" in *Arts, Theology, and the Church: New intersections*, eds. Kimberly Vrudry and Wilson Yates (Cleveland: Pilgrim Press, 2005), 29–45.

Buijs, Govert J. "The Promise of Civil Society," 10 page insert in *Contact* (Sioux Center: International Association for the Promotion of Christian Higher Education, 2005).

Bustard, Ned, ed. *It was Good Making Art to the Glory of God*, revised second edition (Baltimore: Square Halo Books, 2006).

Collins, Jim. *Uncommon Cultures: Popular culture and post-modernism* (New York: Routledge, 1989).

Crimp, Douglas. *On the Museum's Ruins*, with photographs by Louise Lawler (Cambridge: MIT Press, 1993).

Crow, Thomas. *Modern Art in the Common Culture* (New Haven: Yale University Press, 1996).

Derrida, Jacques. "Signature, Event, Context," translated by Samuel Weben and Jeffrey Mehlman (1977), in *Margins of Philosophy* (Chicago: University of Chicago Press, 1982).

Dollot, Louis. *Culture individuelle et culture de masse* (Paris: Presse Universitaire de France, 1974/1993).

Dooyeweerd, Herman. *In the Twilight of Western Thought: Studies in the pretended autonomy of philosophical thought* (Philadelphia: Presbyterian and Reformed, 1960).

Dyrness, William A. *Visual Faith: Art, theology, and worship in dialogue* (Grand Rapids: Baker, 2001).

Eagleton, Terry. *The Function of Criticism from the "Spectator" to Post-Structuralism* (London: Verso, 1984).

Goheen, Michael W. and Craig Bartholomew. *Living at the Crossroads: An introduction to Christian worldview* (Grand Rapids: Baker, 2008).

Knight, Cher Krause. *Public Art: Theory, practice and populism* (Oxford: Blackwell, 2008).

Miles, Malcolm. *Art, Space and the City: Public art and urban futures* (London: Routledge, 1997).

Myers, Kenneth A. *All God's Children and Blue Suede Shoes: Christians and popular culture* (Westchester: Crossway Books, 1989).

Poverty 101: From talk to walk (an in-depth conversation with those who live and work among the urban poor), John Perkins and others interviewed by Luke Seerveld and produced for the Christian Community Development Association, 2005. www.seerveldmedia.com/poverty

Seerveld, Calvin. "Antiquity Transumed and the Reformational Tradition: Which antiquity is transumed, how and why," in *In the Phrygian Mode:*

Neo-Calvinism, antiquity and the lamentations of reformed philosophy, ed. Robert Sweetman (New York: University Press of America, 2007), 231–265 {see *AH*: 79–116}.

——————. "Why Should a University Exist?" Insert of 10 pages in *Contact* (Sioux Center: International Association for the Promotion of Christian Higher Education, November 2000) {see *CE*: 29–58}.

Warwick, Rhona. *ARCADE Artists and Place-Making* (London: Black Dog, 2006).

Wink, Walter. *Unmasking the Powers: The invisible forces that determine human existence* (Philadelphia: Fortress, 1986).

Yates, Wilson. "The Theology and Arts Legacy," in *Arts, Theology and the Church: New Intersections*, eds. Kimberly Vrudry and Wilson Yates, (Cleveland: Pilgrim Press, 2005), 1–28.

Zuidema, Sytze U. "Pragmatism," in *Christian Perspectives* 1961 (Hamilton: Guardian, 1961), 133–157.

The Relation of the Arts to the Presentation of Truth

A NEW YORK artist I know is an embittered atheist. His wife and he, as Dutch Jews, were savagely abused by Nazi troops when they occupied Amsterdam. No Christian God could be around, he said, and let such horror take place.

Their one little daughter now in New York once asked him, "Why don't I go to church like the other kids, Daddy?"

"You want to go to church?" he said; "I'll take you to church."

On Sunday he took her to the Metropolitan Museum of Art. They entered and went sight-seeing through the galleries. "Is this church?" his girl asked.

"Yes."

Later on the little one said, "Can I see God?"

"His room is upstairs," answered her father, "but he's not in right now."

This brief history demonstrates what it means to lie. What happened there in New York was false not because language was used inconsistent with accepted conventions, nor even because the proposed information was contrary to verifiable fact: the lie to the episode lodges in this, that there was a deeply misleading, God-damning violation of the Truth, the Word of God, at work. God is always in to those looking for God, and that father is a false witness who keeps his children away.

A Biblical understanding of truth

To circumscribe Truth we do well to work at it from out of a biblical apriori, if we really intend to get our talk and thought and understanding of what is true cleaned up rather than held captive by centuries of apostate reflection.

According to the Scriptures, Truth is the way God does things. As God of Truth (2 Chronicles 15:3), Yahweh is the utterly steadfast, firmly establishing-covenanting God who has staying power for ever and ever

---

This essay originally appeared in *Truth and Reality*, Festschrift for H. G. Stoker (Braamfontein: DeJong, 1971), 161–175.

and ever. God's deeds show Truth in that they hold, have an ordering reality that is able to stand whatever traffic bears down on them. The Word of the Lord, at its very funding bottom, is epitomized by Truth (Psalm 119:160) because that Word God speaks, whether the Law at Sinai or the Commands in the beginning, is completely trustworthy, certain of fruit, effecting what will last. Wherever the Truth appears, there is a God-revealing, a faithful healing dynamic that enriches those who are responding to its development. This is why the biblical expression "to stand and walk in the Truth" is pregnant with meaning:

> Bring me along till I am walking in your Truth (Psalm 25:5). Covenanting God! teach me your Way so that I may walk in your Truth; pull my heart together till it fear (only) your name (Psalm 86:11).

To experience or declare what is True gets one actively caught up in the fabric of protecting, strengthening, senses-opening communion with the almighty holy One.

By contrast, the usual pagan and secular conceptions of Truth are poverty-stricken indeed. The most it has been conceived to be is a relation of correspondence sustained by a mental affirmation with noetic forms, like capital B Beauty, for example. The scholastic version put εἴδη like Beauty in God's mind and permitted well-meaning Christians a little mystical leeway if they wanted to think God's thoughts after God to get at truth. The modern reduction of such Realism is simply: determine whether the proposition is verifiable by a sensible matter of fact; if so, you are in business concerning truth. More limited God-less conceptions of truth have pegged it as a determinable quality of rectitude inhering in certain kinds of human acts or sometimes as just the function of consistency in a given person's activities. But no matter which, whether it would be an exacting objectivistic theory of approximation or plain subjectivistic sophistry, neither allows much breathing room for discussing "true . . . art." In fact, the most prevalent notion current, that true and false are characteristics only of propositional affirmations,[1] or that "true" is a concessive signal like "yes, yes," the cat is on the mat: such rigorous reductions of Truth to manipulations of logical properties and language games asphyxiates this very topic and stops one from facing the relation of art to the presentation of Truth.

You always get that when biblical light has gone out, been extinguished from careful reflection about reality: distortion, oversimplification, checkmate. When the biblically revealed heart-depth to man is not

---

[1] John Hospers. *Meaning and Truth in the Arts* (Hamden: Archon, 1964), 158–160.

seen, he gets split into a body and soul at variance. When the Truth-depth to human experience is not recognized, one's consciousness gets split into factual knowledge versus opinion—which leaves art such a bad choice artists have often tried to jump over both horns of the dilemma and claim revelational character for their pedestrian work. This stymied epistemological situation concerning art in philosophy has sifted down into the "common sense" of the Occident so that today, like as not, if you are talking art and truth, people will mean that art can be "true-to-life," photographically matter-of-fact, or "true art" has certain "religious values," vague, ineffable, but "spiritual" and high-fallutin, most appropriate, if you like that sort of thing. The idea is that "truth" is an attribute affixed to art, under certain conditions, and sometimes lacking. But such a conception will never confront us with what actually is the state of affairs with art in God's world.

Again, according to the Scriptures, Truth is the matrix within which God's creatures are to live and move and have their meaning. Truth is accepted, lived, acted out, or disobeyed; it is not something there that can be just conceptually grasped or mistaken. The Word of God incarnate, Jesus Christ, is called the Truth (John 5:33); He is the Way, the Truth, the Life wherein God's gracious love and judgment is given (John 14:6). God "wants all men and women to be saved," writes Paul (1 Timothy 2:4), "that is, come into an experiential discernment of the Truth," so that they might be consecrated, prayed Jesus, truly set apart (John 17:17–19). "If you stay within my Word," said Christ, "you will experience the Truth, and the Truth shall make you free" . . . from sin! (John 8:31–32, 34).

Godly revealed reality, the Truth, gloriously manifesting in law-bound ways the just Grace of the Lord: this is what calls us humans to a response of allegiance, love, exhilarated involvement. And that is the biblical explanation for the jealous, exclusive character of Truth, so out of taste with our latitudinarian age. Untruth is not nothing. Lack of truth is not zero; opposite the great Amen! is not a blank, but when it comes to the fundamental habit of a man, silence, ignorance, not-truth (albeit different in measure from intentional deceit) is still nose-thumbing at the Lord God. Because we humans are made to walk in the Truth, for a person not to present the Truth is a damnable business, anathema! enslaving and darkening human consciousness (cf. John 8:44). This is a biblical understanding of what is at stake in the matter of Truth.

Horizons and ways of human knowing

When it comes to human knowing, that integral act of the full bodied person apprehending objects with understanding, the first thing to be said is that the most fundamental, the largest, final horizon within which human knowing necessarily takes place is the Truth. No knowledge ever just is. The fact that an individual human subject gets to know an object structured according to creational order is all pointing directly to the Truth within which the whole operation is framed and which it is to embody.

That is, human knowing of trees and women, hedgehogs and stones, has built-in to the noetic enterprise an unbreakable, cohering ontic relation that gives the whole object trustworthily to the full human subject. Trees and women are not only accessible to the act of knowledge, but things are set up so by God that knowable objects are indissolubly bound together with knowers and are given gloriously open to discovery. The fact that ordinary human knowing enjoys a rich involvement in becoming acquainted with things in their full, complexly simple wholeness (something the Bible recognizes when it says Abram went in and "knew" his wife Sarah)—this unaffected, natural wholeness that is a mark of "everyday" human knowing experience witnesses to the kind of reliable, integrating bond the Truth, the Word of God, holds bounding and structuring human knowledge.

This creational grip of the Truth also holds firm for knowing that denies being conditioned by God-created structure and ascribes creative meaning-guaranteeing power to its own purely human thought processes. But proud theorizing, fragmentized learning, even sinful thinking cannot sunder the creational, time-enduring bond linking subjects and objects in the cosmos that makes knowledge possible. At bottom this matter of fact, a handiwork of the Lord, reveals God's provident faithfulness for all men and women (cf. 1 Timothy 4:10).

Given such a context, it is very important to distinguish the different horizons to knowledge, the varying structural apriori's that limit and require obedience of human knowledge.[2] Beside the root law of Truth are what I shall call the test of cosmic correctness and the criterion of accuracy.

1. Achieved knowledge is *true* if the product develops Christ's lordship of the world (rather than the devil's) and pleases God.

---

2 Cf. especially paragraphs 2–3 in chapter IV ("The structural horizon of human experience and of created 'earthly reality'") in Herman Dooyeweerd: *A New Critique of Theoretical Thought*, volume II (Amsterdam: H. J. Paris, 1955).

If the act and product of knowing is manifestly Holy Spirit-filled and shows God's redeeming presence—how light God's yoke of love is to live under in the world, what a world-wide, glorious, earthy prospect is open for the adopted children of God—then you could cautiously call it true knowledge, one that will lead you into the Truth. If a critical understanding and sense of sin permeates the knowledge, and if it has an edifying thrust, one that builds up in the faith those who receive it, then that knowledge is standing, working, being established in Truth.

2. Knowledge gained is *correct* if the relative states of affairs known are kept relative, limited, related to the rest of the world in its (proper) place.

Abraham Kuyper says that sin tends to make us be mistaken about reality so that we absolutize or minimize what is known beyond its rightful place. John Calvin stated too that unless knowledge serve God in Truth it shall turn into idolatry. That is so. But if the meaning gotten at is still apprehended in a fashion that subjects it to its temporal context (willy-nilly formed by Truth), to some specific law-norm for its functioning, and therefore upholds the defined relationality of matters, then it is meaningful to call such knowledge correct knowledge, for it has been constrained by cosmic order.

3. Knowledge obtained is *accurate* if the subject's knowing agrees with the structural laws (needing to be more-or- less correctly posited by humans in the light of Truth) concerning a particular feature or function of a knowable object.

The result of such approximating discernment will be accurate knowledge.

One might compare these horizons of knowledge with the range of horizons and distinctness Old Testament prophecies have, how they deal with the immediate situation, also reach out to the return of the Jews from captivity, really eclipsing the coming of Christ into the picture, both Christ's incarnation and the second coming. Human knowledge has these varying dimensions because God has varying holds on God's creation: God gives a thing its individual identity, bound by many universe-wide orderings, all before God's holy face. So the shadows of the varied encompassing horizons superimpose themselves, as it were, on every knowing subject and situation. As a result, human knowledge becomes a very complicated affair in which men and women may fail, partly or wholly.

These varying horizons hold for all the kinds of human world-knowing activity there be, whether it be scientific x-ray type knowledge or knowing that is not scientific.

Accurate scientific description of a given tree's metabolism processes may be correctly restricted to the biological frame of reference and be related biotically to the rest of life as it impinges on the actual tree. But theoretical, biological analysis can also be set incorrectly into a hypothesis that posits, as Huxley does, that protoplasmic flow of life is a continuum identical for plant-animal-man. Such distorted biologistic knowledge does not need too much rope before it has hanged itself on the Lie that life is absolutely sacred and God is expendable.

On the other hand, it is also possible for a good Christian believer to know truly that trees are planted by God and ultimately distinct from animal life, yet have such an inaccurate knowledge of their organic workings you would not trust him to graft the two fruit trees in your front yard.

A man could also naively look outdoors and see a row of hickory trees he planted once to conserve the earth, keep it replenished. He knows offhand that the sun and water God sent during the season makes them grow strong enough to withstand the winter cold. It crosses his mind what good logs one of them would make in the fire place, although they stand there in the autumn, bare of leaves, so majestically straight. A man could be hanged on such trees, whether a runaway slave or the Savior. How will it be when those hickories clap their hands as Isaiah prophesied (55:12)? And so on and on a person might truly muse about trees.

But a man's everyday cognizance of his hickory trees could be mistaken if he spent an inordinate amount of time fertilizing, trimming, babying his lovely hickory trees, the way Paul says some men spend too much time on their wives. Such incorrect awareness of your prize trees could grow until you practically worship them, like a fetish, as if one finger became your whole hand; and then your knowledge would have become vain, distorted, untrue.

The point then is this: the different ways humans are busy knowing things are all subject to the varying structural horizons that condition them all. While it is so that the rainbow-rich nature of creation, as manifestation of the Truth, is grasped only by a childlike, obedient faith in the Lord of creation, nevertheless: as a matter of fact, because every human inhabits God's world, created states of affairs can be apprehended by unbelievers as well as by Christ-believers. Things and events are apprehended by Christ-believers searching *out of* the Truth: things and events are mis-taken, taken awry, apprehended accurately perhaps, but distortedly, if not downrightly unrightly, unrighteously, by those who disbelieve the Truth.

Truth is a matter of direction, thrust, ordering dynamic that is shaping historically the developing human subject. Therefore you can have false, incorrect, brilliantly accurate knowledge about metabolism; you can have damnably good political savvy—which in spite of itself witnesses to God's ordering of creation—but is not pleasing to the LORD God. Those who make believe the Truth is not there are not therefore ignoramuses. All knowledge, no matter how God-damning, is also caught up in unfolding our Lord's creation. But only humbled knowledge, obedient within the religious perspective of Truth, is counted for righteousness and makes God happy. It is knowledge obedient to the Truth, not correct, cultural sacrifices, nor epistemological successes either, that pleases the Lord.

One must be aware that there is always the tendency inside knowledge to grow rich in Grace or proudly shrivel up, impoverished. Art, as imaginative, symbolically qualified knowledge, faces the same conditioning.

Art: imaginative symbolical knowledge

Art, christianly conceived, is not something esoteric. Just because artistry demands training and its performance catapults at an audience the result of much, specially gifted work, does not make art something mysterious and hard to understand.

There are no biblical grounds either for the usual talk about artistic "creation." Comparisons between God as capital A Creator Artist and the human as small, image-of-God creator artists are only speculative and misleading. To turn analysis of "what now is human artistic activity?" into a theo-logical discussion on the unique "creativity" of God is no help at all in determining the nature and place of art on the earth. Such a would-be christian approach is caught in the age-old trap of *analogia entis*. Once you work in that problematics you have to be a Roman catholic casuist to escape the heresy of mysticism, deism, or a covert blasphemy. Man is not God's image, a finite parallel to an infinite Perfection. Only Christ is a spitting image of God. The fact that humans are made *in* the image of God means that men and women carry inescapably around with them a restless sense of allegiance to. . . . And this structural, worshipping restlessness remains to plague them until they finally, as Augustine puts it, are rested with commitment in the Truth. But *imago Dei* and "creation" obfuscate understanding art because it looks too hard, and overlooks the limited, serviceable, *knowing* craftsmanship character to artistic activity.

An artist, like anybody else, is aware of what surrounds them, whether it be the breathing of men, the hurt of some woman, or a blossoming apple tree. And like any other human Subject who responds to reality and tries to capture and present the meaning of what one apprehends, the artist too translates the reality perceived into a product embodying what he or she understood its meaning to be. What sets artistic knowledge off from scientific concepts and ordinary nonscientific notions, insights, and judgments is that the artistic product has a suggestive, symbolizing finish to its knowing operation and the results of the process.

The artist addresses oneself to something in a specially focused way that allows all kinds of playful associations and related meanings to crowd in, get juxtaposed and integrated with what is under intuited scrutiny. The artist calls to attention in capital, cursive letters, as it were, what usually flits by in reality as fine print. There is a type of exploratory, uncovering, at-the-frontier element prevalent in an artistic probing of meanings. Its imaginative character consists not in being "fictional" but in presenting whatever reality is fascinating the artist, presenting that meaning *symbolically*, with emphases highlighting and setting in relief certain crucial nuances of the thing, event, or action grappled with. Having such suggestive control qualifying the perception, the artist aims at heightening, intensifying the meaning obtained, not making it signpost "plain"; and that very elusive, artifactual presentation of the meaning is what makes art "imaginative."

The fact that the constructs produced by this kind of specially qualified, aesthetically normed grasp of reality are often couched in pre-analytic and pre-lingual media, like gestures, colors, sounds, and shapes, does not indicate such products are void of knowledge content. It simply points out how different the mode is in which aesthetically qualified action conveys meaning from the way in which conceptually determined knowledge operates. There is no reason at all to force products of artistic endeavor into categories of either "incompleted cogitation" or "ineffable experience." The ways humans grapple, learn, and show an acquaintance with reality are modally much richer than the single analytic way of making distinctions. When a human consciously assumes an imaginative stance toward acts or things and gets busy in the aesthetically led act of symbolizing, then he or she is busy, along with the results of their work, subject to the horizons of knowledge just as biologists and hickory tree observers are.

Once one is freed from the idea that Truth is logical consistency or an imitational correspondence between concepts and object, and once one is also extricated from the supposition that knowledge has to be analytically qualified, then one's theory is saved from countless dilemmas in explaining that the metaphorical ambiguity and nonrepresentational symbolic suggestiveness of art is indeed a glorious vehicle for knowledge and possible embodiment of the Truth.

In fact, the imaginative per-ception of reality and its peculiarly symbolically focused expression of the artist subject's response to the world *in* (or out-of) the Truth is the peculiar wonder of artistry. The suggestiveness and coherent symbolical richness of artistic production does not make it unreliable: that would be so only if scientific precision and casual pedestrian notice of events had a corner on accurate, correct, and true knowledge—which they do not. Symbolically enriched knowledge may take more time to read and unravel to see how it stands before the Truth, but that is its glory, not a weakness.

The skeleton in our epistemological closet is not the imaginative suggestiveness of artistic prehension but rather sin! The anti-creational, ruinous power of sin to break down whatever it shadows, affects art as well as science and everyday knowledge, but does not plague art more so than the others. The distortion, deception, and aimlessness sin works into what God's creatures know of the world and themselves and even God's Grace must not be identified with the pre-distinct, "pre-clear" subtlety and undifferentiated complexity of symbolical knowledge. Beclouding of knowledge that sin effectuates is one of perspective, not structuration. Because ideas are clear does not make them true; because concepts are logically distinct does not give them necessarily the status of correct knowledge: because apprehension of meaning is *aesthetically* ambiguous (multi-referential) does not make the understood result bad or inaccurate—it depends on the measure of religious obedience! or disobedience spiriting the symbolizing product.

An illustration from painting and from song
One could document many times the thesis that historically, as a matter of fact, art has worked out of the Truth or the Lie and been subject specifically to the cosmic horizons of knowledge, while maintaining its peculiar artistic (suggestive) integrity. I shall just sketch in for reference a well-known item from Mondrian's painting and make a note on the song and lyrics collaborated on by Kurt Weill and Bertolt Brecht.

The tree portraits Mondrian (1872–1944) painted and drew before

1912 show a fascinating preoccupation with the range of plant vitality, organic growth, atmospheric involvement, their earthy, dirt-situated, arbory and blossoming fruit-bearing reality. A joyful, visionary comprehension of trees comes through even when the tree "figure" has been dissolved into just verdant colors and billowing shapes.

The Red Tree painting [#88][3] looks almost like a burning bush . . . that is not consumed. It has sinewy energy, as if you see the blood coursing hard through its arteries—an almost anatomical treatment, so you can see it is not a quiet, gnarled, placid, decorative piece. The red tree has vigor, heart, a strong root-like character. It has a Van Gogh intensity to its life beat; there is excitement. Its branches catch and cradle patches of the sky and act friendly enough for a flock of birds to rest on and sing before they move on. It is a hard-working tree, too burdened to be gallant but roughhewn and workaday in its glory. The growing lines and gusts of blue and tangled pattern are not like mussed up hair but show that there is a lot of unfinished business to do for this tree.

Around 1915, however, Mondrian came into the grip of a cultural dynamic that emaciated his painting of creation and had him experimenting in skilled architectonic formulas of black horizontal and vertical lines, gray and white spaces, and the basic complementary colors. Whereas formerly he had used line, space, figure, movement, mass, and color to disclose suggestively, for example, rich meanings trees have, in *De Stijl* he deliberately stopped curves ("too emotional"), modulated colors ("sentimental"), and ascetically tried to reach universal rational patterns with the elements that make up painting—lines, planes, colors. [#89][4] After 1918 he used a little more color, but there is no play to it, no brush strokes visible to suggest tension, life, the world. Purely geometric surfaces, sometimes absorbing blue light, sometimes red, and that is it.

There is a kind of confession to it all, a plea to have our pell-mell, technologically complex zoom of an age straighten itself out, clean and simplify its life, recapture what is elemental. This may be why Mondrian's late style so influenced the modern glass and steel line of architecture. But the point is: after 1915 Mondrian turned his back, with a religiously

---

3 The Mondrian/Holtzman Trust, c/o HCR International USA, does not permit images of Mondrian's work to be rendered in black and white. A full-color image of *Avond: The Red Tree* (1908–1910) can be accessed at this url: http://www.gemeentemuseum.nl/collection/item/1160

4 The Mondrian/Holtzman Trust, c/o HCR International USA, does not permit images of Mondrian's work to be rendered in black and white. A full-color image of *Composition with Large Red Plane, Yellow, Black, Grey and Blue* (1921) can be accessed at this url: http://www.gemeentemuseum.nl/collection/item/6496

Spinozistic, consequent rationalism, on a world of *Red Cloud* (1907) and *The Red Tree,* and froze his knowledge puritanically to color-less compositions of lines and panes. Only near his death did *Broadway Boogie-woogie* (1943) betray a sense of what was lost.

Brecht-Weill's "Havana Song" and "Alabama Song" (1928–29) in *The Rise and Fall of the State of Mahagonny* epitomize their trenchant grasp of evil surrounding them.

> *Ach, bedenken Sie, Herr Jakob Schmidt,*
> *Ach, bedenken Sie was man für dreissig Dollar kriegt,*
> *Zehn Paar Strümpfe, und sonst nichts . . .*
> *Ich bin aus Havana*
> *Meine Mutter war eine Waise.*
> *Sie sagte oft zu mir,*
> *„Mein Kind, verkauf Dich nicht*
> *für ein paar Dollar Noten sowie ich es tat;*
> *„Schau Dir an was aus mir geworden ist."*
> *Ach, bedenken Sie, Herr Jakob Schmidt,*
> *Ach, bedenken Sie, Herr Jakob Schmidt . . . .*
> *O! Show us the way to the next whiskey bar!*
> *. . . O! Moon of Alabama, we now must say goodbye . . .*
> *. . . and have whiskey or know why!*

The melody snugly reinforces the lyrics. It has a half-cabaret, half-tenement character, sensually pulling you along (O! moon of Alabama) or tenderly, sorrowfully, saxaphonely sobbing (Ach, bedenken Sie, Herr Jakob Schmidt), always with the abrupt, jerky ending that dumps you as you start to relax, with a sarcastic laugh.

The prostitute is a bit of reality Brecht keeps coming unforgettably back to: a human being with promise . . . violated! An evil, malicious predicament! Brecht has no prostitute-with-a-heart-of-gold romanticism. Don't kid me, he says, this is a business and I accuse those with the money! they are the guilty ones. The girl is a victim. Hence the bottomlessly sad plight of daughter like poor mother in the hands of the next moon-struck, touristy, away-from-his-bourgeois-wife, American capitalist who wants whiskey, women, and song. Ruthless, crass materialists, all in the name of Western civilized Christian freedom . . .

Fake! says the syncopated, jazz-beat rhythm and cliché- ridden, colloquial language as it mocks symbolically those wide-roaming adventurers who plunder the morals of the poor and down-trodden.

Both artists Mondrian and Brecht-Weill demonstrate significant artistry in these examples mentioned and are symbolically coherent and articulate. (Sometimes Brecht violates the aesthetic norm by trespassing into propaganda and Mondrian's later work often seems to be alphabetizing rather than symbolizing.) But what world purview, allegiance, and slice of grasped knowledge shows up inside the flesh and blood of their specific arts, in the colors and compositioned shapes, the melodied word?

The beginning of an answer would go something like this: When Mondrian deliberately turns away from the red-tree artistry that presents a world with God-enlarging consciousness, that shows trees in their glory albeit plagued by sin waiting for the *eschaton:* when he leaves this bewondering expression of created things for the promise of mathematicized color and line, then he has impoverished his art and saved over only a barren world. His artistry becomes content with presenting less than the Truth, remains ignorant of the rich diversity of the cosmos, and gradually puzzles accurately with geometricized components of the painter's trade. The open, correct sharpness of his original, gifted vision gradually becomes darkened, stereotyped, because of a considered, primitivistically reduced openness to God's world.

Brecht and Weill's songs, from the start, are not conceived in Truth. Their eye does correctly spot how a bodiless Christianity ruins the creaturliness God made, and their keen sense of evil accounts for the accurate bittersweet meaning of the song—they are simultaneously attracted and repulsed by the humanistic, free disorder seen at work in society. But Brecht and Weill never come further than a goddamit to the evil all around. They do not know the biblical meaning of sin, and therefore do not have the artistic strength and vision to be compassionate rather than just pitying. A certain largeness of vision keeps the symbolic mastery gesticulate, but it stays stymied. Because they do not honor creational norms for us humans, the threat of prosaic preachment, and a life interpreted merely as tossed animal instincts constantly threatens to undo the insights they have been granted.

Concluding thought and directive to Christ's body

The relation of the arts to the presentation of Truth is a complicated one because the creational setup of the Lord is complex and because historical development under our Merciful Judge of a God is real. Christ-believing human knowledge, set in the Truth, is relativized *by* its temporality (not *to* its temporality); and unbelieving, disbelieving, untrue human knowledge is *sustained by* its temporality.[5] Christ's Grace continues to show the redeeming Creator God's glory to men and women, but it is blindly seen by the unbeliever (no eye of faith), being suppressed in unrighteousness

---
5   Ibid 561.

or ignored, to one's own damnation and the sterilization of his art.

Art as human knowledge is indeed either a true witness to the Lord or a betrayal of the Truth; but we must not deal with either art or Truth abstractly, forgetting the dynamic to the matter. At its root knowledge is vanity or fear of the Lord, says Ecclesiastes; the direction of Truth or Lie conditions correct knowledge, which frames accurate knowledge. There is no air-tight, (neutral) accurate knowledge, more-or-less correct, plus-or-minus true insights. But human knowledge and art too is always en route. Without a biblically directed faith knowledge that has one standing in the Truth, one's knowing grip on the world has it disintegrating: you can count on that, also for art!

It must also be said: knowledge with a true horizon (because the Subject accepts = lives God's Word) must be bodied forth with correct shape and executed in accurate detail or one is not a faithful workman of Jesus Christ. That is, unless men and women, according to their talents and despite their sin, give earthy historical body to the vision of our Lord's rule upon the earth in art, if they are artists in Christ's body, they then have the dead faith without works James talks about.

Without a working vision of the Truth in Western culture, art has become increasingly a burden and a highly civilized seduction. Today the direction of art untouched by the reforming light of the Truth wavers between superficial amusement (robbed of its "logical service"), bootless, polished technique (a would-be noncommittal routine), and an evil, psychedelic regression, casting helplessly about for the original hallelujah fabric of art. Our critically Christian left hand needs to reveal the insidious God-damning workings that are affecting human consciousness in its leisure. To the pure all things are pure does not mean that to those with the Holy Spirit nothing is carnal. We must test whether the art before us be of God, revealing God's creational richness or not. Art is not excluded from the test of Truth as if it were simply a collected insight in a realm outside of verifiability. Art has stigmatic noetic character for those who fashion, perform, or undergo it.

But we adopted sons and daughters of God must also use our right arm. We were not made creatures only to criticize, and we were never given the leeway to pray that we be taken out of this world. We who believe that Yahweh is the LORD of heaven and earth, and that God's Will must be done *on earth* as it is done in heaven, must live by faith. Cultural endeavor, including art, is now done in tears because of the Evil one and the weight of sin that plagues the world, including our own lives; but we may never abandon the world of the psalms to disbelievers. We *cannot* deny our cultivating task. Therefore, despite the humbling weakness of our hallelujahs, we children afoot in God's theatre must be still and trust the leading of the Truth, put our hand to the cultural plow of art, not looking back, putting our hope only in the Lord. And we must show those ignorant of art the vital, critical importance it is playing and shall play to the third and fourth generation of those who hold to God's covenanting promises; otherwise we will win the battle of confession of faith in church, but lose the war for the believers' life time.

A Few Background Sources

de Rougemont, Denis. "Religion and the Mission of the Artist," in *Spiritual Problems in Contemporary Literature,* ed. S. R. Hopper (New York: Harper, 1957), 173–83.

Dooyeweerd, Herman. "The Epistemological Problem in the light of the Cosmonomic Idea," *A New Critique of Theoretical Thought* (Amsterdam: H. J. Paris, 1955), II: 429–598.

Holtrop, Philip. "Introductory, selected comments on the nature of Truth," paraphrase and comment upon J. H. Vrielink's dissertation, *Het waarheidsbegrip* (1958). Unpublished mimeograph, 1964. 20 pp.

Hospers, John. *Meaning and Truth in the Arts* (Hamden, Connecticut: Archon, 1964).

Jordan, Robert. "To Tell the Truth," *The Christian Scholar* 47 (1964): 295–314.

Morgan, Douglas N. "Must Art Tell the Truth?" *Journal of Aesthetics and Art Criticism* 28:1 (1967): 17–27.

Quell, Kittel, and Bultmann. "ἀλήθεια," *Theologisches Wörterbuch,* 1: 233–51.

Rookmaaker, Hans R. *Art and the Public Today* (1968), in *The Complete Works of Hans Rookmaaker* Volume 5 (Carlisle, UK: Piquant, 2003): 167–203.

Seerveld, Calvin. *A Christian Critique of Art and Literature* (Sioux Center: Dordt College Press, 1995).

Steenland, Mary. "Provisional Analysis of Aesthetic Knowledge and Aesthetic/Symbolic Objectification." Unpublished baccalaureate thesis for Hope College, Michigan, 1968. 34 pp. with 4 charts and 16 illustrations.

Van der Walt, P. D. *Die Calvinis en die Kuns* (Potchefstroom: Instituut vir Bevordering van Calvinisme, n.d.).

A Turnabout in Aesthetics to Understanding

Dear People of God, and Guests who may be strangers:

Somewhat like a *Qohelet* of Old Testament times to a folk gathering I should like festively to tell you today what I hope to be about academically at the Institute for Christian Studies, and then pledge before God and yourselves to carry out that calling as a man of flesh and blood open to the leading of the Spirit of our Lord.

To begin I read you the biblical poem called Psalm 147. What you hear now is the Word of God:

> Hallelu Yahweh!
> for it is just a good thing to play upon strings and sing to our God!
> Doxologies are great! simply the right thing to be going on!
> because the LORD God Yahweh IS building up Jerusalem,
> God IS collecting the scattered outcasts of Israel, getting them back together!
> The LORD IS healing those whose religion-gut was ripped to fibers;
> their aching bruises and open wounds God is binding up with gauze
> —the God who determined how many stars there be and gave them all names—
> Great is our Lord! inexhaustible Might! God's penetrating insight cannot be quantified!
>
> The LORD God helps straighten up again those who were forcibly pressed down,
> and God knocks right down to the ground those who thumb their nose in God's face.
> Get up and sing responsively thank-you songs to the LORD God Yahweh!
> Play for our God with guitar [—the Lord!]
>   who tucks the blue sky in with a cover of clouds,

This ICS inaugural address was originally published separately by the Institute for Christian Studies in Toronto in 1974 (26 pages).

>   who faithfully makes rain ready for the earth,
>   who lets the mountain sides grow green with grass,
>   who gives the wild beast what it needs to eat,
>   even the baby raven what it caws for.
> But the LORD is not impressed with the strength of a war horse;
> the athletically muscled calf of a man is not what God is after:
> what makes the LORD God Yahweh happy are men and women who
>   stand in awe of God,
> that is, those who are expecting great things from GOD's covenantal
>   love!
>
> Doxology the Lord, Jerusalem! Hallelu your God, O Zion!
> Yes, let God make the cross bars of your city gates impregnable;
> let God give your children wholeness, the coming generation of
>   your community.
> [Doxology the Lord!] the One who can circumscribe your territory
>   with shalom,
> Who may give you more than enough of the best of grain,
> Who lets God's proclaiming Word go stretch to the earth
> —quick as a flash runs God's commanding Word!—
>   giving away snow like wool,
>   scattering hoarfrost about as if it were dust,
>   jaggering God's ice down in splinters
>   (Can anyone withstand the freezing cold ice of the Lord?)—
>   but let God speak out the Word and the Word melts the ice.
>   If the LORD blow God's wind back and forth, it ripples the wa-
>   ter. The LORD has made God's Word particularly clear to Jacob;
> God's ordinances and commands for what's right God has been
>   making known specially to Israel—
> God has not dealt this way with any other folk:
> they simply do not know the LORD's ordinances for what is right!
>
> Oh, yes! Hallelu the Covenanting God Yahweh! Hallelujah!

Quite simply and very seriously, it is within the world setting of this God—the God of snow and justice, healing and playing instruments—it is within the cosmic, Worded wonder of this redeeming God I wish to find a home and a task and a new tack for professional, teaching research in aesthetics.

Historical predicament

To be frank, aesthetics, as a scientific discipline, has been largely suspect to professional thinkers ever since it got laboriously born through the midwifery of dilettante virtuosi of taste and poetic criticism in the eighteenth century. Baumgarten's coinage of aesthetics for "the science of sensitive knowledge," a lower down form of knowledge theory (*gnoseologici inferior*) stuck.[1] Although Kant wedged aesthetic judgment firmly into the breach of his influential philosophical problematics, and German Idealists like Schelling made aesthetic intuition the capstone of philosophy, more sober logic-heads prevailed. How can reflection about something so tenuous as "intuitive sensitivity" or so subjective as "beauty"—if that is what aesthetics is all about—how can reflection on such matters show the rigor needed to be scientific? Especially when nineteenth century Positivism revived the old seventeenth century mechanistic, logical fix with a new vengeance and demanded that any serious investigation—psychology, sociology, or whatever—test out with an experimental laboratory method or purely mathematical logical calculation before it could be admitted to the bar of science and speak with the authority of having valid knowledge: aesthetics had to pretend at science by becoming some kind of clinical tabulation of sensations or flounder in the cultural backwater.

That dominant Positivism in scholarship came to seem somewhat hard-nosed and superficial to the twentieth century European mentality after two world wars had been fought on its grounds. If you want to compress what counts into a logic-tight, mental closet and sweep the rest of human culture under the rug of "the emotive," you may get a tidy room, but it is quite bare, sterilized. Yet that severely Positivistic spirit, with its inherited prejudice against a bona fide aesthetics, has persisted, especially in Anglo-Saxon circles of philosophy. It was pointed out once in *Mind* (1951), British philosophers of that prestigious journal have for generations acted as Philistine toward aesthetics as the most narrow-minded christian stereotype who rejects aesthetic theory and art out of hand as of little or of no particular importance, witness the want of space given it (not without reason, of course) in their pages.[2] Since about 1960 the tolerance level for aesthetics has risen among professional philosophers and sundry scientists by dint of aesthetics' having its own journals, international congresses, and de facto age; but aesthetics theory does well even today to disguise itself in analytic probing of concepts possibly useful for talk about art, or it runs the risk in the halls of scientific academia

---

1 "Aesthetica (theoria liberalium artium, gnoseologia inferior, ars pulcre cogitandi, ars analogi rátionis,) est scientia cognitionis sensitivae" (#1) in Alexander Gottlieb Baumgarten, *Aesthetica* [1750] (New York: Georg Olms, 1970), 1.
2 J.A. Passmore, "The Dreariness of Aesthetics," *Mind* 60 (no. 239, 1951): 318.

of seeming to be a displaced orphan, not to say, a professional bastard.

But the historical predicament of a general homelessness to aesthetics goes much deeper than winning accreditation before an established elite, and to find itself as a fruitful discipline, I dare say, aesthetics shall need a much more solid foundation than learning to play the latest logical game in fashion.

For centuries the reality of aesthetic life and the normal workaday service of art in society has been misconceived by the theoreticians and other cultural leaders in Western civilization, including sometimes the great master artists themselves. No wonder, if aesthetic reality has been denied existence theoretically and art has been idolized or categorically damned for its presence in human-kind by influential spokesmen, no wonder you have trouble on your hands in those areas, afortiori in reflection upon such matters. Whenever a facet of creation—aesthetic, sexual, cultic, labor—is denied its due, or whenever a definite task integral to the cultural response of humans is mistaken, people trundled along under such mismade vision begin to limp, actually limp and bodily stumble-bum around in God's world. And it is that kind of fundamental, grass-roots distortion, encrusted by years of learned confusion, compounded by traditions of pride and error amid all the brilliance that has left us out of joint here and makes it so difficult for aesthetics to find its home in the encyclopedia of the sciences.

I do not intend to detail the complex ins and outs of what has led to this predicament—hangups always have a long history—but there are certain crucial developments that need to be recognized so that any turnabouts in aesthetics indeed be toward understanding, setting the root things straight, and not be just another ballyhooed twist and turn out of a superficial dead end.

For example, there have been times, especially long ago, among tribes and peoples, when the whole societal life showed a fascinating, mythopoeic cast. No science, no general theoretic investigation was done; nobody definite, no specific institution called the shots in such "archaic cultures," as historians call them today, although priests and chiefs and bards who sang the epical sagas of the heroic feats of their race were partially distinct as posts of authority: the whole, undeveloped, usually agriculturally settled life of the people was typified by the periodic feasts and quasi liturgical plays they held with music, song, and dance, to appease daemonic powers and worship Mana. That is, characteristic and epitomizing a stage of certain undifferentiated cultures has been a kind of sacrally veiled aesthetic life experience, which they unembarrassedly, bluntedly trusted.

I mention it not to give credence to the old Durkheim-Levy Bruhl thesis of sociologistic evolution, and certainly not to support those who are horrified at the disintegrating, barren rigidity secularization has brought to culture and want to remythologize our life. No, the fact that in the devolutionary vicissitudes of apostate society, under the encircling, darkening closure of human life shut off from adoring its Creator, the fact that the built-in push we humans have to initiate control of our surroundings, once engaged, triggers this vaguely aesthetic sensibility, however distorted: that genetic fact of unfolding human society just documents how abidingly real and native to humanity is an aesthetic life dimension, quite distinct from "art" as we know it.

Again, that condition of an indigenous, fermentative aesthetic activity in human society is not something to be shucked, gotten beyond as unbefitting a scientifically responsible mentality (the melioristic position of Cornford *c.s.*). It is also not evidence (as Johan Huizinga claims) for making "sacred play" index to the most pure, complete exercise of human nature[3]—as if what is primeval be normative. Also, any sustained move to recapture that mythologizing aesthetic cohesion to life is simply stupidly burying your head in the historical sand! Because next to the powerful, integrating biblical faith perspective of Psalm 147 and its open, gritty reality, the mythopoeic cohesion of yore is merely a spider web. And only when aesthetic life is freed from every mythicized mongrelization will it be able to laugh and unobtrusively feed our whole societal life complex with a liberating surprise and praise, unconstrained.

The Greek polis setup, as you might expect, exorcized mythopoeic world-and-life views out of civilized existence, so to speak. At least the demythologizing of aesthetic life that the formidable Plato and Aristotle effected, canonizing in its stead a mathematically conceived idol of Beauty and intellective perfection, indeed blocked any primitivistic, Dionysian unraveling of things, but it also, for all purposes, squelched development of any genuine aesthetic life, declaring it fundamentally illegitimate.

This is not some bit of esoteric ancient history I am rehearsing. It is most intimately related to the fact that the twentieth century church has a nineteenth century hymnody, and that people who like to paint autumn landscapes for their living room often *cannot* see the guts of a ghetto as they walk past and think that abortion is a concept rather

---

3 "*In* den vorm en *in* de functie van het spel, dat een zelfstandige qualiteit is, vindt het besef van 's menschen begrepen zijn in den kosmos zijn eerste, zijn hoogste, zijn heiligste uitdrukking" in Johan Huizinga, *Homo Ludens: Proeve eener bepaling van het spel-element der cultuur* [1938] (Haarlem: H.D. Tjeenk Willink & Zoon, 1952), 18.

than raw anguish of skin. What I am talking about is the root cause why young Christians today gifted by the Lord to be professional artists cannot put bread on the table for their wife and child. This is not a game of academic marbles this afternoon. The ghost of Plato has spooked the church for ages, and the curse of the undeniably great, honorable Philosopher Aristotle has been untold mystification about poetry, music, and the arts, a knotted tangle that admits of no solution. And it always seems so harmless, it's just ideas . . . about Beauty and Inspiration . . . But ideas can kill people inside and mixup societies to their ruin, because there is always credo in human reflection and perception, with impact for the streets—shalom or misery.

Greek theoreticians Plato and Aristotle set the mold for millennia of cultural leaders in church, governing royalty, and even industrial entrepreneurship: art is a menial, lower middle-class skill, that is good or bad depending upon whether it promotes the ideals of *polis über alles* (St. Peter's, Louis XIV, the Rothchilds *über alles*); while the noble, arduous quest for Beauty, once it tiptoes past the sensuous danger zone, has ecstatic potential—"The poet's eye, in a fine frenzy rolling"—which Aristotle dignified as man's divine! activity, seeing things *sub specie universitatis*.[4] Illegitimate, I said, because it rips aesthetic life out of the fabric of daily living, as well as separating it from artisanship, incidentally, and transmogrifies that suggestion-rich, playful dimension of our creaturehood into an amorphous, mental, speculative exercise in would-be divine, leisurely Creativity, effortlessly concerned with ultimate Harmony and everlasting Perfection.

I do not mean art did not get done. Aristophanes' comedies packed in the hoi polloi like Canadian hockey. The paved roads, bridges, theatres, and baths of the Roman artisans are monuments to craft with integrity. The anonymous men called to decorate the churches of Eastern Christianity amazingly bent the ascetic, opposed-to-illusion *mimesis,* Plotinian influence into mosaic brilliance, the jewel-like colors of Byzantine sumptuousness and all that is artistically glorious about Ravenna. Lowly art made its own way.

But aesthetic life, the ordinary allusive, merry human ability to respond to the glory of God's creation, which had been mythopoeically smothered, now was robbed of any existence itself because it was intrin-

---

4 διὸ καὶ φιλοσοφώτερον καὶ σπουδαιότερον ποίησις ἱστορίας ἐστίν ἡ μὲν γὰρ ποίησις μᾶλλον τὰ καθόλου, ἡ δ' ἱστορία τὰ καθ' ἕκαστον λέγει. Aristotle, *Poetica* 9, 1451b 5–7. Cf. *Ethica Nicomachea* 10,7: 1177b 31–34: οὐ χρὴ δὲ κατὰ τοὺς παραινοῦντας ἀνθρώπινα φρονεῖν ἄνθρωπον ὄντα οὐδὲ θνητὰ τὸν θνητόν, ἀλλ' ἐφ' ὅσον ἐνδέχεται ἀθανατίζειν καὶ πάντα ποιεῖν πρὸς τὸ ζῆν κατὰ τὸ κράτιστον τῶν ἐν αὐτῷ·

sically theologized, in the original, bad meaning of the term. Medieval Christendom took the world to be a theophonous ladder and understood human activity to be naturally disposed to all manner of theodicy;[5] that is, orthodox Christianity, for more than a thousand years, lamentably took the distorting half-turn in perspective that flipped creation from being revelation of God and an instigation to praise into a programmed blueprint for gnostic contemplation, praying pride. So the feature of human life that was particularly open to surprise, ambiguity, a transcendental excitement of human sensibility—aesthetic activity—seemed made to order for incorporation into this scheme of *itinerum mentis ad Deum*, and therefore the aesthetic was neatly expropriated into an intellectualized *sursum corda*.

The crunch to this whole malformed buildup came later, when the high road of sinless Beauty, secularized a tincture so that macrocosmic Nature rather than God self came to be the focus: the crunch came when the high road of Beauty worship and the low road of the arts, also come of *secular* age, meshed with a vengeance of pent-up, unjustly disqualified cultural force.

For the long time before the Renaissance, art was a trade like making armor, wool-cutting, and navigation or a propaedutic study like grammar and geometry needed as training to get into the growing universities. But in sixteenth century Florence, Vasari organized painters, sculptors, and architects away from the guilds of druggists, goldsmiths, and carpenters—we are trying to do something different—into a special *Accademia del Disegno*.[6] From then on, over the next two hundred years, these arts now differentiated from the "mechanical" crafts, along with time-honored poetry and music, gradually established themselves as *beaux arts*, the fine arts, arts dealing with "the beautiful"! This happened in Medici circles, society of the grand Louis of France, around the wealthy patrons of Rembrandt's day who preferred landscapes, still lifes, and flattering portraits. It took place while "disinterested taste," part and parcel of Aufklärung deism, became the mark of connoisseurs in these very arts struggling for a peculiarly "aesthetic" identity, *beaux arts*. Also, for the first time, proto-journalistic criticism began to comment and compare within this select body of different but related arts specializing in "the beautiful" in order to help the many amateurs going to the opera,

---

5 Cf. Wladyslaw Tatarkiewicz, *History of Aesthetics*, vol. II, Medieval Aesthetics, trans. R. M. Montgomery, ed. C. Barrett (The Hague: Mouton, 1970), 106–109, 287–288.

6 Paul O. Kristeller, "The Modern System of the Arts: A study in the history of aesthetics (I)," *Journal of the History of Ideas* 12:4 (1951): 513–515.

exhibitions, and reading these newfangled novels—comparative art criticism germinated the systematic science of aesthetics.[7] But the point here is that although certain arts were winning a measure of distinct, "beauty" identity, they were still on the leash of their royal patrons, landed gentry, wealthy business men, and Tory and Whig politicians in early eighteenth century England who wanted a satiric poet punster on their payroll. That is, the important differentiation of art as a definite, aesthetically qualified product (here defined in eighteenth century terms of "beautiful harmony") did not lead immediately to independent art action in society.

It took the swaggering élan of Romanticism and its Faustian break with the Beauty-fix of Versailles, heroic couplets, and Winckelmann, plus the corrosive, thoroughly secularistic acid of Positivism and the enormous societal upheaval of modern Industrialism to set the stage for full-fledged autonomous art. That means: artists came forward who personally assumed all the divine attributes and prerogatives formerly ascribed to other-worldly Beauty and who then, in the name of natural aesthetic activity, demanded of its devotees the most artificial, burning gem-like sensations screwed up to the wrenching point, that is, an artisticized life—"aesthetes" they were called. Further, art was to be in bond to no man: art is not for the infallible pope and his red hat church, it is not for the kings—may they be decapitated—and keep your money! art is for nobody! art is good for nothing! art is for art's sake! *Épater les bourgeois* (to shaft—flabbergast the middle class) was the frustrated spirit of *l'art pour l'art*.[8] Gautier, Baudelaire, the *Tachtigers*, Pater, Oscar Wilde, Beardsley . . . during the reign of Queen Victoria.

The pathos to that cry of "art for art's sake" should make Christians weep. Because these gifted men knew that aesthetic life belongs to a full humanity, and that art should not be in bondage to an intellective, spiritualistic Beauty somewhere out of this world, ironically tied to the power strings of worldly prestige and money; but because they themselves identified aesthetic life with art and accepted "beautiful harmony" as the art norm, albeit drastically, secularly reinterpreted, often sensationally: they could not get art freely there nor their aesthetic life uncontorted. Art for *God's* sake, the God of Psalm 147, and a mature, unsophisticated aesthetic life simply were not possible in their view of reality. So they were stymied.

But they stymiedly persisted, with tremendous cultural power; for

---

7   Paul O. Kristeller, "The Modern System of the Arts: A Study in the History of Aesthetics (II)," *Journal of the History of Ideas* 13:1 (1952): 44–46.
8   Cf. Ruth Saw and Harold Osborne, "Aesthetics as a Branch of Philosophy," *The British Journal of Aesthetics* 1 (1960–1961): 11–12.

they were on target historically, trying to differentiate and individuate the art task and also plugging for the legitimacy of peculiarly aesthetic life. The fact that there was no reconciling-integrating vision to the important, formative work of these "aesthetes" and no community of contemporary Christians able or willing to pick up the ball in a radically biblical, cohesive way—the lack of center that could hold—did not stop the explosive, centrifugal movement they launched (what we call "modern art," after Daumier and Manet) from captivating and dominating, by and large, the hearts of men and women in art ever since. So the touch of supercilious alienation or aimless caprice or undefined hatred inside so many brilliant artistic experiments in the twentieth century—truly provocative, I think, because the constrictive back of traditional Beauty was finally broken and the reality of playful ambiguity, suggestion, even the crypto-metaphorical symbolic was freshly explored, however perversely—but the art-for art's-sake homelessness, bankrupting so much contemporary painting, for example, is indigenous to the tortuous historical predicament I have been trying to lay before you as the real background to the homelessness of aesthetics as a science:

(1) There has been no clear sense of the "aesthetic" field since it was first begun to be isolated about 250 years ago, or it has suffered under the false, world-flight idea of Beauty, which forced any reflection upon "aesthetic" into some brand of speculative, deistic theology.

(2) The "aesthetic" dimension of human life, for the last century, has been equated with "artistic" activity, thereby crowding normal aesthetic life with a kind of precious artificiality and optional character, so that systematic reflection upon "aesthetic" at best becomes a philosophy of criticism, with a tendency toward specialization, maybe esoteric.

And (3) the strong secularist dynamic of autonomy (=a law to itself) that happenstantially attended the differentiation of "art" and "aesthetic life" historically stands ever ready to subvert thought about "the aesthetic" and "art" into a self-sufficient discipline doing its own little thing, a law to itself.

The upshot then to the analysis of this historical hangup, given the actual setting of our predicament, is this: who in the world needs aesthetics? Not the autotelic, subjectivistic, fervently anti-intellectual artists of today who have enough troubles without mumbo jumbo scientific jargon barging into their studios. And not the North American public whose amateurism has been encouraged by the do-it-yourself, democratic ethic: you know what you like, what tastes good to you or not, don't you? you don't need somebody to tell you what to think about a painting, poem, or the nature of music, do you? Aesthetics is obviously also not needed by the many academic philosophers and scientists I mentioned, busy chopping logic or selling out to the technocratic establishment, or clinging like ivy to hoary traditions. —Do God's people need aesthetics?

I have genuine sympathy for all those Christians, in so far as they are ruled by biblical belief, who have an uncertain distrust about the whole complex business of aesthetics and art. Parents who would prefer to have their boy or girl go through life with one eye rather than end up in hell with a portfolio—I respect that, and challenge anybody who doesn't to read the New Testament gospels to find out the truth. There has always been much too much *adoption* of the going culture surrounding the christian community, with our intention of reforming it—as if it were heaven that is paved with good intentions. Quite specifically: many well-meaning Christians today, aware of our aesthetic deficiency, push art, as if exposure to art itself will make a person refined, humane, and richly alive. But that is the intricate lie of Schiller! Art—doing, viewing, or buying it—*can* make a man a prig, parasite, a nauseating, self-satisfied, elegant bore. Educated Christ-believers have better things to do than copy Renaissance Humanists, under the sign of the cross, or while adding the formula "for the glory of God." Besides, a rich aesthetic life—having a developed playful element in one's family, style to one's feelings and loving, a lilting range and catch to your prayers—is something different (though related) from being a little art connoisseur. But that is ahead of the story for today.

If aesthetics is just going to cut up more logical mustard and promote art as the fount of sweetness and light that our barbaric, materialistic culture is missing, nobody needs it, certainly not the christian community. But if aesthetics as a rigorous scientific discipline shall indeed give a winsome account of the aesthetic hold the Lord God has for creaturely existence, so that humans may order their everyday lives more obediently, then that aesthetics can be a blessing to God's people, society at large, artists too, every other science, and even other institutions within society.

That is, if there can be a turnabout in aesthetic theory to help set the root things straight—

For example: to show that "aesthetic" is not just there, a category, a property, or quality that is optional to humanity, but that "aesthetic" is a cosmic dimension, a certain way the Lord asks us to respond to God, that everyone has a definite aesthetic-calling-to-obedience—which does not mean everyone has to be an artist (or an aesthetician) any more than you must assume the job of acrobat or philosopher because you are made to move and think in obedience to Yahweh. Art is a specially imaginative type of gifted aesthetic work for which not everyone has talent: aesthetic life, I would venture to point out, is a matter of the ordinary playful, and when opened up, styleful life zone of our creatureliness[9] whose nuclear meaning is "suggestion." Every man or woman is called to unfold the supple, oblique-implicant, suggestion-rich moment latent in his or her life action—in speech, walk, dress, reactions, doctrine. . . . (Art normed and spirited to serve this human calling is very valuable.)

If aesthetic theory can be God-thanking analysis turned to Understanding, turned to reclaiming creation misappropriated by idolators pretending autonomy, turned to opening up to healing and wisdom our wayabout in the world, bringing the Lord God's reconciling lordship down as close as a wink, playing catch, and our sweat, then aesthetics is very needful and will be a joyous affair. Then too, with its rightful task, aesthetics will be at home.

That brings us face to face with a knotty, critical problem—the rightful task of aesthetics as a science. How is aesthetic theory to be related to everyday affairs and to practicing artistry? Concretely, how are aesthetic theorists on the fourth floor of the Odd Fellows Building to interact with the man on the street, the art fellows at Patmos Workshop and Gallery, and practicing art historians, not to speak now of the institutional church, *Toronto Star*, disturbed children's therapy, carpenters, and the Trudeau government? What is the right relation between (aesthetic) theoretical thought doing and non-theoretical action?

Rightful task

There is a history of bad blood, in general, between theoreticians, specialized (practicing) craftsmen, and the so-called pop and hot dog masses. Since the days of Pythagoras the theoreticians, whether figuring out the geometric course of heavenly bodies or simply trying to redefine piety, presumed to be wiser than thou and know it all. Especially the academic brand of theorist in the wake of lecturer Aristotle learned to split metaphysical hairs, ipse dixit answers categorically on all and sundry topics while puffing on the professorial pipe, and turned out to be often wrong. Meanwhile, the hoi polloi and non-theorizing practitioners went about their own daily business: we have no need of you, theoretician. Each thought his all-absorbing task to be more important than the other's.

---

9   Paul G. Schrotenboer, *Man in God's World* (Grand Rapids: International Reformed Bulletin, 1967), 11–22.

The jostling and estrangement was not ended by the imposition of a churchly brotherhood. Augustinians could still identify theoretical contemplation with Mary the mother of God, and put practical charity out in the kitchen with Martha. Duns Scotus' disciples teeter-tottered the other way: theological theory must become "practical," since we are saved by "doing," not by gnostic knowing. The polar opposition between theory and practice smoldered on because there was no single, underlying vision able to relativize both idols back into a common, united endeavor.

The trouble became more acute after the seventeenth century when theoretical knowledge took on a scientific edge, made claims that impelled action, and when the non-scientist, no longer so cowed by the church organization, asked scientific theory to prove itself by results beneficial for praxis, for the whole human's active, practical life. Then the learned theoretician could no longer go his contemplative way, safe by fiat; he had to show what his theoretical science could do, and if theory rubbed the influential, and later, revolutionary layman the wrong way, there gradually came to be back-talk and back-action, however tardy and impotent. The point is: diffidence and enmity between theory and praxis, of theorists at large with the many non-theorists caught up in the press of life, has been a disturbing trait of Western civilization.[10]

Artists, in their famous wrangle with "theoreticians" of the Royal French Academy, seem to document the bad blood with an example par excellence.

Richelieu founded the Academy to get standards worthy of the French nation in language, poetry, and literature, and to protect them. When painting and sculpture were chartered at the same institution in 1648, breaking up the job monopoly of the master artist guilds in France, a brave new world for art seemed in the making. But doctrinaire head Charles La Brun, with the backing of Louis XIV's minister Colbert, laid down rules for artists to follow, wrote learned treatises that had to be discussed, and armed with a gradual monopoly on commissions, dictated as reigning theoretician (and former student of Poussin) what was orthodox art and what artists had to learn to be approved members of the estab-

---

10 Nicholas Lobkowicz, *Theory and Practice: History of a concept from Aristotle to Marx* (University of Notre Dame Press, 1967). Cf. also Jürgen Habermas: "Die eigentliche Schwierigkeit im Verhältnis der Theorie zur Praxis erwächst freilich nicht aus dieser neuen Funktion der Wissenschaft, die zur technischen Gewalt wird, sondern daraus, dass wir zwischen technischer und praktischer Gewalt nicht mehr unterscheiden können," in "Dogmatismus, Vernunft und Entscheidung—Zu Theorie und Praxis in der verwissenschaftlichten Zivilisation," *Theorie und Praxis* (Berlin: Luchterhand, 1963), 232.

lishment. After a generation or two of ruling theoreticians, Academy art ran stuck; it got the dynastic pallor of formula. Artistic innovators were forced into salons, and the eighteenth century saw a scramble of artists doing their anti-establishment ritualistic thing in the Corpus Christi spring at Place Dauphin in Paris. But the Academy and its authoritarian theoreticians really kept French art in check until the nineteenth century Impressionists broke its restrictive hold.

This striking affair is sometimes cited as evidence for the basic inimicability of art with *theory* of art, between art and *normative principles* of art criticism, art and *aesthetics* as a scientific analysis. Art that stays alive is beyond analysis, isn't it? Style and taste cannot be disputed nor rightly determined by fiat, isn't that so? Any infringement of the artistic sphere by theory, theoretical reflection, kills art's spark of vitality! There is no "rightful task" or wholesome relation possible for aesthetic theory toward practicing art, except second-guessing what has "happened…."

What is at stake here again is no less than the legitimacy of aesthetics as a science. Or you grant it an ivory tower license and a ceremonial task, but damn it to irrelevance, so far as artists are concerned. Laissez faire. The less theoretical aesthetics the better for art.

But the French Academy is an unfortunate example, I think, for trying to justify the fight in history between theory and art as if it be structurally inevitable. What you had there in seventeenth and eighteenth century France were *artists* appointed as "theoretical" watchdogs for a monarchical showpiece. Charles La Brun was an artist-politician, *le premier peintre du roi*, with an ax to grind and a style to cuddle—*le bel antique.* What buffeted up-and-coming young artists who wanted formative training in art was not aesthetic theory, but bureaucrats in an artistic institution that had lost its voluntary association character and become an appendage of the state. Art initiative in the studios of France was stymied because style was controlled by autocratic dictum more than by the leading, competent positing, as it were, of norms by big artists, uncorrupted by court patronage. Artists should be able to interact with theoreticians, whose professional analysis and questions may lay artistic things bare; but theoreticians cannot police art because they are not artists.

In fact, I wonder whether academic theorists of art and literature—not artists turned administrative or teaching bureaucrats—but analysts and historiographers of art have ever been a massive threat to the practice of artistry. Have aestheticians ever called the shots like Church Councils used to and business conglomerates do today? At present what constricts novelists, poets, film makers, painters, and song writers is the Mass Media

Bloc with its monopoly on distribution and public communication, and whatever one may accuse them of, it is not in-depth theoretical reflection about "the aesthetic."

The recurrent challenge mounted by art and artists to the very validity of professional aesthetic's task since its eighteenth century differentiation can be traced, in my judgment, to two root matters. (1) The fearful, unproved, Romantic credo that theory kills initiative, theory violates art's "creativity," is a deep conviction of many artists. This Idealistic Romantic credo is often compounded by a thin-skinned Individualism of studio artists, which makes them believe that the greatest stimulus to success is to be independent, with nobody else in the act. This individualism is further often replete with the pervasive subjectivism of our times that *assumes* there are no norms for art but our own selves.[11]

I cannot share that position, often abetted by historicistic art historians. Besides making aesthetics impossible, it embodies a deep lovelessness for one's neighbor and spite for God's ordering of the world. It continues to kick up clouds of mystification around art so useful to its practitioners when they form arty cults that live as if beyond the call of any law, but which is death to christian cultural development. We have got to get rid of the bohemian bug to art if it indeed wants to serve God and one's neighbor.

It is true, theoretical pontification about art that has not been experienced will be detrimental to its performance, if such "theory" is listened to. However, we must get one thing straight: art is no more recalcitrant to analysis than a salmon's nervous system. Aesthetic analytic judgment is no more arbitrary than calculation of stereometric geometry problems. If art is intelligible, a human artifact, the artwork may be analyzed. And

---

11 Cf. Albert Dresdner's important background book, *Die Kunstkritik: Ihre Geschichte und Theorie.* Erster Teil: Die Entstehung der Kunstkritik (München: Bruckmann, 1915). Also, Hans R. Rookmaaker, *De Kunstenaar een profeet?* (1965), translated as "The Artist as Prophet?" in *Modern Art and the Death of a Culture: The Complete Works of Hans R. Rookmaaker*, vol. 5 (Carlisle: Piquant, 2003), 169–187. Karl Kuypers notes that "artistic" as an adjective describing a creative artist-genius first shows up with Goethe in 1786 and then with Hegel. "Dank der Romantik, die das schöpferische und ursprüngliche Element als unergründlich und an keine verstandesmäßige Regel gebunden als wesentlich für alle schöne Kunst und das Kunstwerk verherrlicht und den Geniebegriff noch mehr als zuvor mit dem dichtenden und die Wirklichkeit durch die Macht der Einbildungskraft umformenden Künstler identifiziert, verschwindet nach Hegel, der von seiner Philosophie des Geistes und der Kunst her dieser Auffassung die erforderliche philosophische Untermauerung gab, die Notwendigkeit, der Dreiheit Kunst, Kunstwerk und Künstler zur Unterscheidung das Adjektiv 'schön' beizufügen" in *Kants Kunsttheorie und die Einheit der Kritik der Urteilskraft* (London: North-Holland Publishing, 1972), 26 and 26n.2.

if art products can be analyzed, such reflection can be systematically thought together in a theory of art. Theory of art does not replace art or presume to make it superfluous any more than a prose paraphrase supplants a poem. Also, you do not cut the model of aesthetic theory on the method of marine biology or mathematics, and more than analysis goes into grasping artistic activity and its results. But aesthetic theoretical thought is not a charade.[12] Both theoretical aesthetic analysis and the fashioning of art belong to the same cultural family, and are called upon to sustain one another in their quite different tasks, not build walls between themselves.

Still—there is something about a poem, a painting, a symphony, that doesn't like . . . aesthetic analysis, despite all the assurances. Great aesthetician Jacques Maritain can start talking about a poem and before you know it, his pages are filled with "participation in the uncreated divine light . . . which is in every man" and jargon like "epiphanies of creative intuition."[13] John Dewey made a heroic effort to undo the fallacies and confusion surrounding the arts, to reconstruct (construct back) the identification of aesthetic life with artistic doing; despite many insights and forceful examples, "artistic" gets dissolved into *"an* experience," any single, successful adaptation in the dialectical stream of living organisms interchanging with the environment. Does every aesthetician, by nature, says an exasperated artist, simply touch down upon the arts for documentation, prostituting them into examples substantiating his apriori metaphysical superstructure!

One could apologize for Maritain: yes, he does obfuscate art into being oracular utterances, and John Dewey does common-ize art away into being the best possible salvation experience in the world;[14] and they

---

12 Cf. Edward G. Ballard, *Art and Analysis: An essay toward a theory in aesthetics* (The Hague: Nijhoff, 1957). Gadamer's "Kritik der Abstraktion des aesthetischen Bewusstseins" in *Wahrheit und Methode, Grundzüge einer philosophischen Hermeneutik* [1960] (Tübingen: Mohr, 3.A., 1972), correctly challenges a Scientialistic treatment of art and recognizes the perspectival subject world objectified in an art piece, but Gadamer wrongly leaves a critic existentialistically mute before art.

13 Jacques Maritain, *Creative Intuition in Art and Poetry* [1954] (New York: Meridian, 1955), 71 and especially chapter 4.

14 E.g., John Dewey, *Art as Experience* [1934] (New York: Capricorn, 1958), 270–271: "Expression strikes below the barriers that separate human beings from one another. Since art is the most universal form of language, since it is constituted, even apart from literature, by the common qualities of the public world, it is the most universal and freest form of communication. Every intense experience of friendship and affection completes itself artistically. The sense of communion generated by a work of art may take on a definitely religious quality. The union of men with one another is the

are both wrong. But the doubts of the artist and curiosity of the bystander will persist past specific apologies, even if other aestheticians cut back simply to making sporadic theoretical points, without any obvious cohering systematics, because: (2) secularized aesthetic theory has an intrinsic bent to serve itself and swallow the grist of its analytic mill whole. The best aesthetic theorists, like Maritain and Dewey, whether captured by the grand Scholastic, intellectualistic tradition, an old-fashioned Rationalism, the driving Spirit of a technocratic pragmaticism, or some other Name under heaven: they *believe* their theory in such a way as to trust it deep down as if it be the Good News itself, revealing the Truth. Hence there is naturally a ruthless certainty to each man's systematic theses, however politely formulated, which brooks no resistance, certainly not from artists who have no head for theory. And it is that hidden reverence for the theory in all fundamentally secular aesthetics that is intolerable to all non-theorists (and to all theorists disbelieving that particular Thomistic or Naturalistic aesthetics or whatever sort it be).

The turnabout in aesthetics for which I am speaking is in earnest to not only scotch that snake of overbearing apocdicity but kill it, without losing the edge of conviction, being a committed aesthetics. With all our getting of knowledge in aesthetics we must gain the Understanding that will humble aesthetic theory enough to bind it into one body with art practice and the many people who distrust it sight unseen.

Perhaps a homely illustration will let me present the rightful task of aesthetics, as I see it, and firm up the way to discuss its extramural relations [D#8].

The science of aesthetics is first of all (as the inner petal indicates) not analysis of art but of "the aesthetic" dimension of reality—"aesthetic life" I have called it. Hard-core (modal) aesthetics, you might say, is meant to piece out what "the aesthetic" be, how it shows up in a marriage or family, church worship services, a business, government, men and women at

---

source of the rites that from the time of archaic man to the present have commemorated the crises of birth, death, and marriage. Art is the extension of the power of rites and ceremonies to unite men, through a shared celebration, to all incidents and scenes of life. This office is the reward and seal of art. That art weds man and nature is a familiar fact. Art also renders men aware of their union with one another in origin and destiny."

Susanne K. Langer believes similarly that art reveals the final meaning of things to men and women: "The only way we can really envisage vital movement, the stirring and growth and passage of emotion, and ultimately the whole direct sense of human life, is in artistic terms. . . . Self-knowledge, insight into all phases of life and mind, spring from artistic imagination" in "Artistic Perception and 'Natural Light,'" *Problems of Art* (New York: Charles Scribner's Sons, 1957), 71.

Diagram #8: Uncomplicated sketch of a specifically academic flower, responding to Psalm 147 and Proverbs 8.

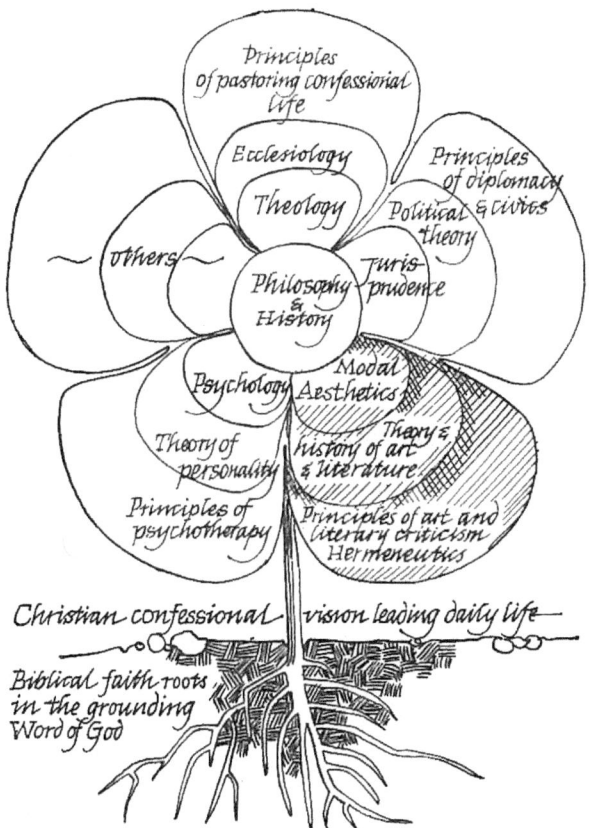

large digging ditches, arranging flowers, selling insurance, flirting in the library, and how rocks, plants, fish, and wild animals disclose an "aesthetic" openness. That is, very abstractly, theoretically, aesthetics tries to get scientifically precise, to approximate the moment of *aesthetic* structuring and functioning in the world, how it definitely unfolds as an intramodal factor in the complexity of creatural existence, in order to help us know how God wills such activity to be done within all the ways we are and creation is called to flourish.

The science of aesthetics shall also analyze art and literature, and develop a methodology for historiography of the various kinds of art and literarily qualified products. Art-theory (typical individuality-structure) aesthetics needs to determine what makes art be art, and needs to search out the peculiar configuration, constitutive infra-structure and full-orbed functioning of music, poetry, dance and architecture, sculpture, typography, novels and painting, cinema and the rest—to figure out what and how the different arts and literature can be normed and anti-normatively shaped, permeated by the artist's dated, committed perspective.

N.B. Theory and historiography of art and literature (that second petal), like all theory and historiography, is reflective, has a strong after-the-fact character: it does not prescribe out of the blue but does examine what artists are doing these days, what drama is coming across the boards, and what of substance is being written; and if Webern, late Messiaen, and Boulez are weaving sounds Mozart and Beethoven could not have dreamt of, a sound aesthetician does not say Mozart and Beethoven had the definitive word on music.

The key to relating aesthetic theory and artistic practice is for both to realize that the apriori of art structure and the aesthetic, imaginative norm for art is not a theoretical construct, also not an historical given: it is ontic; and a monopoly for positing its discovery belongs to neither theoretician nor artist.

Fundamental disputes on what art is are not jurisdictional, but when irreconcilable, come down to vision and stance—where does a person finally choose to stand. So, from a biblically christian viewpoint, the closest consultation on the definitive issues among art theorists, art historians, and artists, who understand their field as a calling to serve the Almighty Lord's Rule on earth here and now—not to speak of art critics and knowledgeable art viewers who work out of a christian perspective—such willing, communal research would be a mark of happy obedience and a step toward experiencing communion of the saints as a professional reality too. Leadership in the area of art and literature would then be a co-forming responsibility of practicing art theorists, art historiographers, critics, and actual performing and producing artists.

Finally, in my judgment, if it be rightfully considered, hermeneutics is a province of the science of aesthetics (the outer petal); and it is study in these principles of art and literary criticism where the outreach of theoretical aesthetics becomes most clear, as it serves within the flower of an academic, educational ministry.

Again, *artists* depict things, dramatize events, go after meaning-reality in its individuality-structured positioning. Artists are not busy theoretically, but with their special imaginative attitude they aesthetically form artifacts which, if properly normed, in turn lead others to notice nuances of meaning and fine lineaments of the world lost to a surface consciousness. Workaday *critics,* as journalists, for example, have the task to prepare an audience to receive a specific artwork.[15] Whether showing a larger or smaller awareness of historical context, their propadeutic activity is neither artistic nor properly theoretic, but demands an intuiting, ferreting-out discrimination, an aesthetically founded analysis that attempts to forge a trustworthy bond between art product and public at large.

The *hermeneutical aesthetician,* however, pulls back abstractly—the nature of theory!—to get at the principles, that is, the mainsprings of interpretation *überhaupt.* While hermeneutic aesthetics will again and again touchstone its investigations with particular criticisms, its theoretical investigation is intent upon positing the structural norms for reading, seeing, and hearing art, the generally applicable guidelines for interpreting texts and pieces of art. The hermeneutical aesthetician is wary of formulae for instant judgments, not in order to be esoteric or stubbornly obnoxious to artists and viewers who deal in this piece of art or that one and want direct advice, but, true to his theoretical calling, the (outer petal) aesthetician, in this reformationally christian setup, works slowly at developing a systematic body of methodical, critical principles that will shore up and deepen the literary or art critic in his piece work by helping him anticipate, remember, and oversee what he is actually about.

A christian hermeneutic will also be conceived so as to respect the office of the reader or audience, so they may learn to respond themselves rather than follow recipes. Also if they are truly wise, theoretically formulated principles of criticism may lead the artist as artist to self-examination: is what he or she means to be about conducive, in the larger cultural horizons, to being attentively understood. . . .

I realize that this brief outline and "job description" of the rightful task of aesthetics does not insure it be done with a foundational thrust and christian insight. You cannot build a concern for exploring the transcendental problems of aesthetic activity, art, and interpretation, in order to reach clarity and insight on the fundamental categories: you cannot build that sense of task into the demeanor of practicing aestheticians, anymore than you can build an openness to artistic innovation into a conservative public mind by reminding them they must respect the office of artistic leader. No more than you can build the humbled, communal dimension into an artist's work by telling him he belongs to a faith community. A carefully outlined aesthetics cannot save art. But the science of aesthetics is also not to be a luxury permitted to a chosen few epiphenomenally busy in the Odd Fellows Building [where the Institute

---

15 C. Seerveld, *A Christian Critique of Art and Literature* [1963] (Toronto/Sioux Center: Toronto Tuppence/Dordt College Press, 1995), 121–130.

for Christian Studies has its home] or closeted in plush seminar rooms at the University of Toronto. Instead, aesthetic theory as a science that is couched and executed in the spirit of a limited service within God's variegated flower garden (see D#6, page 176), called to examine the aesthetic categories that discipline and set human aesthetic consciousness (= foundational studies, cf. παιδείᾳ καὶ νουθεσίᾳ of Ephesians 6:4), will no longer suffer from the old, false dichotomy of theory versus practice and therefore, with its rightful task assured, making earnest with its christian freedom, will have the structural wherewithal to *help* set up healing in aesthetic life and artistic calling. Such an aesthetics may concentrate on a new tack of becoming a doxological aesthetics.

A new tack
A new tack—that has manifesto character; but I do not have it all spelled out. By a doxological aesthetics I mean this: within the limiting confines of its rich zone of creation, engaged according to its educational formative nature, not abandoning at all any of the tentative caution proper to theoretic work, not short-changing in the least its conceptual knowledge-getting, yet within all that knowledge-getting, an aesthetics that gets Understanding. Aesthetic theory that is transcendentally open to the structuring faithfulness of the Lord, unashamed to join its hand in leading God's weak little people in developing a biblically reforming, wide-open christian culture, a minority culture in our post-christian age. Doxological aesthetics will be aesthetic theory that builds up the praise in the world for the Lord by breaking open a consciousness of the deadends: the stunting, historically assumed deadends in aesthetic life that make one's whole behavior rigid; deadends in the art world you can find everywhere—in gallery, museum, disc-jockeyed radio, and showplace exhibitions of the party-line, hard-edge disciples; conceptual deadends of out-dated beauty theory, "disinterestedness," "creativity," "post-object art"....[16] A low profile theory that by analytic deeds invites the aesthetic lost in to serve with joy on what is fruitful aesthetically, artistically, and

---

16 Cf. for example, Jose Ortega Y Gasset, "The Dehumanization of Art" (1925), *The Dehumanization of Art and other essays on Art, Culture, and Literature* (Princeton University Press, 1968); Peter Viereck, *Dream and Responsibility: Four test cases of the tension between poetry and society* (University Press of Washington D.C., 1953); Roy McMullen, *Art, Affluence and Alienation: The fine arts today* (Toronto: Mentor, 1968); Joseph Grange, "The Decay of Symbols and Youth's Unrest," dittograph paper read at the annual meeting of the American Society of Aesthetics at the University of Colorado, 1970; Harold Rosenberg, "The Art World, Thoughts in Off-Season," *The New Yorker* (24 July 1971): 62–65.

can be blessed.

I mean to give more than slogans even though I am unready to detail a program. Doxological aesthetics will be aesthetic theory spilling over to give leadership like: fashioning games that are not cruelly competitive but full of surprise for catching a child with discoveries, unawares; researching how families and friends may celebrate church and state holidays with style and imagination rather than crass food and drink, sermons, and firecrackers. A doxological aesthetics will openly argue for the necessary crafted character to art, for art to be deep, and try to build up evidence for the importance of the art *product*, next to the craze of momentary experiences repeated or the unrepeatable "performance," which allow no room for suggestion and symbolical subtleties to take effect, building upon a continuum, but settling for the profoundly anaesthetic flurry of unfocused, intensified impressions similar to the drug scene. Doxological aesthetics will be theoretic study with post-theoretical "fall-out" for underlining the wholesomeness of asking artists, "Paint me something for my study, for the kitchen, for the death of my child, for my becoming a Christian, for a rainy day—" rather than let them stare at a studio wall, paint out their unengaged frustrations, or, in the wan hope of striking it rich with the Canadian Council, potboil their psyches. That is, an aesthetics that shows by its theory the normality of taking artists up into our daily life *as freemen artists,* not as commissioned slaves, or "free-lance" individuals. Doxological aesthetics should graduate a consciousness that would ferment getting the school or the church to teach children to dance Psalm 23 and Psalm 127–128 and Psalm 148 in the worship liturgy, that would encourage not pop art satire of Campbell soup cans but designing a more playful and nuance-rich label, that would support the moves to change musea from being temples where artifacts are rootlessly admired back into schools with historical context.

A doxological aesthetics assumes a willingness to pick up the Groen van Prinsterer–Abraham Kuyper reformation perspective, with its special grit among all the many christian traditions, which puts the Old Testament cosmic sense of a redemptive peoplehood and the New Testament call to break down everything puffed up against the experiential knowledge of Jesus Christ and reconcile all things back to God's ordering: putting that to work. Without Kuyper's confessional Idealism (or the Positivistic antipode of a specialistic expertise practiced by devout Christians). We followers of Christ in the world of 1970 AD may have and shall have, if we are faithful, the shalom of a minority culture that has broken with mainline Western Humanism. I think we can learn much on that point from the Blacks south of the border and from the Trotsky-Marxist endeavor to do just that, have a minority culture; both the principled Blacks and Trotsky never relegated their faith to the backyard or left it as a wedding veil packed in the trunk with other trinket souvenirs—a faith that is vital, relevant, and misguided.[17] Christian believers today should not be so squeamish about being forthrightly, scandalously, humbly, and openly christian, also in their aesthetics. Otherwise we cut down the doxology in anticipating the Rule of the Lord.

Aware of how unripe I am for the foundational work ahead and of how few, actually, in the Reformation tradition—which is my tradition—have investigated specially in these matters; aware that I shall need much reading to gather insight from christian attempts outside the tradition of Reformation and evangelical Christianity; aware that starting my year with close analysis of Kant's *Kritik der Urteilskraft* seems like a long way from doxology: so that one not lose heart but get a willingness to hope, a vision of joyful labor and the long pull for generations so inclined, happy to see the strength and blessing of the communion-building and academic healing beginning in concert here in Canada: before I make my last remarks, let us listen once more to the refreshing Word of God.

I read to you what the voice of Understanding, Wisdom itself, says at the close of Proverbs 8:22–36. It is so childlike and simple, deeply comforting, it makes you smile, unafraid of anything, with the certainty of our salvation. This Proverbs 8 passage gives color to what the New Testament reports when it says that the man-child of Mary who died and

---

17 Cf. Ralph Ellison, "Twentieth-Century Fiction and the Black Mask of Humanity" (c.1946) in *Images of the Negro in American Literature*, eds. S. L. Gross and J. E. Hardy (University of Chicago Press, 1966), 115–131; Jeff Donaldson, "The role we want for black art," *College Board Review* 71 (Spring 1969): 15–18; *The Black Aesthetic*, ed. Addison Gayle, Jr. (New York: Anchor, 1972). Leon Trotsky's *Literature and Revolution* (1924) (Ann Arbor paperback, 1960) bristles with certainty and knowledge on what to do, for example: "Our Marxist conception of the objective social dependence and social utility of art, when translated into the language of politics, does not at all mean a desire to dominate art by means of decrees and orders. . . . Of course the new art cannot but place the struggle of the proletariat in the center of its attention. But the plough of the new art is not limited to numbered strips. On the contrary, it must plow the entire field in all directions. Personal lyrics of the very smallest scope have an absolute right to exist within the new art. Moreover, the new man cannot be formed without a new lyric poetry. But to create it, the poet himself must feel the world in a new way. . . . The proletariat has to have in art the expression of the new spiritual point of view which is just beginning to be formulated within him, and to which art must help him give form. This is not a state order, but an historic demand" (170–171). Cf. especially chapter 6, "Proletarian Culture and Proletarian Art," and chapter 8, "Revolutionary and Socialist Art."

rose again in history was the first, the foremost, the final lord of creation (cf. Colossians 1:15, Revelation 3:14): the *son* of God whose cosmic saving Word offers a life more abundant than we are wont to know.

What you hear now is the Word from the mouth of Understanding, the Word of the Son of God:

> The LORD God Yahweh set me up as the starting point of what God was doing,
> the very first of God's great deeds long, long ago;
> from everlasting, yes—from the very origin, I was officially there,
> even before the beginning of the earth!
>
> When there were no whirlingpool expanses of water yet,
> I was already broken in
> —even when there did not exist sources of water, springs swollen to flow. In the dawn before the mountains were settled into place,
> in front of the foothills—there I was ! —
> The LORD God had not yet made the earth,
> neither the [wild] outdoors nor a beginning on all the dirt [needed] for the continents.
> When God straightened up the sky, I was right there!
> When the LORD God staked out a horizon for the whole ocean expanse,
> When God firmed up the thunder clouds so they wouldn't fall,
> When the underground springs swelling the unruly ocean waters started to get too powerful
> and the LORD set God's ordinance for the bodies of water
> so that they would not overstep God's Word,
> When God said "Let there be—" to the very underpinnings of the earth, [I was right there!]
> Yes, I was God's very own protégé.
> And I was enjoying myself day after day, playing around all the time in front of God's face,
> playing through the hemisphere[s] of God's earth,
> having fun with all of humankind. . . .
>
> So now, listen to me, you children
> —how happy it will be for those who walk along the way I give the guidelines for ! —
> all of you, listen obediently to the paideia [of truth, right, troth, gentleness, fearing the LORD][18] so that you become men and

---

18 Cf. Proverbs 8:3–21.

women with understanding!
—don't let it just blow away in the air—
That man or woman will be a happy one who really listens to me
so that they are daily on the lookout for the door to understanding,
so that person is continually knocking on the doorposts where understanding is to be discovered:
[that person will be a happy one] because whoever finds me has found life!
—that person shakes blessings away, as it were, from the LORD God Yahweh!
But whoever misses me has wasted oneself:
all those who disdain Understanding love what is dead.

Students, whose lives have touched or will still someday touch mine in our brief histories:
For however much time God may give me with you—fifteen Hezekiah years more or less—to knock on the cosmic door to Understanding, I pledge to you to do it with the sweet intensity of play so that the hard professional work, whose end we cannot oversee, never be nervous or routine, but itself be received and enjoyed as a fruitful gift of the Lord. Without a student a teacher is nothing; without a sense of a christian student generation taking up the task, reforming and building upon the older generation's life-offerings, anchored in the trust of our Lord Jesus Christ's return: without that Understanding our labor would be dead-ended. I thank God that with you at the graduate Institute for Christian Studies LIFE has been found in scholarship.

Curatorium of the Institute:
Before God I accept from you the office to do research and teaching in the systematics and history of aesthetic theory, still somewhat overwhelmed that in 1972 a man can be given this post publicly in downtown, metropolitan Toronto for Christ's sake! no strings attached but to find out what shall bring shalom into the aesthetic life of men and women and their doings with art and literature. I am happy you know it will take some time for me to get my bearings, to take stock of the turnabout to Understanding I envision in the field, to develop a limited mastery of its particulars so that I may move with care and speak with wisdom. I thank God that "inauguration" means a solemn beginning, so I need not yet give an account of the trust you have placed in me. I promise to be a faithful steward, God strengthening me.

Colleagues Hart, Olthuis, Zylstra, De Graaff and Runner:
I have found in you men a singleness of mind and an utter purity of faith that has quietly humbled me again and again, and made me ache to have such sterling, seeking dependence upon the Will of the Lord. My journey to this Toronto spot, as you know, has been a circuitous one; the forming of a synthetic christianity dies hard. I hope not to be arrived as an Erasmus in a den of reformers, but to be here so gratefully, with my heart showing, that you will be able to teach me that the Holy Spirit can rub out the last spot of what a man will not give up to make him whole before the Lord. Thank you that I may be one with you in this joyful calling; I pray that you use me up in whatever way will best praise the Lord.

To my immediate family and loved ones and the few men and women whom I thank God for as friends, especially my parents here present, my wife Inès, and the children:
That your supporting love for me—in the jewels of so many cups of tea, the goodnight kiss, and halting honest prayer—has not diminished over such a long time, that you have uncommonly protected me from evil and distraction, and held steady a love communion rare in our days, I should simply like to acknowledge all that here on this day and offer it all up to God with great thanksgiving so that all the love, including mine for you, may splash down like sunshine over us all again and make us laughing together as we look expectantly to see what God has in store.

People of God gathered here, your Trustees in the Association for the Advancement of Christian Scholarship, and especially the artists present:
I had wanted so much to lay before you a five-year plan that was a detailed blueprint. That I was unable to do that now is maybe what I had to learn before you today: that while I understand in some detail where we are in time and why, finding a home for the contours of aesthetics, able to look past the wrinkles in the specific task—though the doxological direction to take is clear—I do not have the answers cased. Mine is going to have the character of a pilgrimage into a far country to which I trust the Lord will lead. So I am not going to mastermind reformation of the North American art world; but what could be as earth-shaking: I ask you as fellow believers to pray for me and to join me, in your calling, whatever it be, to hold up some candlelight for those who have lost the way in art or never known (consciously) the healthy role of aesthetic activity in the life God gave us to live, that is, start giving consecrated leadership that shall be fruitful for the coming of our Lord's Rule, who has done and

will do great things for God's people.

Finally, Guests present who may be strangers to the work of the Institute for Christian Studies and the vision it stands for:
Let me ask that you try to hear the ring of truth in our upstart critique, and if possible, become curious enough to give us a second hearing as we mature in the scholarly work. Western civilization, in plain language, is in a mess, fleeing pell-mell from deadends of its own making, with nowhere to go hide. As T.S. Eliot says somewhere:

> In a world of fugitives
> the person taking the opposite direction
> will appear to be running away.

Against the main stream of secular scholarship the graduate Institute for Christian Studies joyfully dares to ask for a turnabout, also in aesthetics, couched in the indicative of Psalm 147 and responding to the imperative of Proverbs 8, a turnabout to understanding in aesthetics—along with philosophy, history, political science, psychology, theology, economics—so that God be praised with reverence deep, the God of our salvation!

Philosophical Aesthetics at Home with the Lord:
An Untimely Valedictory

If the title misled you to think these remarks would be like a serene posthumous letter from heaven, then Gioia's dance translation of Tracy Chapman's song "Why?" as introduction should have started to correct your expectations. My title is also not exactly playing off the discouraged prisoner, apostle Paul's remark to the Philippian believers that he'd rather be with Christ than teaching at 229 College Street West in Toronto, but it's better for you that I show up regularly with my backpack of books and muffins from Inès (cf. Philippians 1:12–26).

"Why is a woman not safe?" Dance by Gioia Seerveld. Photo by Robert E. VanderVennen

"Philosophical aesthetics at home with the Lord" has Psalm 91 for its orientation—a psalm the devil particularly hates and has memorized cold (Matthew 4:1–11), and a psalm that is the favorite of our saintly Ross Mortimer (to whom I dedicate the final song). Doing theoretical scholarship *can* be at home with the Lord even in a brutal world with the mass starvation of children, the elderly urban dweller in loneliness, the subtle terrorization of women, and the practice of Saussure's slipknot linguistics, which holds that signifiers have no certain extra-lingual signified reality so that in our duplicit world "love is hate / war is peace / no is yes / and we're all free."

As an older sinful scholar saved by the resurrected Jesus Christ's

---

This ICS exaugural address was originally published separately by the Institute for Christian Studies in Toronto in 1996 (31 pages).

sacrifice on the cross in history, I am gratefully at home with the merciful Lord here and now. And I should like to highlight certain things I understand obedient Christian scholarship to be amid the troubled historical sputtering of these last days, in order to give the next generation food for thought as *they* covenant with the LORD in our *dürftige Zeit* (to use Heidegger's phrase, "during our impoverished," not to say, with Adorno, "damaged-life times").[1]

Many evangelical Christians become homeless, cannot go home again once they have actually been faced with the rich power of current cultural diversity. And many secular disbelievers make a virtue out of being philosophical nomads, when really, I think, they are historical refugees, unable after the acid of Americanization to recapture the cloth of the European habit or the simple life of non-Western traditions. So let me try to describe theoretical study—its dynamic, prerequisites, and criteria—that will be at home with the Lord in a ruthless secularized culture, and then focus down on the field of philosophical aesthetics.

My remarks are a valedictory of sorts, saying goodbye to the Institute for Christian Studies. I call them "untimely," not because they are particularly "untimely ripped . . . from the womb" (Shakespeare, in *Macbeth,* V, viii) although, since there is no end to the making of speeches as well as of books, in any event there is always a measure of premature unripeness to the figs one serves. Sparking off from Nietzsche's *unzeitgemässe Betrachtungen*—without Nietzsche's affront to the intelligence of his audience—I recognize that my farewell remarks are not fashionable, do not fit in with the times, and might be considered out-of-step with the current drummers drumming. But "Why?" be on "the cutting edge" of scholarship—a terribly revealing, aggressive metaphor that masks Darwinian power one-upmanship.

Philosophical theory at home with the Lord might better offer a glass of fresh, unpolluted conceptual water to those whose throats are parched for knowledge, rather than adopt the conquistador ethic of cutting up new terrain.[2]

---

1   Heidegger uses the phrase in "Hölderlin und das Wesen der Dichtung" (1936), for example, to describe somewhat portentously that time "im Nichtmehr der entflohenden Götter und im Nochnicht des Kommenden." Adorno's subtitle to *Minima Moralia* is "Reflexionen aus dem beschädigten Leben" (1951).

2   Cf. William Rowe's careful conclusion to "Society after the Subject, Philosophy after the Worldview," in *Stained Glass* (1989): "What finally validates rules—especially the rule of postmodern research—is the promise of paralogy: not merely new theories but new logics, and therefore the promise of endless alternative paradigms. This is science gone to market in a big way—that is, as an industry—bent on satisfying if possible

Dynamic of scripturally directed learning and the next generation of Reformational philosophical theory

I do not hear so much anymore about "scripturally-directed learning." Except for John Kok's keen exposition of "Vollenhoven and 'Scriptural Philosophy'" (*Philosophia Reformata* 53:2 [1988]: 101–42), the phrase seems to have faded into disuse behind other concerns, like whether you are "modern" or "postmodern." But "scripturally-directed learning" always struck me as a key to the dynamic of Reformational Christian philosophy. Our theoretical thinking did not need a Cartesian methodological skepticism to cast about for an Archimedean point in the winds of change.[3] The anchor of the Creator God in Jesus Christ reliably witnessed to by the Holy Spirited Bible held as a clear, invigorating starting point, and was "*intrinsically* related"—H. Evan Runner pounded it out from the beginning—to our theoretical, scientific grasping of reality.[4] So one's daily way of life in society, one's committed vision of place and professional task in God's world, and even those called to become philosophical scholars had rough contours provided apriori by the Word to

---

the infinite, mass desire for the new and for seeing things in a new way: philosophy as vision quest, research as hallucinogen. It is difficult to distinguish this industry from entertainment. And one fails to see what is so *post-*modern about research conducted in the 'columbian' spirit of exploration, fuelled, as always, by the desire not for justice (as Lyotard claims), but for colonization of the unknown" (180).

3   Herman Dooyeweerd's brief for an Archimedean Point as inescapable prerequisite for the philosophical task is not unusual. Descartes in "Méditation II" (1641) stated: "Archimède, pour tirer le globe terrestre de sa place et le transporter en un autre lieu, ne demandait rien qu'un point qui fût ferme et immobile; ainsi j'aurai droit de concevoir de hautes espérances si je suis assez heureux pour trouver seulement une chose qui soit certain et indubitable."

Martin Heidegger stated in 1943: "Wenn daher schon nach der Wahrheit gefragt werden muss, dann verlangt man die Antwort auf die Frage, *wo wir heute stehen* [CS: my italics=*pou sto*]. Man will wissen, wie es heute mit uns steht. Man ruft nach dem Ziel, das dem Menschen in seiner Geschichte und für diese gesetzt werden soll. Man will die wirkliche 'Wahrheit.' Also doch Wahrheit!" *(Vom Wesen der Wahrheit* [Frankfurt am Main: Vittorio Klostermann, 1967], 6).

Special about Dooyeweerd's argument is his Augustinian—*inquietum est cor nostrum donec requiescat in te* (cf. *Wijsbegeerte de Wetsidee/New Critique of Theoretical Thought* [hereafter *WdW/NCTT*] 1:14–15/1:11–12)—slant that the choice of one's *pou sto* underlying philosophical thinking must be pre-philosophical, and is an uncontestable religious decision in the face of *the* Ἀρχή *of all meaning, namely,* God (*WdW/NCTT* 1:8–25/1:7–21). Cf. C.A. van Peursen on Dooyeweerd, "Dooyeweerd en de wetenschappelijke discussie" (1994) translated by John Kok, "Dooyeweerd and the Discussion About Science," in *Pro Rege* 24:1 (1995): 11–17, especially 16–17.

4   H. Evan Runner, "The Relation of the Bible to Learning," *Christian Perspectives 1960* (Pella: Pella Publishing, 1960), 86–93, 100–17, 133–37, 146.

PSALM 91

Whoever feels at home in the presence of the Most Glorious God
shall be able to pass the night
in the shadow of the Almighty One,
for that person can say to the LORD God,
"My sanctuary! My Place-to-stand!
    My God in whom I am trusting!"

The LORD God shall extricate you from the trap of the Hunter!
God will save you from the sting of Death!
The LORD shall cover you with God's wings;
under God's wings you can run to hide.
Do not be afraid of midnight terror
or of sickness that stalks people in the daytime
or of pain that creeps up (on one) in the twilight
or of crippling disease that strikes while the sun shines:
a thousand may collapse right next to you,
ten thousand may be struck down; but you shall not perish—
God's truth shall protect you, fence you in,
while letting you see with your own eyes
how the godless are paid in full.

You have said, "The LORD God is my sanctuary!"
You have taken the Most Glorious God as your At-home!
Therefore Destruction cannot get you;
disaster shall never enter (the door) where you are living:
for God Almighty has made you a charge of God's angels,
ordering them to guard you in all that you do.
They shall hold you up by their hands
so that you do not even stub your foot against a stone,
so that you can walk past roaring lions and poisonous snakes,
so that you can step on and crush the lion and even . . . the Dragon!

"Because he or she has held fast to me, I shall save them!
Because she or he knows my name, I shall deliver them!
I will hear each one when that person cries out to me;
I will be with them in the terribly dark days,
free them from the Darkness, and bring them glory!
I will let him and her live peacefully on and on,
because I shall let them see my salvation!"

Translation by Calvin Seerveld, 1965

which one was faith-convicted.

That self-consciously *thetical* orientation holds enormous promise for fruitful, edifying, and critical theoretical studies, because you communally have a headstart in knowledge (Proverbs 1:7, 9:10). You know the LORD's *chesed* posits discoverable ordinances for all facets of creatural human life, and ontic structural limits for developing institutional powers in history, which as divine love constraints, keeping human authority relative, are violated with cruel outcomes. You know ahead of time that physical, sensitive, technical, and aesthetic affairs as well as analytic, political, and economic matters are called to be holy, normed by the compassionate Rule of Jesus Christ acoming, which affords joy in thinking, justice in feeling, truth in advertising, and peace-making speech. The educative fun comes in spelling out concretely what this biblically-directed vision means for us traditioning creatures today, and patiently unearthing *our* errors—*philosophia Christiana reformanda est.*

It's been good fun for many years, as the variety of theses and dissertations I have been privileged to mentor show, not because the cross-generational research always got it right and was trouble-free, but because the work together was informed by the dynamic that this offering of theoretical analysis is for the Lord, for God's supportive people, and any inquisitive neighbor, whether the stuff be the belabored parataxic thought-moves of Adorno, the incisive bright *Lehrstücke* of early Brecht, the wide-ranging humanist cultural theory of Ortega y Gasset, the fine-tuned notebooks and paintings of Paul Klee, the graphic cries of Käthe Kollwitz, Derrida's painstaking rereading of Plato's *Phaedrus,* or the lethal phantasmic world of Baudrillard.

The Reformational dynamic of being at home with the Lord in strange and sometimes fearsome academic places comes through best, I think, when someone who has Psalm 91 in the blood can pass it on imperceptibly, with corporeal presence, like mouth-to-mouth resuscitation or a holy kiss that takes two, three, or more years of intimate struggle with material you want to understand, honor, exorcize, transform, bring captive to the Truth (2 Corinthians 10:3–5). That you do academic work in the grip of something more powerful than yourself becomes very real, if I may be personal for a minute, when your friends and colleagues are untimely taken away. But you know Howard Rienstra, Robert Carvill, Peter Steen, Stanley Wiersma, Bernard Zylstra—Destruction did *not* get them! (You'd say it in faith before the devil self!) So you continue the endeavor of scholarly obedience under a glorious host of witnesses.

The generation of Reformational scholars coming up does well to hear the passion. If you have not self undergone the hardship experienced by those founding the Association for Reformed Scientific Studies, or suffered the ridicule Gerald Vandezande and Harry Antonides originally did in charting policy for the Christian Labour Association of Canada; if you have never had to sing Luther's song ad-libbing (as some of us colleagues could have done, earlier on) "let *wife,* goods and kindred go," you might miss the genius of Reformational scholarship and cultural activity, and suppose it comes down to holding certain orthodox tenets.[5] The dynamic of "scripturally directed learning" is selflessly single-minded service (Philippians 1:9–1 1), has *nothing* to do with careers or fringe benefits, but comes with the high cost of *communal* struggle as sinful people to be obedient together in making a *redemptive difference* on the secular educational scene.

I felt confirmed on this point upon reading writings by Ignacio Ellacuria and Ignacio Martian-Boró, Jesuit professors of the University of Central America, José Simeón Cañas (begun 1965, about the time of the Unionville Study Conference of our Association), who were murdered six years ago yesterday by a U.S.-trained elite army corps of El Salvadorean soldiers. "¿es posible una universidad distinta?" "Is a different kind of university possible" that gives preference to the *exploited* poor majority of people in the country, asked Ellacuria ten years after its inception? And there are fascinating, unflinching reflections, about how university experience does not lead to democratic socialization but fosters societal differentiation (Martian-Boró, 223). You don't seem to serve the economically poor peasants in the land by admitting the intellectually poor as students to the university (Ellacuria, 198). How do you combat the undeniably bourgeois structure of the university—privileged, propertied, self-interested and get beyond importing foreign models, short-sighted pragmatism, and gradual acclimation to what is (diabolically) "normal"? they asked (Ellacuna, 193–94, 218).

I make no judgment on how ICS is faring with respect to the pressures of assimilation to what is expected by our good neighbor secular peers, the pros and cons of being domesticated to the Learned Societies format of learning, or the temptation to be different because you make no difference. My initial point is that the dynamic of "scripturally-directed learning" is very precious, blowing where it lists. Now it is time

---

5 It is instructive to notice how Scriven needs to modify John Howard Yoder's rather absolute position on designating nonviolence to be the crux of the Anabaptist attitude and practice, in order to avoid an unbiblical legalism on Anabaptist identification (188–90).

for us older ones to encourage the younger ones: you may not need to reinvent the wheel that racked the body of legendary St. Catharine of Alexandria, but it is your turn now to be faithful, forgiven leaders in not being conformed to current fashions but to be metamorphosed by the radical renewal of your consciousness to discern more deeply what the good, satisfied will of God be for learning what and how and why (Romans 12:1–2).

Prerequisites: the structure of Christian scholarly knowledge
As to the prerequisites and criteria for thorough-going Christian scholarship, which might give sight to the culturally blind and speech to those mute from disorientation in the world, let me be terse and incomplete, aware that my own mix of New York fishmonger sensibility and an embarrassment of European riches shape my predilections.

Prerequisites for giving *scholarly* body to a biblically shaped vision are at least: (1) ingrained historical knowledge, (2) multilinguality, (3) encyclopedic purview, and (4) knowing what time it is on the streets.

First of all, scholarly learning takes time because it respects the fact that cultural knowledge did not begin when you as a person entered the world. An apprentice scholar goes prospecting for precious stones in the rubble of civilization, develops a detective sense for what is hidden and connected, and gradually becomes aware, like a connoisseur, of the location and dated environs formative upon what is discovered, the human travail embodied in artifacts and in only-once-upon-a-time events, good or bad. Christian scholarship is not in a hurry, does not jump to conclusions, but cherishes sifting the evidence, being open to insightful contributions by twisted people loose in God's world. A result of such patient re-searching investigation of the complicated, convoluted, cumulative past of human accomplishments is a historical consciousness where you lose the prominence of yourself in order to gain yourself in the context of the ages. So the scholar can come to perceive that there is nothing really new under the sun, except those offerings born again by the gospel of Jesus Christ; yet God's grace shines down upon the unjust as well as upon the just cultivators of the earth (cf. Matthew 5:45); therefore, blanket historiographic judgments are wrong.

This historical consciousness constitutive for Christian scholarship keeps one cautious but enables one to make fine, critical distinctions, with feelers (*Gereformeerde voelhorens*/Reformational antennae) that notice subliminally where things are coming from and where they are going. The historically aware Christian scholar will be saved from the anachronistic mistake, for example, of reading Thomas Aquinas' *ratio humana* as if it be the narrow-minded post-Cartesian *cogito* of Rationalism, equally dismissible by us post-Enlightenment figures. And a would-be scholar errs, says Gertrude Himmelfarb, if you jettison centuries of philosophical reflection because of its dead-white-male bias, proudly missing untold knowledge (151–55). It is fairly clear that one cannot fault Aristotle for not reading Foucault, and we should not badger Kant for omitting Kristeva. But the shallowness of the homo-up-to-datum intellectual who lacks historical consciousness turns ugly when it comes to giving leadership, because intellectual enablement without a fortified historical humbledness—if one is thrust into power without historiographic seasoning—normally evidences, I'm afraid, arbitrary, special interests rather than a discerning wisdom.

Second, a blessing in God's judgment upon the Babel of Bible times (Genesis 11:1–9) is the prismatic richness of varied mother tongues. To hear modern Greek, Polish, or Chinese spoken to your face, which you do not understand, deeply confronts you with a neighbor who is "other" than yourself. It is a mark of scholarship, I contend, to realize that human language is the soul of story-telling and the literature of a specific people's culture; and foreign languages are *not* capricious games or snags that need a fix-it, but are invitations to leave behind one's parochiality and to enter into fantastic new worlds that help provide the sharpness of depth-vision. Facility in several languages has always been good for renewing scholarly precision: Humanist Lorenzo Valla (1405–57) showed that the neo-Platonist Greek texts of Dionysius revered as canonic by a millennium of Latin-reading Christians was *not* the Areopagite brought to Christ by the apostle Paul (Acts 17:32–34); reformer Martin Luther (1483–1546) changed a church's perception of *Busse,* distinguishing "repentance and conversion" from "penance," because he could probe behind the Vulgate into the original biblical languages.[6]

---

6 In the 1518 commentary on his 95 Wittenburg theses, Luther points out the error of reading the Latin Vulgate translation of the Greek μετανοεῖτε(be converted, be at heart turned around, e.g., Matthew 4:17, Romans 12:2) *poenitentiam agite,* as meaning "do penance": ". . . ex ipso verbo graeco 'Metanoite,' id est poenitentiam agite, quod rigidissime transferri potest 'transmentamini,' id est 'mentem et sensum alium induite, resipiscite, transitum mentis et phase spiritus facite,' ut scilicent nunc caelestia sapiatis, qui hucusque terrena sapuisti" (*Conclvsio* I.1). Therefore, said Luther, the church prescription of penance as a sacrament earning indulgence, thanks to the intervention of clerics, is not Scriptural. "When our Lord and Master Jesus Christ said *poenitentiam agite,* he willed the whole life of believers to be one of repentance" (*Conclvsio* I).

In a prefatory letter to John Staupitz, with the hope that Staupitz will submit the

I am not promoting the old humanist trust in the power of languages to save Western civilization as Matthew Arnold (Greek) and Alfred North Whitehead (Latin) did.[7] Technological expertise with directions in American-English has become practically the *lingua franca* of worldwide culture anyhow. But I hear the frustrated cry of Ojibway Basil H. Johnson who says to earnest liberal white academics, "If you want to understand us 'Indians,' learn our languages! Then you might not translate the raven as a 'trickster,' and treat our sacred myths like Walt Disney 'Little Red Riding Hood' nursery tales."[8] And Johnson's plea holds true for anyone willing to meet diverse ethnic cultural traditions deserving respect around the globe, whether it be Dutch, Russian, Venda, Swahili, or Arabic. Scholarship gives one the time it takes for a person to learn to navigate in languages foreign to one's mother tongue but not strange to God's ear. That's why scholarly knowledge can have the bouquet of vintage wine rather than the monolingual fizz of a diet coke.

Third, scholarly knowledge, as I understand it, has durance, the interconnected, systematic settledness that is there for the long haul. Even when the study concerns something very definite, there will be a philosophical, encyclopedic overview present that situates the knowledge genially. It is the nature of bona fide scholarship not to be single-issue oriented, not to play the power moves of centering and marginalizing, politicizing knowledge; but like a good basketball player the scholarly investigator develops peripheral vision that is universe-wide and cross-culturally primed during any focused examination.

Such an integrative perspective is considered totalitarian by many current theorists prone to "fragmatics," as my colleague Bob Sweetman has called it.[9] And the very pressured hurry to life with which our information-ridden society formats knowledge tends to force one to *petits*

---

commentary to Pope Leo X, Luther credits his old professor (Staupitz) with first giving him the idea that *poenitentia* meant "a change of heart God induces" rather than endless "rites of contrition" exacted of people. From being the most bitter word in the Bible, "Nunc nihil dulcius aut gratius mihi sonet, quam *poenitentia*" (Letter to Staupitz, 30 May 1518, 1:17).

7 Cf. the concluding paragraphs of Matthew Arnold's "Literature and Science," in *Discourses in America* (1885), and "The Place of Classics in Education," chapter 5 in Alfred North Whitehead's *The Aims of Education* (1929).

8 Cf. Basil H. Johnson in "One Generation from Extinction," 99–104. In my judgment the 1991 official Canadian video that celebrates Bill Reid's sculpture, "Spirit of the Haida Gwaii," given pride of place at the Canadian embassy in Washington, D.C., trivializes Haida creation myths by telling its creed in cartoon style.

9 Robert Sweetman, "Of Tall Tales and Small Stories: Post-modern 'fragmatics' and the Christian historian" (1994).

récits, says Bob Goudzwaard in his most recent writing, since you only have time to worry about saving your own skin (29) with the cutback of your job rather than to worry about a "world" of misery and the burgeoning national debt out there.

Whoever is tempted in graduate studies to follow the tune of piecemeal, topical issues must be prepared to pay the pipers Stanley Fish, Haydon White, and others who have repudiated, in my judgment—while living off it!—scholarship that assumes reliable wholeness and eschatonic continuity because of the sovereign provident LORD who will be returning in Jesus Christ to see what we sinful and redeemed humans have made of God's good creation.

Fourth, what distinguishes the specialized kind of theoretical research that results in scholarly knowledge from pedantry is that scholarship breathes the pulse of concrete experience and aches to put the pell-mell rush of daily life into perspective.[10] William Butler Yeats excoriates the old, learned, respectable pedantic annotators of lines—

> All shuffle there; all cough in ink
> All think what other people think. . . .
> Lord, what would they say
> Did their Catullus walk that way.

But Nietzsche's philosophy has verve and passion. Johan Huizinga's *Herfstij der Middeleeuwen* (1919) has details laden with blood and fire and insight. George Steiner scholarship exhaustively probes the matter of "translation" (in *After Babel,* 1975) until you see how the very quality of life depends upon it. Kwame Anthony Appiah's in-depth analysis of Africa in the philosophy of culture (*In my Father's House,* 1992) wrestles through to contested theoretical conclusions that convict the reader that we stand at a crossroad in our philosophical scholarship.

I am not advocating that scholarly knowledge be the most important kind of knowledge. To be street-smart and know the Manchester stride (which I have taught my Junior Members, to avoid being mugged on city streets walking between art galleries),[11] or to have the split-second presence of mind to answer redemptively, as a Citizens for Public Justice representative answers a journalist's wrong-headed question, can be at

---

10 The section on "scholarship" in the Institute for Christian Studies' founding educational creed says we confess that "The task of the scholar is to give a scientific account of the structure of creation and thereby promote a more effective ordering of the everyday experience of the entire community" (c. 1965).

11 This burly walk was taught me by Martin Evans, a former director of the Greenbelt Festival in England, in 1982.

times much more valuable than the slow, reflective scholarly knowledge that can back-up one's stance in the world. But Christian scholarship does not happen in a vacuum just because it is done in a basement study or library carrel: scholarship, if it is right, has existentiality, is circumstantially aware of what time it is. I do not mean the time on your watch, or even the time on the *Toronto Star* headlines. I mean the time of profound skepticism in the streets, the deteriorating pragmatist stage of our cultural tuberculosis—the consumptive North American time—the delusionary time in academe that we are post-ideologies. (What time one thinks it is, deeply affects the character of your scholarship.) Christian scholarship, I believe, does not become like the times it inhabits, but spends its honest-to-God identity winsomely, like a fool, weeping and laughing as needed with those in the times that are passing away (cf. 1 John 2:15–19).

Criteria: the Septuagintal norm
for an institution geared to Christian theoretical learning
The criteria for theoretical study at home with the LORD in our rapacious, parasitic day can be put succinctly: let there be a Septuagintal community of field-specific scholars consecrated to the LORD in faithfully edifying the rising generation.

That may sound old-fashioned and homespun to some, but it is incredibly radical for an academic institution today to be a university rather than a collection of fiefdoms in power struggle for money and pride of place (Said, 140–43): an actual street address where specialized scholarly work is conceived to be wedded to the colleague's scholarly work so that interdisciplinary rigor is normal, exciting, not just for the apprentice scholars but for the mentors themselves. "Septuagint" is my metaphor for having seventy or ten scholars united for the slow, difficult task of translating a biblical vision and Christian thought-tradition with a corpus of sources into new languages so that a living past of fallible, sanctified scholarly witnesses known veritably in your blood comes to fructify present and coming generations with wisdom, while we augment, correct, and serve it to both friends and enemies.

I posit Septuagintal criteria as *norm* for a Christian institution doing theory, not as a utopian ideal; just as I meant to describe the *structure* of Christian scholarly knowledge, not sketch a possible scenario. Septuagintal translation as guiding norm for Christian theoretical study can, of course, be debated, defaulted on, as well as enjoyed. I firmly believe, from within the inheritance of the historical Reformation, the Septuagintal calling is a light yoke and a great gift made possible only by the presence of the Holy Spirit, since each of us all-too-human creatures is continually tempted to prefer the Holy Spirit's absence.

A Septuagintal community for doing theory means the music of philosophical jargon will fill the air, because it takes more than a shared worldview to mediate disciplinarily honed scholarship: it takes a common, operative philosophical systematics. I know, "geneticistic interactionary monism" and "anticipatory analogical aesthetic functions" sound like glossolalia to the uninitiated, but technical philosophical terms embody as precise and fearsome a necessary shorthand as the medical vocabulary of *retinitis pigmentosa* and embolism. In-house jargon, whether it be Vollenhovian or Derridean, betrays the speaker's affiliation, communicates to the faithful, and builds up a universe of discourse that allows a community of scholars to explore intricate realities (or get lost in a scholastic labyrinth of words).

What keeps a Christian Septuagintal philosophical scholarly endeavor in touch with the world of pain and insight is that the fine-tuned, intellectual exorcism that is essential to Christian scholarship is not done as Pharisaic putdown, but aims to restore wholeness to what is damaged and give good direction to what has been mistaken or unjustly suppressed. The Christian Septuagintal agenda is at heart passionately redemptive, intent upon giving flesh and blood to Christ's gentle Rule upon concepts, images, arguments, sensations (cf. Philippians 1:9–11!), hunches that can kill people or bring life even before the ideas grow legs. And it is that aura of restoring creatural praise of God and a perception that the ungainly theoretical results are a sweet-smelling offering to the LORD through all the jargon smoke that rallies around the Septuagintal community of irregular scholars the watershed of folk who follow the Christ, including that endangered species called *de kleine luyden*.[12]

Whoever spends a lifetime in scholarly work that meets the criteria of a Septuagintal community knows what Psalm 91 means about being at home with the LORD. That peace always needs to be troubled, however, by Kwame Appiah's remark that "the real battle is not being fought in the academy" (179). I think the real power struggles of sin are being fought in institutions of theoretical learning, too, but Appiah means that conceptual warfare is not the only battle in town, so scholars need to remember with modesty that they and their books are not Shelley's

---

12 *"De kleine luyden"* is a Dutch phrase, "the little fellows," which refer to ὁ λαός ("the lay people"), to use Jesus Christ's term of endearment, the uneducated folk who lived close to the Bible whom Abraham Kuyper led to support the formation of a Christian political party, a Christian university (free from state and church), a Christian newspaper (*Trouw*), and other cultural endeavors in the Netherlands during the 1880s.

Whoever Shelters with the LORD

1. Who-ev-er shel-ters with the LORD and lives with-in the Al-might-y's shade can say, "My God, in whom I trust, your ref-uge makes me un-a-fraid!"
2. The faith-ful LORD will spare you death. God's wings will cov-er you from harm. No ter-ror, sick-ness, night or day, will ev-er cause you grave a-larm.
3. Though thou-sands per-ish at your side, such pun-ish-ment shall not touch you. Be-cause the LORD serves as your home, God's grace will al-ways see you through.
4. God gives his an-gels charge of you to guard from those who per-se-cute. You shall not trip a-gainst a stone, but tram-ple ser-pents un-der-foot.
5. "Be-cause you cleave to me in love and know my name to call in need, I shall pro-tect and keep you safe with bless-ing, glo-ry, life in-deed."

Text: Psalm 91; vers. Calvin Seerveld, 1985, ©
Tune: Grenoble Antiphoner, 1753

LM
DEUS TUORUM MILITUM

"legislators of the world"; "intellectuals" should not assume the role of a secular clergy.

That said I am still impressed with the role played among God's people, as well as in the Egyptland of the pharaohs, Nebuchadnezzar's Babylon, and political cabinets today, by the educated *hakamim* (wise men and women, counselors for leaders), especially when prophets, priests, and royal rulers become corrupt. So, in our highly diversified society there is a good place waiting for professional scholars humbly driven by the biblical Reformational dynamic and chastened by the Septuagintal norm, to give away wise untimely counsel to those caught in our cultural times of disarray and inscrutable, wildcat harassment.

Pledges of Jubilee (Eerdmans, 1995) is an example of philosophical aesthetics at home with the Lord. Everything I have enunciated today is there: a steady, unobtrusive Reformational dynamic wrapped in love, scholarly professionality with historiographic depth, different lingual universes, encyclopedic reach, and awareness of racist monuments, proverb poetry, psaltery, pop-rock, cinematic, and technotronic artistry. I find an amazing concordance in the variety of what the eighteen women and men have written (and I know it would also be there for the shadowy figures who did not make the publishing deadline). I have not yet read everything, but I have read enough to know it reaches out gloriously beyond anything I may have sparked, and to my surprise and joy fulfils the hope of my inaugural for a turnabout in aesthetics to understanding. With intimations of doxology *Pledges of Jubilee* takes a load off my shoulders: I do not have to weigh myself in the balance as to whether *I* have come through on my task commissioned by the curatorium and Association twenty-three years ago. Thank God! Here is a quiver full (Psalm 127) of evidence for what almost always remains invisible—that intimate, inter-generational transfer of a focused vision, which now seems to sparkle fresh like grass in the sun after a spring rain (cf. 2 Samuel 23:3–4).

From my vantage point of making an institutional exit, I will not sketch out my ten year work program taking shape, if God is merciful. But I should like to end by noting five problems I think will need attention, if not priority, in the field of philosophical aesthetics by you Jubilee-oriented generation.

First, if trust in scientific reason supposedly deteriorates further—I am not convinced this will be so, inside or outside the academy—and if Jacques Ellul's *word* more and more succumbs to McLuhan's electronic media *image,* then stock in imaginativity will soar, and there will be jobs galore for aestheticians! Lyotard typically transmogrifies Kant's conception of the sublime into a handy paralogical device that makes truth-knowing essentially a matter of incommensurable discourses (1984:77–79; 1988:19, 48–50, 168–69, 179–80). So an aestheticism may try to fill the vacuum left by scientism and legitimate as ethical whatever hangs fire, so long as it be imaginative.

Philosophical aestheticians at home with the LORD will need to state clearly the peculiar (modally preverbal, cogitative, I happen to think) valid knowledge of nuanced reality objective to the imagining personal subject, and show that the aesthetic faceting of truth has its own glory, though it is neither discursive nor intrinsically revelational. Maybe the idea of "allusivity" as core orientation and my current study on "wicked beauty," along with Estrada's emphasis on "ugliness" (675–737), may help define aesthetics phenomenologically as a particular discipline in a flexible way that will support Zuidervaart's fashioning a normative aesthetics that aims to hold disturbing final truth in many-splendored tension with actual historical art.[13]

Second, given a penchant for artistic event over art object in the last few generations, and a trend to recess art products behind artistic process, there is even some urgency for theorists to face the problem again whether artistry, which has modulated its character for centuries, has a nature. I am not talking here about whether arts like music, theatre, and sculpture are ever "prime" or not:[14] I am talking about whether a chamber orchestra concert, a theatre troupe presenting Brecht's *Mutter Courage,* and a bronze woman mould cast by Henry Moore, have a constructed structure distinct from noise, a good discussion, and smelted ore—a constructed structure appealing to an ontic kind of entity/event that is historically artistic in nature.[15]

Milan Kundera reports how Ionesco's *Bald Soprano* and *The Lesson* liberated Czech society in the 1960s from experiencing theatre as an educational, moral, and political instrument (260); it took an "absurd" piece like *Rhinoceros* to free theatre to be theatre-as-such, an exhilarating, imaginative wonder that sideswiped totalitarian rule and bureaucratic doublespeak without moving a political muscle. Such bona fide artistic reality deserves ontological backup, I think, to forestall colonialization by semiotics, media studies, or to have artistry get lost in the shuffle of important non-artistic affairs like gender, nationality, and technological

---

13 Cf. Zuidervaart's careful dialogue with Adorno's struggle on truth in art, "History, Art, and Truth" (1991:275–307).

14 I need to think through Jim Leach's incisive judgment in *Pledges of Jubilee* that "Seerveld overestimates the irreducibility of each art-kind" (44), because "the distinctive character of an art-kind often importantly involves extra-aesthetic facets" (49). Leach is correct, it seems to me, that one's ontological ordering needs the flex to meet historical actualities as they develop (50). Whether "there are no 'prime' arts," as he contends (52), is for me still moot.

15 Granted that entitary kinds evolve historically in ways that irreducible modal orderings for creatural existence do not—and we must avoid a Platonic doctrine of *eidē* for entities—can we not discern sorts of typical cultural configurations such that they constitute an ontic kind able to harbor important "phaenotypical" (Dooyeweerd, *WdW* 3 :53–641/*NCTT* 3:76–98) differences, comparable to the fairly fixed, typical nature throughout history of families, of political governance, of cities, of commercial institutions? Jim Leach is again correct, I think, to ask us to distinguish ontic "aesthetic analogues" from a "spectrum of the arts" (*Pledges of Jubilee,* 52), but the playful historical clutter to constellations of arts in God's world is not wholly arbitrary, would be my hunch.

innovation, which do indeed impinge upon art.

Sorting out this foundational matter of defining artistry in a changing world is practically hopeless, I think, if an artistic event/artwork is conceived conventionally and only in terms of its functions. Precisely because there are now so many more professional Christian artists who have questions about their task, it behooves aestheticians at home with the LORD in God's world to come through with supportive rationale and wisdom for the artist's specific, multifaceted calling.

Third, it has been my privilege as philosophical aesthetician to work in an aesthetics lab for twenty years: at *Patmos* with Willem Hart, Mary Steenland, and a few others, 1969–79, where the vision of Christ's Rule in art hit the rocky road of having actual, manual graphic artists before your face whose lives were dislocated in and by society; and a decade on a committee with Bert Polman, Emily Brink, and nine others who became intimates in forging a new *Psalter Hymnal* for the Christian Reformed Church, 1977–87, where the principle of aesthetic integrity and liturgical appropriateness was not theoretical, but came down to concrete decisions on selecting this or that melody, and which versified texts. (The *Psalter Hymnal* may be the single most important cultural thing I will have done in my lifetime.)

Since the assignment a few months ago to think through the necessity of Christian public artistry, I have discovered for myself a way to bring "aesthetic lab" concerns, along with aesthetic life at large, and especially "popular culture and art"—artistry encapsulated within the enlarging social complex of bona fide entertainment—more forcefully to the fore for critical appreciation and examination.[16]

Because non-artistic institutions like business, state, church, "first-nation" bonds, municipalities, media, and schools will need to act if the

---

16 "The Joys Are Simply Told" by William D. Romanowski in *Pledges of Jubilee* (31, 35–36) very charitably credits the idea of "aesthetic life" in my *Rainbows for the Fallen World* (1980) with the goods to avoid the elitism associated with certain Christian communities and with various secular art theories that have not taken the "popular arts" seriously. Indeed, the watershed of ordinary playfulness (I spent an academic year on "Theory of Play" in a graduate seminar at ICS, 1981–82), imaginativity ("Imaginativity" in *Faith and Philosophy* 4:1 [1987]: 43–58 {supra pp. 27–44}), "taste" ("Both More and Less than a Matter of Taste," in *Acta Academica* 25:4 [1993]:1–12 {supra pp. 135–144}), and "style" I consider basic realities needing analysis by theoretical aesthetics. Romanowski is also certainly correct to note that the problem of evaluating "commercial art," as he himself has incisively done in *Dancing in the Dark: Youth, popular culture and the electronic media* (coordinated by Quentin Schultze, edited by Roy Anker [Grand Rapids: Eerdmans, 1991]), goes beyond any exclusive "aesthetic criterion" (*Pledges of Jubilee*, 33).

art world can be reshaped for integration in society, there are genuine philosophical aesthetic problems that need sorting out. In a generation where all kinds of boundaries are being erased, it would be good to demonstrate how careful theoretical distinctions—cultural work, aesthetic events, art-as-such, encapsulated art—can build bridges rather than throw up fences.[17] As Vàclav Havel says: the public dominant culture is decisive in a land (134–35). So public culture is territory that Christian aesthetics must hold in steady view in order to have its voice heard there.

Fourth, most fraught is the writing of art history, because both a connective narrative and the focus of an artistic/literary canon are hotly contested.[18] Artistry and literature are always inextricably intertwined with the changing societal cultural life extant, and themselves come of age variously, like mutants from cultic rites, artisanry, oral story-telling, decorative engraving, work chants, and what not. So the difficulty for history-keeping is to decide what kind of opossum it is you are trying to catch in order to detail its pedigree and lineage, physiognomy, habitat, working contribution, prospects, and issue. There are multiple, legitimate stories for one to tell and write down like maps for later visitors to ponder as they retrace the trails, for example, of frescoes, the "novel," European painting, cinematic art, the oeuvre of Picasso, Inuit carving.

Because neo-idealist "art histories" like the keen, minute studies of cultural schematicist Erwin Panofsky dissolve art into a sign-language for *zeitgeistig* approximations of "intrinsic meaning . . . essential to human mind," such iconographic art history writing has been unable, I think, to

---

17 Cf. C. Seerveld, "The Necessity of Christian Public Artistry," in *Christian Public Culture: The arts, democracy, and community*, eds. Lambert Zuidervaart and Henry Luttikhuizen (London: Macmillan Press / New York: St. Martin's Press, 2000), 83–107 {see *RA*: 1–28}.

18 In *Rethinking Art History. Meditations on a Coy Science* (1989) Donald Preziosi states that "the art of art history is inextricably grounded in a logocentric paradigm of signification" (16); so the very idea of a "disciplinary" art history writing must be put in question (17–20). Preziosi reads the diversity and (politicizing) conflict of "guiding metaphors in art historical practice" to demonstrate "the ironic status of the discipline of art history as a form of institutionalized knowledge" (157).

In his conclusion to *Principles of Art History Writing* (1991) David Carrier states that "traditional narrative strategies no longer seem effective" (240). ". . . I have argued that traditional art history ends when art historians recognize the inescapably rhetorical character of their narratives" (242).

For a judicious analysis of the status quo in theoretical reflection on "canon" and an extensive bibliography cf. Jan Gorak, *The Making of the Modern Canon: Genesis and crisis of a literary idea* (London: Athlone, 1991). Also, cf. a special issue of *The Journal of Aesthetics and Art Criticism* on "Philosophy and the Histories of the Arts," 51:3 (1993): 299–523.

correct the neo-Positivist evolutionistic determinism of geneticist Riegl who did make an important advance in proposing that *art* history deal with peculiarly *artform* matters.[19] Today the very task of detecting a story line has been so discredited by earlier, facile teleologistic scenarios with millennial endings (Hegel, Arnold Hauser) that certain serious investigators doubt standard art history writing can be anything other than a celebrative reifying, fictional ploy of panoptic ideologues (Bryson, Preziosi, Carrier).

An aesthetics at-home with the LORD, however, knows that the reality of an eschatonic fabric to change provides a non-logical, turbulent but connected storyline of fruit and waste for human endeavor, including the committed material works and events of artists' hands. It is so that artworks have an implacable, affective nature, which must be noted in keeping their history, and the disruptive innovations that take place between successive generations busy in the same artistic field are critical for art history-telling;[20] but to tell a history of something one needs horizons beyond the stark art object/artistic event present, horizons of spirited vision that palpably enfold the very human artistry and literary narrative pieces one is examining in sequence.

I may still think "cultural periods" conceived as conflicting, contemporary, eventful happenings that inhabit historians as well as artists of diverse traditions, spiriting the direction of their contributions, will help order the googolplex of factors one needs to sift through in a remembering that will do justice to the committed artistic footprints of strangers. But it's true, the best art historiographic vessels for loving the neighbor while toasting the Lord will be chalices of alabaster.[21]

---

19 Lorenz Dittmann seems to me to offer an exemplar for art history writing that meets Henry Luttikhuizen's important demand to "look for the visual strategies employed, which were produced to persuade a particular audience to accept certain beliefs as their own" (*Pledges of Jubilee*, 96), in Dittmann's painstaking analysis of how color showed up in the changing figures and times of European painterly art; cf. *Farbgestaltung und Farbtheorie in der abendländischen Malerei, Eine Einführung* (Darmstadt: Wissenschaftliche Buchgesellschaft, 1987).

20 "...the *historical* is to be found in what a new generation makes of its inheritance. The crux to be noted by an historian of art is not so much what is given as what is taken. The *historical connection* is the unpredictable innovative modification made across the break in continuity" (my "Vollenhoven's Legacy for Art Historiography," in *Philosophia Reformata* 58:1 [1993]: 64–65 {see *AH*: 47–48}. Kurt Badt's judgment on "Der kunstgeschichtliche Zusammenhang" (1966–67) hints in this direction; cf. *Kunsttheoretische Versuche* (Köln: Verlag M. DuMont Schauberg, 1968), 148, 167–68.

21 As a practicing art historian Henry Luttikhuizen finds that "Periodization has lost its legitimacy in art history, for it has proven to be impossible to keep periods distinct from one other" (*Pledges of Jubilee*, 91), and details various evils to which the carto-

Fifth, somehow there needs to come a realignment, I believe, in the mentality as well as terminology of those who advocate a "theological aesthetics" and a "theology of the arts," because "theological aesthetics" short-sheets the very genuine desire to have human artistry praise God and serve the neighbor in all of life. My complaint goes back to biblical basics: the doctrine of a good creation precedes and grounds the doctrine of redemption from sin; so you do need a Christian philosophy of culture before you think about a missiology of culture. How can we in the Reformational Christian tradition make convincing that doing justice in the city of Jerusalem should not be reduced to worship in the temple at the hub of the city activity? How can we make convincing that the *Basileia tou theou* is the biblically mandated, primal horizon for the body of Christ on earth, and such primordial context calls us to the ministry of reconciliation (cf. 2 Corinthians 5:17–19), and is not in competition with or subservience to the *ekklesia*, its mother?[22]

Perhaps the difficulty for even Christians to conceive the radicality of the biblical gospel for full-time diaconal aesthetic and artistic service *outside* the church walls lies in the fact that many Christian thought traditions have only domesticated the Greco-Roman inheritance and then hewn out a transcendent "theological" realm for theory and the arts that would go an additional, special extra mile of "grace," rather than be driven to instigate an in-principle conversion by the Hebraic-Christian revelation of the Greco-Roman impulse we Western Christians have inher-

---

graphic methodology may be prone. I agree that art-historical rigor is never neat, but I would argue that actual art-historical writing like "Telltale Statues in Watteau's Paintings" (*Eighteenth-Century Studies* 14:2 [1980–81]: 151–80 {see *AH*: 171–195}) is never meant to be an instantiation of an art historiographic theory; yet one's operative art-historiographic methodology normally enframes (or de-frames!) and provides the horizons for what the historian of art finds, describes, and exposits. Cf. Henry Luttikhuizen's forthright critique in "Serving Vintage Wisdom: Art Historiography in the Neo-Calvinian Tradition," *Pledges of Jubilee*, 87–92, 104.

22 I have in mind the intriguing Christian reflection of figures like Gerardus van der Leeuw, *Wegen en Grenzen: Een studie over de verhouding van religie en kunst* (Amsterdam: H.J. Paris, 1932); Nathan A. Scott, Jr., ed., *The New Orpheus: Essays toward a Christian poetic* (New York: Sheed & Ward, 1964); Jeremy S. Begbie, *Voicing Creation's Praise: Toward a theology of the arts* (Edinburgh: T & T Clark, 1991); an ambitious three-year, international project, "Toward a Missiology of Western Culture," currently funded by the Pew Charitable Trust fund.

I am at a loss at how to argue that promotion of a general spiritualization of art, or a liturgical cast to art, or an evangelizing requirement for art, as the most Christian task misses, I think, the grounding biblical insight that art as normal creatural service can be a restored and redemptive, holy act, so artistry does not need an "extra," theologically explicit insignia to be truly full-fledged service by Christ's body-at-large.

ited. As the plethora of non-European ethnic cultures cry out for justice, maybe the time is opportune for God's people in the West (or East) to challenge both Athens and Babylon at their very rootage in vanity, and go biblically simple, with a historical feasting in post-resurrection creaturehood that also comprises the rigor of exorcizing prayer and fasting (cf. Mark 9:14–29, Isaiah 25:6–9).

After this tumble of words, do you know what it all comes down to, asked Qohelet (Ecclesiastes 12:11–14)? It's as simple as that a mother and father are called to give their daughters and sons bread, and not a stone (cf. Matthew 7:1–12).

"Offering of bread rather than a stone"
Photo by Ines and Calvin Seerveld

It is the responsibility before God of each generation toward the next following generation, whatever its appointed tasks be, to know the difference and to bake good bread.

Lambert Zuidervaart, Henry Luttikhuizen, Barbara Carvill, William David Romanowski (whom I privately think of as the Jubilee Gang-of-Four): *Pledges of Jubilee* has been an uncommon blessing to me, not only the excellent, traditioning book (to use Bill Rowe's phraseology), but also the generating conception: raising up a kind of stele to mark an end with new beginnings. A teacher with students who lovingly, critically carry on one's work can "graduate" in peace.

Gratefulness to God wells up in me too for the young men and women in whose lives of reflection I have been a living part. A good number are bodily present or in spirit here tonight as dedicated professors, college administrators, reliable curators/designers/novelists/artists/figures in the art world, "independent scholars" (the euphemism for those still not gainfully employed), and many from varied walks of life. A person has only one lifetime. So far, because of you students and Junior Members—I still have a couple!—at both Trinity (Chicago) and the Institute (Toronto), my professional lifelines have indeed fallen "in (very) pleasant places" (Psalm 16). Inès and I say, "Thank you all dearly."

Senators, Trustees, President Fernhout and administrators, indefatigable staff of the Institute for Christian Studies, with the whole Gideon band of Institute supporters in Canada, the USA, and around the world: The trust you gave me back in 1972 and the prayers attached to money you have offered up to God for me, my family, and the little working community of scholars in Toronto, is quietly overwhelming. The miracle of the Institute's existence has rested on the LORD's blessing-response to the heartfelt desires of mostly you few Dutch immigrants, slowly augmented by those who caught the Reformation vision for university-level education, who have rowed with incredible persistence against the secularist stream.

It has been a wonderful trust for me to be freed for the task of translating that goodly heritage—sometimes discovering for the first time its educational bread for the world—into the precarious field of aesthetics. God will judge the faithfulness, and I know it is unfinished. But there are pockets of artists, theorists, and young educators throughout the world—Australia, South Africa, Indonesia, Greece, Spain, England,[23]

---

23 There is a recent formation of a Christian Studies Centre in Melbourne, Australia, by an incorporated Association for Christian Higher Education in Australia (1995), under the leadership of Keith Sewell and Bruce Wearne.

A Christian Worldview Network in South Africa (since 1991) has published a Manifesto on *Christians and the Arts in South Africa* (1993), holds national conferences, and puts out a *Many to Many (M2M)* newsletter, originally spearheaded by Craig Bartholomew; and there is a (1994) Christian Action Research Project (CARP) at the Department of Philosophy of the University of the Orange Free State, led by Gideon Strauss and Gerrit du Preez, with an e-journal, NUANCES, on the World Wide Web.

Iskandar Saher carries on as chaplain to the General (philosophy) Studies faculty at the Christian university of Satya Wacana in Indonesia. A Union of Greek Christian Artists, predominantly professional musicians, has been incorporated in Thessaloniki/Athens, Greece, presided over by Phedon Kaloterakis. There is a loose relationship of mostly graphic, media, and performance artists in Barcelona united by Joyce and Jim Phillips, with David Estrada Herrero as mentor.

Peter Smith (Surrey), Kate and Martin Rose (Sheffield), and Paul Martin (Rugby)

as well as the USA and Canada—who have been stirred with hope to give their aesthetic life and imaginative thought to the Lord as a sweet-smelling offering.

If there be any guests present for whom this all sounds strange, I hope you will test the spirit of the ICS, and join this crazy group of Chaucerian pilgrims telling jokes and stories of troubles together on the turbulent, earthy road to the new Jerusalem.

Inner circle of colleagues: The last few years at ICS have been at times difficult, as we all know. I respect each one's Christian faith-guts very much, and I am deeply grateful for pristine acts of love I have experienced from you over the years. I am also struck and deeply saddened by how fragile communion can be. I've sometimes thought amid the struggles to wield power that we were all individually rephrasing Augustine's agonized prayer to God: "*Da mihi castitatem et continentiam [et humilitatem], sed noli modo*" (*Confessiones,* 8,vii,17).

I am glad to say goodbye now while I still have life and health to give away my imaginativity perhaps in other ways and places, although Bob Sweetman has put a restraining arm on my sleeve, so I will sit in on his Vollenhoven seminar this winter, *per diem pro Deo.* So I take my leave now from you, Henk, Jim, George, Paul in absentia, Bob, Ken, Brian and Sylvia, Marcille, with a phrygian melody Genevan psalm, a poem I once overheard Luci Shaw speak at Oxford, a Bach chorale, and a twelfth-century plainsong with a second advent text to be sung by all those festively gathered here—all together a sort of hopeful, untimely answer from the thesaurus of our living past to the Tracy Chapman "Why?" song danced at the beginning.

---

keep a tenuous connection going in the practice and reflection on their artwork since they were caught by the vision of the late Hans Rookmaaker.

Genevan 141

I am cry - ing, LORD, please come quick - ly!
Guard my lips from mouth - ing words twis - ted.
When a trust - ed per - son cor - rects me,
Your con-cern and pow - er a - maze me:

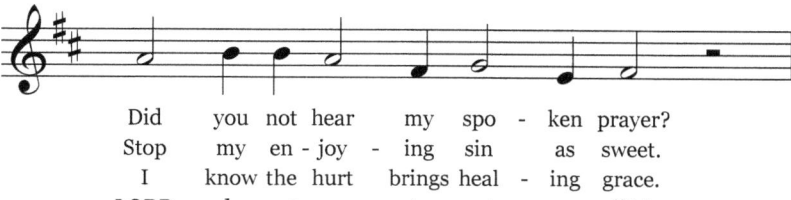

Did you not hear my spo - ken prayer?
Stop my en - joy - ing sin as sweet.
I know the hurt brings heal - ing grace.
LORD, do not emp - ty out my life!

I deep - ly yearn to know You care.
LORD, strip my deeds of sly de - ceit.
How sad when judg - ment is not faced
Frus - trate each wil - y temp - ter's vice--

My lift - ed hands still bring thanks-giv - ing--
Keep my poor heart from turn - ing wick - ed.
un - til one's crook - ed life is wast - ed.
let me walk past their traps in safe - ty.

Text: Psalm 141, vers. Calvin Seerveld, 1989, © 9889
Tune: Genevan Psalter, 1562 GENEVAN 141

Judas, Peter

because we are all
betrayers, taking
silver and eating
body and blood and asking
(guilty) is it I and hearing
him say yes
it would be simple for us all
to rush out
and hang ourselves

but if we find grace
to cry and wait
after the voice of morning
has crowed in our ears
clearly enough
to break our heart
he will be there
to ask us each again
do you love me?

Luci Shaw, 1981, in *Polishing the Petoskey Stone*.
Wheaton: Harold Shaw Publishers, 1990

Bibliography

Appiah, Kwame Anthony. *In my Father's House: Africa in the Philosophy of Culture* (New York: Oxford University Press, 1992).

Estrada Herrero, David. *Estètica* (Barcelona: Editorial Herder, 1988).

Carrier, David. *Principles of Art History Writing* (University Park: Pennsylvania State University Press, 1991).

Dooyeweerd, Herman. *De Wijsbegeerte der Wetsidee,* vols. 1 and 3 (Amsterdam: H.J. Paris, 1935, 1936 [hereafter *WdW*]), translated William S. Young and David Freeman. *A New Critique of Theoretical Thought*, vols. 1 and 3 (Philadelphia: Presbyterian and Reformed, 1953, 1957 [hereafter *NCTT*]).

Ellacuria, Ignacio. "The Challenge of the Poor Majority," "Is a Different Kind of University Possible?" and "The University, Human Rights, and the Poor Majority," in Part III, "The University and Social Justice," in *Towards a Society that Serves its People: The intellectual contribution of El Salvador's murdered Jesuits,* eds. John Hasselt and Hugh Lacey (Washington, D.C.: Georgetown University Press, 1991), 171–219.

Goudzwaard, Bob. "Richting geven in een stuurloze wereld," in *Zoeken naar een nieuwe taal: Communicatie over inspiratie en geloof* (Amsterdam: VU Uitgeverij, 1995), 26–44.

Griffioen, Sander. "Het hachelijke van levensbeschouwelijke filosofie," *Beweging* 59:2 (1995): 44–45.

Guinness, Os. "Mission modernity: Seven checkpoints on mission in the modern world," in *Faith and Modernity*, eds. Philip Sampson, Vinay Samuel, and Chris Sugden (Oxford: Regnum/Lynx 1994), 322–52.

Havel, Vàclav. *Living in Truth* [1986], ed. Jan Vladislav (London: Faber & Faber, 1989), 3–195.

Himmelfarb, Gertrude. *On Looking into the Abyss: Untimely thoughts on culture and society* (New York: Knopf, 1994).

Johnson, Basil H. Selections in *An Anthology of Canadian Native Literature in English*, eds. Daniel David Moses and Terry Goldie (Toronto: Oxford University Press, 1992).

Kuiper, Roel. "Wereldbeschouwelijk denken als opgave" and response by Gerrit Glas, "Wereldbeschouwing als gave," in *Beweging* 59:2 (1995): 46–51.

Kundera, Milan. "Candide had to be destroyed" (1980), translated K. Seigneurie, in *Living in Truth*, ed. Jan Vladislav (London: Faber & Faber, 1989), 258–62.

Luther, Martin. "Resolutiones disputationum de indulgentiarum virtute" (1518) in *Luthers Werke in Auswahl*, ed. Otto Clemen (Bonn: A. Marcus und E. Weber's Verlag, 1925), 1:15–147.

Lyotard, Jean-Francois. "Réponse à la question: qu'est-ce que le postmoderne?" in *Critique*, no. 419 (April 1982), translated Régis Durand, "Answering the Question: What is Postmodernism?" in *The Postmodern Condition: A report on knowledge* (Minneapolis: University of Minnesota Press, 1984), 71–82.

―――. *The Differand: Phrases in Dispute* [1983] translated by Georges Van Den Abbeele (Minneapolis: University of Minnesota Press, 1988).

Martin-Baró, Ignacio. "Developing a critical consciousness through the university curriculum," in Part III, "The University and Social Justice," in *Towards a Society that Serves its People: The intellectual contribution of El Salvador's murdered Jesuits*, eds. John Hasselt and Hugh Lacey (Washington, D.C.: Georgetown University Press, 1991), 220–42.

Norris, Christopher. *Uncritical Theory: Postmodernism, intellectuals, and the Gulf War* (Amherst: University of Massachusetts Press, 1992).

Preziosi, Donald. *Rethinking Art History: Meditations on a coy science* (New Haven: Yale University Press, 1989).

Rowe, William. "Society after the Subject, Philosophy after the Worldview," in *Stained Glass: Worldviews and social science*, eds. Paul A. Marshall, Sander Griffioen, Richard J. Mouw (Lanham: University Press of America, 1989), 156–83.

Said, Edward W. "Opponents, Audience, Constituencies and Community," in *The Anti-Aesthetic: Essays on postmodern culture*, ed. Hal Foster (Seattle: Bay

Press, 1983), 135–59.

Scriven, Charles. *The Transformation of Culture: Christian social ethics after H. Richard Niebuhr* (Scottdale: Herald Press, 1988).

Seerveld, Calvin. *A Turnabout in Aesthetics to Understanding* (1974) {supra pp. 233–258}.

"Spirit of the Haida Gwaii" (video, 48 minutes, 1991). Directed by Alan C. Clapp, scripted by Robert Bringhurst, produced by Deluxe Production Canada Ltd. in Vancouver, funded from the Montreal Office of the Royal Bank of Canada.

Sweetman, Robert. "Of Tall Tales and Small Stories: Postmodern 'fragmatics' and the Christian historian." Typescript of a keynote address given at the Lilly Foundation Regional Conference on "The Future of Christian Scholarship in a Postmodern World," held at Calvin College, Grand Rapids, Michigan, 21–23 June 1994, 19 pp.

Zuidervaart, Lambert. *Adorno's Aesthetic Theory: The redemption of illusion.* (Cambridge: MIT Press, 1991).

Zuidervaart, Lambert and Henry Luttikhuizen, eds. *Pledges of Jubilee: Essays on the arts and culture, in honor of Calvin G. Seerveld* (Grand Rapids: Eerdmans, 1995).

"Blowing bubbles on graduated time, 1995"
Photo by Bert Witvoet

A REVIEW: KANTS KUNSTTHEORIE

KUYPERS, KAREL. *Kants Kunsttheorie und die Einheit der Kritik der Urteilskraft*. Amsterdam/London: North-Holland, 1972, 191 pages, £5.91.

Discovering the historical Kant may seem to be slim returns for an expense of effort today. But the spate of new books setting straight our benign neglect of Kant's *Critique of Judgment* points up the contribution made here by Dutch scholar Kuypers.

By and large, argues Kuypers, readers to date have assumed the prejudiced Romantic interpretation of Kant's *Critique of Judgment,* as if it were a philosophy of fine art mysteriously yoked to a treatise in theoretical (teleological) biology. But that is not what Kant did and it is not what he said he was doing; therefore it is no wonder the whole army of Kant's little helpers has been unable to get the third *Critique* back together again. The fact that the first introduction to the *Critique of Judgment*—which holds the key to its interpretation, according to Kuypers—was not properly available to commentators until 1889 (120) has added to the confusion. Not until we grasp the integral unity of Kant's *Critique of Judgment,* says Kuypers, will we be able to (1) see its cornerstone place in Kant's critical philosophy, (2) unravel the false problems critics have brought to Kant's exposition of taste, and (3) recapture Kant's dated but living contribution to aesthetic theory.

Kuypers sets out to prove his thesis that the *Critique of Judgment* is a unity by showing from the texts what Kant means by "art" and why "Technik der Nature" posited by (reflective) judgment excited Kant so. "Art" for Kant means any man-made artifact embodying a prior plan, idea, or purpose (25). In the nineteenth-century wake of Goethe and Hegel, art came to be synonymous with "fine art" (*schöne Künste*); but for Kant "art" still means any artifact manifesting purposive system, *seinsollende Werke,* of which there be different sorts (*CJ,* secs. 42–46). Thus it was most natural for Kant to explain the cohering network of empirical laws, which our particular experiences assume for classifying things, as a system

---

First published in *Journal of Aesthetics and Art Criticism* 34:2 (1975): 208–10.

"by analogy with art" (first intro. *CJ*, secs, 1, 12). Kant makes explicit that

> the representation of nature as art is a mere Idea, which serves as a principle for our investigation, and hence is only subjective. (first intro. *CJ*, Haden trans., Library of Liberal Arts, 11)

Kuypers points out that this explicit affirmation of "the technic of nature," "purposiveness of nature," or "artistic knowledge," as a postulate characteristic of reflective judgment (first intro. *CJ*, secs. 2, 5, 6) is a new feature in Kant's critical philosophy (61). In fact, *Urteilskraft*, which authenticates this treatment of nature as if it were "art," that is, more than an aggregate, replaces *Vernunft* as the unifying source of human experience (65–66). It is finally in the third *Critique*, according to Kuypers, that Kant resolves the split world with which his first *Critique* seemed to end, between mechanically determined nature and the pure freedom of practical reason (47–48). *Urteilskraft* mediates between *Verstand* and *Vernunft*, and judgment-ability's a priori ascription of purposiveness to nature links the realm of sense-knowable objects and the realm of supersensible morality (146–47).

The whole third *Critique*, Kuypers posits again and again, is governed by Kant's single-minded, *critical* exposition and deduction of the purposiveness of nature, analogous to "art," as a necessary presupposition of the reflective judgment (51, 71, 89, 92–96, 122, 132, 173; cf. *CJ*, sec. 23).

Working out of this hermeneutical principle, Kuypers shows how important features of the third *Critique* fall into place. First of all, the crux of Kant's exposition is the deduction of the pure aesthetical judgment, because Kant inherited the tradition that taste (beauty-judgments) must be empirical, and how can something empirical assume a priori authority (92, 123–24)? Kuypers demonstrates that Kant found the concept of purposiveness to be the key to validation since, when the purposiveness or design of Nature was felt, such reflective *Gefühlsurteile* carried autonomous, albeit subjective, final authority (35–37, 132–35). Relevant correspondence prior to 1790, such as the 28 December 1787 letter to Reinhold, documents that the nexus of teleology and feeling-of-delight enlarged Kant's conception of Nature and judgment found in the first *Critique* and formed the background to his retitling the projected "Critique of Taste" a *Critique of Judgment* (29–30, 46). Kant makes the link explicit:

> It is really only in taste, and I mean taste for objects of Nature, that judgment-ability shows itself to be a faculty which has its own peculiar principle and thus grounded claim to a place in the general critique of the higher cognitive faculties, which one perhaps might not have credited it. (first intro. *CJ*, sec. 11, my translation; cf. Haden, 48)

It becomes clear, then, Kuypers explains, since the crux of the third *Critique* is the validation of taste-judgments by reference to the purposive system of Nature and its felt universal communicability, that *Naturschönheit* is what interests Kant (31, 125–26; cf. first intro. *CJ,* sec. 12). It becomes clear why Kant calls his analysis of the sublime "a mere appendix"—the sublime lacks the requisite "objective" purposiveness to be of direct help in the deduction (34, 96–97; cf. *CJ,* sec. 23). Then one also realizes how the third *Critique* is misread if one thinks its core feature is about genius (O. Schlapp) (155) or "beauty in the arts" (e.g., even H. Cohen and P. O. Kristeller) (121, 160–61). Most importantly, it becomes clear that aesthetical judgments and teleological judgments are natural complements of reflective judgment—the two main parts of the third *Critique* form a unity (137). While pure aesthetical judgment has an essential priority for Kant, because of its noncognitive, transcendental, subjective autonomy, which constitutes its own particular, totally critical compass, teleological judgment is still the necessary context for such aesthetical judgment, for teleological judgment lays heuristic claim to the whole of human moral freedom united regulatively with the natural world (96–98, 109–10, 115, 118, 145–47; cf. second intro. *CJ.* sec. 8).

Kuypers rebuts Romantic exegesis of Kant throughout his analysis by emphasizing the particularly eighteenth-century climate of Kant's treatise. Kant was oriented toward spectators of gardens and criticasters; he did not have the "creative artist" in view (125). And the fact that the climax to both halves of the third *Critique* is a methodology *(CJ,* secs. 60, 79–91), argues Kuypers, does not mean Kant was weakly repeating himself: the closing sections of the third *Critique* are evidence of Kant's continuing concern to be rigorously "critical" (a kind of agnostic piety), which nevertheless admitted a stern ethic that serves as an idealistic "metaphysics," if you will, in keeping with his overriding, optimistic, cultural humanism (110–12, 139–40. 171–72, 176–77). Taste, for Kant, has its autonomous authority, but belongs to the wider world of being human.

Kuypers' German is knotted by Dutchisms, but his deliberate, painstaking exegesis of Kant's third *Critique* is a model of careful scholarship. It breaks new ground. Although Kuypers does not draw implications from Kant's third *Critique* for today, it seems to me that his insightful analysis shows the relevance of Kant's work for the spectator aesthetics of Dufrenne and phenomenological aesthetic theory in general. Kuypers' exposition even encourages the idea that Kant's approach to aesthetical judgment may be of help to contemporary aestheticians looking for alternate ways to consider some norm for art other than the prevalent ones of demagogic commercialization or arid logicism.

A Review: Truth and Method

Gadamer, Hans-Georg. *Truth and Method,* translation ed. by Garrett Barden and John Cumming. N.Y.: The Seabury Press, 1975, xxvi + 551 pages, $22.50.

Gadamer's major study (1960) of the key features of a philosophical hermeneutics has now reached English, a few years after its third German edition. Translations are by nature treacherous undertakings and are often only the lesser of two evils—a faint facsimile of the original or an unknown quantity in the realm of hearsay. The present rendering of Gadamer's magisterial prose lacks the éclat of Edward Casey's translation (1973) of Dufrenne's *Phenomenology of Aesthetic Experience.* The present rendering does not have the reliable clarity and flow of Ralph Manheim's translation (1955–57) of Ernst Cassirer's *Philosophy of Symbolic Forms.* It is closest, perhaps, in lack of stature, to the old Douglas Ainslie translation (1909) of Croce's *Aesthetic.* The fact that Sheed and Ward, which owns the translation copyright, does not credit any translators by name and only mentions that "the translation was edited by Garrett Barden and John Cumming from the second (1965) edition" does not seem fair either to the importance of the matter or to the enormity of the undertaking. The veiled anonymity is, however, a measure of the product. But *Truth and Method* is too searching a work to be neglected on that account. Gadamer's perspective raises horizons for aesthetics that need to be seen by those confined monolingually to the world of English.

Truth and Method is a model of ordered thinking. Part I is a critique of pure "aesthetic consciousness" as we know it today. Gadamer shows first *historically* (I,A) how, in the grand humanist context of eighteenth-century classical culture and enlightened taste, Kant established the idea of aesthetic disinterestedness with subjective a priori autonomy at the expense of denying its cognitive character (55). He describes how Schiller, Hegel, and others superimposed on Kant a fascination with man's

---

This book review originally appeared in *Journal of Aesthetics and Art Criticism* 36:4 (1978): 487–490.

symbol-making activity as an utterly free source of supersensible meaning. Gadamer asks whether this problematics of a disinterested "aesthetic attitude" (indifferent as to whether its object be real or not) and the cult of artistic genius and soaring creativity do not dogmatically disjoin "aesthetic experience" from historical reality (72–73, 80). Art too affords knowledge, and experience of art is not simply an introduction to uncommitted aesthetic awareness (86–87). What is the fundamental mode of being of art experience?

Then Gadamer conducts a *systematic* examination (I,B) of matters that will elucidate the ontological structure of artworks and our understanding of them. He probes the nature of play with phenomenological acuteness: its absorbing, self-renewing, self-presentational ideality. And human play, says Gadamer, reaches its perfection in art, for then the playing is wholly transformed into the sheer appearance of playing for a potential audience (99). Art lives as performance only, and the definitive event character of play, once recognized, could save us from mistaking art for an "object" of "subjective awareness," instead of the presentation of a world of truth that engulfs one with the joy of recognition (102–104).

Gadamer continues his systematic probing by elucidating the temporality of art in terms of a Kierkegaardian contemporaneity or overwhelming presence and in terms of ecstasy, based on Aristotle's view of the tragic (112–16). Gadamer's structural analysis of "image" (*Bild*) or picture, in contradistinction to "copy," "sign," and "symbol," is fundamental to the whole book and lays the groundwork for his stand on the oracular or ontological power of art, in which the being of truth is presented (and a communion of spectators is fused). It is because "image" is at the core of art that art bears forth truth with an oracular existentiality that simply is not able to be methodically subjected to analytic objectification (121–27, 131–37; cf. 444). Gadamer emphasizes the progressive present tense of art—its existentiality—by insisting that occasionality is a universal characteristic of artworks, epitomized by portraits. And this leads him to affirm architecture as a central art and "the ornamental and decorative" as primary features of representation that has aesthetic structure (138–41).

A North American reader close to the New York gallery scene, or one whose orientation is the psychology of art perception practiced by Gombrich and Arnheim, may be mystified by Gadamer's view of art. But a recent book by Robert Rosenblum on *Modern Painting and the Northern Romantic Tradition* (1975) is a kind of art-historiographic reading of artists from Van Gogh to Pollock and Rothko that would bear out the philosophical analysis Gadamer makes. What art means is more than meets the eye, and the truth of art transcends its artistic character; so one does not understand nor interpret art fully if one rests in formal, aesthetic matters. Therefore aesthetics proper, if it would be complete, must be taken up into general hermeneutics and hermeneutics must be reconceived to do justice to experience of art (144–47).

Part II is a critique of traditional text-hermeneutics and the unexamined assumptions behind "historical consciousness." Gadamer again first *historically* (II,A) weighs Schleiermacher, Dilthey, and Husserl in the balance and finds them wanting. Schleiermacher's belief that interpreters must reconstruct the original world of the art and literature under consideration if one would truly understand them (a position E. D. Hirsch approximates today) asks for an impossibility in view of the total historicity of our being. Dilthey's grappling with human historicality and historical relativity never overcomes the inadequate subjectivity of his starting-point, according to Gadamer. And even late Husserl's concept of life is too schematized to do justice to the ongoing, living reality of past significance, of which artistic and literary texts are an instance.

Then Gadamer again follows up the historical review with a *systematic* exploration (II,B) into the universal conditions for just interpretation, which will not presume interpretation can be ahistorical. Using Heidegger, Gadamer rejects the Enlightenment prejudice against one's having presuppositions and working prejudgments, and the concomitant Enlightenment emasculation of tradition—as if one who does not question the prejudices of his own age is therefore a model knower (239–40; cf. pp. 324, 358). The basic problem for hermeneutics, says Gadamer, is to posit a criterion for distinguishing legitimate prejudices from illegitimate prejudices, so that one's inevitable prejudgments will foster rather than block a fusion of the past with the present that leads to the miracle of understanding, the sharing of a common meaning by temporally distant consciousnesses (246, 258, 260).

The criterion Gadamer posits as the solution to the basic hermeneutic problem is the principle of *Wirkungsgeschichte* (ever-interacting-history). (The Sheed and Ward translation of this technical term is "effective-history" and is obfuscatory unless you hear it as a practical Aristotelian, something like "efficient-causal history." The Kisiel-Palmer circumscription for *wirkungsgeschichtliche Bewusstsein* is better—"historically operative consciousness"; cf. Richard E. Palmer, *Hermeneutics,* 1969, 191.) The attempt to fix upon a text of the past as an hermetically sealed object for which you furnish the conclusive interpretation is a bad prejudice, says

Gadamer, because it treats historical items as if they were dead curiosities and presumes a position for readers that is blind to human finitude (270, 297, 320). Instead, a good prejudice for the right hermeneutical experience would be this: an interpretation that understands a text properly will be a living application of its meaning (274–78). The way a judge creatively supplements canon law to update its original meaning and the way a (Bultmannian) preacher risks demythologizing Scripture in order to have the abiding word of God relevant for a current situation, according to Gadamer, is exemplary for art and literary criticism (292–97, 305). The good interpreter does not try to dominate the text, but lets the text—a piece of ongoing tradition, of history-ever-interacting upon the consciousnesses present to it—speak and convince the receiving interpreter (324–25, 359, 422).

In colloquial parlance one could say that Gadamer is pointing out the philosophical reason why so much literary criticism (not to speak of book reviews) and critical analysis of "the other's" scholarship is judgmental rape of the text, when it should be a love affair, if hermeneutical activity is meant to be humane. Interpretation in the humanities went wrong, and remains obstinately wrongheaded, for Gadamer when it tried to understand art, literature, and research in the cultural sciences as if it were dissecting bugs and smashing atoms. One should treat texts like "images" that reflect the human originator's imperatives, and one should approach texts with a permanent openness that evidences hearing truth the other speaks to us in our reciprocating acknowledgement that our interpretation is only one actualization of its historical potential (299, 336, 428). Correct interpretation will bear the mark of unending dialogue and *remain* a questioning, because knowledge is inherently dialectical and we humans *are* conversations (xxii. 328, 330, 333–34, 340). The interpreter is called to melt into the continuing, enlarging, ever-interacting-history of tradition, or risk hybris (337, 341).

Gadamer concludes his (I) critique of our eighteenth-century, pure "aesthetic consciousness" and his (II) critique of the "historical consciousness" of nineteenth-century hermeneutic theory in Part III with a draft for a twentieth-century ontology of language-in-action. Part III is really a most appropriate challenge to contemporary aesthetic theory: insofar as aesthetics is metacriticism it must accept the responsibility for grounding its analyses in a philosophy of history and an ontology of language that make their peace with the problem of truth, otherwise aesthetic theory hides its philosophical head in methodological sand.

It becomes apparent why the buck stops for Gadamer at *Sprache*, or better, *Sprachlichkeit*. (The Sheed and Ward translation for both terms is uniformly "language" and misses the rich coloring and large dimensions of this key to Gadamer's thought. Palmer reaches for it more imaginatively with "linguisticality"; cf. *Hermeneutics,* 206–7. It is especially at the nodal points where Gadamer's own position comes most to the fore that the Sheed and Ward translation seems most deficient, as if the journeymen in words lacked philosophical antennae. For another example, take "Darstellung" in I,B, which is sometimes correctly rendered "presentation," but again and again becomes "representation"; see e.g., 97–98, thereby muddling unnecessarily Gadamer's rigorous emphasis upon the self-contained "disclosure" character of play, the "revelatory" nature of images, the "eventful" state of understanding, and the "presentational being" of art. To document the serious shortcomings and the slippage in meaning of the Sheed and Ward work, one could contrast its rendering on page 98, with that by Palmer, *Hermeneutics,* 173, of the short paragraph in the original text on page 104, 3rd German ed., 1972). "Language" or structural able-to-speak-ness serves as Gadamer's Ἀρχή and Archimedean point because the universal human speakability or (mother) tongue into which each one is born (and which a priori shapes one's being-in-the-world consciousness), that is, the linguisticality of humankind, is the ontic source of presentifying the past; and language-in-action is a paradigm of the hermeneutical experience—bringing a fund of tradition to new life (401–03, 432–33). Our (mother) tongue bespeaks us, says Gadamer playfully, even before we open our mouths to communicate in talk; in the beginning and at the end is the Word, the final source of meaning, in which one's self and the (human) universe interspeakingly meet as one (429, 431).

Such Heideggerian lingo will sound like glossolalia to those who are bred on the chiseled prose of Hume, and Gadamer's ontological commitment to *Sprachlichkeit* can only cause gnashing of teeth among those who frequent the nominalistic speakeasies of North America. But the day is past when Carnap could poke fun at Heidegger's "Nothing" (1932) and get away with it. It turns out there is more to the world, art, and literature than is dreamt of in the vocabulary of Wittgensteinian epigones. Behind and within the Heraclitan doubletalk (367), the contradictory thesis of Nicholas Cusanus (393, 442), the dialogics of Plato (332, 354–55), the dialectic of Hegel, to which Gadamer is partial (xxiv, 310, 417–18), and the murky terminology of his friend Heidegger lies the insight that the tongue of humankind, which is not of our making, is an amazing gift that makes discourse possible between different persons and beyond the day of one's life (cf. the Rilke quotation used as motto for the whole book). Raising the ante on Kant's critical question, "How in the world is knowledge with certainty possible?" Gadamer raises the question, "*What* in the world makes understanding and *interpreting the other* (with adequacy!) possible?" We have been missing the critical answer and question, Gadamer intimates, because, unlike the Greeks, "we are entangled in the knots of subjectivism" (418) and have been operating with a denatured idea of language as if it were a rational construction and instrument of subjective decisions (365, 375–77, 392, 408).

The living language of humankind, however, is the final, universal ground of meaning in history: it is the heart of humanity, and the very corporeality of thinking. Human speaking is always finite but also always contains a world of unspoken meanings that elicits *and* certifies the fundamental, unending question-and-answer fabric of reality (411, 415–16, 428–29). The continuing speech act from which one can never escape proves that language is not a prison-house but the very mediator of society and culture (363–64, 420–21). This means for interpretation-theory, says Gadamer, that there cannot be any per se correct interpretation of a text (358). If that seems unsettling to art and literary critics, then we have to realize, says Gadamer, that just as Kant's critical philosophy exposed the dogmatist view of "experience," so a truly historical hermeneutics sees through the dogmatist view of "conclusive meaning." Every interpretation is (and should be) a new creation of understanding assimilating the text handed down, just as every act of speech is (thanks to *Sprache*!) a loosening anew of the congealed meaning of traditional discourse (430).

At the very end Gadamer sets sail past the promontories of relativism and eclecticism, which he consciously rejects, as an epistemological conservative, you might say, by invoking what one could call "the law of the conservation of scholarship" or "the inalienable task of humanity to recycle ancient thinking, forever and ever." In fact, he does it by remodeling the old Platonic Idea of the "beautiful" to illuminate, he says, the event character of understanding and the immediacy of hermeneutical experience (434, 441). Gadamer finds his ontology of language and his position on the ambiguous oracle nature of art corroborated by what he hears in Plato's dialogues about the visible image structure and radiance of the beautiful (437–44). To understand a text is like seeing the beautiful: one is charmed out of his prejudices into receiving its presented meaning as an event of truth. One may trust this *method* of open questioning and re-searching to divulge *truth* (446–47).

Aside from the ingenuity and legitimacy and import of writing a history of philosophy this way, where the line between exegesis and eisegesis becomes as fine as a hair, here at the bottom of it all a basic question arises about the "unending dialogue" that Gadamer exemplifies and promotes as hermeneutical norm (xxii). Such a model for interpretation does not allow for finality of interpretation—a text is always only of application to ourselves (559)—but Gadamer still claims the interpreter of texts deals with matters of final seriousness, namely truth (texts are not just expressions of subjectivity) (356). How are we to understand him? If "unending dialogue" is Gadamer's *final* position and credo for guaranteeing the emergence of truth in interpretation (446–47), is there any way to deny that for him at least this is the standpoint beyond all other standpoints (339)? And if texts only present truth and never, for example, a lie, and if interpretations of a text cannot possibly lead to contradictory results (on his dialogic model), but always yield an enlargement of the interpreter's awareness of one's consciousness being formed by the "Thou" of history (xxiii), is there any qualitative criterion for separating good from bad interpretations? And is there any overwhelming reason for attending to the rigorous discipline of interpreting oracular art with fundamental seriousness (aura of sacred play, the tragic of life, etc.) that Gadamer's whole analysis seems to request? Or, if texts can sometimes present the opposite of truth, the lie, and if interpretations of texts can be contradictory, is it human to expect "unending dialogue"? Do there not come times in human life and history when dialogue *must* stop and martyrs ought to appear? And must not a general hermeneutics (and its dependent aesthetic theory), which would have universal horizons and be embedded in actual historical reality, also account for such crisis situations?

Despite the translation, the English reader will profit from going the second mile with Gadamer, the mile of openhearted dialogue. Gadamer will certainly toughen the fiber of one's reflection in aesthetics with a sense of history, for which John Fisher's editorial pleaded (*JAAC,* Summer 1976). Interaction with Gadamer might also stimulate American thought on the philosophical foundations of aesthetic theory, which is of great concern to many European members of the international community of scholars in aesthetics.

List of illustrations▪

© – copyright granted or purchased

    AP – reproduced with the artist's permission
    CS – photograph by Calvin Seerveld
    CSU – © status unknown
    PD – in the public domain

1. *Puer natus est*, Gregorian chant introit for the Christmas mass. PD
2. *The Good Shepherd*, Ravenna mosaics in Mausoleum of Galla Placidia, c.450-500 AD. PD
3. *Deer and shrubs,* detail, Ravenna mosaics in Mausoleum of Galla Placidia, c.450-500 AD. PD
4. Willem Claesz Heda, *Still life* (1633), oil painting, Rijksmuseum, Amsterdam. PD
5. Rembrandt, *De Staalmeesters* (1662), oil painting, Rijksmuseum, Amsterdam. PD
6. Rembrandt, *The Flayed Ox* (1655), oil painting on wood, 94 x 69 cm, Louvre Museum, Paris. PD
7. Rembrandt, *The Bedstead* (1646), etching and burin on paper, 12.6 x 22.4 cm, Rijksmuseum, Amsterdam. PD
8. Georges Rouault, *Fille au miroir* (1906), watercolor, Musée d'art moderne, Paris. © 2013 Artists Rights Society (ARS), New York / ADAGP, Paris
9. Christine Anderson, *Historical Dislocations: the Expulsion (after Massacio)* (1987), oil painting, New York City. AP
10. Christine Anderson, *The Standoff: surveying the Philistines* (1988), oil painting, New York City. AP
11. Ed Hagedorn, *New Growth* (1970), acrylic painting, pipe, mixed media, Colbourne, Ontario [now destroyed]. AP
12. Warren Breninger, *Art as a metaphor for childbirth, no. 2* (1986), photography/painting, mixed media on C-type paper, 45 x 75 cm, North Frankston, Victoria, Australia. AP
    Technical note: By mixed media are meant inks, acrylic, pencils, graphite, and crayons, as additives; subtractive methods are effected with scrapers, sandpaper, and steel wool. By C-Type paper is meant traditional color photographic paper whose emulsion has been light exposed, not ink jet

▪ Links to many of these illustrations in full color can be easily accessed at www.dordt.edu/DCPimagesSeerveld

paper; C-Type paper has a water (ink) absorbent emulsion layer that exists as colored layers. The materials are actually photographic but the methods are both drawing and painting, with some added sculptural methods in regard to stripping away the emulsion layers. The works begin as photo-reproductions of drawings which are printed and then the photo surface is worked on as a drawing or painting.

13 Warren Breninger, *Art as a metaphor for childbirth, no. 1,* photography/painting, mixed media on C-type paper, 45 x 75 cm, North Frankston, Victoria, Australia. AP

14 Joyce Recker, *Murmurs of the Heart* (1990), purple heart wood, found rock, chicken wire. Collection of Inès and Calvin Seerveld. AP

15 Britt Wikström, *Seagull I* (1984), bronze, Rotterdam. AP

16 Britt Wikström, *Seagull III* (1985), bronze, Rotterdam. AP

17 Britt Wikström, *Woman* (1984), bronze. Collection of Inès and Calvin Seerveld. AP

18 Britt Wikström, *Noah's ark,* ceramic relief, 4 x 14 m, Elout School, Rotterdam, The Netherlands. AP

19 Britt Wikström, *Wim de Mol* (1983), gravestone, chiseled granite, Essenhof Cemetery, Dordrecht, The Netherlands. AP

20 Gerard Pas, *Red-Blue Crutch Installation* (1986-87), lacquer painted wood, London, Ontario. AP

21 Gerard Pas, *Vision of Utopia* (1986), watercolor on paper, 85 x 66 cm. AP

22 Karl Bucher, *Waiting Prisoners of War* (1979), petrifying material, Red Cross Museum, Geneva, Switzerland. CS

22 Joe Fafard, *The Pasture* (1985), financial district downtown Toronto. CS

24 Gjon Mili, *Untitled* (1941), photograph, in a Swiss magazine. CSU

25 Henry Moore, *Reclining Figure* (1957-58), outside UNESCO Building in Paris. Reproduced by permission of The Henry Moore Foundation

26 Cigar Box, *Phillies.* CS

27 Robert Fludd, *De tribus prioribus creationis diebus,* from his "Utriusque Cosmi Historia" 1617–19). PD

28 Study desk with books. CS

29 Duane Hanson, *The Tourists* (1970). Reprinted with permission of *Acta Academica.*

30 Zadkine, *De verweoeste stad* (1951-53). CS

31 Ed Hagedorn, *At the sounding of the trumpet* (1972). AP

32 Warren Breninger, *Gates of Prayer* (1993–2008) [detail]. AP

— List of Illustrations —

33 Taj Mahal, India (1632-53). PD
34 Yves Klein, *Anthropometries of the Blue Period,* Paris event (9 March 1960) in the Galerie Internationale de l'Art Contemporain. © 2013 Artists Rights Society (ARS), New York / ADAGP, Paris
35 Sadao Watanabe, *Anointing at Bethany* (1991). CS
36 Jan Sterbak, *Vanitas—Flesh dress for an Albino Anorectic* (1988). CSU
37 Velasquez, *Rokeby Venus* (1651). PD
38 *Abu Simbal Colossi*, temple of Ranses II (1292–1225 BC*)*. CS
39 Myron, *Discobolus* (c.470 BC). PD
40 Utrecht Cathedral side chapel, smashed in 1600s. CS
41 Glid Nandor, Dachau Memorial (1960). CS
42 Käthe Kollwitz, *Woman with dead child* (1903), Kunsthalle, Bremen, Germany. © 2013 Artists Rights Society (ARS), New York / VG Bild-Kunst, Bonn
43 Paul Klee, *Le savant* (1933). © 2013 Artists Rights Society (ARS), New York
44 Hemmed in by books (2006). CS
45 Matthias Grünewald, *Temptation of St. Anthony* (1512–16), oil on panel, 265 x 141 cm. PD
46 Redeemer University College, Ancaster, Ontario (2012). PR
47 Ontario College of Art and Design, Toronto (2007). CS
48 Matt Cupido, "Psalm 46:4" (1996), Redeemer University College, Ancaster, Ontario. AP
49 Rands Afrikaans Universiteit, student mural [detail] (1992). CS
50 Block of $8 Canadian Bear postage stamps. CS
51 Flower of Paradise, South Africa. CS
52 Walrus. Photo by Max Smith. PD
53 Alpine rescue? CSU
54 Wim Botha, *Bible Christ*. Photo by Dirk Van den Berg
55 Rodin, *Le Baiser* (1886), 181.5 x 112.5 x 117 cm. PD
56 Johannes Vermeer, *Delft* (c. 1661-1663), oil on canvas, 96.5 x 117.5 cm. PD
57 François Boucher, *Madame Pompadour* (c. 1750), 212 x 164 cm. PD
58 Anonymous First Nations Canadian carver, *Hewn face with tears* (19 *). CSU

59 Leutze, *Washington Crossing the Delaware* (1851). PD

60 Pablo Picasso, *Two brothers* (1905), 450 x 651. © 2013 Estate of Pablo Picasso / Artists Rights Society (ARS), New York

61 Claude Tousignant, *Accelerator Chromatiques* (1967), National Gallery of Canada, Ottawa. CSU

62 Rembrandt, *Self Portrait* (1659) [detail], 84.5 x 66 cm. PD

63 Top City shanty town outhouse, South Africa (1994). CS

64 Dundas Square, downtown Toronto (2010). CS

65 Henry Hunt, *Kwakiutl* (1973). CSU

66 Matthias Grünewald, *Isenheim Altarpiece* (1506–1515). PD

67 Marcus Aurelius on horse, Rome. PD

68 Whistler, *Nocturne in Black and Gold* (1874), oil on panel, 60.3 x 46.4 cm. PD

69 Aubrey Beardsley, *The Peacock Skirt* (1892). PD

70 Paul Klee, *Dancing girl* (1940). © 2013 Artists Rights Society (ARS), New York

71 Salvador Dali, *Rainy Taxi* (1938). © Salvador Dalí, Fundació Gala-Salvador Dalí, Artists Rights Society (ARS), New York 2013

72 Robert Smithson, *Spiral Jetty* (1970), 15 x 1500 feet. PD

73 Vladimir A. Serov, *The Delegates from the Village Visiting Lenin* (1950). Art © Estate of Vladimir Serov/RAO, Moscow/VAGA, New York

74 Baker Press kitsch tract. CS

75 Maiden form bra advertisement, 1960s.

76 Arc de triomphe, Paris (1806–1836). Photo by Pierre Camateros. CC

77 Frederick Hart, *The Three Soldiers, Viet Nam Memorial* (1984). CS

78 Maya Lin, *Vietnam Veterans Memorial Wall* (1982). CS

79 Gerald Folkerts, *Ralph* (2005). AP

80 Warren Breninger, *Resurrection of the living and the dead, Series II* (2001–2008), mixed media on Arches paper. AP

81 Peter S. Smith, *Fallen Tree* (1989), wood engraving. AP

82 Andries Botha, *Baptism for the fallen . . . and those taken darkly* (1991), metal, thatching grass, soda can tops, 4.46 x 1.83 x 0.94 m. AP

83–85 Dayton Castleman, *The End of the Tunnel* (2005). AP

86 Britt Wikström, *Caritas* (2006). AP

87 Georges Rouault, *Sarah* (1956). © 2013 Artists Rights Society (ARS), New York / ADAGP, Paris

88 Piet Mondrian, *Avond: The Red Tree* (1908–1910), oil paint on canvas, 70 x 99 cm, Haags Gemeentemuseum, The Hague, Netherlands. For the image reference: http://www.gemeentemuseum.nl/collection/item/1160

89 Piet Mondrian, *Composition with Large Red Plane, Yellow, Black, Grey and Blue* (1921), oil paint on canvas, 59.5 x 59.5 cm, Haags Gemeentemuseum, The Hague, Netherlands. For the image reference: http://www.gemeentemuseum.nl/collection/item/6496

The graphics on pages 176 and 249 were done by Willem Hart; those on pages 114, 115, 117, and 174 by Ana Feliciano.

Index

aesthete 93, 108, 132, 161, 240-1
aesthetic activity 79, 88, 99, 101, 108, 118, 124, 143, 160-2, 188, 190, 237, 239, 257
aesthetic affairs 80, 96, 263
aesthetic conscience 128, 134; see taste
aesthetic consciousness 252, 289, 292
aesthetic dimension 241, 248
aesthetic functions 36, 152, 270
aesthetic insight 123, 210
aesthetic judgment 31, 47, 75, 128, 138, 156, 235
aesthetic law 78
aesthetic life 81, 84, 112, 115, 118, 121-2, 125-7, 131-3, 188-90, 192, 236-8, 240-3, 247-8, 252, 274; see imaginativity
aesthetic mode 33, 75
aesthetic norm 152-3, 160, 163, 203, 229, 250
aesthetic obedience 82, 90, 108
aesthetic object-functions (nuances) 35, 42, 74, 189, 202
aesthetic structure 75-6, 79-80, 249, 290
aesthetic subject-functions 35
aesthetic subjectivity 75, 78
aesthetic taste 127-30, 156
aesthetic, the 156-7, 241, 246, 248
aesthetic theory 45, 76-81, 145, 242-3, 245, 247-8, 250, 252, 256, 285, 287, 292, 295
aesthetics 45-9, 74, 78-9, 108, 139, 146-7, 150, 233-6, 240-3, 245, 248-54, 272-3, 291-2, 295
  committed 248
  doxological 165, 252-3
  modal 80, 248
  rightful task of 243, 248, 251
  science of 248-51
  theological 277
  theoretical 155, 163, 245, 247, 250, 274
allusivity 8, 35, 79, 80, 85, 88, 156, 159, 163, 192, 203, 272
ambiguity, normative aesthetic 32, 152, 227, 239, 241
anaesthetic 108, 124, 161-2

Aristotle 9, 28, 50, 63-4, 120, 169, 237-8, 290
art history 275-6
art theory 48-9, 193, 249
artistic activity 4, 35, 77, 79, 88, 159, 162, 188, 190, 225-6, 241, 247
artistry 6, 10, 155, 164, 173, 192-3, 197, 202-3, 210, 225, 227, 229-30, 272-5, 277
artists 5, 10-1, 13, 20, 35, 173, 193, 214, 226-7, 231, 240-2, 244-6, 250-1, 253, 274, 276
artworks 41, 74, 77, 139, 170, 190-3, 202-3, 210, 213-4, 246, 251, 276, 290
artworld(s) 114, 147, 162, 202
as-if, doing 4-6, 11, 27, 32, 35, 37, 114, 126, 188
ascetic 105-6, 108, 112, 238

Baumgarten, A. 47, 136-7, 235
the beautiful 75-6, 154, 157, 159, 208, 239, 294
beautiful harmony 74, 80, 152-3, 156, 240
beauty 9, 47-8, 74-6, 119, 137, 141, 151, 153-4, 156-7, 159, 163, 207, 220, 235, 237-41
  theology of 156, 208
bubbles, blowing 1, 6, 23, 25, 162, 284

Christ, body of 59, 69, 145-6, 163, 230-1, 277
christian life 81, 83-4, 104-6
christian philosophical aesthetics 147, 208
christian philosophy 56, 147, 261, 277
clay jars 173-5, 188; see tin-can
clothes 81, 89-96
consciousness, historical 265-6, 291-2
creativity 225, 238, 246-7, 290

devils 32, 34-6, 108, 222
Dooyeweerd, H. 45-6, 48-63, 65-80, 147, 175, 177, 179, 261

encyclopedia of the sciences 49-52, 54, 79-80, 148, 236

faith-commitment 46, 86, 90, 96, 125, 132
fictions 8, 32, 34, 37-8, 41-2, 70, 226
fun 4, 36, 88, 100, 103, 105, 122, 182, 189, 214, 255, 263

Gadamer, H-G. 135, 140, 247, 289-95
games 4, 81, 96-104, 108, 188, 253
genius, artistic 9, 29, 75-6, 141, 246, 290
grotesque 101, 141, 152, 156-8

haha! Erlebnis 99-103
Hartmann, N. 63-8, 70
heart, human 39, 43, 58, 114, 150, 175, 208, 220, 257, 266
Hegel, G.W.F. 47, 139, 154
hermeneutics 250-1, 291, 293-5
historiography 148, 249-50, 272, 276-7
horizons 60, 72, 222-4, 226-7, 231, 276-7, 289
human knowledge 222-3, 230-1
human nature 5-6, 8, 35, 42, 106, 113, 115-6, 189
Hume, D. 137-8
humor 7, 13-4, 40, 111-2, 122-6, 131-3, 152

images 7-8, 10, 28, 31-2, 77, 290, 292-3
imaginata 31-2, 35, 41-2
imaginating 10-1, 39-42, 190, 272
imagination 2, 5-10, 23, 27-30, 76, 115, 123, 158, 189
imaginativable(s) 33-5, 42
imaginative activity 23, 27, 30-3, 35-8, 122, 126, 133, 152
imaginativity 1, 4-7, 9, 11, 23-5, 27, 33, 35, 38-42, 44, 108, 114, 125-7, 130, 133, 142, 146, 152, 188-9, 210, 272
imaginators, professional 7, 10-1, 23, 25, 188, 193
imaging 27, 31-2, 35-6
imagining 4-6, 8, 27, 30-44, 126, 188-9, 210
imperatives 40, 87-8, 258, 292
  aesthetic 39, 81-2, 87-90, 107
institutions, academic 181-2, 269
interpretation 251, 291-2, 294-5

jokes 4, 114, 122, 126, 188
joy 82-4, 152
  kill-joy 93, 106, 120, 163

Kant, I. 28-9, 31, 47, 64-5, 138-40, 156, 285-7, 289
  Critique of Judgment 28-9, 138-9, 140, 142, 192, 254, 285-7
kitsch 162, 192, 204
knowledge
  accurate 223-5, 231
  correct 223, 227, 231
  imaginative 6, 8, 12-3, 34, 225-7
  nuanced 4, 10-2, 23, 34, 192, 210
  scholarly 265, 267-9
  symbolical 78, 225, 227
  true 222-3
Kuyper, A. 54-9, 66, 76, 208, 223, 253, 270
Kuypers, K. 246, 285ff.

laughter 36, 101, 103, 123-4, 132-3, 189
law
  modal 38, 45ff., 147-8
  natural 38, 70, 147
learning, scripturally-directed 71, 261, 264
leisure 118-22, 134
lifestyle 81, 89-90, 104, 131-2, 134
literary criticism 250, 292
ludic(ity) 35, 88, 103, 108, 152, 165

making-believe 4, 6, 27, 31, 44, 100, 114, 188
modal aesthetics 80, 248
modal law-spheres, theory of 57ff.
monstrous 152, 157-8
Moore, H. 37, 273

norm for human taste 130, 141, 143
norms 150-1, 250
  for advertising art 203
nuancefulness see allusitivity
nuances 35, 88, 103, 108, 141, 152, 173, 189

ordinances, creational 34, 38, 57-9, 69, 84, 99, 125, 150, 155, 192, 234, 263

periods, cultural   178-9, 276
philosophical aesthetics   146, 150, 156, 159, 259ff.
Plato   7, 9, 27-8, 63-4, 75, 238
play(ers)   31-3, 36, 96, 99-100, 102-3, 108, 255, 290
playfulness   36, 85, 99, 102, 114, 152, 161
playing games   35, 96-8, 100-3, 107, 188
Pledges of Jubilee   272-4, 276, 278
principalities (and powers)   90, 115, 147, 178, 180-1

reformational dynamic   263, 271
Romantic movement   9
Rookmaaker, H.   74, 79

scholarship, obedient/intrinsically christian   59, 61, 265, 269-70
Scripturally-directed learning   71, 261, 264
Septuagintal community   269-71
similation   11, 23, 37, 39, 41
special sciences   45-6, 49, 78
sphere sovereignty   54-6, 58, 60
style   79, 81ff., 108, 114, 131-4
sublime   88, 138, 141-2, 156-8, 272, 287

suggestion-rich   35, 85, 88, 127, 203, 238, 243
symbol(s)   29, 42, 77-8, 190, 290
symbolific   11, 152, 156, 226-7

taste   47, 111ff., 127-44, 192, 239, 286-7
theatre of God   173, 232
theology of the arts   147, 277
tin-can   113-6; see clay jars
tragic   152, 156-8
truth   219-25, 227, 230-2, 290

ugly   152, 155-6, 158-9, 163, 165

Vollenhoven, D.H.Th.   46, 62, 130, 148-50, 179

way-of-life   38, 86, 131-2
De wijsbegeerte der wetsidee (renamed: A philosophy of God's structuring Word)   71; see 41
workaholic   104, 111-2, 115, 119, 132-3
world-and-life vision   86, 175-6, 178-80
worldview   132, 270

www.ingramcontent.com/pod-product-compliance
Lightning Source LLC
Chambersburg PA
CBHW070720160426
43192CB00009B/1259